Regulating Europe

Regulating Europe explains why economic and social regulation is rapidly becoming the new frontier of public policy and public administration in Europe, at both the national and EU levels. Statutory regulation, implemented by independent regulatory bodies, is replacing not only older forms of state intervention but also, to some extent, the redistributive policies of the welfare state. Thus, *Regulating Europe* is an examination of the emergence of the regulatory state as the successor of the Keynesian welfare state of the past.

The contributions emphasize the parallelism of policy developments at the national and European levels. The book is organized into three parts. The first provides the necessary theoretical background, including a new model of demand and supply of EU regulations. The second presents a series of case studies of particular regulatory policies and institutions in the UK, Germany, France, Spain and the EU. The last part evaluates current policy and institutional developments, pointing out how the lack of statutory regulations in Europe affects the design of the new institutions. Special attention is devoted to the issue of the democratic accountability of expert, politically independent agencies.

Regulating Europe makes an original contribution to the current debate on regulatory policy-making in general, and on EU policy-making in particular. The delegation of regulatory powers to politically independent institutions is explained as a solution to the problem of policy credibility. There is a thorough examination of why most European policies are regulatory in nature and special attention is devoted to the role of the European Commission as regulator and as 'policy entrepreneur'.

Giandomenico Majone is External Professor of the European University Institute, Florence. He is also a visiting scholar at the Max Planck Institute of Social Science in Cologne and at the Institute of Advanced Studies in Vienna.

European Public Policy
Edited by Jeremy Richardson, *University of Essex*
European Public Policy Institute, University of Warwick

This series provides accessible and challenging books on three aspects of European public policy:

• the European Union policy process and studies of particular policy areas within the EU
• national and comparative policy studies with a significant interest beyond the countries studied
• public policy developments in non-EU states

Books in the series come from a range of social science disciplines but all have in common the objective of analysing the dynamics of the policy-making and implementation process via empirical work guided by relevant theory, thus furthering our understanding of European integration. Books in the series are accessible beyond the academic and student market to those who are directly involved in public policy within Europe.

Titles in the series include:

Democratic Spain
Reshaping external relations in a changing world
Edited by Richard Gillespie, Fernando Rodrigo and Jonathan Story

Adjusting to Europe
The impact of the European Union on national institutions and policies
Edited by by Yves Mény, Pierre Muller and Jean-Louis Quermonne

Forthcoming titles include:

Remaking Social Europe
Ricard Goma

Policy-making in the European Union
Edited by Jeremy Richardson

The European Commission
Policy styles and policy instruments
Jeremy Richardson and Laura Cram

Making Europe Green
Environmental policy-making in the European Community
David Judge, David Earnshaw and Ken Collins

Policy-making, European Integration and the Role of Interest Groups
Jeremy Richardson and Sonia Mazey

Regulating Europe

Giandomenico Majone

With contributions by Pio Baake, Robert Baldwin, Lluis Cases, Fabrice Demarigny, Michelle Everson, Laraine Laudati, Oliver Perschau, Albert Weale and the editoral assistance of Claire Tame

London and New York

First published 1996
by Routledge
11 New Fetter Lane, London EC4P 4EE

Simultaneously published in the USA and Canada
by Routledge
29 West 35th Street, New York, NY 10001

© 1996 Giandomenico Majone

Typeset in Times by
Ponting–Green Publishing Services, Chesham, Buckinghamshire

Printed and bound in Great Britain by
Clays Ltd, St Ives PLC

British Library Cataloguing in Publication Data
A catalogue record for this book is available from the
British Library.

Library of Congress Cataloguing in Publication Data
Regulating Europe / edited by Giandomenico Majone
     p.   cm. – (European public policy)
    Includes bibliographical references and index.
    1. Trade regulation–Europe.   2. Independent regulatory
commissions–Europe.   I. Majone, Giandomenico.   II. Series.
HD3616.E8R44   1996
338.94–dc20   96–7015

ISBN 0–415–14295–4 (hbk)
ISBN 0–415–14296–2 (pbk)

Contents

Part III Problems of the regulatory state

Tables and figures

TABLES

FIGURES

Notes on contributors

Pio Baake is Research Associate at Humboldt University, Berlin. His current research interests include industrial organization and public finance.

Robert Baldwin is Reader in Law at the London School of Economics and Political Science. He is currently researching European regulation and its implementation.

Lluís Cases is Professor of Administrative Law at the Universidad Autonoma of Barcellona. He is currently researching economic administrative law, and European administrative law and its impact on the national system of public law.

Fabrice Demarigny is an economist and received his doctorate in Political Science from the Instut d'Etudes Politiques in Paris. His current work focuses on relations between the state and the market.

Michelle Everson is Research Associate at the Zentrum für Europäische Rechtspolitik at the University of Bremen where she is at present researching the evolution of European Union citizenship.

Laraine Laudati holds an MBA from Cornell University and a JD from Fordham University, and is a member of the bars of Washington DC and California. She is Ph.D candidate in the Law Department of the European University Institute, Florence and currently working as a consultant to DG IV.

Giandomenico Majone is External Professor of Political Science at the European University Institute, Florence, visiting scholar at the Max Planck Institute of Social Sciences in Cologne and at the Institute of Advanced Studies in Vienna. His current research interests include general theories of regulatory policy-making with specific reference to the European context.

Oliver Perschau is Research Associate in Public Finance at Berlin Polytechnic University. His current research includes public choice, public finance and empirical macroeconomics.

Albert Weale is Professor of Government at the University of Essex and co-editor of the *British Journal of Political Science*. His current research interests include the Single European Market and environmental policy.

Clare Tame, the editorial assistant on this book, is Research Associate in the Department of Social and Political Sciences at the European University Institute where she works as a social sciences editor.

Series editor's preface

From the early 1980s, deregulation, liberalization and privatization have emerged as the dominant policy fashion in Western Europe. These concepts have been presented as common solutions to a vast range of public policy problems by governments of left and right alike. More recently, this policy fashion has spread to the former Soviet bloc countries in Eastern Europe. This now dominant trend emerged as a contrast to the long period of postwar history which saw the emergence of 'big government' in Western Europe and the seemingly inexorable extension of state regulation. As a reaction to the alleged failure of this approach, new ideas – often from outside existing policy communities – emerged, which have gradually captured the middle ground of politics. Thus, a superficial analysis might suggest that the era of big government is over and that it has been replaced by a new regime of liberalized and unregulated markets, following a European-wide 'bonfire' of state controls.

The reality is quite different, as this volume so clearly demonstrates. Thus, Giandomenico Majone rightly points out that much of the deregulatory process has in fact been more about regulatory reform than the claimed deregulation. The so-called 'big bang' in the City of London is, perhaps, the most spectacular example of this phenomenon. Rather than ridding City institutions of public controls, Mrs Thatcher's reforms replaced one set of controls with another often more burdensome regulatory regime. The new regime was intended to force a change in the behaviour of City institutions in order to prevent the decline in the competitive position of Britain's financial markets in the face of global trends. Rather than a retreat of the state in Western Europe, we have often seen a rather more interventionist state, re-writing regulatory rules as a means of addressing a range of reform deficits enshrined in existing regulatory bargains. In practice, the idea that the state should do less has been implemented by the state doing more by way of intervention in rather long-standing regulatory regimes.

A second policy fashion has been for states to attempt to constrain and then reduce public expenditure. 'Throwing public money' at problems is seen as a 1960s fashion and as no longer an option. States have been reluctant to use this policy instrument as a general response to public policy problems and have, therefore, denied themselves one of the traditional levers on society. Paradoxically, this has made regulation a more attractive policy instrument, as it transfers costs to private actors. In the case of the European Union, the Commission has never had access to big budgets (apart from the Common Agricultural Policy and the Structural Funds) and so, as Professor Majone's own research has demonstrated, it has resorted to regulation as a major resource in the process of European integration.

A third policy fashion, also analysed in detail in this volume, is that the institutions for the 'delivery' of regulation have changed. Much greater emphasis is now placed on the role of different types of agency in the design and oversight of regulation. Combined with the 'Europeanization' of regulation, this trend has reduced the direct controls which national governments can exercise over the regulatory process. Hence, an important focus of this volume is the traditional issue of accountability. As Professor Majone suggests, this raises two theoretical problems: namely, why have governments been willing to create new regulatory systems over which they may have less control, and what are the implications of this delegation for democratic legitimacy and accountability? As the case studies in this volume show, these issues have been especially complex because of the fluid and uncertain relationships between national and European regulation. This has created both problems and opportunities. On the one hand, it is difficult to weld together so many different regulatory styles and traditions, but on the other hand it provides an ideal opportunity for policy learning and policy transfer.

The issue of democratic control is central to this major theoretical and empirical review of regulation in Europe. Professor Majone concludes that non-majoritarian institutions are bound to play an increasingly important role in Europe. This leads to a struggle between governments and agencies, leaving the accountability and democratic control problems unresolved. Attempts to resolve this age-old problem are certain to be one of the central features of European and national level politics into the next century. Our hope is that this weighty volume will be seen as a major contribution to our understanding of how an efficient and democratic solution might be found.

Preface

This volume attempts to close a serious gap in the literature on comparative policy-making in Europe. As every student of the subject knows, in America regulation has long been recognized as a distinct type of policy which has given birth to a distinct theoretical and empirical literature. Indeed, in political science and economics the study of regulation has been elevated to the status of a sub-discipline, while American administrative law is co-extensive with the study of regulatory law and the regulatory process.

The situation is quite different in Europe. Here, for historical reasons which will become clear to the readers of this book, research on the economics and politics of regulation – especially statutory regulation by independent agencies – is still in its infancy; only legal scholars have recently begun to produce book-length treatments of this topic. As a result, political scientists and political economists who wish to understand the growth of statutory regulation in Europe have to rely on conceptual frameworks originally developed for the study of regulation in America.

Although the century-old American experience with this mode of policy-making has immense heuristic value for European scholars and practitioners, it is clear that models developed with a particular political and institutional setting in mind cannot be applied directly to quite different contexts. The aim of this volume, therefore, is to make an original contribution to the comparative study of regulation in Europe, at both the national and supra-national levels, by presenting theoretical and empirical analyses which are sensitive to the idiosyncratic features of current regulatory developments on this side of the Atlantic.

The preparation of this volume has been made possible by the generous support of the Research Council of the European University Institute. My students in the Department of Social and Political Science at the EUI have endured several drafts of a manuscript in continuous evolution. I thank them warmly for their patience, support and their often incisive criticisms.

Several colleagues in the Law Department of the EUI have been extremely helpful with their comments and suggestions. I wish to extend especial thanks to professor Renaud Dehousse, Christian Joerges and Francis Snyder for their continuous interest and support in this project.

In different, but equally important, ways the following persons have contributed to the successful conclusion of this project: Marie-Ange Catotti, a fixed and indispensable reference point in an institution in a state of perpetual flux such as the EUI; Michelle Everson and Laraine Laudati who not only contributed their own excellent case studies, but also translated, both literally and conceptually, the French, German and Spanish case studies; and Clare Tame who has done a superb job of editing a composite and initially much too lengthy manuscript.

Giandomenico Majone
Florence, November 1995

Acknowledgements

Professor Majone would like to acknowledge the following copyright holders for their permission to reprint extracts of his own material from the following publications: Cambridge University Press ('Cross-national sources of regulatory policymaking in Europe and the United States', *Journal of Public Policy*, 1991, XI: 79–106); Kluwer Law International ('Independence and accountability: Non-majoritarian institutions and democratic government in Europe', in *The Collected Courses of the Academy of European Law* (forthcoming); Frank Cass & Co. Ltd ('The rise of the regulatory state in Europe', *West European Politics*, 1994, 17, 3: 77–101); Blackwell Publishers ('The European Community between social policy and social regulation', *Journal of Common Market Studies*, 1993, 31, 2: 153–70); and Routledge Publishers ('Paradoxes of privatization and deregulation', *Journal of European Public Policy*, 1994, 1, 1: 53–69).

Introduction

At the end of the period of reconstruction of the national economies shattered by the war, income redistribution and discretionary macroeconomic management emerged as the top policy priorities of most Western European governments. The market was relegated to the ancillary role of providing the resources to pay for this government largess, and any evidence of market failures was deemed sufficient to justify state intervention, often in the intrusive forms of centralized capital allocation and the nationalization of key sectors of the economy. Indeed, centralized management and unfettered policy discretion came to be regarded as prerequisites of effective governance.

This social democratic consensus about the relative roles of state and market in the managed economy began to crumble during the 1970s. The combination of rising unemployment and rising rates of inflation could not be explained within the Keynesian models of the day, while discretionary public expenditure and the centralized welfare state were increasingly seen as part of the problem rather than the solution. It is at this point that we witness the appearance of the notion of government – or public sector – failure with public-choice theorists identifying various types of government failure, just as previous generations of economists had produced an ever-lengthening list of market failures. Nationalization policies seemed to provide striking empirical evidence of public sector failure – in one country after another, publicly owned firms came under fire for failing to achieve not only their economic, but also their social, objectives.

That such criticisms were not always fair or objectively justified is immaterial – the fact is that an increasing number of voters were convinced by them, and were willing to support a new model which included privatization of many parts of the public sector, more competition throughout the economy and greater emphasis on efficiency and decentralization in the provision of social services. The failure of the socialist experiment of President Mitterand in 1981/2 was seen as conclusive proof that redistributive Keynesianism was no longer possible for countries which, like France, were closely integrated in the European and global economy.

In addition to privatization, market liberalization and welfare reform, the new model of policy-making which emerged in the 1980s is commonly thought to include deregulation. It is true that in Europe, as in the United States, traditional structures of regulation and control were breaking down under the pressure of powerful technological, economic and ideological forces, and were dismantled or radically transformed. This is often referred to, rather misleadingly, as 'deregulation'. What is observed in practice is never a dismantling of all regulation – a return to a situation of *laissez-faire* which in fact never existed in Europe – but a combination of deregulation *and* re-regulation.

Thus, in Britain and elsewhere, the privatization of the public utilities has been followed by price regulation, while the newly privatized firms have lost their pre-existing immunity from national and European competition law. In fact, in industries such as telecommunications, the power of the incumbent operators (and former monopolists) to fight off would-be rivals is so great that governments have to intervene to restrain it. As a result, competitors frequently owe their existence to regulatory constraints imposed on their larger rivals.

Deregulation may also mean less restrictive or rigid regulation. Thus, the rationale for government intervention has seldom been challenged in the increasingly important area of 'social regulation' – environment, health, safety and consumer protection. Here the issue is not deregulation, but rather how to achieve the relevant regulatory objectives by less burdensome methods. For example, the substitution of environmental standards by economic incentives in the form of pollution charges does not do away with environmental regulation, but only introduces different and, hopefully, more efficient policy instruments.

In short, the last fifteen years have been a period less of deregulation than of intense regulatory reform, where the latter term is used to denote the apparently paradoxical combination of deregulation and re-regulation. Regulatory reform is the phenomenon with which this volume is concerned. Traditional forms of regulation and control in Europe included public ownership, the assignment of regulatory functions to departments of government under the direct control of political executives, and various self-regulatory arrangements, often corporatist in nature. These modes of regulation are being gradually displaced by statutory regulation administered by expert agencies which are in theory independent of direct political controls (the practice is complicated by the persistence of older regulatory philosophies, as shown by the case studies in the second part of this volume). At the same time, important regulatory powers previously exercised by national governments have been transferred to the European level – a striking example of deregulation followed by re-regulation. Now, the Treaty of Rome enjoins European regulators to 'neither seek nor take instructions from any Government or from any other body' in the performance of their duties.

Thus, a central feature of regulatory reform in Europe, at both the national and the supranational levels, is the delegation of significant policy-making powers to independent institutions. That this is not an isolated feature but part of a more general trend is shown by other recent events such as the growing independence of the national central banks, and the exceptional status granted to the future European Central Bank by the Maastricht Treaty on European Union. The Bank will be able to make regulations that become European and member-state law without the involvement of either European legislators or of national parliaments.

These developments pose two key theoretical problems analysed in the first and third parts of this book. First, how can we explain the willingness of political leaders to limit their own policy discretion – so highly in the past – and to accept the consequent diffusion of state power? Second, what are the implications of delegation for democratic legitimacy and public accountability?

Doubts concerning the wisdom of unchecked government discretion were first raised in the course of a long-running debate on rules versus discretion in monetary policy: should governments tailor policy to current economic conditions or conduct policy according to pre-announced rules, such as a constant rate of monetary growth? In the 1960s, critics of government discretion argued that governments and central banks lack the knowledge and flexibility necessary for successful discretionary policy. Hence the risk that discretionary policy could actually make the economy less, rather than more, stable. The debate was given a new twist in the late 1970s when the credibility of policy-makers – rather than insufficient information – emerged as the key issue: fixed rules are preferable because they increase policy credibility, while discretion leads to 'time inconsistency'. As regards the latter, without a binding commitment holding them to the original plan, governments will use their discretion to switch to what now appears to be a better policy. But if other policy actors anticipate such a policy shift, they will behave in ways which prevent policy-makers achieving their original objectives.

Time inconsistency is clearly a general phenomenon, not limited to monetary policy. If its significance for all areas of policy-making has been recognized only recently, the explanation may be the increasing openness of national economies. Growing economic, ecological and political interdependence among nations has the effect of weakening the domestic impact of national policy actions and strengthening their impact on other countries. Thus, domestic policies are increasingly projected outside the national borders, but can achieve their external objectives only if they are credible. This is because the traditional alternative to persuasion – state coercion – cannot normally be applied beyond the national borders.

Even in purely domestic terms, however, the growing complexity of public policy reduces the effectiveness of the traditional control-and-command techniques of government bureaucracy. Until fairly recently, most of the tasks undertaken by national governments were simple enough to be organized along classical bureaucratic lines. Once a programme was enacted, the details of its operations could be formulated and appropriate commands issued by highly centralized command centres. By contrast, the single most important characteristic of the new forms of economic and social regulation is that their success depends on affecting the attitudes, consumption habits or production patterns of millions of individuals and thousands of firms and local units of government. The new tasks of government are difficult not only because they deal with technologically complicated matters, but also because they attempt to modify individual expectations and behaviour. Hence credibility tends to replace coercive power as the essential resource of policy-makers, even at the domestic level.

Unfortunately, credibility is problematic for elected politicians. In part this is because in a democracy political executives have shorter time horizons than their counterparts in the private sector, so that the effectiveness of reputational mechanisms for achieving credibility is more limited in the political sphere. Moreover, a legislature cannot bind a subsequent legislature and a majority coalition cannot bind another, so that public policies are always vulnerable to reneging and hence lack of credibility. In such a situation, delegation to an extra-governmental agency is one of the most promising strategies whereby governments can commit themselves to regulatory policy strategies whilst maintaining political credibility.

The desire to achieve credible commitments moreover explains a puzzling feature of policy making in the European Community/European Union (EC/EU). It is not *a priori* obvious why the member states – traditionally so jealous of their sovereignty – would be willing to delegate it to the European institutions with regulatory powers extending well beyond the level required by the founding treaties or by the functional needs of an integrated market. We know from the theory and practice of international relations that market failures with international impacts, such as transboundary pollution, can in principle be managed through intergovernmental agreements, without delegating regulatory powers to a supranational body such as the European Commission. However, when it is difficult to observe whether governments are making an honest effort to enforce a cooperative agreement, the agreement lacks credibility. Thus, the delegation of regulatory powers to an independent institution is – once again – a means by which governments can commit themselves to regulatory strategies that would not be credible otherwise.

If delegation solves, at least in part, the credibility problem, it simultaneously creates another. A basic principle of democratic theory is that public policy be subject to control exclusively by persons accountable to the electorate. Independent agencies would appear to violate this principle and hence are viewed with suspicion by the advocates of direct accountability to parliament. The technocrats who head such agencies are appointed – not elected – officials and yet they yield enormous power. How is their exercise of that power to be democratically controlled? The same question can be raised concerning all 'non-majoritarian' institutions – institutions which, by design, are not directly accountable either to voters or to elected politicians:

not only independent regulatory or executive agencies, but also independent central banks, supranational bodies such as the European Commission or the World Trade Organization, and even courts and administrative tribunals.

The challenge is to develop a concept of accountability that is consistent with democratic principles but which does not negate in practice the very rationale of non-majoritarian institutions. The solution suggested here divides the general problem into two parts: first, the type of issues that can be legitimately delegated to independent experts; and, second, the means by which indirect accountability may be enforced. Concerning the first I argue that delegation is legitimate in the case of efficiency issues, that is, where the task is to find a solution capable of improving the conditions of all, or almost all, individuals and groups in society. On the other hand, redistributive policies, which aim to improve the conditions of one group in society at the expense of another, should not be delegated to independent experts. The technical arguments behind these normative statements are presented in the concluding chapter.

Turning to the means by which accountability in the sphere of efficiency issues may be enforced, we begin by noting that the tendency to assume that independence and accountability are mutually exclusive is inspired by a traditional, hierarchical view of control which is quite inappropriate for the highly technical and discretionary activities delegated to regulatory agencies. A more appropriate concept should contemplate a network of complementary and overlapping checking mechanisms instead of assuming that control is necessarily to be exercised from any fixed place in the system. In practice, this means that an independent agency can be monitored and kept democratically accountable only by a combination of control instruments: clear and narrowly defined objectives; accountability by results; strict procedural requirements; professionalism; transparency; public participation; and even inter-agency rivalry and regulatory competition. Legislative and executive oversight are not of course excluded, but any attempt to 'micro-manage' the agency should be firmly resisted. We shall argue that this analysis of the legitimacy problem, like the previous analysis of the delegation problem, is as applicable to the European as to the national level.

In sum, the aim of this volume is twofold: it seeks to inform the reader about the far-reaching regulatory reforms currently taking place in Europe, but goes beyond this to present a theoretical framework for analysing the reasons and the broader implications of those reforms. In support of this, the case studies, whilst limited in number and scope, raise the major problems and paradoxes of practical regulatory activity, in particular, the contrasting demands of policy and politics in practical regulation, and the importance and interplay of independence, accountability and legitimacy in any balanced future development of regulatory reform in Europe.

Part I

The political economy of regulation

1 Regulation and its modes

Giandomenico Majone

INTRODUCTION

Regulation, in the sense of rules issued for the purpose of controlling the manner in which private and public enterprises conduct their operations, is of course as old as government. Moreover, the normative justification of regulation – the correction of what are today called 'market failures', for example, monopoly power – is hardly new: Machlup's chronology of anti-monopoly regulation, for example, includes an edict of the Roman Emperor Zeno from AD 483, prohibiting all monopolies, combinations and price agreements; the decision of an English court in 1603 (*Darcy* v. *Allin*) declaring a monopoly in playing cards void as against common law because it results in higher prices and lower employment; and the decree of the Massachusetts Colonial Legislature in 1641 that 'there shall be no monopolies granted or allowed among us but of such new inventions as are profitable to the country, and that for a short time' (Machlup 1952: 152–7).

What have changed in time are less the functions than the modes of regulation. When one speaks of regulation today, in America and increasingly also in Europe, one usually refers to sustained and focused control exercised by a public agency, on the basis of a legislative mandate, over activities that are generally regarded as desirable to society (Selznick 1985: 363–4).

In this definition the reference to socially desirable activities excludes, for example, most of what goes on in the criminal justice system; it also suggests that market activities are 'regulated' only in societies that consider such activities worthwhile in themselves and hence in need of protection as well as control.

The reference to sustained and focused control by an agency, on the basis of a legal mandate, implies that regulation is not achieved simply by passing a law, but requires detailed knowledge of, and intimate involvement with, the regulated activity. One of the most distinguished students and practitioners of regulation in the New Deal era put it as follows:

[t]he art of regulating an industry requires knowledge of details of its operations, ability to shift requirements as the condition of the industry may dictate, the pursuit of energetic measures upon the appearance of an

emergency, and the power through enforcement to realize conclusions as to policy.

(Landis 1966 [1938]: 25–6)

Statutory regulation by independent boards or commissions has a long tradition in the United States – at the federal level it goes back to the 1887 Interstate Commerce Act regulating the railways and setting up the corresponding regulatory body, the Interstate Commerce Commission – but is a fairly recent phenomenon in Europe. Ideology is not the sole, but certainly an important, factor in this difference. American-style regulation, which leaves ownership of industry in private hands, expresses a widely held belief that the market works well under normal circumstances and should be interfered with only in specific cases of market failure.

In Europe, on the other hand, the market system, and the structure of property rights which such a system entails, have been accepted by a large majority of voters only recently. For most of the period between the great depression of 1873–96 and the Second World War, large segments of public opinion were openly hostile to the market economy, and sceptical about the capacity of the system to survive its recurrent crises. Hence in industry after industry, the response of most European governments to perceived cases of market failure was a very intrusive form of control, that is, nationalizations rather than American-style regulation.

The European response to market failures has also been shaped by a long tradition of state dirigisme and bureaucratic centralization. Even where regulatory instruments such as price control or licensing, rather than public ownership, have been used, there has been a general reluctance to rely on specialized, independent agencies. Instead, regulatory functions have been assigned with a few exceptions, such as the one discussed in the chapter by Everson, to ministries or inter-ministerial committees, or to semi-public corporatist bodies. The absence of independent single-purpose agencies, the confusion of operation and regulation, the preponderance of informal procedures for rule-making, and the opaque quality of corporatist self-regulatory arrangements, are all factors that explain the low visibility of regulatory policy-making in Europe in the past, and the consequent lack of sustained scholarly attention.

Things have changed considerably over the last two decades as shown not only by the proliferation of regulatory bodies at both the national and European levels, but also by a growing body of specialized literature of European origin on regulation as a distinct type of policy-making. Traditional ways of thinking and patterns of behaviour are not easily changed, however, and if one wants to understand the limits of current policy and institutional innovations one must be aware of the legacy of older approaches. For this reason the present chapter compares statutory regulation – with which the remainder of the book is concerned – with two other modes of regulation which have been historically important in Europe: nationalization and self-regulation. The comparison leads to the conclusion that, in spite of some defects that have been extensively discussed in the academic literature and in the deregulation debate, statutory regulation by expert and independent agencies represents a definite improvement over previous practices.

REGULATION THROUGH PUBLIC OWNERSHIP

Historically, public ownership has been the main mode of economic regulation in Europe. Although public enterprise can be traced back to the seventeenth century, and in some parts of Europe to even earlier periods, its use became widespread only in the nineteenth century with the development of gas, electricity, the water industry, the railways, the telegraph and, later, the telephone services. These industries, or parts of them, exhibit the characteristics of natural monopolies: situations where, because of the economies-of-scale phenomenon, it is more efficient for production to be carried out by one firm, rather than by several or many. Public ownership of such industries was supposed to give the state the power to impose a planned structure on the economy and to protect the public interest against powerful private interests.

It is important to keep in mind that the nationalization of key industries in the nineteenth and twentieth century has been advocated on a variety of grounds: not only to eliminate the political power and economic inefficiency of private monopolies, but also to stimulate economic development, to favour particular regions or social groups, to protect consumers and foster democratic accountability, to ensure national security and even to punish (Renault, Charbonnages du Nord and other French enterprises were nationalized after the Second World War because their owners had collaborated with the Germans). Moreover, the ideological roots are quite varied. It would be wrong to assume that nationalizations always reflected collectivist values and goals – Bismarck, Mussolini, Franco and De Gaulle have been among the most energetic nationalizers of European history.

Regardless of the multiplicity of objectives and ideological justifications, the central assumption was always that public ownership would increase government's ability to regulate the economy and protect the public interest. Public enterprises would shape economic structure directly through their production decisions and indirectly through their pricing decisions. In the early days of nationalization it seemed axiomatic that the imposition of prices and quality standards in the public interest could be achieved more effectively by the flexible decision-making inherent in the public ownership framework – considerable managerial discretion, subject only, in theory, to political accountability – than by formalized legal controls imposed by an external agency (Ogus 1994: 267–8).

Subsequent experience, however, demonstrated that public ownership and public control cannot be assumed to be the same thing. Indeed, the problem of imposing effective public control over nationalized enterprises proved so intractable that the main objective for which they had been created – namely, the regulation of the economy in the public interest – was almost forgotten.

After the Second World War, the legislation in France, the United Kingdom, and other European countries which brought many large enterprises into public ownership tended to stipulate objectives of a general nature and saw the role of managers of public enterprises as that of trustees of the public interest. The managers were supposed to decide at arm's length from government, although government was accorded certain powers over them, notably power for the sponsoring minister to appoint board members and chairman, to issue general directions, and to approve investment programmes.

However, the idea of an unproblematic notion of public interest proved to be a will-o'-the-wisp (Prosser 1989: 136). Perceptive economists, such as W. Arthur Lewis (1951) soon recognized the dangers of an institutional arrangement in which objectives were ill defined and in which it was very difficult to determine *ex post* whether or not they had in fact been achieved. The incentives built into such an arrangement might lead public sector managers to maximize the scale of operations, subject to external financing constraints, or to seek a quiet life untroubled by changes in working practices or difficulties in labour relations, rather than to pursue a rather vague notion of public interest (Kay, Mayer and Thompson 1986: 9).

As early as 1951, Lewis had pointed out that:

> [t]he appointing of public directors to manage an undertaking is not sufficient public control. . . . Parliament is handicapped in controlling corporations by its lack of time. . . . Neither have Members of Parliament the competence to supervise these great industries. . . . Parliament is further handicapped by paucity of information . . . for example, less information is now published about the railways than was available before they were nationalized.
>
> (Lewis 1951, cited in Machlup 1952: 50)

In Britain dissatisfaction with the performance of nationalized industries led to repeated attempts by government to prescribe more specific objectives. A theme common to Treasury White Papers in 1961, 1967 and 1978 was greater emphasis on commercial rather than public interest considerations, and on external financial controls. Despite the intentions of the authors of such papers, detailed scrutiny by government of the day-to-day activities of nationalized enterprises had tended to increase rather than the reverse, and the autonomy of the latter in decisions regarding investment, planning and industrial relations had been steadily eroded (Kay, Mayer and Thompson 1986: 9–10). Thus, ministerial interference was frequent and pervasive, albeit of an informal nature. Moreover, the ministerial power to issue general directions, though little used for its true purpose, was often invoked as a means of avoiding responsibility for unpopular decisions (Wade 1988: 161).

The French nationalizations of 1982/3 gave rise to essentially the same problems as earlier waves of nationalization: the objectives were not clearly defined either before or after the 1981 presidential elections; and the degree of government influence over the nationalized industries became a bone of contention. In May 1983, Mitterand asserted that 'the nationalized industries should have total autonomy of decision and action' (*Le Monde*, 28 May 1983, cited in Hall 1986: 204). Of course, comments Hall, the newly nationalized enterprises would never operate totally autonomously, but it was equally hard for the state to acquire effective control over them. In fact, these enterprises had the worst of both worlds – they lacked adequate direction from the state to guide long-term strategy, and at the same time they were subject to sporadic government intervention in their daily operations. And because the nationalized enterprises faced more intense political pressures to avoid lay-offs than did private firms, the capacity of the state to restructure French industry might have been reduced, rather than strengthened, by nationalizations (Hall 1986: 205).

Nationalization has failed not only with respect to its objective of economic regulation and control, but also with respect to the socio-political objectives of consumer protection and public accountability. For example, the British nationalized enterprises tried harder than the public corporations of other countries to create mechanisms for the protection of consumers. The 1940s witnessed the creation of consumer councils or consultative committees which handled complaints and commented on price increases and other policy proposals, and some of the most active councils even attempted to undertake consumer audits. Their powers were modest, however, because of the official view of managers of public enterprises as the trustees of the public interest.

Indeed, the record of these consumer councils has generally been dismal. They rarely used records of complaints to argue for general policy changes, and, although in some cases there was a statutory requirement that they be consulted before price increases and on the boards' general plans, such consultation has been late and cursory. Underlying these and other problems has been the fundamental difficulty in obtaining information from the enterprises (Prosser 1989: 137–8).

Detailed ministerial interventions in the decisions of public managers, particularly in pricing and personnel decisions, had perverse effects in terms of public accountability. Because such interventions were usually exercised through informal and even secret processes, rather than by official directions, accountability was reduced to vanishing point. In fact, how could accountability be enforced if it was not clear where responsibility for decisions lay – with the public managers or with the government? The very multiplicity of objectives assigned to nationalized companies made it impossible to define clear criteria of evaluation. Company executives could always argue that the poor performance of their companies was due not to poor management but to the political constraints imposed on their personnel, investment and pricing decisions.

At any rate, accountability to parliament was always more of a myth than a reality since, as Arthur Lewis noted, parliaments have neither the time nor the expertise and information necessary to supervise great industrial enterprises. Governments, on the other hand, generally resisted proposals that public corporations should be treated in the same way as private monopolies. This has meant generous exemptions from antitrust legislation – see, for example, the chapters by Baake and Perschau, and by Cases, in this volume – but also, given the traditional reluctance of European judges to regard matters of economic and social policy as justiceable, from judicial review of the decisions of public managers. Thus, the European consumer was less well protected *vis-à-vis* public corporations than the American consumer was *vis-à-vis* private monopolies subject to legal controls imposed by an independent regulatory body.

In the privatization debate, attention has tended to focus exclusively on the relative efficiency of public and private enterprises. Rigorous tests of the common assumption that private firms are more efficient then publicly owned ones are often difficult because of comparability problems: government-run enterprises may differ systematically from those that are privately run. Where comparisons are meaningful, several empirical studies suggest that public enterprises are not necessarily less efficient than private ones, as long as they operate in a competitive environment. A Canadian study, for example, found that there was no significant difference in the efficiency of Canada's two main railway systems, the privately owned Canadian Pacific and the publicly owned Canadian National (Daves and Christensen 1990). Similarly, a study carried out in Australia, comparing the public Trans-Australia Airlines and the private Ansett Airlines of Australia, found very little difference in the performance of the two companies. Such conclusions indicate that there is nothing intrinsically more efficient about private ownership (Kay, Mayer and Thompson 1986).

If this is true, then the current crisis of nationalization policies in Western Europe is less a problem of productive efficiency than the failure of a particular mode of regulation. Public ownership not only reduced government's ability to regulate the economy, but also interrupted a policy-learning process which could have produced, half a century ago, the kind of regulatory institutions that Europe is now struggling to develop. In late nineteenth-century Europe there are instances of the public control of particular industries by means of regulatory agencies or tribunals. For example, just a year after the United States Congress passed the Interstate Commerce Act (1887) regulating the railway industry and creating the first federal regulatory commission, an Act of the British Parliament provided the first effective regulation of railway rates and established the Railway and Canal Commission as successor to the Railway Commission of 1873. Some thirty years later, the UK Electricity Supply Act established a body – the Electricity Commission – with extensive regulatory powers.

Such commissions were often court-like tribunals rather than regulatory agencies in the modern sense. In England, tribunals:

[p]roved so common that by 1933 the regulation of British public utilities was viewed by some as considerably impaired by this reliance on the quasi-judicial method and by the resulting failure to develop the administrative commission. What was absent was a powerful agency that applied a special expertise, employed its own secretariat and regulated (in the sense of imposing a planned structure on an industry or social issue). Regulators, instead of instituting action, responded to the competing proposals of private interests.

(Baldwin and McCrudden 1987: 15)

Dissatisfaction with the quasi-judicial approach to regulation could have stimulated institutional innovations, as it did in the early 1970s when the failure of the court-like Air Transport Licensing Board as an all-purpose agency led to the creation of the relatively powerful Civil Aviation Authority. Instead, the nationalization of the utilities tended to confuse the roles of manager and regulator, subordinating the latter to the former – questions of agency design literally disappeared from the public agenda.

STATUTORY REGULATION BY INDEPENDENT AGENCIES

The failure of public ownership as a mode of regulation explains the current popularity of an alternative mode whereby public utilities, and other industries deemed to affect the public interest, remain in private hands but are subject to rules developed and enforced by specialized agencies or commissions. Such bodies are usually established by statute as independent authorities, in the sense that they are allowed to operate outside the line of hierarchical control or oversight by the departments of central government. This mode of regulation represents a new frontier of public policy and public management in Europe and other parts of the industrialized world.

By contrast, however, it has a long history in America where the tradition of regulation by means of independent bodies combining legislative, judicial and executive functions (rule-making, adjudication and enforcement in the terminology of American administrative law) goes back to the Interstate Commerce Act of 1887 at the federal level, and even earlier in states such as New York, Massachusetts and Wisconsin. The rejection by American political leaders of nationalization as a politically and economically viable option reflected the generally held belief that the market functions perfectly well under normal circumstances, and that interference should be limited to clear cases of market failure. The expert commission represents the institutional embodiment of this belief.

Faith in the power of expertise as an engine of social improvement – technical expertise which neither legislators or courts nor bureaucratic generalists presumably possess – has always been an important source of legitimation for American regulators. For writers of the New Deal such as Merle Fainsod, regulatory commissions emerged and became instruments of governance for industry precisely because Congress and the courts proved unable to satisfy the 'great functional imperative' of specialization and expertise. Independent regulatory commissions, 'commended themselves because they offered the possibility of achieving expertness in the treatment of special problems, relative freedom from the exigencies of party politics in their consideration, and expeditiousness in their disposition' (Fainsod 1940: 313).

Among the important reasons for the establishment of regulatory commissions mentioned by Cushman (1941) is the greater ease in recruiting experts for an independent agency than for executive departments. Landis finds an even closer relationship between expertise and the regulatory commissions: '[t]he demand for expertness, for a continuity of concern, naturally leads to the creation of authorities limited in their sphere of action to the new tasks that government may conclude to undertake' (Landis 1966: 23).

Conversely, as the supply of goods creates its own demand, according to Say's law, so the supply of regulation creates its own demand of expertise:

> With the rise of regulation, the need for expertness became dominant; for the art of regulating an industry requires knowledge of details of its operations, ability to shift requirements as the condition of the industry may dictate, the pursuit of energetic measures upon the appearance of an emergency, and the power through enforcement to realize conclusions as to policy.
>
> (Landis 1966: 25–6)

Certainly, the New Deal advocates of regulation knew that, as Fainsod put it, the expertness of the regulatory bureaucracy is not always above suspicion. Still they insisted that issues of fact should be handled by experts, using whatever methods appeared the most appropriate. Judicial review of the evidence used in reaching a regulatory decision would be a serious threat to 'the very virtue of specialized knowledge which constitutes one of the chief justifications of the establishment of commissions' (Fainsod 1940: 3–4). Moreover, the 'great functional imperative' of specialization and expertise led to a blurring of the distinctions stressed by the classical doctrine of the separation of powers.

For example, with the Interstate Commerce Act, the United States' Congress delegated its own power to regulate an important part of interstate commerce, namely interstate railway traffic, to an agency designed especially for the purpose – the Interstate Commerce Commission (ICC). This was an important institutional innovation, at least at the federal level. As Landis would comment some fifty years later, the novelty with respect to traditional administration consisted not only in the precise definition of the scope of the activities of the ICC – a particular industry – but especially in regard to the responsibility given the commission for the exercise of those powers. In the words of Landis: '[i]n the grant to it of that full ambit of authority necessary for it in order to plan, to promote, and to police, it presents an assemblage of rights normally exercisable by government as a whole' (Landis 1966: 15).

Precisely because of this broad delegation of executive, legislative and judicial authority, however, the independent regulatory commissions (IRCs) have been accused of constituting a politically irresponsible 'fourth branch of government' never envisaged by the framers of the United States' Constitution. We shall come back to this debate in Chapter 13. Here it suffices to note that while in Europe sustained criticism of nationalization policies developed only fairly late, '[t]he single constant in the American experience with regulation has been controversy' (McCraw 1984: 301). This striking characteristic of American-style regulation is explained by McCraw as follows. Many of the diverse functions assigned to regulatory commissions were regarded by legislatures as essential tasks, but very difficult for existing governmental institutions to perform. Because legislators did not wish to burden themselves with such duties, they passed the responsibility to specialized agencies. But an agency receiving the assignment was also forced to accept the intrinsic controversy that had created the task in the first place. Hence, this author concludes, 'controversy became attached to regulation like a Siamese twin' (McCraw 1984: 301–2).

This is only a partial explanation, however. The origins of the IRCs must also be understood in the context of a continuing struggle over policy-making between the US president, on one side, and Congress, powerful interest groups, and occasionally the Supreme Court, on the other. The IRCs were created by Congress not only to deal with some complex technical problems, but also to limit presidential control over important policy areas. In fact, the independence of the important regulatory bodies created during the New Deal – the Federal Communications Commission, the Securities and Exchange Commission, and the Civil Aeronautics Board, among others – was the price President Roosevelt had to pay for acceptance by Congress and the Supreme Court of far-reaching public intervention in the economy. The president would have preferred to assign the new functions to executive departments under his immediate control, but the other branches of government were not willing to accept this (Shapiro 1988). Conflict over regulation is also the result of the conflictual nature of the US political system.

In the 1970s, the legal, political and economic criticisms of American-style regulation found expression under the label 'regulatory failure'. Just as the market fails in certain circumstances to serve the public interest, so does public regulation. Hence, it was argued, market failure is not a sufficient justification for government intervention since regulatory failure may have more serious consequences than market failure. We shall evaluate these arguments in the next chapter. The aim of the present chapter is to assess the advantages and limitations of different modes of regulation, and so it is appropriate to compare the ways in which both statutory regulation by independent agencies and regulation by nationalization can fail. This is done in Table 1.1.

Table 1.1 Comparing two types of regulatory failure

American-style regulation	Regulation by nationalization
capture of regulators by regulated firms	capture of public managers by politicians and trade unions
overcapitalization (the so-called Averch–Johnson effect)	overmanning
anti-competitive regulation	public monopolies
vague objectives ('regulate in the public interest')	ambiguous and inconsistent goals given to public managers
poor co-ordination among different regulators	poor co-ordination among different public enterprises
insufficient political accountability of independent regulatory agencies	no effective control over public enterprises by parliament, the courts or the sponsoring minister

As Table 1.1 shows, there are striking analogies – in fact one can detect a one-to-one correspondence – between the major defects of these two modes of regulation. Thus, the 'capture' of the regulatory agencies by the regulated interests corresponds to the 'capture' of the nationalized firms by politicians, bureaucrats and trade unions; overcapitalization in the regulated utilities (the tendency to use too much capital in production, induced by the method used by American regulators to control the prices charged by the utilities) is the counterpart of overstaff in the public sector; severe problems of account-ability and coordination arise in both cases. Again, according to some critics of American regulation, managers of regulated firms develop a cost-plus mentality which is inimical to innovation – but surely this cannot be worse than the bureaucratic mentality of public managers who know that their firms will never face bankruptcy.

Because of these analogies, it has been argued that there is not a marked difference between public monopolies, such as the European Post and Telecommunications Ministries, and privately owned but publicly regulated monopolies, such as the American Telephone and Telegraph Company before deregulation. Such analogies, however suggestive, cannot be pushed too far. It is true that American regulation has often restricted competition among existing enterprises and limited new entry, but in Europe the monopolistic position of public enterprises is often defined in law and, in some countries, for example Germany, even guaranteed by constitutional provisions. Publicly owned monopolies can neither go bankrupt nor be taken over by other firms. If technological progress allows a more competitive organization of the industry, competition will eventually emerge and end the rule of private monopolies. If monopolies are public, however, the entry of newcomers and competition by new substitutes will be either delayed or prevented altogether. The deregulation of telecommunications in the United States and privatization of the same industry in Europe offer a striking illustration of this difference.

PRIVATIZATION AND DEREGULATION COMPARED

In order to understand better the nature of a given policy it is useful to examine what happens when the policy is reversed (Majone 1994). American deregulation has proved to be considerably more forceful than European privatizations in introducing competition and restructuring key sectors of the economy, and points to a number of additional observations concerning the relative merits of the two modes of regulation. To make the discussion more concrete, I examine the deregulation of telecommunications in the United States and the privatization of the same industry in Britain, the pioneer of privatization in Europe.

The story of the American deregulation of the telecommunications industry leading to divestiture of one of the most powerful companies in the world (the Bell system) has been told many times (Derthick and Quirk 1985; Temin 1987; Joskow and Noll 1991). For our purposes it is sufficient to recall the main points of this extraordinary reversal of public policy.

Before divestiture, the Bell system included the American Telephone and Telegraph Company (AT&T), the twenty-three Bell Operating Companies, providing local and regional telephone services, and other companies such as Western Electric, producer of telecom equipment, and the Bell Telephone Laboratories. The Federal Communications Commission (FCC) – the agency responsible for regulating telecommunications at the federal level – began allowing competition to AT&T in long-distance communications in the late 1950s, several years before pro-competitive deregulation acquired widespread political support in Washington. Important decisions taken by the FCC in the pre-divestiture period include the *Above 890* decision of 1959, authorizing private long-distance microwave systems, which could use the frequency spectrum above 890 megahertz; the *Carterfone* decision of 1967, allowing use of a radio telephone that was not manufactured and owned by AT&T; and the *MCI* decision, later the same year, allowing a company to sell long-distance telephone connections to a multiple business over a single, independent network.

Thus, by the mid-1970s, AT&T had been forced to allow its customers to own their own telephones, to construct their own private networks and to buy point-to-point connections from alternative carriers. Despite this, the liberalizations from the late 1950s to the early 1970s did not fundamentally challenge the structure of AT&T. The company still bought equipment only from itself and the vast majority of ordinary telephone calls – both local and long-distance – still went through the AT&T network.

The turning point came in 1974, when the Antitrust Division of the

Department of Justice filed an antitrust suit against AT&T (the third such suit in AT&T's history) requesting that the company be divested – that is, that local service, long-distance and manufacturing be broken up into three separate, unrelated businesses, and further dividing local services into several companies. The suit was filed despite opposition from several other federal agencies, including the Department of Commerce which was concerned about the economic consequences of divestiture, and the Department of Defense which favoured a single, integrated long-distance carrier for reasons of national security.

The company began a five-year lobbying campaign in Congress seeking legislation that would force the antitrust case to be dropped and cancel the licences of AT&T's long-distance competitors. The campaign seemed close to achieving its objectives when President Reagan was elected in 1981. In fact, the Reagan administration did oppose the antitrust case, but was unable to stop it. The Assistant Attorney General for Antitrust, William Baxter – a former law professor at Stanford University and a strong advocate of competition – succeeded in keeping total control of the litigation. In 1984, AT&T gave up the fight, offering a settlement that gave the Antitrust Division most of what it wanted. In retrospect one can see that the ability of the FCC to take gradual liberalizing actions opened up the way for the more radical changes that took place later.

These developments were followed with great interest in Europe, where national governments had traditionally granted authority over telecommunications to a single monopolist, usually the Ministry of Posts, Telegraph and Telephones (PTT). Now an emergent coalition of computer and service industries saw the chance to challenge the traditional postal-industrial complex. The strength of the service sector in Britain – banking, insurance, trading, publishing and media – may explain why this country was the first to follow the American example. The British Telecommunications Act 1981 established British Telecom (BT) as a public corporation with an exclusive right to operate public networks and to regulate the industry. The Post Office, which had been the monopoly supplier of telephone services from 1912 to 1981, retained responsibility for postal services. In a 1982 White Paper the Thatcher government announced its intention to sell just over half of BT's shares.

The Telecommunications Act 1984 abolished BT's involvement in regulation. In August of that year, BT plc took over the business of the public corporation and, after a massive publicity campaign, three billion shares were sold to the public at the end of November 1984. The 1984 Act had been preceded by two important reports to the Secretary of State for Industry on telecommunications policy: the Littlechild Report, proposing a new scheme for the regulation of BT's profits (Littlechild 1983), and the Beesley Report on the liberalization of telecom services (Beesley and Littlechild 1989). The latter report is particularly significant for the present discussion.

The Report recommended, *inter alia*, that unrestricted sale of BT's capacity should be allowed. This would enable competitors to make the most efficient and innovative use of capacity. As was to be expected, BT opposed unrestricted sale, appealing to many of the same arguments that AT&T had used against the FCC's requirements: the loss of revenue with adverse effects on investment; reduced ability to cross-subsidize services such as local calls; the problems of standardization and compatibility of different equipment. These arguments had no more validity than when they were first produced by AT&T, but the government chose not to follow Professor Beesley's opinion that the advantages to customers of unrestricted sale would outweigh any potential problems for BT. In July 1984, the Minister announced that, as a general principle, simple resale would not be licensed before July 1989, allegedly in order to give time to Mercury – the only licensed competitor to BT – to construct its rival network. The government also announced its intention not to license any other operators until November 1990. As Vickers and Yarrow note (1988: 233) this constituted a remarkable restriction of competition, especially since the terms of BT's licence gave the company the opportunity to restrict and distort competition in various ways. Even more momentous was the government's decision not to restructure BT before privatization. It will be recalled that, in America, AT&T underwent far-reaching restructuring as part of the settlement with the Antitrust Division and the FCC.

The legacy of nationalization is apparent not only in the limited scope given to competition, but also in the design of regulatory institutions for telecommunications and other privatized utilities. The Secretary of State retains important regulatory powers and the operation of the regulatory body is dependent on prior decisions of the Minister as to the principles to be applied. On the other hand, the far-reaching reforms achieved by the American deregulation movement have been greatly facilitated by a style of regulation characterized by independence, expertise and policy entrepreneurship. We have already noted the role of the FCC in the radical restructuring of the telecommunications industry. Two other regulatory commissions played a leading role in the reversal of traditional regulatory policy: the Civil Aeronautics Board (CAB) and the Interstate Commerce Commission (ICC). The pro-competitive stance of these bodies is especially remarkable considering that as late as the early 1970s both the CAB and the ICC had followed a highly protectionist course.

The CAB not only succeeded in bringing about an almost complete deregulation of the airline industry – after spring 1980 carriers deemed fit were essentially free to enter the industry at will and to determine their routes and fares. Even more significantly, its chairman, Alfred E. Kahn, persuaded Congress to abolish the agency – the only major federal regulatory agency to pass beyond old age unto death (Reagan 1987: 45). The ICC did not ask to be abolished, but its staff dropped from 2,000 in 1976 to 1,300 in 1983 (Derthick and Quirk 1985).

That these three commissions undertook to change policy themselves, and to change it in a deregulatory, self-denying way, tells us something about the nature of independent regulatory commissions as instruments of governance. First, in all three cases, the chairmen provided powerful leadership in bringing about policy change. This may seem surprising at first, given the collegial nature of the commissions. In fact, after organizational reforms in the 1950s and 1960s, the chairmen have emerged as the chief executives and dominant figures. As chief executives they generally expect, and are expected by others, to have a well-defined agenda, and to measure their success by the amount of the agenda they accomplish (Derthick and Quirk 1985: 65).

Moreover, the commissions, although nominally independent, are in various ways heavily dependent on the three branches of government. They owe their existence to Congress, whose statutes govern them and from which they receive not only financial but, more importantly, political, support. Federal courts review the quality of their decision-making and can, if necessary, overturn their decisions. Finally, the commissioners and their chairmen owe their appointments to the president, even if he cannot remove members at will, and in particular not for disagreement over policy, but only for serious misconduct. Thus, when important elements of the three branches adopt a common approach to an issue such as deregulation, chairmen and commissioners are likely to respond.

Perhaps even more surprising was the fact that the staffs of the three commissions – primarily lawyers and economists – actively supported, or at least did not oppose, the pro-deregulation stance of their superiors, even when the consequences of the new policy for the size of the staff and even for the survival of the organization were apparent. As Derthick and Quirk suggest (1985: 93–4), this open-mindedness may be due to the recent rise of professional policy analysts using widely shared standards of argument and problem-solving styles, and to the growing influence of public interest groups, both of which factors balance the influence of bureaucratic ideologies and traditional patterns of behaviour.

The leading role of the commissions in the deregulation movement is a serious challenge to theories of 'capture' of the regulators by the regulated interests, and of self-seeking bureaucratic behaviour (see the following chapter). The historical record shows that when American regulators enjoy the support of the courts, of key committees and sub-committees of Congress, and of academic and public opinion, they can overcome the resistance of the regulated industries and of important elements of the executive branch, including the president (recall President Reagan's opposition to the divestiture of AT&T). I have suggested that this is due to the relative independence of the commissions, to the high level of professionalization of their staffs and to the political entrepreneurship of their chairmen. On the other hand, a long tradition of ministerial interference in managerial decisions, and a preference for assigning important regulatory responsibilities to central government departments rather than to independent regulatory bodies, have produced hesitant and, in some cases, seriously flawed policy changes in Europe.

Two conclusions may be derived from this comparison. First, the great paradox of nationalization is that public ownership has weakened, instead of strengthening, the regulatory capacity of the state. By confusing the roles of manager and regulator, and effectively subordinating the latter to the former, public ownership has impeded the development of specialized regulatory institutions. Moreover, the persistence of old habits of thought and patterns of behaviour – especially the habit of ministerial interference and secrecy – inherited from the age of nationalizations, has had a negative effect on the design of new institutions (see Chapter 3). On the other hand, a mode of regulation emphasizing independence and expertise not only produces more incisive regulatory policies but, as our examples show, can also push through deregulation when economic and technological changes make public over-sight no longer necessary. Despite its conflictual beginnings and the criticism to which it has been subjected for more than a century, the American model of statutory regulation by independent agencies has proved to be remarkably resistant, and in fact has been widely imitated internationally.

SELF-REGULATION

Regulation can also be achieved by delegating responsibilities to private or semi-private bodies, in which case one speaks of self-regulation. This mode of regulation has a long tradition among the crafts and the professions, but in recent times it has extended into other areas such as technical standard-ization, industrial safety and financial services.

With or without approval by a public authority, it plays a significant role in highly technical areas such as standardization and whenever product quality is an important consideration. For example, major international firms in accountancy promise their customers higher standards of service than the minimum assured by professional bodies and attempt to maintain standards by common procedures and internal quality control (Kay and Vickers 1990: 321).

Self-regulation offers a number of important advantages with respect to other modes such as regulation by an independent public body, but it also suffers from severe limitations. To begin with the advantages, a self-regulatory organization (SRO) can normally command a greater degree of expertise and technical knowledge of practices within the relevant area than a public agency. A second advantage is that the rules issued by a private body are less formalized than those of public regulatory regimes. This informality reduces the cost of rule-making, facilitates quick adaptation of the rules to new technical knowledge and changing economic conditions, and permits more flexible enforcement.

Another attraction of SROs in a period of fiscal austerity is that the administrative costs of self-regulation are normally internalized in the trade or activity which is subject to regulation, while the cost of public agencies are typically borne by the taxpayer (Ogus 1994: 107)

In terms of speed and efficiency, the advantages of self-regulation over direct governmental regulation can be quite significant. Thus, under the terms of the US Securities and Exchange Act 1934, an SRO, the National Association of Securities Dealers (NASD), inspects the offices, books and records of its members for violations of Securities and Exchange Commission (SEC) regulations. In 1968, 45 per cent of NASD members were inspected under this programme. By way of contrast, in 1969, SEC inspectors surveyed only 5.5 per cent of the dealers who were not members of the NASD (Katz 1976, quoted by Ayres and Braithwaite 1992: 104).

Again, before passage of the US Occupational Safety and Health Act of 1970, standards for toxic substances in the workplace were set by the American Conference of Governmental Industrial Hygienists (ACGIH) – a private organization in spite of its name. The OSH Act established a new public agency, the Occupational Safety and Health Administration (OSHA), to replace the ACGIH as the main standard-setting body (OSHA standards are legally binding whereas ACGHI threshold limit values are voluntary or 'consensus' standards). Under the terms of the Act, Congress told OSHA to use a list of approximately four hundred limit values established by the ACGHI in 1968, as its initial set of toxic substances standards. By the mid-1980s OSHA had reduced the exposure limits for ten substances and established 'work practice' standards for thirteen other chemicals, while the ACGIH had reduced the exposure limits for about two hundred more (Mendeloff 1988: 82).

Perhaps the most authoritative acknowledgement of the benefits of self-regulation comes from the European Commission – a body often criticized from its alleged centralizing tendencies. Following the adoption of the General Programme for the Removal of Technical Trade Barriers in May 1969, the Commission had attempted to harmonize technical standards across the member states of the European Community by means of directives providing detailed technical specifications for single products or groups of products. However, this approach to technical harmonization failed completely. A serious regulatory lag developed from the outset: because of the technical complexity of the issues, it took an excessive amount of time to produce harmonizing directives which often would cover only a small range of products. Thus, it took ten years to pass a single directive on gas containers made of unalloyed steel, while the average time for processing fifteen harmonizing directives which were passed as a package in September 1984, was 9.5 years (Eichener 1992). In the same period, private or semi-private standardization bodies in the member states were producing thousands of technical standards each year.

Acknowledging the failure of the traditional approach, the EC Council in 1985 approved a 'New Approach to Technical Harmonization and Standardization'. Under the new approach, Community regulation is restricted to essential safety and health requirements that a product must satisfy in order to secure the right of free movement throughout the Common Market, while technical specifications are spelt out by standards, which are not legally binding, set by European standardization bodies: the European Committee for Standardization (CEN); the European Committee for Electro-technical Standardization (CENELEC); and the European Telecommunications Standards Institute (ETSI). Since these are private-law associations, the new approach *de facto* delegates technical regulation to SROs.

At the national level, technical regulation has been delegated to private organizations for a long time in most European countries – as well as in Australia, Canada and the United States – with generally good results. Especially in Germany, since the beginning of the twentieth century technical safety has been regulated by standards and other norms set by a variety of SROs of which DIN (Deutsches Institut für Normen) is the most important. Some authors argue that this delegation to private organizations of responsibility for the safety of the citizens and the quality of the products they use is not acceptable either legally or politically. However, these arguments assume a distinction between the public and the private sector, which in the area of standard setting is far from clear-cut.

Many technical standards are set through a consensus process which often requires government officials as well as industry representatives to be made party to any consensus. With the exception of proprietary standards developed by a particular firm, governments are usually an integral part of the process leading to what is eventually considered a private standard. Thus, the Canadian Standardization Authority (CSA) requires government officials to take part in the standard-setting process, while its US counterpart, the American National Standards Institute (ANSI) requires accredited standards organizations to follow a process that gives ample opportunities to government departments and others to become involved in any eventual consensus. In Germany the federal government regulates its relationship with DIN on a contractual basis, as does the European Community/European Union (EC/EU) with the European standardization bodies. Under the latter arrangement, the standardization bodies have agreed that all interested parties (industry, users, consumers, trade unions and state agencies) shall have a chance to participate in European standard-setting.

Thus, in the area of technical standards, the important distinction is not between public and private, but between mandatory and voluntary standards. Even in sensitive areas such as occupational health and safety, the superiority of mandatory standards is far from clear. As John Mendeloff (1988) has shown in the context of American regulation of the workplace, federal standards are usually too strict and costly to justify the benefits they confer. At the same time, the slow pace of standard setting means that many serious hazards are never addressed at all: over-regulation causes under-regulation. As we saw, the same phenomenon of over-regulation (in the sense of excessive legal harmonization) leading to under-regulation convinced the EC authorities to adopt the new approach to technical standardization.

A serious problem of self-regulation is the risk of capture of the regulators by the regulated interests. We saw above that this is also a problem for other modes of regulation, and we shall examine the capture theory more closely in the next chapter. But, as one economist put it, 'with self-regulation, regulatory capture is there from the outset' (Kay quoted in Ogus 1994: 108). Precisely in order to reduce this risk, most standardization bodies, including CEN and CENELEC, are now required to allow all interested parties to participate in standard-setting. However, this requirement may not be sufficient to give adequate representation to diffuse, ill-organized interests. As we shall see in a later chapter, public regulatory bodies may provide better protection of such interests than an SRO.

Monitoring is another potential problem. As already mentioned, an important, perhaps the main, advantage of entrusting regulation to SROs is that practitioners are likely to be better informed than the public authorities about what is happening in their field of activity: their ability to discover and expose malpractice is superior. The disadvantage is that the willingness of an SRO to publicize and punish wrongdoers is likely to be less than that of a public regulator (Kay and Vickers 1990: 240). A possible solution is a two-tier system where a public agency acts chiefly as a regulator of regulators, with the SROs handling day-to-day rule-making and supervision.

This is the regulatory structure set up in Britain under the 1986 Financial Services Act. A public body, the Securities and Investment Board (SIB) supervises a number of SROs regulating various financial services such as the management of pension funds or the sale of life insurance. However, recent examples of regulatory failure, such as Robert Maxwell's unchecked theft from his companies' pension funds, or the widespread mis-sale of life insurance, show that the system is not very effective. Most reform proposals advocate strengthening the control of the SIB over the SROs. Such proposals draw on the experience of America's Securities and Exchange Commission – a powerful single regulator.

This shows that even in areas where self-regulation may be presumed to enjoy a comparative advantage, the presence of a forceful public regulator is needed in order to 'guard the guardians'. Where the market failure to be corrected is a lack of competition or a negative externality, self-regulation is clearly inappropriate. In conclusion, self-regulation may be a useful adjunct to statutory regulation, but cannot replace it. Hence the focus of this book on *statutory* regulation administered by *independent* public bodies.

REFERENCES

Ayres, I. and Braithwaite, J. (1992) *Responsive Regulation*, Oxford: Oxford University Press.

Baldwin, R. and McCrudden, C. (1987) *Regulation and Public Law*, London: Weidenfeld & Nicolson.

Beesley, M. and Littlechild, S.C. (1989) 'The regulation of privatized monopolies in the United Kingdom', *Rand Journal of Economics* 20, 3: 454–72.

Cushman, R.F. (1941) *The Independent Regulatory Commissions*, Oxford: Oxford University Press.

Daves, D.W. and Christensen, L.R. (1990) 'The relative efficiency of public and private firms in a competitive environment: the case of Canadian railroads', *Journal of Political Economy* 88: 958–76.

Derthick, M. and Quirk, P.J. (1985) *The Politics of Deregulation*, Washington (DC): The Brookings Institution.

Eichener, V. (1992) 'Social dumping or innovative regulation? Process and outcomes of European decision-making in the sector of health and safety at work harmonization', Florence: European University Institute, EUI Working Paper, SPS 92/28.

Fainsod, M. (1940) 'Some reflections on the nature of the regulatory process', in Friedrich and Mason (eds) *Public Policy*, Cambridge (MA): Harvard University Press.

Hall, P. (1986) *Governing the Economy*, New York and Oxford: Oxford University Press.

Joskow, P. and Noll, R. (1991) 'Regulation in theory and practice: an overview', in Fromm (ed.) *Studies in Public Regulation*, Cambridge (MA): MIT Press.

Katz, R.N. (1976) 'Industry self-regulation: a viable altnernative to government regulation' in Katz (ed.), *Protecting Consumer Interests*, Cambridge (MA): Ballinger.

Kay, J.A., Mayer, C. and Thompson, D. (eds) (1986) *Privatization and Regulation: the UK Experience*, Oxford: Oxford University Press.

Kay, J.A. and Vickers, J. (1990) 'Regulatory reform: an appraisal', in Majone (ed.) *Deregulation or Re-regulation? Regulatory Reform in Europe and the United States*, London: Francis Pinter.

Landis, J.M. (1966) [1938] *The Administrative Process*, New Haven (CT): Yale University Press.

Lewis, W.A. (1951) 'Recent British experience of nationalization as an alternative to monopoly control', cited in Machlup *The Political Economy of Monopoly*, Baltimore (MD): The Johns Hopkins University Press.

Littlechild, S.C. (1983) *Regulation of British Telecommunications Profitability*, London: HMSO.

McCraw, T.K. (1984) *Regulation Reconsidered*, Cambridge (MA): Belknap Press of Harvard University.

Machlup, F. (1952) *The Political Economy of Monopoly*, Baltimore (MD): The Johns Hopkins University Press.

Majone, G. (1994) 'Paradoxes of privatization and deregulation', *Journal of European Public Policy* 1, 1: 53–69.

Mendeloff, J.M. (1988) *The Dilemma of Toxic Substance Regulation: How Over-regulation Causes Under-regulation at OSHA*, Cambridge (MA): MIT Press.

Ogus, A.I. (1994) *Regulation – Legal Form and Economic Theory*, Oxford: Clarendon Press.

Prosser, T. (1989) 'Regulation of privatized enterprises: institutions and procedures', in Hancher and Moran (eds) *Capitalism, Culture and Economic Regulation*, Oxford: Clarendon Press.

Reagan, M.D. (1987) *Regulation: The Politics of Policy*, Boston: Little, Brown.

Selznick, P. (1985) 'Focussing organizational research on regulation', in Noll (ed.) *Regulatory Policy and the Social Sciences*, Berkeley and Los Angeles: The University of California Press.

Shapiro, M. (1988) *Who Guards the Guardians?*, Athens (GA): University of Georgia Press.

Temin, P. (1987) *The Fall of the Bell System*, Cambridge: Cambridge University Press.

Vickers, J. and Yarrow, G. (1988) *Privatization: An Economic Analysis*, Cambridge (MA): MIT Press.

Wade, W. (1988) *Administrative Law* (6th edition), Oxford: Clarendon Press.

2   Theories of regulation

Giandomenico Majone

INTRODUCTION

Until the early 1960s the prevailing theory of regulation regarded market failure as the motivating reason for regulatory intervention. Statutory regulation or public ownership were supposed to eliminate or reduce the inefficiencies engendered by particular types of market failure. Behind the notion of market failure is one of the most celebrated results of neoclassical economics which has come to be known as the fundamental theory of welfare economics. This theorem states that, under some assumptions, competitive markets lead to an efficient allocation of resources, that is, to a situation where there is no rearrangement of resources – no possible change in production and consumption – such that someone can be made better off without, at the same time, making someone else worse off. Such a situation is said to be Pareto-efficient (or Pareto-optimal), after the Italian economist and sociologist Vilfredo Pareto (1848–1923) who first formalized the notion of economic efficiency.

We speak of market failures when the conditions for the validity of the fundamental theorem are not satisfied, so that markets do not lead to efficient outcomes. For example, in a perfectly competitive market, firms expand output to the point where price equals marginal cost – the cost of producing an additional unit of their product. However, a monopolistic firm, if unregulated, will curtail production in order to raise prices. By setting prices at levels other than the competitive level, the firm distorts resource allocation. Moreover, monopolists lack sufficient incentive to minimize production costs since they do not feel the pressure of competitors who would lower their own costs in order to capture sales. Thus *monopoly power* is an important cause of market failure.

Again, the resource allocation provided by the market may not be efficient when there are *negative externalities*, that is, when the actions of one individual or firm impose a cost· on other individuals or firms without a corresponding compensation. Since individuals or firms do not bear the full cost of the negative externalities they generate, they will tend to engage in an excessive amount of such activities. Air and water pollution are probably the best-known examples of negative externalities. Without some method of internalizing the cost of pollution, too many of society's resources are attracted into polluting processes and products, and too few are attracted into pollution-free processes and products. Arguably, government intervention is needed to help reduce the gap between the private costs of polluting activities and the true cost to society.

Another necessary condition for a competitive market to function well is that buyers have sufficient information to evaluate competing products. This condition is satisfied in many cases, but the increasing complexity and sophistication of new products and production processes often exceed the capacity of consumers, workers or small investors to evaluate the consequences to them of exercising choice in different ways. When the information needed for an informed choice is either lacking or asymmetrically distributed – for example, between firms and their customers, or professionals and their clients – one speaks of *information failures*. A number of government activities, from consumer protection legislation and safety standards to labelling requirements for medical drugs and foodstuffs, and reporting requirements for financial firms, are motivated by information failures and the belief that the market, by itself, will supply too little information.

Finally, there are some goods that either will not be supplied by the market or, if supplied, will be supplied in insufficient quantity. Examples are national defence, public health, environmental protection, and public administration. Such goods are called (pure) public goods. These have two critical properties: first, it does not cost anything for an additional individual to enjoy the benefits of a public good; second, it is difficult or impossible to exclude individuals from the enjoyment of such goods. Because of these characteristics there is insufficient economic incentive for the market to produce sufficient levels of public goods. This lack of incentive to produce what people desire is another type of market failure: *inadequate provision of public goods*.

There are other situations where the market does not perform as well as predicted by the fundamental theorem of welfare economics – indeed, only the imagination of economists sets a limit to an ever-lengthening list of market failures – but the four types mentioned above are those with which this book is mainly concerned. The empirical question, however, is whether the normative categories of welfare economics are capable of explaining the reality of regulatory policy-making.

A frequent criticism of the market-failure approach is precisely that it is a normative, rather than a positive, theory. It provides a basis for identifying situations where the government ought to do something, tempered by considerations of regulatory failure (see Table 1.1, p. 18). Many political scientists and economists argue that analysts should focus their attention not on normative issues but on describing the consequences of government programmes and the nature of the political processes which produce such programmes. Normative analysis, it is argued, is irrelevant since policy outcomes depend on such factors as the rules of the political process, the incentives facing various participants in the process and changing configurations of power and interests in society, rather than on consideration of allocative efficiency or ideas of the public interest.

According to the positive or economic theory of regulation popularized by George Stigler (1971), regulation is not instituted in the public interest, that is, for the protection and benefit of the public at large or some large sub-class of the public, but is acquired by an industry and designed and operated primarily for the latter's benefit. How else could one explain the price and entry regulation of basically competitive industries such as airlines, road haulage, banking and insurance, long-distance telephone services or the anti-competitive licensing of so many trades and professions?

In the first part of this chapter, we compare the relative merits of the normative and the positive theory of regulation, also in the light of the recent experiences of deregulation. Deregulation raises questions that are in a sense opposite to those with which Stigler and other 'positive' theorists of regulation were concerned – why should firms wish to forgo the advantages of regulation? Why has deregulation succeeded in some areas and failed in others? Hence, deregulation has provided a unique opportunity for assessing the predictive power of the two traditional theories. The comparison leads to the conclusion that, while positive theory has greatly enriched our understanding of the political economy of regulation, it has not made the normative theory obsolete. Basically, this is because in social science, as in politics, the distinction between positive and normative standpoints is much less sharp than old and new positivists would have us believe (Majone 1989). For example, the normative theory of regulation has considerable predictive power, while the more sophisticated versions of the positive theory leave ample room for normative concerns about efficiency and aggregate welfare (see below).

On the other hand, a serious limitation of both theories is that they are essentially institution-free. They largely ignore the complex institutional environment in which regulators operate, and treat regulatory bodies as black boxes or automata programmed either by interest groups or by public-minded executives. As a consequence, both theories are silent on crucial aspects of the regulatory process such as the limits of political control of regulatory discretion, judicial review, the requirements of accountability, the entrepreneurial skills of key individuals in the regulatory bureaucracy, and the importance of reputation and credibility.

It is however, impossible to explain the behaviour of regulators, as well as specific policy outcomes, without taking these and other institutional variables into consideration. Thus, we saw in the preceding chapter that the success of deregulation in the United States, at least in the areas of transportation and telecommunications, owes much to the policy entrepreneurship of some key regulators. Similarly, in Chapter 4 it will be shown that, in order to explain the enormous expansion of regulation at the European level, it is necessary to consider the policy entrepreneurship of the European Commission, the role of the European Court of Justice, the limited control which the member states of the EC/EU can exert through the Council of Ministers, the low credibility of intergovernmental arrangements in regulatory matters and so on.

In sum, both the positive and the normative theory of regulation provide important insights, but are not sufficiently rich to explain the complex dynamics of regulatory policy-making. What is needed are institutionalist theories of regulation. Although such theories are still in their infancy, considerable progress has been made in recent years thanks to advances in related areas of research such as neo-institutionalism, the economic theory of organizations, and the theory of repeated non-cooperative games. Some results of particular relevance for the arguments to be developed in this book will be presented in the second part of the present chapter.

THE ECONOMIC THEORY OF REGULATION

The economic theory (ET) traces its lineage to George Stigler's 1971 article, 'The economic theory of regulation'. This seminal paper was an attempt to provide a theoretical foundation for the notion – introduced earlier by political scientists like Marver Bernstein (1955) – that regulatory agencies are captured by producers. In Stigler's theory, political actors are presumed to be utility maximizers. Their utility function is not spelt out in detail, but certainly includes securing and maintaining political power. To achieve this objective the politician needs votes and money. These resources can be provided by groups positively affected by regulatory decisions.

However, shared interests do not automatically give rise to effective interest groups (Olson 1971). Because of the costs of organizing collective action, concentrated business interests have an overwhelming advantage over more diffuse groups (consumers or taxpayers) in mobilizing for regulatory politics and getting what they want. Business interest groups may be too small to offer enough votes, but can provide other valuable resources, including money, which the politician can use to finance his electoral campaign.

Thus, a politico-economic exchange takes place between self-interested politicians and organized interests: favourable regulatory decisions for votes or money. What matters to the participants, is their wealth or utility, rather than aggregate welfare. It follows that, for the ET, regulation is not about enhancing efficiency by correcting market failures, but about redistributing income from some groups in society (typically, consumers and diffuse interests) to others (producers and politicians).

Stigler writes as if regulatory agencies were captured by the strongest, best-organized interest group – a particular industry or profession. Generally speaking, however, no single economic interest captures an agency. Compact, well-organized groups will tend to benefit more from regulation than broad, diffuse interests, but the winning coalition usually includes some subsets of consumers. For example, in the pre-deregulation era, the rates of local telephone service were subsidized by the heavy users of long-distance service, typically firms. Similar regulatory regimes protecting individual consumers prevailed in all the public utilities, as well as in the energy and transport industries. Stigler's theory does not explain this pervasive phenomenon of cross-subsidization. A more general model was needed, and this was provided by Peltzman (1976).

According to this author, as long as some consumers can offer votes or money for a small departure from a regulatory regime protecting only producer groups, pure producer protection will not, in general, be the dominant political strategy. Politicians, or regulators acting on their behalf, will allocate economic benefits across producer and consumer groups so that total political utility is maximized. Peltzman then investigates the effect of changes in demand and cost conditions in the regulated industry on the nature of the resulting equilibrium. He predicts a tendency for regulation to offset the effect of market forces on the division of rents between producers and consumers, as well as a tendency toward systematic, cost-based cross subsidization.

Peltzman (1989: 21–37) illustrates these tendencies by several concrete examples. One puzzle remains, however. Stigler's central thesis is that regulation is acquired by an industry and designed and operated primarily for its benefit. If this is true, it ought to follow that both naturally competitive and naturally monopolistic industries should attract economic regulation. In fact, most structurally competitive industries are not subject to price and entry regulation – a fact which Peltzman's model, like Stigler's, seems incapable of explaining. In this respect, a 1983 article by Gary Becker marks a significant advance.

Becker shares the basic assumption of his Chicago colleagues that regulation, like other political instruments such as taxes and licences, are used to raise the welfare of more influential pressure groups. Thus, he too regards regulation as basically an instrument of redistribution and rent-seeking. However, Becker adds the important insight that deadweight losses act as a constraint on inefficient regulatory policies. Deadweight loss – a measure of the inefficiency of redistribution – is the difference between the winners' gains and the losers' losses from regulation-induced change in output. These gains and losses are what motivates the competing interest groups to exert pressure on the political process. Rising deadweight loss progressively enfeebles the winners relative to the losers. This is because the pressure the winners exert for each extra unit of benefits must overcome steadily rising pressures from the losers to avoid the escalating losses. Becker concludes that the political process will be drawn toward efficiency-enhancing regulation: 'policies that raise efficiency are more likely to be adopted than policies that lower efficiency' (Becker 1983: 384). Neither winners nor losers would rationally oppose changes that eliminate some deadweight loss.

Becker's argument establishes an interesting link between the ET and the normative theory of regulation. As already mentioned, market failures create incentives for regulation, according to the normative theory. But if regulation can correct the inefficiency resulting from market failure, there will be more wealth to distribute. This extra wealth can induce greater pressure for regulation from winners and can attenuate the opposition from losers. In contrast to the normative theory, the ET says that the regulation will not maximize the extra wealth, because producers and consumers are not, in general, equally well organized politically. But faced with a portfolio of potential areas to regulate, the political process will be attracted to industries where it can increase wealth as well as to those where deadweight losses are small (Peltzman 1989: 13). This explains why monopolistic industries are subject to economic regulation much more frequently than structurally competitive industries.

Becker's theory, with its emphasis on economic efficiency and correction of market failure as an important motive for regulation, comes close to merging with the normative theory. In a sense, the difference between the two theories is analogous to the difference between a first-best and second-best solution. In welfare economics a first-best solution corresponds to the maximization of a social welfare function, subject only to a production constraint. If one or more additional constraints are imposed on this welfare function (such as the political and distributional constraints considered by the positive theory of regulation), the result of the maximization exercise is a second-best solution (Mishan 1976). Thus, Becker's theory may be seen as a second-best version of the normative theory.

The important point, at any rate, is that the normative theory also has an empirical basis and some predictive power. In a useful survey paper entitled 'Regulation in theory and practice', Joskow and Noll (1991) call attention to these aspects by calling the traditional theory 'normative analysis as a positive theory' (or NPT). One of the founders of the ET has acknowledged the continued relevance of the NPT in the following words:

> If there is an empirical basis for the NPT's continuing attraction for economists, it is probably its apparent success as an entry theory. Consider Hotelling's classic statement in 1938 of the natural monopoly version of the NPT. In this purely theoretical piece, railroads and utilities are presumed, without much evidence, to be the main real-world examples of natural monopoly. They also occupied most of the regulatory (including public ownership) effort when Hotelling wrote. This correspondence between the NPT and the real-world allocation of regulatory effort seems striking. Now consider the postwar expansion of regulation. In terms of the resources involved, the biggest single chunk is probably accounted for by environmental regulation, where the externalities aspect of the NPT scores another success.
>
> (Peltzman 1989: 17, footnote omitted)

Peltzman also compares the ET and the NPT in light of the deregulation policies of the two past decades. He finds that most cases of deregulation can be explained by the ET, but with two important exceptions: road haulage and telecommunications. The former industry was *de facto* deregulated when substantial rents were being earned by owners and workers who formed the heart of the dominant political coalition. Not only were the rents substantial, but there was no evidence of their having suffered any serious erosion. Long-distance telecommunications were deregulated after the technological threat to existing rents became clear but before substantial erosion took place (Peltzman 1989: 39).

Other authors come to conclusions that are more broadly favourable to the NPT. Thus, in none of the cases of deregulation studied by Derthick and Quirk (1985) did the regulated industries decide that regulation was no longer in their interest; nor was the defeat of the regulated industries brought about primarily by other well-organized groups that stood to gain from reform. Instead, these authors argue that the regulatory reforms of the late 1970s and early 1980s would never have occurred without the policy entrepreneurship of some key regulators, and the sustained intellectual critique of previous regulatory policies developed by economists – including, paradoxically, Stigler and other prominent critics of the public-interest theory of regulation – in the previous decade (Derthick and Quirk 1985: 238–46; see also Vietor 1994).

In conclusion, positive and normative theories of regulation should be viewed as complementary rather than mutually exclusive. Positive theories, especially the ET, have greatly improved our understanding of the regulatory process and of the constraints facing even the most public-spirited regulator. But even when regulation is best explained by the political or economic power of groups seeking selfish ends, those who attempt to justify it must appeal to the merits of the case. Legislators, administrators, judges, scholars and the public at large wish to know whether the regulation is justified. All of them seek standards against which to judge the success of a policy and the merits of specific programmes initiated within the framework of that policy (Breyer 1982).

INSTITUTIONALIST THEORIES OF REGULATION: THE CONTROL PROBLEM

Both the NPT and the ET are basically institution-free theories of regulation. This is particularly evident in the ET, where only economic interests and resources are truly fundamental, while institutions are largely epiphenomenal. As mentioned above, Stigler's aim was to provide a theoretical foundation for the notion of 'regulatory capture'. But any theory of capture must treat regulatory institutions as passive entities. This is the logical consequence of a presumed chain of control: interest groups control politicians and politicians control regulators, so the groups get what they want. Regulatory policy will reflect the underlying balance of power among economic interests. If one assumes such a chain of control, there is little to be gained by modelling the behaviour of political and bureaucratic institutions which simply operate to provide a smooth, faithful translation of private interests into policy. But as the example of deregulation in the US shows (see Chapter 1), the institutional and behavioural characteristics of regulatory bodies – their independence, expertise and policy entrepreneurship – may be important in explaining certain policy changes. In turn, regulators operate in a complex political environment which includes, in addition to economic interests, political executives, legislators, rival agencies, political parties, judges, the media, public-interest groups and – increasingly in Europe – supranational authorities.

No model capable of representing the political environment in all its complexity yet exists, but some recent work in the positive theory of institutions (PTI) – a theory which draws on concepts and insights from public choice, the new institutionalism, and the new economics of organization – is beginning to look inside the economists' black box to trace the political and bureaucratic linkages by which interests are translated into public policy (Moe 1987). This research has already made significant progress on two key issues of regulatory policy-making: political control and the delegation problem.

While the economic theory of regulation assumes that control is unproblematic, a major component of the PTI has to do with the issue of political control of the bureaucracy: to what extent and by which means are politicians able to guide and control regulatory bureaucracies? A closely related issue, largely ignored by the ET, has to do with delegation of power to regulators: when will political sovereigns delegate policy-making powers and when will they choose to make policy themselves? We discuss the issue of political control in this section, that of delegation in the next.

Most studies conducted by American political scientists before the 1980s saw neither the President nor Congress as effective institutions for central control of the bureaucracy. Several presidential studies came to the conclusion that, in general, presidents lack the resources and also the interest to monitor and control the federal bureaucracy effectively (Fenno 1959; Neustadt 1960; Noll 1971). Similarly, the literature on Congress described difficulties with legislative control mechanisms. For example, a well-known empirical study of congressional committee members as agency overseers found that members of Congress are concerned more with satisfying voters than with overseeing the bureaucracy (Scher 1960). Other studies raised questions about the quality of congressional control noting that it is uncoordinated, fragmented and *ad hoc* (Mayhew 1974).

According to a number of scholars, the situation is not very different in Europe. A parliamentary party is unlikely to use parliamentary institutions to monitor seriously the administrative activities of the government which it supports, while opposition parties lack the information and resources necessary for effective legislative oversight. On the other hand, the policy initiatives of cabinet ministers can be blocked by the opposition of civil servants often allied to powerful interest groups (Thoenig and Friedberg 1976; Hayward 1982; Dyson 1982; Page 1992 provide a useful comparative analysis of political control of the bureaucracy in France, Germany and Britain, as well as in the USA and the EC).

In the 1980s, views about the possibility of political control of the bureaucracy began to change for a number of theoretical and practical reasons: new developments in formal modelling of the control problem; more sophisticated statistical analyses correlating time series of agency outputs with various indicators of the preferences of political principals; greater attention given to the design of control mechanisms, in the spirit of the new institutionalism in politics and economics; and, not least, the rise to power of political leaders, such as President Reagan and Prime Minister Thatcher, committed to the goal of rolling back the state and reducing the role of public bureaucracies.

An important theoretical development of this period was the application of agency theory to the study of bureaucratic discretion. The starting point of agency theory is that in a principal–agent relationship information is asymmetrically distributed. Agents usually have more information than principals about the details of the tasks assigned to them, as well as about their own actions, abilities and preferences. Agents can take advantage of the high costs of measuring their characteristics and performance to engage in opportunistic behaviour. Such behaviour imposes costs on the principal who finds it in his or her interest to monitor agent's behaviour and structure the contract in a way that reduces 'agency costs'.

The applications of agency theory to the problem of political control make two key assumptions. First, bureaucratic agents are bound by contract to serve democratically elected principals; their primary duty is faithful implementation of the law. Second, over time the interests of politicians and bureaucrats tend to diverge. This is because political coalitions change from those existing when democratic principals adopted a certain policy, and also because bureaucracies develop separate interests as a result of institutionalization and external pressures. Thus, when politicians try to control policy implementation, bureaucrats will often try to shirk their demands (Wood and Waterman 1991: 802–3).

The question is how (or whether) politicians can overcome this shirking tendency as well as the tendency of bureaucrats to use their information advantage to manipulate the choice of their political superiors. Agency theory suggests that sophisticated politicians recognize these dangers and can take countermeasures. Political control is possible because elected principals create bureaucracies:

They design bureaucracies with incentive structures to facilitate control. Political principals also monitor bureaucratic activities to offset information imbalances. When bureaucratic activities stray from the desired result, policymakers apply sanctions or rewards to bring them back in line. Thus, the theory is dynamic, positing well-informed central decision makers who systematically mould the preferences of bureaucratic agents.

(Wood and Waterman 1991: 803)

In fact, several empirical studies carried out during the 1980s found evidence of the capacity of democratic institutions to control policy formulation and implementation. Thus, Moe (1982) analysed annual outputs from the Federal Trade Commission (FTC), the National Labor Relations Board (NLRB) and the Securities and Exchange Commission (SEC), and found that the outputs of these regulatory bodies varied with changing presidential administrations. In a later study, the same author, using quarterly data on NLRB decisions, found that they were influenced by all three major political institutions – the president, Congress and the courts (Moe 1985).

The importance of congressional control is emphasized by Weingast and Moran (1983). Using annual data on FTC decisions, these authors show that the policy preferences of members of congressional committees with over-sight responsibilities play an important role in determining the agency's actions: shifts in these preferences are what causes changes in agency policy. Similarly, in a detailed legislative and legal history of antitrust policy-making from 1969 to 1976, Kovacic (1987) argues that the FTC, rather than ignoring congressional preferences as suggested by older theories, chose antitrust programmes that were consistent with, and responsive to, the policy preferences of its oversight committees in Congress.

POLITICAL CONTROL WITH MULTIPLE PRINCIPALS

The economic theory of agency is used mainly to analyse hierarchical relationships where one principal attempts to control the behaviour of one or more agents. However, the studies mentioned above make clear that a political theory of agency should pay special attention to the case of multiple principals with different and possibly conflicting objectives. A good illustration of this possibility is a study of the FTC during the period 1981–4 when President Reagan attempted to introduce major regulatory reforms and policy changes, including reduction of the agency's budget, application of cost-benefit tests and the adoption of a less confrontational approach to compliance with antitrust legislation. The study found that despite some success in reducing the budget of the agency, the reform agenda remained only partially implemented by 1984. This was due mainly to congressional opposition to budget cuts. No longer able to use budget increases to induce the agency to comply with their wishes, the appropriations committees used legislative language in budget resolutions to impose their own performance standards, specifying precisely both those activities to be provided and those not to be provided by the FTC (Yandle 1987).

A more general theory of agency faces a number of new questions concerning, for example, the relative influence of different principals, the effectiveness and efficiency of various instruments and strategies of control, and the possibility of coalitions between regulators and subsets of principals. Recent research, both theoretical and empirical, is beginning to provide answers to such questions. As noted above, early applications of agency theory maintained that among principals, legislators are the most influential ones, since it is statutes that create regulatory agencies and provide the structure of incentives that should minimize the divergence between legislative intentions and bureaucratic outputs. It has been found, however, that legislators find it more efficient under severe time constraints to monitor bureaucratic performance indirectly rather than through oversight hearings. To a large extent, legislators rely on programme recipients, lobbyists and interest groups to provide information on bureaucratic performance (McCubbins and Schwartz 1984).

Compared to Congress, presidential control is more direct. The most important instrument of executive control appears to be the power of appointment and removal. Other important instruments of executive control are administrative reorganizations and the ever-increasing use of the President's managerial arm, the Office of Management and Budget. The already mentioned study by Wood and Waterman (1991) of seven regulatory agencies from the late 1970s through most of the 1980s carefully compares various control instruments including political appointments, budget increases and decreases, congressional oversight hearings, administrative reorganizations and legislation. All seven agencies appeared to be responsive, at least in the period examined. The data show, that among the tools of political control, the power to appoint is the most effective and most frequently used: in five of the seven cases examined, agency outputs shifted immediately after a change in agency leadership. Reorganization, congressional oversight and budgeting are also important.

The authors conclude that the evidence for active political control is so strong that controversy should now end over whether political control of the regulatory bureaucracy is possible. Instead, future research should concentrate on a detailed analysis of the various mechanisms of control (Wood and Waterman 1991: 822). They also note, however, that:

> [a]gency responsiveness and stability can roughly be arrayed along a continuum which aligns nicely with certain bureaucratic attributes. The agencies most responsive to executive influence, gauged by the magnitude and duration of change, were those situated in the executive departments. . . . On the other hand, the agencies with the most stable outputs were the independent regulatory commissions.
>
> (Wood and Waterman 1991: 823)

This is of course what one would expect since, as we saw in Chapter 1, the IRCs were created by Congress precisely to ensure agency independence from presidential control and short-term political considerations.

The Wood and Waterman list of control mechanisms does not include potentially important instruments such as the formal and informal influence of the public (for example, through public hearings), the media, professional opinion and, especially, judicial review. Omission of the latter factor seriously weakens another interesting study by Jeffrey Hill (1985). Using public-choice arguments, Hill shows that bureaucrats can influence policy outcomes by colluding with latent legislative majorities. Specifically, in a complex situation where policies must be described by at least two dimensions, a senior bureaucrat can build an implementation coalition that differs from the original legislative coalition.

For this to be possible, it suffices for the bureaucrat's preferred alternative to be closer to the 'ideal points' of a majority of legislators than the bill which they helped pass. Thus, the discretion of the bureaucrat derives not from defying legislative intent but from the possibility of constructing new majorities. As Bendor (1990) notes, this is a very interesting result from the theoretical point of view because it shows that bureaucratic discretion, and hence control problems, can arise even when there are no information problems. In Hill's model, problems arise solely from the legislature's difficulty in reaching stable collective choices, without the need of making the standard assumption of agency theory that information is asymmetrically distributed between agents and principals. However, the model effectively assumes that the courts will not punish administrative deviations from a statutory mandate. On the other hand, if legislators know in advance that judicial review is likely, they would be committed to the policy originally chosen. Hence the formal analysis conveys an impression of greater administrative discretion than is empirically plausible (Bendor 1990: 392–5).

In conclusion, two main lessons can be derived from recent (mostly American) work in the PTI. First, political control of regulatory bureaucracies is possible, so that delegation of important policy-making powers to expert agencies need not entail a loss of democratic accountability. Equally important is the second lesson that the conventional view of control as 'self-conscious oversight, on the basis of authority, by defined individuals or offices endowed with formal rights or duties to inquire, call for changes in behaviour and (in some cases) to punish' (Hood 1991: 347) is quite inappropriate for a highly technical and discretionary activity such as regulation. Earlier research implicitly assumed that such a mode of control was the only relevant one: hence its negative conclusions about the possibility of monitoring and controlling bureaucratic discretion.

A more appropriate notion of control is one which Christopher Hood has called 'interpolable balance': a view of control that takes as its starting point a need to identify self-policing mechanisms which are already present in the system, and can contemplate a network of complementary and overlapping checking mechanisms instead of assuming that control is necessarily to be exercised from any fixed place in the system (Hood 1991: 354–5).

The new institutional theories of regulation show precisely that regulators can be monitored and kept politically accountable only by means of a combination of control instruments: oversight by specialized congressional committees, presidential power of appointment, strict procedural requirements, professional standards, public participation and judicial review. When such a system works properly, no one controls an independent agency, yet the agency is 'under control' (Moe 1987).

THE DELEGATION PROBLEM

Why political sovereigns may choose to delegate policy-making powers to an independent agency rather than making policy themselves is another issue which is receiving increasing attention by neo-institutionalist scholars. The attention is fully deserved because, as we shall see in the following chapters, the importance of delegation is growing in many countries and at all levels of government. Take, for example, the future European Central Bank (ECB). When the Bank is established, presumably at the end of the century, it will have sweeping statutory powers. According to the Treaty on European Union (Maastricht Treaty), the ECB can make regulations that are binding in their entirety and become European and member-state law, without the involvement of the main law-making body of the European Union – the Council of Ministers – or of national parliaments. The Bank has a single objective, monetary stability and the freedom to pursue this objective in complete independence of the other European institutions and of the national governments.

Moreover, since the governors of the central banks of the member states of the Union are members of the ECB Council, they too must be insulated from domestic political influences in the performance of their task: they can no longer be players in the old game of pumping up the economy just before an election. In short, in the future European monetary union, issues of macroeconomic management that have been the lifeblood of Western politics, determined the rise and fall of governments and affected the fate of national economies, are to be decided by politically independent experts (Nicoll 1993: 28).

Why did the same politicians who always preferred to have a hand on the monetary lever, suddenly opt to delegate such far-reaching powers to an independent technocratic institution? *Mutatis mutandis*, the same question can be raised in many other areas, from competition and trade policy to health and safety regulation. In particular, the delegation problem is crucial for understanding why the member states of the Union have been willing to transfer such extensive powers to the European Commission even when the transfer was not really required by the functional needs of the single European market.

One can find in the literature several partial and more or less *ad hoc* explanations of the delegation problem. Thus, it has been said that independent agencies are justified by the need of expertise in highly complex or technical matters, often combined with a rule-making or adjudicative function that is inappropriate for a government department; that agencies' separateness from government is useful whenever it is hoped to free public administration from partisan politics and party political influence; that an agency structure may favour public participation, while the opportunity for consultations by means of public hearings is often denied to government departments. Agencies are also said to provide greater policy continuity than cabinets because they are one step removed from election returns, while the exercise of a policy-making function by an expert agency should provide flexibility not only in policy formulation but also in the application of policy to particular circumstances. Finally, it is argued that independent agencies can protect citizens from bureaucratic arrogance and reticence, and are able to focus public attention on controversial issues, thus enriching public debate (Baldwin and McCrudden 1987; Teitgen-Colly 1988; Guédon 1991).

These explanations have merit, but they are not theoretically well grounded and are not sufficiently general to explain important cases of delegation such as the ECB. I shall argue that the central aspect of the delegation problem today is the issue of policy credibility. This issue first attracted sustained analytic attention in the 1970s. A landmark paper published in 1977 provided the first rigorous statement of the problem (Kydland and Prescott 1977). This contribution was part of the long-running debate on rules versus discretion. The question is whether governments should tailor policies to current economic conditions (discretionary policy) or conduct policy according to pre-announced rules, such as a constant rate of monetary growth.

Critics of government discretion such as Milton Friedman argued that governments and central banks lack the knowledge and information necessary for successful discretionary policy. Moreover, there is often a considerable lag between the moment when a policy decision is announced and its actual implementation. Hence there is a risk that discretionary policy could make the economy less, rather than more, stable. The argument advanced by Kydland and Prescott was based on quite different considerations. According to these scholars, the central problem of public policy is its credibility: fixed rules are preferable because they increase policy credibility while discretion leads to 'time inconsistency'. Time inconsistency occurs when a policy which appears optimal at time t_0 no longer seems optimal at a later time t_n. Without a binding commitment holding them to the original plan, governments will use their discretion to switch to what now appears to be a better policy. The problem is that, if people anticipate such a policy change, they will behave in ways which prevent policy-makers achieving their original objectives.

To illustrate, suppose that at time t_0 parliament enacts strict anti-pollution legislation. This seems to be, at the time, the optimal response both to the severity of pollution problems and to the wishes of the voters. After passage of the law, however, there is a sharp economic downturn, so that inflation and unemployment replace environmental quality as the main concern of voters. Especially if an election is imminent, the government will be tempted to ask parliament for the law to be amended in order to make it less stringent and hence less costly to implement. Or, more simply, the government may decide to reduce the level of implementation by cutting the budget of the pollution inspectorate. But industrial polluters, predicting such developments, will assume that they can violate the relevant regulations with impunity and the original policy objectives will not be achieved. The policy lacks credibility because it is seen to be time-inconsistent: the incentives of the policy-makers at time t_n differ from their incentives at time t_o.

The growth of economic, financial, ecological and political interdependence, in both the international and the domestic spheres, explains why policy credibility has become so important today. However, credibility is quite problematic for elected politicians and for bureaucrats under their direct control. In part this is because in a democracy political executives have shorter time horizons than their counterparts in the private sector, so the efficacy of reputational mechanisms (see below) is more limited in the political sphere. We also know from Arrow's impossibility theorem and much recent research in public choice (Mueller 1989) that in any situation of collective choice there are many possible majorities, that their respective preferences need not be consistent, and that one majority cannot commit a subsequent majority. Because a legislature cannot bind a subsequent legislature, and a majority coalition cannot bind another, public policies are always vulnerable to reneging and hence lack credibility (Shepsle 1991: 255).

Now, the theory of non-cooperative games helps to analyse situations where binding commitments are either impossible or too costly. A standard result is that a non-cooperative game such as the prisoners' dilemma has no Pareto-efficient solution if it is played only once. If the game is played an indefinite number of times, however, 'cheating' is no longer the dominant (but inefficient) strategy. This is because a collapse of trust and co-operation carries a cost in the form of a loss of future profits. If this cost is large enough, cheating will be deterred and co-operation sustained. For this to be the case, the discounted value of all future gains must be larger than the short-run gain from non-cooperation. Co-operation and credible commitments are hard to achieve in politics precisely because the time beyond the next election counts for little.

To illustrate, let us consider the following situation, appropriately called the *trust game* (Kreps 1990; Milgrom and Roberts 1992). Player A must first decide whether or not to trust player B. If A chooses to trust B, B is made aware of this and has the option either to honour that trust (in which case both players gain ten utiles), or to abuse it (in which case A loses five utiles and B earns fifteen). If A decides not to trust B then both A and B obtain zero (zero being the value arbitrarily assigned to whatever the two players might do in the absence of trust), see Table 2.1.

If the game is played only once we can predict that A will not offer trust and B will not honour trust when it is offered – a sub-optimal outcome. The situation is quite different if the game is played repeatedly. For example, A can inform B that he or she will begin by offering trust and will continue

Table 2.1 The trust game: payoffs to: (A, B)

		B	
		honour A's trust	abuse A's trust
A	trust B	10, 10	-5, 15
	don't trust B	0, 0	0, 0

doing so as long as B honours that trust. The moment B abuses the offered trust, however, A will never trust B again. Now it is in B's interest to honour the trust: abuse in any round will increase the payoff in that round by five utiles, but the payoff will be zero in all subsequent rounds (if any occur). Thus, if B's discount rate is not too high, so that he or she has a substantial stake in the future, the combination of strategies (Trust B, honour A's trust) is a Nash equilibrium since neither player has an incentive to deviate from that pattern of behaviour: the 'contract' between A and B is self-enforcing.

So far it was assumed that the same individuals engaged in a transaction repeatedly. This would seem to limit the game's applicability since many transactions between individuals (or organizations) do not recur frequently or even recur only once. But as Kreps (1990) has shown, this assumption is not necessary. If the same B faces a series of individuals A_1, A_2, and so forth who each offer trust only if B honoured trust when it was last offered, then B's calculation about whether to honour trust is exactly the same as if B were repeatedly facing the same A. The resulting arrangement is again self-enforcing, as long as B's opportunities in later transactions can be tied to his or her behaviour in earlier transactions (Kreps 1990: 106). In each transaction B honours trust in order to maintain a reputation for honesty that will encourage future trading partners to offer trust. Moreover, in many situations it is convenient to think of B as an organization (an independent regulatory agency, for example) so that the system of reputation does not depend only on individual behaviour, but is supported by the entire history of the organization as well as by its 'corporate culture' and *esprit de corps*. In this perspective, an organization is an intangible asset carrying a reputation that is beneficial for efficient transactions, conferring that reputation upon the present and future members of the organization (Kreps 1990: 108–11).

In the trust game, reputation is the mechanism that keeps the game going. We now examine the role of reputation in more complex situations. In the contracting approach to the economics of organizations (Williamson 1985), one distinguishes between complete and incomplete contracts, where 'contract' does not denote only a legally enforceable promise, but also an informal or even tacit agreement. A complete contract would specify precisely what each party is to do in all possible circumstances, and how the realized benefits and costs are to be distributed in each contingency. Such a contract would be self-enforcing because each party would find it optimal to abide by the contract's terms. Of course, complete contracts are an abstraction. In most ongoing transactions, contingencies will arise that have not been accounted for because they were not even imagined at contracting time. Thus, actual contracts are usually incomplete and unenforceable.

Incomplete contracting leads to problems of imperfect commitment. There is a strong temptation to renege on the original terms of the contract because what should be done in case of an unforeseen contingency is left unstated and ambiguous and thus open to interpretation. The problem of time inconsistency analysed by Kydland and Prescott is of course the policy equivalent of imperfect commitment in incomplete contracting. In both cases the root difficulty is the fact that the incentives of policy-makers (or contractual partners) in the implementation phase may no longer be the same as their incentives in the planning stage. Hence, not only the temptation to renegotiate, but the possibility of renegotiating, deprives the original agreement of its credibility and prevents it from guiding behaviour as intended.

One response to contractual incompleteness is an arrangement (known as 'relational contracting') where:

> [t]he parties do not agree on detailed plans of actions but on goals and objectives, on general provisions that are broadly applicable, on the criteria to be used in deciding what to do when unforeseen contingencies arise, on who has what power to act and the bounds limiting the range of actions that can be taken, and on dispute resolution mechanisms to be used if disagreements do occur.
>
> (Milgrom and Roberts 1992: 131)

Crucial to this approach is the choice of the mechanism for adapting the relationship to unforeseen contingencies. In many transactions one party will have much more authority in saying what adaptation will take place. But if the other contractual partners are to delegate such discretionary authority, they must believe that it will be used fairly and effectively. The source of this belief is, once again, reputation. The party to whom authority is delegated should be the one with the most to lose from a loss of reputation. This is likely to be the one with the longer time horizon, the more visibility, and the greater frequency of transactions (Milgrom and Roberts 1992: 140). In the public sector, it will often be an expert, politically independent regulator rather than a politician or a bureaucratic generalist.

Thus, the delegation of regulatory powers to some agency distinct from the government itself is best understood as a means whereby governments can commit themselves to regulatory strategies that would not be credible in the absence of such delegation (Gatsios and Seabright 1989: 46). In Chapter 4, I shall use the analytical framework developed here in order to explain the delegation problem in the European context.

REFERENCES

Baldwin, R. and McCrudden, C. (1987) *Regulation and Public Law*, London: Weidenfeld & Nicolson.

Becker, G.S. (1983) 'A theory of competition among pressure groups for political influence', *Quarterly Journal of Economics*, 98: 371–400.

Bendor, J. (1990) 'Formal models of bureaucracy: a review', in Lynn and Wildavsky (eds) *Public Administration*, Chatham (NJ): Princeton University Press.

Bernstein, M. (1955) *Regulating Business by Independent Commissions*, Princeton (NJ): Princeton University Press.

Breyer, S. (1982) *Regulation and its Problems*, Cambridge (MA): Harvard University Press.

Derthick, M. and Quirk, P.J. (1985) *The Politics of Deregulation*, Washington (DC): The Brookings Institution.

Dyson, K. (1982) 'West Germany: the search for a rationalist consensus', in Richardson (ed.) *Policy Styles in Western Europe*, London: Allen & Unwin.

Fenno, R.F. Jr (1959) *The President's Cabinet*, New York: Vintage Books.

Gatsios, K. and Seabright, P. (1989) 'Regulation in the European Community', *Oxford Review of Economic Policy* 5, 2: 37–60.

Guédon, M.-J. (1991) *Les autorités administratives indépendantes*, Paris: Libraire Générale de Droit et de Jurisprudence.

Hayward, J.E.S. (1982) 'Mobilizing private interests in the service of public ambitions: the salient element in the dual French policy style', in Richardson (ed.) *Policy Styles in Western Europe*, London: Allen & Unwin.

Hill, J. (1985) 'Why so much stability: the role of agency determined stability', *Public Choice* 46: 275–87.

Hood, C. (1991) 'Concepts of control over public bureaucracies: "comptrol" and "interpolable balance"', in Kaufmann (ed.) *The Public Sector*, Berlin and New York: de Gruyter.

Hotelling, H. (1938) 'The general welfare in relation to problems of taxation and of railway and utility rates', *Econometrica* 6: 242–69.

Joskow, P. and Noll, R. (1991) 'Regulation in theory and practice: an overview', in Fromm (ed.) *Studies in Public Regulation*, Cambridge (MA): MIT Press.

Kovacic, W.E. (1987) 'The Federal Trade Commission and congressional oversight of antitrust enforcement: a historical perspective', in MacKay, Miller and Yandle (eds) *Public Choice and Regulation*, Stanford (CA): Hoover Institution Press.

Kreps, D.M. (1990) 'Corporate culture and economic theory', in Alt and Shepsle (eds) *Perspectives on Positive Political Economy*, Cambridge: Cambridge University Press.

Kydland, F. and Prescott, E. (1977) 'Rules rather than discretion: the inconsistency of optimal plans', *Journal of Political Economy* 85, 3: 137–60.

McCubbins, M.D. and Schwartz, T. (1984) 'Congressional oversight overlooked: police patrols *vs.* fire alarms', *American Journal of Political Science* 28: 165–9.

Majone, G. (1989) *Evidence, Argument and Persuasion in the Policy Process*, New Haven (CT): Yale University Press.

Mayhew, D.P. (1974) *Congress: The Electoral Connection*, New Haven (CT): Yale University Press.

Milgrom, P. and Roberts, J. (1992) *Economics, Organizations and Management*, Englewood Cliffs: Prentice-Hall International.

Mishan, E.J. (1976) *Cost Benefit Analysis*, New York: Praeger.

Moe, T. (1982) 'Regulatory performance and presidential administration', *American Journal of Political Science* 26: 197–224.

Moe, T. (1985) 'Control and feedback in economic regulation: the case of the NLRB', *American Political Science Review* 79: 1094–116.

Moe, T. (1987) 'Interests, institutions and positive theory: the politics of the NLRB', *Studies in American Political Development* 2: 236–99.

Mueller, D. (1989) *Public Choice II*, Cambridge: Cambridge University Press.

Neustadt, R.E. (1960) *Presidential Power*, New York: Wiley.

Nicoll, W. (1993) 'Maastricht revisited: a critical analysis of the Treaty on European Union', in Cafruny and Rosenthal (eds) *The State of the European Union*, Boulder: Lynn Rienner Publishers, 2: 19–34.

Noll, R. (1971) *Reforming Regulation*, Washington (DC): The Brookings Institution.

Olson, M. (1971) [1965] *The Logic of Collective Action: Public Goods and the Theory of Groups* (2nd edition), Cambridge (MA): Harvard University Press.

Page, E.C. (1992) *Political Authority and Bureaucratic Power*, New York: Harvester Wheatsheaf.

Peltzman, S. (1976) 'Toward a more general theory of regulation', *Journal of Law and Economics* 19: 211–40.

Peltzman, S. (1989) 'The economic theory of regulation after a decade of deregulation', *Brookings Papers on Economic Activity*, Washington (DC): Brookings Institution, 1–41.

Scher, S. (1960) 'Congressional committee members as independent agency overseers: a case study', *American Political Science Review* 54: 911–20.

Shepsle, K.A. (1991) 'Discretion, institutions, and the problem of government commitment', in Bourdieu and Coleman (eds) *Social Theory for a Changing Society*, Boulder: Westview Press.

Stigler, G.J. (1971) 'The theory of economic regulation', *Bell Journal of Economics and Management Science* 6, 2: 3–21.

Teitgen-Colly, C. (1988) 'Les autorités administratives indépendantes: histoire d'une institution', in Colliard and Timsit (eds), *Les autorités administratives indépendantes*, Paris: Presses Universitaires de France.

Thoenig, J.-C. and Friedberg, E. (1976) 'The power of the field staff: The case of the Ministry of Public Works, Urban Affairs and Housing in France', in Leemans and Dunsire (eds) *The Management of Change in Government*, The Hague: Martinus Nijhoff.

Vietor, R.H.K. (1994) *Contrived Competition: Regulation and Deregulation in America*, Cambridge (MA): Harvard University Press.

Weingast, B.R. and Moran, M.J. (1983) 'Bureaucratic discretion or congressional control', *Journal of Political Economy* 91, 5: 765–800.

Williamson, O. (1985) *The Economic Institutions of Capitalism*, New York: The Free Press.

Wood, D.B. and Waterman, R.W. (1991) 'The dynamics of political control of the bureaucracy', *American Political Science Review* 85, 3: 801–28.

Yandle, B. (1987) 'Regulatory reform in the realm of the rent seekers', in MacKay, Miller and Yandle (eds), *Public Choice and Regulation*, Stanford (CA): Hoover Institution Press.

3   The rise of statutory regulation in Europe

Giandomenico Majone

INTRODUCTION

Statutory regulation by independent agencies – sometimes called, for historical reasons, 'American-style regulation' – is rapidly becoming the most important mode of regulation, indeed the leading edge of public policy-making in Europe. The aim of this chapter is to explain the relatively sudden growth of statutory regulation, as well as the lateness of its arrival on the European political stage.

Consider the regulation of anti-competitive behaviour. The first important piece of antitrust legislation in the United States was the Sherman Act of 1890, the implementation of which was delegated to the Antitrust Division of the Department of Justice. The regulatory system was completed just before the First World War with the Clayton Act and the Federal Trade Commission Act. In Germany a cartel law comparable to, and in fact inspired by, the American legislation was approved by the Bundestag only in 1957, after a difficult political debate which lasted almost ten years. A Federal Cartel Office was created to implement the 1957 law and subsequent amendments (see Chapter 7).

At that time only Britain had an analogous, although significantly weaker, regulatory body – the Monopolies and Mergers Commission created in 1948. The treaty establishing the European Economic Community (EEC) had just been signed in Rome (25 March 1957), and the Competition Directorate-General of the European Commission (DG IV) could not begin to implement the competition articles of the Treaty of Rome (especially Article 85 prohibiting cartels and restrictive practices, and Article 86 prohibiting 'abuse of dominant position', that is, misuse of monopoly power) without an explicit set of procedural rules. These were adopted only in 1962, in the form of the famous Regulation 17 (see Chapter 11). Today, more or less independent and powerful competition authorities exist in France (see Chapter 8), Spain (see Chapter 9) and in practically all other member states of the European Union, as well as in the countries of Eastern Europe which wish to join the Union.

The growth of statutory regulation implemented by agencies operating outside the line of hierarchical control or oversight by the central administration, has greatly accelerated during the last two decades, in an increasing number of policy areas (Majone 1994 and 1995). In France, for example, the expression 'autorité administrative indépendante' was used for the first time by the law of 6 January 1978 creating the Commission Nationale de l'Informatique et des Libertés, although several independent regulatory agencies already existed prior to that date: the Commission de Contrôle des Banques created in 1941 and transformed into the Commission Bancaire by the law of 24 January 1984; the Commission des Opérations de Bourse (1967), whose powers have been significantly extended by the law of 2 August 1984; the Commission des Infractions Fiscales (1977); the Commission des Sondages (1977); and the Médiateur (1973), the only single-headed regulatory agency created in France to date. Today there are almost twenty independent agencies including, in addition to those already mentioned, the Commission d'Accès aux Documents Administratifs (1978), the Commission de la Sécurité des Consommateurs (1983), the Conseil de la Concurrence (1986), and the Commission de Contrôle des Assurances (1989) (Guédon 1991).

In Britain, too, the 1970s have been a period of significant institutional innovation, especially in the area of social regulation. The Independent Broadcasting Authority (1972), the Civil Aviation Authority (1972), the Health and Safety Commission (1974), the Equal Opportunities Commission (1976), and the Commission for Racial Equality (1976) are only some of the regulatory bodies created in this period (Baldwin and McCrudden 1987). Despite the hostility of Conservative governments towards any kind of 'quangos' (quasi-governmental organizations), a number of regulatory agencies were set up in the 1980s and early 1990s, partly because it was realized that in many cases privatization would only mean the replacement of public by private monopolies unless the newly privatized companies were subjected to public regulation of profits, prices, and entry and service conditions. Hence the rise of the new breed of regulatory offices for the privatized public utilities: the Office of Telecommunications (created in 1984); the Office of Gas Supply (1986); the Office of Water Services (1989); and the Office of Electricity Regulation (1990). These regulatory offices combine a number of functions: they administer price regulation; they ensure that the privatized firms comply with the terms of their licences; and they act as a channel for consumer complaints and as promoters of competition in the industry they regulate. Detected instances of monopoly abuse are referred to the Office of Fair Trading and to the Monopolies and Mergers Commission (MMC). Thus privatization also had the effect of increasing the power of the competition authorities, and in particular of the MMC because of the power given to this agency to impose modification of licence terms and to reset the price caps for the privatized utilities.

Parallel, if slower, institutional developments are taking place in all other European countries. The reasons given for the rise of independent regulatory bodies are strikingly similar from country to country, as well as being strongly reminiscent of the arguments of earlier American writers (Majone 1994). Some of these functional explanations have already been mentioned in Chapter 2: the need for expertise in highly complex and technical matters, combined with a rule-making or adjudicative function that is inappropriate for a government department; agencies' separateness from government is useful to free public administration from partisan politics; agencies provide greater policy continuity than political executives because they are one step removed from election returns, while the exercise of a policy-making function by an expert agency should provide flexibility, not only in policy formulation, but also in the application of policy to particular circumstances; and finally, the ability of independent expert agencies to focus attention on controversial issues, thus enriching public debate (Baldwin and McCrudden 1987; Teitgen-Colly 1988; Guédon 1991).

Such explanations, although valuable, are *ad hoc* rather than theoretically grounded and hence are not sufficiently general to address issues such as the delegation problem – under which conditions political principals are willing to delegate important policy-making powers to independent bodies – and policy credibility. Moreover, such functional explanations are too narrow to account for the main political, economic and technical factors which have transformed the role of the state in the economy and the nature of regulatory policy-making in Europe during the last three or four decades. Although a full discussion of such factors is beyond the scope of this book, the following ones should be mentioned: external, mostly American, influences; the crisis of interventionist policies; the already mentioned regulatory framework needed for privatization; and, in particular, the cumulative impact of a growing body of Community regulations.

Early American influences

American regulatory philosophy and practice have exerted a particularly strong influence on European policy-makers in three distinct periods: during the formative years of the European Community; in the 1970s, the period of rapid expansion of social regulation, especially environmental and consumer protection, and risk management; and in the early 1980s, the era of deregulation and privatization.

Before analyzing these influences in some detail, it may be useful to recall the basic characteristics of American regulation. While European scholars traditionally tended to identify regulation with the whole realm of legislation, governance and social control, within the framework of American public policy and administrative law the term has been given a more specific meaning. To use again Philip Selznick's formulation, regulation refers to sustained and focused control exercised by a public agency over activities that are socially valued (Selznick 1985: 363). The definition suggests that market activities can be 'regulated' only in societies that consider such activities worthwhile in themselves and hence in need of protection as well as control. The main difference between the American and the traditional European approach to economic regulation has been ideological, rather than technical or institutional. The American rejection of nationalization in favour of statutory regulation expressed a widely held belief that the market works well under normal circumstances and should be interfered with only in clearly defined cases of market failure (see Chapter 1). In Europe, on the other hand, popular acceptance of the market as an engine of progress is a more recent phenomenon. Peter Jenkins (1988) exaggerated only slightly when he wrote that only now, for the first time in the twentieth century, do the governing classes of Europe no longer assume that socialism in some form is what history has in store. Hence, as was seen in Chapter 1, economic regulation in Europe tended to replace the market, for example through public ownership, rather than to increase its efficiency by correcting specific forms of market failure. For the same reason, the commitment to competition policy has never been as strong in Europe as it has in the United States. Indeed, cartels and restrictive agreements were traditionally accepted either as an expression of the freedom of contract, as in Britain, or as instruments of rationalization and industrial policy, as in Germany.

Powerful external pressures were needed to modify such deep-seated attitudes, and these were applied by the United States after the Second World War. During the reconstruction period, Washington's successful effort, in Europe as in Japan, was to ensure the primacy of economics over politics, and thus to de-ideologize issues of political economy into questions of output and efficiency (Maier 1978: 23–48). Partly because of such effort, the Treaty of Paris establishing the European Coal and Steel Community (ECSC) in 1951 rejected the option of (inter)nationalizing the ownership of the means of production in coal, iron and steel in favour of a common market in these products achieved by removing custom duties, quotas and other obstacles to free trade.

It is well known that the anti-cartel clauses of the ECSC Treaty – which Jean Monnet considered to be the first European antitrust law – were significantly influenced by the American model represented by the Sherman Act, the Clayton Act and the Federal Trade Commission Act. Washington, represented by the US High Commissioner for Germany, John McCloy, and his cartel expert, Robert Bowie of Harvard University, insisted more than once on a particular wording of individual articles (Berghahn 1986: 144). Monnet was familiar with American antitrust legislation and there are striking similarities between his original draft of the Treaty, which envisaged a general ban on cartels without exceptions, and the principles of American competition policy.

In spite of these influences and pressures, the anti-cartel clauses of the ECSC were not an exact copy of the American model. Elements of the European cartel tradition survive in the Treaty, even if in covert form. Thus, Article 65 bans agreements and practices which restrict or distort competition in the common market for coal and steel, while Article 66 follows the

American example in prohibiting the formation of monopolies, but not concentrations short of monopoly. However, the High Authority of the ECSC could, in certain circumstances, permit horizontal agreements in order to improve productivity or the distribution of individual products. Moreover, Articles 59 and 61 endow the High Authority with interventionist powers in crisis situations. In short, the governments of Western Europe were not prepared to rely completely on the mechanisms of competition (Berghahn 1986: 144–5).

Competition rules occupy an important position also in the 1957 Treaty of Rome. Article 3(f) of the Treaty calls for 'the institution of a system ensuring that competition in the Common Market is not distorted'. Articles 85–94 provide the foundation for the competition or antitrust policy of the Community. The competition rules are directed both against private companies and against national governments. Policy towards private companies is controlled by Articles 85 and 86 which, as many legal scholars have pointed out, are remarkably similar to Articles 1 and 2 of the Sherman Act. However, American influence on the Rome Treaty is not quite as strong as in the case of the earlier Treaty of Paris. For example, the power to control mergers is explicit in the ECSC Treaty (along the lines of the anti-merger section of the Clayton Act), but not in the Treaty of Rome. Article 86 of this treaty is a poor instrument to control mergers since it requires a firm to be in a dominant position before it can be invoked. An explicit merger control regulation was approved by the EC Council only at the end of 1989, after almost twenty years of political dissension between the European Commission and the member states, unwilling to surrender control over what they considered to be an important instrument of industrial policy (see Chapter 11).

One important reason for the disparity between the two treaties was the changing motivation for a competition policy. Initially, under pressure from the United States, the major objective was to ensure that in the new coal and steel market the potential of large German firms would continue to be controlled along the lines of the allied policy of deconcentration. Strict competition rules reflected the political objective of preventing a revival of trusts and cartels in German heavy industry. By the mid-1950s fears of a resurgent Germany had diminished, and the new climate of opinion combined with a lack of enthusiasm for strong supranational powers to produce the rather weaker competition rules of the EEC Treaty (Allen 1983: 212).

Discussion on a German anti-cartel law began before the signing of the Treaty of Paris, in the autumn of 1949. Ludwig Erhard, who as Minister for Economics was responsible for drafting the law, had the difficult task of mediating between the American insistence on a strict ban on cartels and the opposition of German industry which hoped for a return to the old legal framework (Majone 1991).

A compromise was eventually found, but the debate lasted until 1957. Erhard had reason to be thankful for the American insistence on a strict cartel ban, which he himself favoured. It is quite possible that without American pressure this principle would have been rejected outright (Berghahn 1986: 173). The law finally approved by the Bundestag in 1957 has been compared to a Swiss cheese, prohibiting cartel agreements in principle, but granting so many exceptions that the ban often slipped through the numerous holes (Hardach 1980: 149). The fact remains that the Kartellgesetz went considerably beyond previous legislation such as the cartel decree of 1923 (see Chapter 7). An important institutional innovation was the creation of a specialized regulatory agency, the federal cartel office (Bundeskartellamt) with powers of investigation and enforcement.

Later influences on social and economic regulation

With the waning of America's 'consensual hegemony' in Europe, the kind of direct influence evident in the cases just discussed became increasingly impossible. However, American models remained important for European regulators in the 1960s and 1970s, especially in new policy fields like the environment, nuclear safety and consumer protection, that is, in social regulation. The leading role of the United States in economic regulation is not difficult to explain, given the ideological reluctance to nationalize, on the one hand, and the early development of mass production and the concentration of economic power which was already well advanced in the 1880s, on the other. But leadership in social regulation cannot be explained in the same way. It is certainly not the case that in the 1960s the environment was more polluted or the consumer less protected in the United States than in Europe.

A suggestive hypothesis (Majone 1991) is that, because the United States was a 'welfare laggard' compared to Europe, it could devote to social regulation the financial and political resources which in Europe were absorbed by the growing needs of the welfare state. Such an explanation focuses on the inherent tension between social regulation and traditional welfare policies based on the universal provision of social services and large-scale transfer payments. Budgetary limitations are one obvious cause of tensions: current estimates of the costs of various programmes of social regulation, particularly environmental and health and safety regulation, show that these represent a significant and growing percentage of GNP in all industrialized countries (for the United States see, for instance, MacAvoy 1992). Sooner or later, voters have to choose between expanding or even continuing welfare programmes and devoting sufficient resources to environmental protection and other types of social regulation.

However, the roots of the latent conflict between traditional social policy and social regulation go deeper than budgetary limitations. While the programmes of the welfare state are largely concerned with the provision of 'merit goods' (housing, medical care, education, retirement income and so on), the aim of social regulation is to provide 'public goods', like environmental protection, product safety or consumer information.

Public provision of merit goods raises delicate issues about government paternalism and consumer sovereignty. Moreover, most merit goods can also be supplied, often more efficiently, by the market. On the other hand, there is general agreement that public goods cannot be produced in sufficient quantities by the market. Indeed, as we saw in Chapter 2, inadequate supply of public goods is precisely one of the types of market failure which regulation is meant to correct. Hence social regulation is politically less controversial than social policy in a country like the United States where the ideology of free markets and consumer sovereignty has always received widespread support.

American methods and instruments of social regulation have been widely imitated in Europe. Examples range from the adoption of US emission standards for cars and of the methodology of environmental impact assessments – first defined by the US National Environmental Policy Act of 1969 and introduced into European legislation about a decade later – to the advocacy of environmental cost-benefit analysis, of tradeable permits and pollution taxes. In addition, the integrated pollution inspectorates and environmental agencies created in a number of European countries in the 1980s (for Britain, see Chapter 6) are clearly inspired by the model of the American Environmental Protection Agency established in 1970. In addition, European regulators have often been 'free riders' on the results of American regulatory research, while activist-driven emulation has played a significant role in the development of environmentalist movements in Europe.

Such influences are bound to become less important in the future, as environmental policy in Europe, both at the national and at the EC level, approaches maturity. Other aspects of the American experience, however, will remain important or even grow in significance. Thus, as the EC moves more squarely into the environmental arena, American regulatory federalism – which finds expression, for example, in the balance between localized implementation and a strong federal enforcement presence – may present an increasingly relevant model (Mott 1990).

As mentioned above, American regulatory philosophy and practice have continued to inspire policy developments in Europe during the phase of privatization and deregulation in the 1980s. The worldwide significance of the American deregulation of telecommunications has already been mentioned in Chapter 1. One of the important lessons for Europe was the need for a clear separation of regulatory and operational responsibilities. Thus, the formal separation of telecommunications from the Post Office, the establishment of British Telecom (BT) as an independent but regulated entity, and the creation of a specialized regulatory agency (OFTEL), were among the key policy objectives of the British 1984 Telecommunications Act. The 1987 Green Book on Telecommunications of the European Commission also stressed the importance of an institutional separation of regulatory and managerial functions – a principle now accepted also by countries such as France and Germany which have not yet fully privatized their telecom services.

A second lesson was that neither deregulation nor privatization could mean a return to *laissez faire*. Just as deregulation in the United States had not meant an end to all regulation – for example, airlines have not been deregulated with respect to safety, and all newly deregulated industries have lost their pre-existing statutory immunity from the antitrust laws – so it was soon realized that privatizations in Europe would have to be followed by regulation of prices and by a widening of the scope of the competition agencies. Prior to privatization, such agencies did not have the power to examine the potentially anti-competitive practices of the nationalized industries. Moreover, regulation of the competitive behaviour of the privatized industries is further strengthened by the availability of EC competition law which offers more powerful remedies than are available under the laws of most member states (Veljanovski 1987).

In fact, since in Europe nationalization has been the functional equivalent of American-style regulation, at least in the case of natural monopolies (see Chapter 1), it follows that privatization is best thought of as re-regulation – the replacement of one mode of regulation, public ownership, by another mode, statutory regulation. As a consequence of such re-regulation, the role of the state changes from that of a producer of goods and services to that of an umpire whose main function is to ensure that economic actors play by the agreed rules of the game.

From the Keynesian welfare state to the regulatory state

The growth of regulation in Europe must be understood not only as a shift from one mode of regulation to another, but even more as a reordering of public priorities. To examine the latter, it is useful to distinguish three main functions of government in the socio-economic sphere: income redistribution, macroeconomic stabilization and regulation.

The *redistribution function* includes all transfers of resources from one social group to another, as well as the provision of merit goods, that is, goods that the government compels individuals to consume, such as elementary education or publicly financed medical care.

The *stabilization function* is concerned with the preservation of satisfactory levels of economic growth, employment and price stability. The main instruments to achieve these objectives are fiscal and monetary policy, labour market policy and industrial policy.

Finally, the *regulatory function*, as we saw, attempts to increase the allocative efficiency of the market by correcting various types of market failure: monopoly power, negative externalities, failures of information or an insufficient provision of public goods (see Chapter 2).

All modern states engage in income redistribution, in macroeconomic stabilization and in economic and social regulation, but the relative importance of these functions varies from one country to another and from period to period. Thus, until recently most European countries attached greater political significance to redistribution and to economic stabilization and development than to the correction of market failures through competition and other regulatory policies. These priorities are reflected in such labels as 'welfare state', which emphasizes the redistributive function of the state, or 'Keynesian state', which emphasizes the stabilization function, or even 'Keynesian welfare state', combining what were considered to be the two main functions of the modern state.

On the other hand, American scholars often refer to the US federal government as a 'regulatory state' (see, for example, Seidman and Gilmour 1986; Sunstein 1990; Rose-Ackerman 1992). This terminology – a neologism in Europe – suggests that in the United States the regulatory function has been more important than the other two functions. In fact, prior to President Roosevelt's New Deal and to the fiscal revolution that took place between the presidencies of Herbert Hoover (1929–33) and Lyndon Johnson (1963–9), the United States government played a very modest role both in redistribution and in macroeconomic stabilization. In United States there was no 'colbertist' tradition of state interventionism as in France, and no bureaucracy accustomed to support domestic cartels while innovating in social policy, as in Germany; and the small size of the federal budget (like the small budget of the European Union today) prevented the development of economic and social policies, even on a modest scale. However, the Commerce Clause of the US Constitution allowed the federal judiciary to create a single continent-wide market by regulating interstate commerce. There is here an obvious analogy with the role of the European Court of Justice under Articles 30–4 of the Treaty of Rome prohibiting quantitative restrictions on imports and all equivalent measures, between member states.

Partly because of these analogies, it is not misleading but actually heuristically useful to think of the EC/EU as a 'regulatory state'. Also at the national level, however, redistributive and interventionist macroeconomic policies no longer occupy the central position they once had. In the decades immediately following the end of the Second World War, ambitious economic and social policies were legitimized by the widespread belief that governments could control the economy by manipulating key macroeconomic variables and, at the same time, ensure social justice and greater equality in the distribution of wealth.

But full employment and the welfare state could be maintained only as long as the economy was expanding. The stagflation of the 1970s showed that growth could not be taken for granted. Keynesianism was proclaimed dead: monetarism and supply-side economics became the new orthodoxy. The rejection of demand management and fine tuning of the economy implied also the rejection of more direct forms of public intervention: not only nationalizations, but also national and regional planning and, increasingly, industrial policy.

Moreover, unprecedented increases in the costs of redistributive programmes during the 1960s and 1970s, and the explosion of powerful special interest lobbies – the main theme of Mancur Olson's controversial book entitled *The Rise and Decline of Nations* (Olson 1982) – were widely perceived by both Left and Right as a serious threat not only to economic efficiency, but also to the legitimacy of the democratic state. Critics argued that, with time, the growing influence of special interest lobbies and corporatist arrangements distorts prices, restricts competition and slows down economic growth, leading to a condition termed by Andrew McFarland 'interest group stasis', at best a static if not a declining economy (McFarland 1992: 60–5). Also, the increased emphasis on redistributive issues due to the accumulation of special interest groups makes political life more divisive by reducing the significance of common interests. In struggles over redistribution no group can gain without other groups losing as much or more (Olson 1982: 41–7). That one group may lose more than the other group gains is of course due to the fact that redistribution is not costless but usually entails a 'deadweight loss', that is, the social cost of setting up and operating the redistribution system, or of attempting to evade it.

The shift toward economic and social regulation must be viewed against the background of growing criticism of traditional policies. Compared to the traditional forms of state intervention, statutory regulation by independent agencies was increasingly perceived as being less bureaucratic and more independent of party political influences – more committed to a problem-solving, rather than a bargaining, style of policy-making, and better able to protect the diffuse interests of consumers rather than those of producers – management and trade unions who have been the national partners of politicians in managing the Keynesian welfare state. The growth of this mode of regulation owes much also to a new awareness of the mismatch between existing institutional capacities and the growing complexity of policy problems: policing financial markets and enforcing competition rules in an increasingly interdependent world economy; controlling the risks of new products and new technologies; reducing environmental pollution; and protecting the health and economic interests of consumers without impeding the free flow of goods, services and people across national boundaries. It is sufficient to mention problems such as these to realize how significant is the supranational dimension of the new economic and social regulation. Not surprisingly, a good part of national regulations are today of European origin or are produced in order to implement European legislation. As explanatory variables of the growth of statutory regulation in the member states, EC directives are even more significant than the factors mentioned so far – American influences, privatization policies and the crisis of the Keynesian welfare state.

THE IMPACT OF COMMUNITY REGULATION

The stupendous growth of EC regulations since the 1960s represents a major theoretical puzzle for the student of European integration (see Chapter 4).

Our aim in this chapter, however, is only to give an idea of the quantitative and qualitative dimensions of regulatory growth in the EC and of its impact at the national level.

Consider, first, the almost exponential growth of the number of directives and regulations produced by the Brussels authorities, on average, each year (recall that directives are addressed only to member states, and are binding only as to the result to be achieved, leaving to the national authorities the choice of methods for achieving the result; while 'regulations' lay down general rules which are binding both at the Community level and at the national level). By the year 1970, the average was twenty-five directives and six hundred regulations per year; by 1975, this figure had risen to fifty and one thousand respectively; between 1985 and the early 1990s, eighty directives and one and a half thousand regulations per year.

To compare: in 1991, the European authorities in Brussels issued 1,564 directives and regulations as against 1,417 pieces of legislation (laws, ordinances, decrees) issued by Paris, so that by now the Community introduces into the corpus of French law more rules than the national authorities themselves. Moreover, according to some estimates, today only 20 to 25 per cent of the legal texts applicable in France are produced by the parliament or the government in complete autonomy, that is, without any previous consultation in Brussels (Conseil d'Etat 1993). Presumably, an analogous situation prevails in all the other member states.

Reporting such statistics, the French Conseil d'Etat speaks of normative drift (*dérive normative*) and luxuriating legislation (*droit naturellement foisonnant*), doubting that any government could have foreseen, let alone wished for, such a development. It also points out, however, that the same member states that deplore the 'regulatory fury' of the Brussels authorities are among the major causes of over-regulation with their demands for Community interventions in the most varied areas of economic and social regulation.

Another suggestive indicator of the continuously expanding agenda of the Community is the number of specialized Councils of Ministers, which rose from fourteen in 1984 to twenty-one in 1993. Recall that the Council is the body which takes the final decision on most European legislation. It consists of a representative of each member state at ministerial level. When general matters are discussed, member states will normally be represented by their foreign ministers, but other ministers will be sent for specialist discussions. Meetings of ministers other than foreign ministers are referred to collectively, as 'specialized' or 'technical' Councils. In addition to the traditional Councils of the ministers of economics, finance, agriculture, trade and industry, we have now regular meetings of the ministers of the environment (since 1974), education (since 1974), research (since 1975), tourism (since 1988), civil protection (since 1988) and telecommunications (since 1988).

Again, of seven important areas of current policy development – regional policy, research and technological development, environment, consumer protection, education, cultural and audiovisual policy, and health and safety at work – only the latter was mentioned in the Treaty of Rome (Article 118), and then only as an area where the Commission should promote close co-operation among the member states. Environmental policy provides a striking illustration of the rate of growth of EC regulation. In the two decades from 1967 to 1987, when the Single European Act (SEA) finally recognized the competence of the Community to legislate in this area, well over one hundred directives, regulations and decisions were introduced by the Commission and approved by the Council. Budgetary crises, intergovernmental dissensions, and the Europessimism of the 1970s and early 1980s hardly seemed to affect the development of Community environmental regulation. From the single directive on 'the approximation of laws, regulations, and administrative provisions relating to the classification, packaging and labelling of dangerous substances' of 1967 (Directive 67/548/EEC), we pass to ten directives/decisions in 1975, to seventeen just in the six months preceding passage of the SEA (Johnson and Corcelle 1987).

Today, European environmental regulation includes more than two hundred pieces of legislation, and in many member states the corpus of environmental law of Community origin outweighs that of purely domestic origin. Moreover, while the first directives were for the most part concerned with *product* regulation, and hence could be justified by the need to prevent that national standards would create non-tariff barriers to the free movement of goods, later directives increasingly stressed *process* regulation (emission and ambient quality standards, regulation of waste disposal and of land use, protection of flora and fauna, environmental impact assessments), and thus aimed explicitly at environmental rather than free-trade objectives.

To appreciate the impact of these developments on the member states, one must keep in mind that, according to the jurisprudence of the European Court of Justice, Community acts made under the authority of the founding treaties take precedence over the domestic law of the member states. Even more, under conditions which have become increasingly less stringent over time, Community acts have 'direct effect', that is, pass directly into the domestic law of the member states, without the need of any intervening action on their part. Thus, if a Community act, such as a directive, is directly effective, a private citizen can invoke it against a public authority in a member state, often the central government, and even against another private individual (Hartley 1988).

In addition to the supremacy and direct effect of European legislation, membership in the EC/EU has other important implications. In particular, the mutual recognition of national rules and standards (to be discussed in more detail in Chapter 4) does not involve the transfer of regulatory powers to the Community, but nevertheless restricts the freedom of action of national governments which cannot prevent the marketing within their borders of a product lawfully manufactured and marketed in another member state. Accordingly, the principle of mutual recognition introduces competition among national regulators, and, with this, a way of assessing the costs and benefits of different regulatory approaches. For example, suppose that two countries, let us say France and Germany, use different technical standards for colour television sets. If the German standards are cheaper to implement but German television sets are considered just as good as the French ones by consumers, French producers will lose market share. Hence they will put pressure on their own government to change national standards. In the end the most cost-effective standard will prevail, but this *ex post*, market-driven harmonization is quite different from the *ex ante* harmonization of national regulations which had been the main objective of the Community in the three decades after the coming into force of the Treaty of Rome.

Thus, the influences of the EC/EU on regulatory developments in the (present and future) member states are pervasive. Some influences are direct, others, like mutual recognition, indirect. The important point is that the transfer of regulatory powers to the European level has not reduced, but actually increased, regulatory activities at the national level. This apparent paradox is easily explained. In the policy-making system created by the Treaty of Rome, implementation of most Community rules is the responsibility of the member states. Moreover, Community legislation has not just replaced national regulations, but has actually created new regulatory responsibilities. This is true not only in competition law, but also in a number of other policy areas such as consumer protection, product safety, food and drugs, and (especially in the countries of southern Europe) environmental protection, health and safety at work, and equal rights for male and female workers.

In order to take part in the formulation of all these new rules in Brussels, and then to implement them at the national level, member states have been forced to develop new regulatory capacities on an unprecedented scale. Economists distinguish between 'trade creation' and 'trade diversion' in a customs union. Trade creation represents a shift to a more efficient producer as a result of the establishment of the customs union, while the opposite is true of trade diversion. By analogy, we can say that, in the field of regulatory policy-making, European integration has meant 'rule creation' – new and generally better rules both at the national and supranational levels – rather than simply 'rule diversion' from one level of government to another.

REFERENCES

Allen, D. (1983) 'Managing the Common Market: the Community competition policy', in Wallace, Wallace and Webb (eds) *Policy-making in the European Community*, London and New York: John Wiley & Sons.

Baldwin, R. and McCrudden, C. (1987) *Regulation and Public Law*, London: Weidenfeld & Nicolson.

Berghahn, V. (1986) *The Americanization of West German Industry*, Leamingston Spa and New York: Berg.

Conseil d'Etat (1993) *Report of the Conseil d'Etat 1992*, Paris: Documentation Française.

Guédon, M.-J. (1991) *Les autorités administratives indépendantes*, Paris: Libraire Générale de Droit et de Jurisprudence.

Hardach, K. (1980) *The Political Economy of Germany in the Twentieth Century*, Berkeley and Los Angeles: University of California Press.

Hartley, T.C. (1988) *The Foundations of European Community Law* (2nd edition), Oxford: Clarendon Press.

Jenkins, P. (1988) *Mrs Thatcher's Revolution*, Cambridge (MA): Harvard University Press.

Johnson, S. and Corcelle, G. (1987) *L'autre Europe 'verte' – la politique communautaire de l'environnement*, Brussels: Labor.

MacAvoy, P.W. (1992) *Industry Regulation and the Performance of the American Economy*, New York: W.W. Norton & Co.

McFarland, A.S. (1992) 'Interest groups and the policymaking process: sources of countervailing power in America', in Petracca (ed.) *The Politics of Interests*, Boulder: Westview Press.

Maier, C. (1978) 'The politics of productivity: foundations of American international economic policy after Second World War', in Katzenstein (ed.) *Between Power and Plenty*, Madison (WI): University of Wisconsin Press.

Majone, G. (1991) 'Cross-national sources of regulatory policymaking in Europe and the United States' *Journal of Public Policy*, XI, 1: 79–106.

Majone, G. (1994) 'The rise of the regulatory state in Europe' *West European Politics* 17, 3: 77–101.

Majone, G. (1995) 'Independence and accountability: non-majoritarian institutions and democratic government in Europe', to be published in Weiler, Dehousse and Cassese (eds) (forthcoming) *Collected Courses of the Academy of European Law*, London: Kluwer Law International.

Mott, R. (1990) *Federal–State Relations in U.S. Environmental Law: Implications for the European Community*, Florence: European Policy Unit of the European University Institute, Working Paper no. 90/2.

Olson, M. (1982) *The Rise and Decline of Nations* New Haven (CT): Yale University Press.

Rose-Ackerman, S. (1992) *Rethinking the Progressive Agenda: the Reform of the American Regulatory State*, New York: The Free Press.

Seidman, H. and Gilmour, R. (1986) *Politics, Position and Power: From the Positive to the Regulatory State* (4th edition), Oxford: Oxford University Press.

Selznick, P. (1985) 'Focusing organizational research on regulation', in Noll (ed.) *Regulatory Policy and the Social Sciences*, Berkeley and Los Angeles: University of California Press.

Sunstein, C.R. (1990) *After the Rights Revolution: Reconceiving the Regulatory State*, Cambridge (MA): Harvard University Press.

Teitgen-Colly, C. (1988) 'Les autorités administratives indépendantes: histoire d'une institution', in Colliard and Timsit (eds), *Les autorités administratives indépendantes*, Paris: Presses Universitaires de France.

Veljanovski, C. (1987) *Selling the State*, London: Weidenfeld & Nicolson.

4 The European Commission as regulator

Giandomenico Majone

INTRODUCTION

In the preceding chapter it has been suggested that the enormous quantitative and qualitative growth of Community regulation since the 1960s, far from being a necessary outcome of the integration process, actually poses a major theoretical puzzle. In fact, aside from competition rules and measures necessary for the integration of national markets, few regulatory policies or programmes are explicitly mentioned in the Treaty of Rome. As already noted, environmental and consumer protection were not even mentioned as Community policies, while health and safety at work was identified as an area where the Commission should only promote close co-operation among member states. On the other hand, agriculture, the European Social Fund, economic and social cohesion, and development co-operation, which together account for more than 80 per cent of the EU budget, are redistributive rather than regulatory policies.

The extraordinary growth of Community regulation is puzzling for several reasons. First, as we saw in the preceding chapter, member states complain about over-regulation, yet they are strongly represented at every stage of decision-making and their approval is required for most Commission proposals before these become European law. Again member states strive to preserve the greatest possible degree of sovereignty and policy-making autonomy, as shown for example by their stubborn resistance to Community interventions in areas such as macroeconomic policy and taxation. At the same time, however, they have accepted a number of regulatory interventions which were neither foreseen by the treaties nor strictly necessary for the proper functioning of the common market.

Finally, concerning the qualitative rather than quantitative dimension of regulatory growth, it is surprising that policy innovation is at all possible in a system where the formal rights of initiative of the Commission, as well as its executive functions, appear to be so tightly controlled. There can be little doubt as to the determination of the member states to limit the Commission's discretion at every stage of policy-making. Political initiative comes from the heads of state or government in the European Council; political mediation takes place in the framework of the Committee of Permanent Representatives of national governments (COREPER); formal adoption is the prerogative of the Council of Ministers; and implementation is in the hands of national administrations.

Before final adoption by the Council, a Commission proposal will typically have been discussed in a working group comprising for the most part national officials; submitted to an advisory committee which includes national experts; transmitted to COREPER for discussion in the working group of national officials it sets up; reviewed by COREPER once more, and finally placed before the Council for approval (Peters 1992). In addition, the Commission's discretion in the exercise of powers delegated to it by the Council has been tightly regulated by Council Decision 87/373/EEC on the 'comitology' system. It is common practice for the Council to lay down the general principles to be followed on a given issue and to delegate the power to deal with detailed questions. Under the comitology system, the Council may establish a committee, composed of representatives of national governments, to which the Commission must submit drafts of measures it intends to adopt under the delegated power. There are two main types of such committees: advisory and oversight. The latter are again subdivided into 'management' and 'regulatory' committees. Regulatory, and to some extent also management, committees can block a Commission proposal and transmit the case to the Council which can overrule the Commission or postpone a decision indefinitely.

Not surprisingly, many students of European integration have concluded that policy innovation in the EC/EU is highly unlikely. At most the Commission can hope 'to generalize and diffuse solutions adopted in one or more member states by introducing them throughout the Community. The solutions of these member states normally set the framework for the Community solution' (Rehbinder and Stewart 1985: 213). For intergovernmentalist writers, policy innovation is not just unlikely but actually impossible, since the Commission is little more than an international secretariat set up to facilitate bargaining among the member states. Their model is one of least-common-denominator bargaining – a sort of Ricardian theory of Community policy-making. As in Ricardo's theory of economic rent the price of a good is determined by the unit cost of the output produced by the marginal firm so, according to intergovernmentalists, the quality of policy decisions in the EC/EU is determined by the preferences of the least forthcoming (or marginal) government. Hence, barring special circumstances, the outcome will converge towards a least-common-denominator position.

In spite of these pessimistic assessments, we shall see that genuine policy innovation is not, in fact, impossible. It is not very frequent, certainly, but then incrementalism is also a pervasive feature of domestic policy-making. Thus, a satisfactory model of regulatory policy-making at the European level should be able to explain not only the quantitative growth of Community regulation, but also the ability of the Commission to innovate with respect to the regulatory practices of all or most member states. The aim of this chapter is to develop such a model.

THE SELECTIVE EXPANSION OF EUROPEAN COMPETENCES

The continuous growth of regulatory policies at the European level appears all the more striking when one observes that other policies mentioned in the Treaties (such as transport, energy, research and development, education and, most notably, social policy) have remained largely underdeveloped. This highly selective expansion of European competences is precisely what neo-functionalist theories fail to explain. Ernst Haas, the founder of neo-functionalism, explained the growth of Community competences in terms of the 'expansive logic of sectoral integration'. Haas assumed a process of functional 'spillover', in which the initial decision of governments to delegate policy-making powers in a certain sector, such as coal and steel, to a supranational institution inevitably creates pressure to expand the authority of that institution into neighbouring policy areas such as trade, competition and labour market policies. Since all sectors of the economy are inter-dependent, the logic of functional spillovers would eventually bring about a general transfer of policy-making powers to the supranational institutions (Haas 1968).

Subsequent developments showed that such a process is neither inevitable nor automatic, but Haas and his followers never provided a satisfactory explanation of the selective nature of the expansion of supranational competences. The distinction they sometimes drew between 'high' and 'low' politics is not relevant here since we are not considering foreign and security policy, or other sovereign functions such as justice or taxation. Rather, the methodological mistake of the neo-functionalists consisted in the failure to distinguish between different policy *types* or, even more simply, between regulatory and direct-expenditure programmes.

For the purpose of our argument it is sufficient to distinguish three policy types closely related to, but not identical with, the three functions of government discussed in the preceding chapter. The three relevant types are: redistributive policies, distributive policies, and regulatory policies (Lowi 1979). Redistributive policies transfer resources from one group of individuals, regions or countries to another group, while distributive policies, such as public works or research and development, allocate public resources among alternative users.

As several critics have pointed out, Lowi's classification is neither exhaustive nor mutually exclusive, but this is not a serious limitation for the present discussion. The important distinction for us is between regulatory policies and those non-regulatory policies (such as distributive and re-distributive) which require the direct expenditure of public funds. The distinction is based on the fact that budgetary constraints have only a limited impact on regulatory policy-making, while the size of non-regulatory, direct-expenditure programmes is determined by budgetary appropriations and, ultimately, but the level of government tax revenues. The public budget is a soft constraint on regulators because the real costs of regulatory programmes are borne not by the agencies but by the individuals, firms or governments who have to comply with the regulations.

As Christopher DeMuth, a former administrator for regulatory affairs in the US Office of Management and Budget, writes:

> Budget and revenue figures are good summaries of what is happening in welfare, defense, or tax policy, and can be used to communicate efficiently with the general public over the fray of program-by-program interest group contention. . . . In the world of regulation, however, where the government commands but nearly all the rest takes place in the private economy, we generally lack good aggregate numbers to describe what is being 'taxed' and 'spent' in pursuit of public policies. Instead we have lists – endless lists of projects the government would like others to undertake.
>
> (DeMuth 1984: 25)

The significance of this structural difference between regulatory policies and policies involving the direct expenditure of public funds, cannot be over-stated. Moreover, the difference is even more crucial at the European than at the national level since not only the economic costs but also the political and administrative costs of implementing European rules are borne, directly or indirectly, by the member states. As we show below, these structural characteristics of regulatory policies go a long way towards explaining the regulatory bias of Community policy-making.

THE SUPPLY OF COMMUNITY REGULATION

In the following pages we will develop a simple demand-and-supply model of Community regulation (Majone 1995). Because of its right of legislative initiative, the Commission plays the main role on the supply side, in spite of the fact that most Commission proposals have to be formally approved by the Council of Ministers (see below). We start by assuming that the Commission has a utility function which it attempts to maximize, subject to constraints. What is the nature of this utility function? Public-choice models of bureaucracy usually assume that officials try to maximize the size of the agency as measured by various parameters. One of the best known among such models takes the agency's budget as the maximand (Niskanen 1971). In Niskanen's model, the size of the budget is positively related to such goals of a bureaucrat as 'salary, the prerequisites of office, public reputation, power, patronage and output of the bureau' (Niskanen 1971: 38). Now, an administrative agency can maximize its own budget, subject to the constraints that the budget covers the cost of producing a given level Q of service, because only the managers of the agency know the true cost of producing Q, that is, the cost function

$C(Q)$. The funding body – say, the parliament – knows only its utility function $U(Q)$ and thus cannot determine the level of Q such that the necessary condition for utility maximization (equality of marginal utility and marginal cost) is satisfied. This allows the agency to request a budget larger than the one that maximizes the net benefits of those who provide the funds.

Niskanen developed his model bearing in mind line agencies administering direct-expenditure (for example, distributive or redistributive) programmes (Dunleavy 1991). Budget maximization may be a plausible objective for such agencies, but certainly not for regulatory agencies where the budget constraint is relatively unimportant, as noted above. In fact, not even economic theories of regulation (see Chapter 2) make use of the budget-maximization hypothesis in modelling the behaviour of regulatory agencies. In these models, regulators maximize their utility not by concealing their true cost function – which largely consists of personnel costs that the funding body can estimate fairly accurately – but by providing regulatory benefits to a variety of interest groups.

Moreover, both Niskanen's model of budget maximization and economic theories of regulation assume that the type of service provided by the agency, though not the level of activity, is fixed. In other words, the administrative or regulatory tasks have already been assigned; the models attempt only to predict how the given tasks will be performed. But in the case of a new and still developing bureaucratic organization, the central issue is the definition of competences. Hence our model assumes that what the European Commission attempts to maximize is its influence, as measured by the scope of its competences.

The available empirical evidence, as well as casual observations, seem to support the hypothesis that the utility function of the Commission is positively related to the *scope* of its competences rather than to the *scale* of the services provided or to the size of its budget. For example, the great expansion of Community competences since the mid-1980s in areas such as the environment, health and safety at work, consumer product safety and the regulation of financial services has been accompanied by a significantly less than proportional increase of expenditures for administration – from 4.35 per cent of the total Community budget in 1985 to 4.8 per cent in 1994 – while the number of directives has more than doubled in the same period. Thus, budgetary appropriations per unit of regulatory output have actually decreased, suggesting that the Commission prefers task expansion to budgetary growth.

Of course, the scope of Community competences could be expanded in different directions: our model in no way implies an *a priori* preference for regulatory policies. What restricts the freedom of choice of the Commission is the constraints it faces, especially the budgetary limitations. Despite a significant growth in recent years, the budget of the European Union represents only 2.4 per cent of all the public sector spending of the member states, and less than 1.3 per cent of the gross domestic product (GDP) of the

Union. By comparison, between 45 and 50 per cent of the wealth produced in the member states is spent by the national and local governments. The EU budget is not only very small, but also quite rigid: almost 70 per cent of total appropriations consists of compulsory expenditures. These resources go for the most part to the Common Agricultural Policy (CAP) and to a handful of distributive and redistributive programmes. What remains is insufficient to support large-scale initiatives in politically appealing fields such as industrial policy, energy, transport, research or technological innovation. Given these constraints, the only way for the Commission to increase its influence is to expand the scope of its regulatory activities: regulatory policy-making puts a good deal of power in the hands of the Brussels authorities while, at the same time, giving the possibility of avoiding tight budgetary constraints imposed by the member states.

This completes our discussion of the supply side of the 'market' for Community regulation. We consider now the demand side, where the member states are the most important, but by no means the only, actors.

THE DEMAND OF COMMUNITY REGULATION

Neo-functionalists were undoubtedly correct in assuming that the functional needs of an integrated European market would necessitate a considerable transfer of policy-making powers to the EC level. However, as already noted, the logic of functional spillovers is unable to explain the full extent of present Community competences. Much social regulation, as well as many distributive and redistributive programmes, cannot be explained in this way. Even in the case of economic regulation, where functional logic is most compelling, the timing and quality of many developments cannot be understood without taking into consideration other factors such as the policy entrepreneurship of the Commission – as in the case of the Merger Control Regulation approved by the Council only in 1989, after more than twenty years of political wrangling; see below – or the activism of powerful actors who cannot wait for incremental task expansion to produce the policy outputs they want.

Thus, multinationals and other export-oriented firms tend to prefer European to national regulations not only to avoid the costs of meeting different and often inconsistent national standards, but also to avoid the risk of progressively more stringent regulations in some of the member states. A similar development has been observed in America. For example, the American car industry decided to support federal regulation of air pollution because of the threat posed by different and inconsistent air-pollution standards, but also because it feared

> [a] kind of political domino effect, in which one state legislature after another would set more and more stringent emission standards without regard to cost and technical difficulties involved. . . . Federal legislation was preferable to state legislation – particularly if federal standards were

based on technical presentations to an administrative agency rather than through symbolic appeals to cost-externalizing politicians.

(Elliott, Ackerman and Millian 1985: 331)

Thus, the car industry, which during the early 1960s had successfully opposed federal emission standards for motor vehicles, abruptly reversed its position in mid-1965: provided that the federal standards would be set by a regulatory agency, and provided that they would pre-empt any state standards more stringent than California's the industry would support federal legislation.

For a European example, consider Directive 79/831 amending for the sixth time Directive 67/548 on the classification, packaging and labelling of dangerous substances. The 1979 directive does not prevent member states from including more substances within the scope of national regulations than are required by the directive itself. In fact, the British Health and Safety Commission proposed to go further than the directive by bringing inter-mediate products within the scope of national regulations. This, however, was opposed by the chemical industry which argued that national regulations should not impose greater burdens on British industry than the directive placed on its competitors. The industry view prevailed, thus ensuring that Community regulation would in fact set the maximum as well as the minimum standard for national regulation (Haigh 1984). German firms, concerned about an environmentally conscious public opinion at home and wishing to avoid the commercial obstacles that would arise from divergent national regulations, also pressed for an EC-wide regulation of toxic substances.

The European chemical industry had another reason for supporting Community regulation. The US Toxic Substances Control Act (TSCA), enacted in 1976, represented a serious threat for European exports to the American market. A European response to TSCA was needed, and the Community was the natural forum for fashioning such a response. In fact, the 1979 directive has enabled the Community to speak with one voice in discussion with the United States and other OECD countries, and has strengthened the position of the European chemical industry in ensuring that the new American law did not create obstacles to its exports. There is little doubt that the ability of the Commission to enter into discussion with the United States has been greatly enhanced by the directive, and it is unlikely that each European country on its own could do so effectively (Brickman, Jasanoff and Ilgen 1985: 277).

Demands for Community regulation also come from public-interest organizations such as environmentalist and consumer-protection groups – particularly ones from countries with a low level of health and safety regulation. Such groups hope to get from Brussels the type of protective legislation which, because of their political weakness, they are unable to get from their own governments.

By far the most important source of demand, however, are the member states themselves. As already noted, quite often the Commission introduces legislative proposals at the suggestion of particular national governments interested in a particular issue. Thus, the British government exerted considerable pressure on the Commission to introduce legislation liberalizing the market for life and non-life insurance, where British insurers enjoyed a competitive advantage over their competitors on the continent, while the German government pushed for the adoption at the European level of its own technology-based approach to air-pollution control.

There are several reasons why a country may want to use Community legislation in order to impose on the other member states its own approach to a particular regulatory issue (Héritier *et al.* 1994). If successful, such a strategy would minimize the costs of legal and administrative adaptation to new Community rules; it would give a competitive advantage to the national industry which is already familiar with, and adjusted to, the particular regulatory regime; and, in the case of countries with a high level of social regulation, it would reduce the cost advantages of countries with lower levels of protection by forcing all member states to adopt the same regulatory standards.

Precisely for these reasons other countries may be expected to oppose the proposal. The final outcome will depend not only on the ability of the proposing country to form a winning coalition in the Council of Ministers but also, and at least equally importantly, on the congruence of the national approach with the regulatory objectives of the Commission. For, although it is true that in a formal sense the Commission proposes and the Council disposes, it is the case that the legislation approved by the Council usually reflects the policy positions of the Commission – a result partly explained by the fact that the Commission can withdraw a proposal at any stage of the policy-making process.

POLICY CREDIBILITY, RELATIONAL CONTRACTING AND THE DELEGATION PROBLEM

Whatever its sources, demand for European regulation can be effective only if the Community is competent to regulate in a given area. This observation brings us back to the delegation problem already introduced in Chapter 2, namely, how can we explain the willingness of the member states to delegate to the European institutions such extensive regulatory powers? According to Article 235 of the Treaty of Rome:

> If action by the Community should prove necessary to attain . . . one of the objectives of the Community and this Treaty has not provided the necessary powers, the Council shall, acting unanimously on a proposal from the Commission and after consulting the European Parliament, take the appropriate measures.

This article effectively confers to the European institutions a general legislative power within the broad policy areas covered by the Treaty. For example, the Commission has used Article 235, in conjunction with Article

100 on the approximation of national laws and regulations, to produce environmental directives even before the Single European Act formally acknowledged the competence of the Community in the field of environmental protection.

The existence of international market failures, such as transboundary pollution, is not sufficient to explain the phenomenon of delegation to supranational authorities. We know from Coase's theorem (Coase 1960) that it is not the externalities as such that constitute a problem for collective action, but positive transaction costs and imperfect information. In a situation where transaction costs are zero and information is complete, affected parties can bargain among themselves to reach an efficient solution: either the externality is 'internalized' by the emitter or, if the costs of eliminating it outweigh the benefits, the externality persists but is shown, *ipso facto*, to be Pareto-irrelevant.

The same argument can be applied to problems of collective choice at the international level. Without transaction costs and given complete information, there would be no need for sovereign states to delegate regulatory powers to supranational bodies. If national regulators were willing and able to take into account the external effects of their decisions; if they were well informed about one another's intentions; and if the costs of organizing and implementing policy co-ordination were negligible, international externalities and other market failures could be managed by intergovernmental agreements, or even by means of non-cooperative mechanisms such as retaliation or tit-for-tat strategies (Majone 1994).

Of course, such conditions are never satisfied in practice and most international agreements are accompanied by the creation of a secretariat to facilitate the exchange of information and reduce the costs of organizing co-operation. The powers delegated to European institutions are much greater than this, however. In order to explain why member states have accepted such far-reaching limitations of their sovereignty, we must examine more closely the different kinds of transaction costs that arise in the formulation and implementation of international regulatory agreements.

In Coase's definition, transaction costs are incurred in order:

> [t]o discover who it is that one wishes to deal with, to inform people that one wishes to deal and on what terms, to conduct negotiations leading up to a bargain, to draw up the contract, to undertake the inspection needed to make sure that the terms of the contract are being observed, and so on.
>
> (Coase 1960: 15)

For our purposes it is necessary to adapt this definition somewhat and, at the same time, to take it a little further. Thus, we shall group all transaction costs under three broad categories: search and information costs; bargaining and decision costs; and policing, enforcement and measurement costs. In the following discussion we concentrate on the third category. This is because any intergovernmental agreement involves search and bargaining costs, but policing, enforcement and measurement costs are especially significant in the case of regulatory agreements. It is the high level of these transaction costs that explains the decision to delegate powers to a supranational authority rather than merely setting up an international secretariat.

Policy discretion is probably the most important reason why policing regulatory agreements is so costly. Unfortunately, discretion in regulation is unavoidable. First, regulation is heavily dependent on scientific, engineering or economic knowledge, but the relevant knowledge is almost always insufficient to permit definite conclusions about the causes and remedies of particular problems. Hence the regulator is forced to exercise policy discretion in choosing among several possible courses of action (Greenwood 1984). Second, regulation consists of applying the general principles stated in a formal document (a statute or an international convention, for example) to particular, and often rapidly changing, circumstances, and this again implies a good deal of discretion.

Again, because regulators lack information that only regulated firms have and because governments are reluctant, for political reasons, to impose excessive costs on industry, bargaining is an essential feature of the process of regulatory enforcement. Regardless of what the law says, the process of regulation is not simply one where the regulators command and the regulated obey. A 'market' is created in which bureaucrats and those subject to regulation bargain over the precise obligations of the latter (Peacock 1984). Since bargaining is so pervasive, it may be difficult for an outside observer to determine whether the spirit of an international regulation has been violated.

In turn, policy discretion facilitates the strategic use of regulation (domestic or international) to gain advantages with respect to other countries or jurisdictions. Notice that internationally relevant policy externalities can arise even in the case of purely local market failures. For instance, problems of safety regulation for the construction of local buildings create no transboundary problems and thus, according to the principle of subsidiarity, should be left to the local authorities. However, if safety regulations specify a particular material produced only in that locality, they amount to a trade barrier and thus have negative external effects. Hence, local regulation of a local market failure may create an international policy externality. Similarly, local authorities have sometimes controlled air pollution by requiring extremely tall smokestacks on industrial facilities. With tall stacks, by the time the emissions descend to ground level they are usually in the next city, region or country, and so of no concern to the jurisdiction where they were emitted.

Regulatory discretion allows local or national governments to blur the distinction between providing public goods for their citizens and engaging in policies designed to advantage the locality or the country at the expense of their neighbours. Centralization of regulatory authority at the higher level of government can correct such policy externalities, but its cost is the homogenization of policy across jurisdictions that may be dissimilar with respect to underlying tastes or needs.

In conclusion, when it is difficult to observe whether governments are making an honest effort to enforce a regulatory policy, the policy is not credible. As noted in Chapter 2, the delegation of regulatory powers to some agency distinct from the government itself is an important means whereby governments can commit themselves to regulatory strategies that would not be credible in the absence of such delegation. This explains the transfer of regulatory powers to the European Commission. Sometimes governments have problems of credibility not just in the eyes of each other but also in the eyes of third parties. For example, where pollution has international effects and fines impose significant disadvantages on firms that compete internationally, firms are likely to believe that national regulators will be unwilling to prosecute them as rigorously if they determine the level of enforcement unilaterally rather than under international supervision.

Hence the transfer of regulatory powers to a supranational authority like the European Commission may, by making more stringent regulation credible, improve the behaviour of regulated firms. Because the Commission is involved in the regulation of a large number of firms throughout the Union, it has more to gain by being tough in any individual cases than a national regulator; weak enforcement would destroy its reputation in the eyes of more firms (Gatsios and Seabright 1989: 49–50). For the same reason, and because of its independence from electoral considerations and party political influences, the Commission is also less likely to be captured by special interests than a national authority.

Finally, it is important to keep in mind that the Treaty of Rome is a 'framework treaty' rather than an international agreement providing a detailed specification of objectives and policy instruments such as the treaties creating the European Coal and Steel Community and Euratom. With the exception of the automatic clauses concerning the elimination of customs duties between the member states, the Treaty of Rome provides only general principles and policy guidelines, and delegates to the European institutions (especially the Commission and the Council) the task of specifying the concrete measures to be taken in order to achieve the broad objectives set out in Article 2. In the language of Chapter 2, this means that the Treaty is best understood as a 'relational contract' among the member states.

It will be recalled that a relational contract does not attempt the impossible task of foreseeing and accurately describing all the relevant contingencies that might arise in the course of the contract. Instead, it settles for an agreement that frames the entire relationship, recognizing that it is impossible to concentrate all of the relevant bargaining action at the *ex ante* contracting stage. Under relational contracting the parties will be particularly concerned with who has what powers to act when unforeseen circumstances arise, and with dispute-resolution mechanisms to be used if disagreement occurs (Milgrom and Roberts 1992).

Thus, delegation is an essential aspect of relational contracting. However, if the contracting parties are to delegate discretionary authority to adapt the relationship to unforeseen circumstances, they must believe that it will be used fairly and effectively. The party to whom authority is delegated should be the one who has the most to lose from loss of reputation, hence the one with the longer time horizon, the more visibility and the greater frequency of transactions (Milgrom and Roberts 1992: 140).

The Commission, supported when necessary by the European Court of Justice, satisfies these requirements in a way that no mere international secretariat, devoid of discretionary authority ever could. Hence the delegation of policy-making powers to the Commission, which was explained above by the lack of credibility of intergovernmental agreements, can be seen to follow, more generally, from the nature of the Treaty of Rome as a relational contract. Article 235 is the appropriate response to the contractual incompleteness which characterizes all constitutional documents.

DISCRETION IN THE POST-DELEGATION STAGE

The relational contracting approach attaches at least as much importance to the post-delegation (or contract execution) stage as to the *ex ante* contracting stage. This emphasis on implementation follows from the observation that, because of contractual incompleteness, it is impossible to concentrate all the relevant bargaining action at the *ex ante* stage (Williamson 1985). Hence, the relational contracting view of control is rather different – more dynamic and less one-dimensional – than the view of the principal-agent theory.

As we saw in Chapter 2, this theory holds that political control of the bureaucracy can be accomplished at the delegation stage since politicians can design bureaucratic institutions with incentive structures to facilitate monitoring and oversight. It is certainly true that at the delegation stage political principals have the freedom to select their agents and impose an incentive structure on their behaviour. Over time, however, bureaucrats accumulate several advantages, including institutionalization and job-specific expertise, which alter the original relationships. Now politicians must deal with agents they once selected, and in these dealings the bureaucrats have a strong bargaining position because of their technical and institutional expertise. As a result, they are increasingly able to pursue their objective of greater autonomy. In the words of Moe:

> Once an agency is created, the political world becomes a different place. Agency bureaucrats are now political actors in their own right: they have career and institutional interests that may not be entirely congruent with their formal missions, and they have powerful resources – expertise and delegated authority – that might be employed toward these 'selfish' ends. They are players whose interests and resources alter the political game.
>
> (Moe 1990: 143)

In sum, the contractual approach provides a better key for understanding the dynamics of delegation and control and the conditions for policy innovation at the European level than either neo-functionalism, with its theoretically ungrounded belief in the automatism of functional spillovers, or inter-governmentalism, with its emphasis on *ex ante* bargaining among national governments and its view of the Commission as a mere facilitating institution. It is of course true that national interests gave rise to European institutions and that national leaders make the final decisions on legislation and institutional reform, but it does not follow that control is unproblematic. As already noted, contractual incompleteness implies that a good deal of delegated discretion is unavoidable. On the other hand, supranational institutions, like their national counterparts, have interests of their own, including survival, growth and security. They take action on their own behalf and on behalf of their supranational objectives, not simply on behalf of the 'underlying' national interests.

Moreover, oversight for purposes of serious policy control is as costly, time-consuming and difficult to do well for the representatives of the member states in the Council of Ministers as for politicians elsewhere. Hence their unwillingness to invest scarce resources in such activities. As was mentioned in the introduction to this chapter, the 'comitology' system was devised in order to control the Commission's discretion in the execution of Council directives. Even in the case of the regulatory and management committees, however, the Commission is not only in the chair, but has a strong presumption in its favour (Ludlow 1991: 107).

According to a detailed empirical study of the comitology system, 'Commission officials generally do not think that their committee significantly reduced the Commission's freedom, and even less that it has been set up to assure the member states' control' (Institut für Europäische Politik 1989: 9).

The same study points out that the Council acts only rarely on the complex technical matters dealt with by the comitology committees, but, when it does, its decisions mostly support the Commission's original proposals (Institut für Europäische Politik 1989: 123). In addition to its reluctance to engage in costly policy control, the Council also suffers from its inability to compete with the expertise at the disposal of the Commission and its Directorates (Peters 1992: 119).

The offices of the Commission responsible for a particular policy form the central node of a vast 'issue network' which includes, in addition to national experts, academics, consumer advocates and representatives of other public–interest groups, economic interests, professional organizations and sub-national governments. Commission officials engage in extensive discussions with all these actors but remain free to choose whose ideas and proposals to adopt. The variety of policy positions, which is typically much greater than at the national level, increases the freedom of choice of European officials. It may even be the case that national experts find the Commission a more receptive forum for new ideas than their own administration. An important piece of safety regulation, the 1989 Machinery Directive 89/392, offers a striking example of this. The crucially important technical annex of the directive was drafted by a British safety expert who originally had sought to reform the British approach to safety in the workplace. Having failed to persuade the policy-makers of his own country, he brought his innovative ideas to Brussels, where they were welcomed by Commission officials and eventually became European law (Eichener 1992: 52).

POLICY ENTREPRENEURSHIP AND THE PROTECTION OF DIFFUSE INTERESTS

Thus, despite the attempts of the member states to limit its regulatory discretion, the Commission is often able to play the role of a policy entrepreneur. Policy entrepreneurs are constantly on the look-out for windows of opportunity through which to push their preferred ideas. Policy windows open on those relatively infrequent occasions when three usually separate process streams – problems, politics and policy ideas – converge. Policy entrepreneurs concerned about a particular problem search for solutions in the stream of policy ideas to couple to their problem, then try to take advantage of political receptivity at certain points in time to push the package of problem and solution (Kingdon 1984).

According to Kingdon (1984: 189–90), successful policy entrepreneurs possess three basic qualities. First, they must be taken seriously either as experts or as leaders of powerful interest groups, or as authoritative decision-makers. Second, they must be known for their negotiating skills. And third, and probably most importantly, they must be persistent. Because of the way they are recruited, the structure of their career incentives, their long-term horizon, and their strategic advantage in policy initiation, Commission officials often display the qualities of a successful policy entrepreneur to a degree unmatched by national civil servants or even politicians.

In particular, the Commission exhibits the virtue of persistence to an extraordinary degree. Most important advances in European policy have been achieved after many years during which time the Commission persisted in its attempts to 'soften up' the opposition of the member states, while waiting for a window of opportunity to open. A textbook example is the Merger Control Regulation approved by the Council on 21 December 1989, after more than twenty years of political wrangling.

As far back as 1965, the Commission argued that the Treaty of Rome was seriously deficient without the power to control mergers. The following year it asked a group of experts to study the problem of concentrations in the Common Market. The majority of the group held that Article 85 of the Treaty could be applied to 'monopolizing' mergers, but the Commission chose to follow the contrary opinion of the minority. It did, however, accept the majority view concerning the applicability of Article 86 to mergers involving one company already in a dominant position in the Common Market. The European Court of Justice followed the Commission's interpretation in the *Continental Can* case (1973).

At the beginning of 1974, the European Parliament and the Economic and Social Committee approved by large majorities a proposal for a merger control regulation, but the national governments were not yet prepared to grant the Commission the powers it requested. A long period of inaction followed. The process was again set in motion by the path-breaking *Philip Morris* Judgement of 17 November 1987 in which the Court of Justice held, against the then prevalent legal opinion, that Article 86 does apply to the acquisition by one company of an equity interest in a competitor where the effect is to restrict or distort competition. The Commission warmly endorsed the Court's decision. It was clear that another important step, after *Continental Can*, had been taken on the road towards the control of merger activities with a 'Community dimension'.

In the meanwhile, the 'Europe 1992' programme for the completion of the internal market had stimulated waves of mergers. This development opened the window of opportunity the Commission had been waiting for so long. Centralized merger control of Community-wide mergers would now be presented as essential for success in completing the internal market. Finally, the convergence of Kingdon's three streams of problems, politics and policy ideas produced the 1989 Merger Control Regulation. This episode in the history of EC policy-making is a clear example of the entrepreneurial skills of the Commission, but also illustrates the more general point that an adequate explanation of policy development in the EC must be rooted in the dynamics of the entire system, and must pay serious attention to the relationship of mutual dependence among European institutions – in some cases, as here, the Commission and the Court of Justice; in others, the Commission and the European Parliament (Dehousse and Majone 1994).

William Riker provides additional insights into the strategies used by policy entrepreneurs to change the *status quo*. He argues that through agenda-setting, strategic behaviour, and especially through the introduction of new policy dimensions to the political debate, the entrepreneur can break up existing equilibria in order to create new and more profitable policy outcomes. The successful entrepreneur 'probes until he finds some new alternative, some new dimension that strikes a spark in the preferences of others' (Riker 1986: 64).

An example of this strategy is the Commission's advocacy of the concept of 'working environment'. This concept opens up the possibility of regulatory intervention in areas such as ergonomics, traditionally considered to be outside the field of health and safety at work. The already mentioned Machinery Directive, the Safety and Health at Work Directive 89/391 – an important framework directive – and Directive 90/270 on health and safety at work with display screen equipment, are inspired by this regulatory philosophy. In view of the claim of intergovernmentalist scholars that

Community policies are under the control of the most powerful member states, it should be pointed out that these directives extend to the European level the approach of two small countries – Denmark and the Netherlands, which first introduced the concept of working environment into their legislation – and were opposed by Germany in order to preserve the power and traditional approach of its own regulatory bodies (Eichener 1992; see also Chapter 5 below).

Other notable examples of regulatory innovations are the Directive 92/59 on General Product Safety, Directive 89/48 which creates, for the first time in Europe, a single market for the regulated professions, and several old and new environmental directives.

It is interesting to note that some of the best examples of policy entrepreneurship at the European level are in the field of social regulation. This may be explained in terms of J.Q. Wilson's well-known classification of policies according to the pattern of the perceived distribution of costs and benefits (Wilson 1980: 366–72). Wilson's classification may be represented in tabular form as in Table 4.1.

Table 4.1 The politics of policy

| | | Benefits | |
		Diffuse	Concentrated
Costs	Diffuse	majoritarian politics	client politics
	Concentrated	entrepreneurial politics	interest-group politics

Source: adapted from Wilson (1980)

When both costs and benefits are widely distributed (for example, social security, national health care, education and so forth), interest groups have little incentive to form around such issues since no identifiable segment of society can expect to capture a disproportionate share of the benefits or to avoid a disproportionate share of the costs. Hence, such issues are dealt with in the traditional arena of majoritarian politics. In the European context this means that the issues are dealt with at the national rather than at the supranational level. Hence, most traditional social policy remains under the control of the member states.

When both costs and benefits are concentrated, each side has a strong incentive to organize and exercise political influence. EC structural policy is a pertinent example. Although the structural funds aid some industrially declining regions in the wealthier countries, the overall effect of the policy is to transfer resources from one well-defined group of contributing countries to another equally well-defined group of receiving countries. As this example

suggests, the European analogue of interest-group politics is intergovernmental bargaining between two (or more) groups of countries.

When the benefits of a prospective policy are concentrated while the costs
are widely distributed, small, easily organized groups (such as oligopolistic
firms in the car, electronics, chemical or pharmaceutical industries) have
powerful incentives to lobby in order to obtain favourable legislation at the
national or, increasingly, at the European level. On the other hand, consumers
have little incentive to organize since the costs of the regulation are low on
a per capita basis. The label 'client politics' for this particular configuration
of costs and benefits suggests the possibility that the regulators become
captured by the regulated interests.

Finally, a policy may confer general (though perhaps small) benefits at a
cost to be borne chiefly by a small segment of society. Most social regulation
falls into this category. The costs of cleaner air and water, safer products, and
better working conditions are borne, at least initially, by particular segments
of industry. Since the incentive to organize is strong for the opponents of the
policy but weak for the beneficiaries, social regulatory measures can be
passed only if there is a policy entrepreneur who can mobilize public
sentiment (by capitalizing on crises like the Seveso or Chernobyl disasters),
put the opponents of the regulatory measures on the defensive and associate
the legislation with widely shared values – clean air and water, health and
safety, equal rights for men and women.

According to Wilson, the policy entrepreneur 'serves as the vicarious
representative of groups not directly part of the legislative process' (Wilson
1980: 370). This observation helps explain the growing importance of social
regulation at the supranational level, as well as the entrepreneurial role of the
Commission. As we saw in Chapter 3, in Europe the regulatory function, and
social regulation in particular, has been historically less important than the
macroeconomic stabilization and the redistributive functions. Even now the
most powerful political coalitions form around issues of redistribution and
macroeconomic management. Hence national policies always tended to
favour producers – managers, unionized workers, organized professionals –
usually at the expense of consumer and other diffuse interests. Moreover,
political systems characterized by party control of both executive and
legislature, highly centralized public bureaucracies and limited judicial
review of policy decisions, do not leave much room for either the political
representation of unorganized interests or the emergence of independent
policy entrepreneurs.

The situation at the supranational European level is quite different. Here
the redistributive function of government is severely limited by the small size
of the Union budget, and the macroeconomic function almost non-existent.
Hence, redistributive coalitions and corporatist arrangements are weak
(Streeck and Schmitter 1991) – the politics of the Common Agricultural
Policy being the exception which confirms the rule. In such a situation, the
insulation of the Commission from partisan politics and electoral results, the

activism of the Court of Justice, and the interest of the European Parliament in finding a distinctive role for itself, are all factors that explain why diffuse interests are often better represented at the European level than at the national level, and why entrepreneurship is such an important feature of European policy-making. Notice the apparent paradox: the same supranational institutions so often criticized for their 'democratic deficit' or for their distance from domestic political concerns, may in fact be the best advocates of diffuse interests which do not find adequate expression in national political systems. We shall discuss the alleged democratic deficit of European policy-making and other normative issues in the concluding chapter.

REFERENCES

Brickman, R., Jasanoff, S. and Ilgen, T. (1985) *Controlling Chemicals: the Politics and Regulation in the United States*, Ithaca: Cornell University Press.
Coase, R.H. (1960) 'The problem of social cost', *The Journal of Law and Economics* 3: 1–44.
Dehousse, R. and Majone, G. (1994) 'The institutional dynamics of European integration: from the Single Act to the Maastricht Treaty', in Martin (ed.) *The Construction of Europe – Essays in Honour of Emile Noël*, Dordrecht and Boston: Kluwer Academic Publishers.
DeMuth, C.C. (1984) 'A strategy for regulatory reform', *Regulation* 4: 25–30.
Dunleavy, P. (1991) *Democracy, Bureaucracy and Public Choice: Economic Explanations in Political Science*, New York: Harvester Wheatsheaf.
Eichener, V. (1992) 'Social dumping or innovative regulation? Process and outcomes of European decision-making in the sector of health and safety at work harmonization', Florence: European University Institute, EUI Working Paper, SPS 92/28.
Elliott, D., Ackerman, B.A. and Millian, J.C. (1985) 'Toward a theory of statutory evolution: the federalization of environmental law', *Journal of Law, Economics and Organization* I, 2: 313–40.
Gatsios, K. and Seabright, P. (1989) 'Regulation in the European Community', *Oxford Review of Economic Policy* 5, 2: 37–60.
Greenwood, T. (1984) *Knowledge and Discretion in Government Regulation*, New York: Praeger.
Haas, E. (1968) [1958], *The Uniting of Europe* (2nd edition) Stanford: Stanford University Press.
Haigh, N. (1984) *EEC Environmental Policy and Britain*, London: Environmental Data Services.
Héritier, A., Mingers, S., Knill, C. and Becka, M. (1994) *Die Veränderung von Staatlichkeit in Europa*, Opladen: Leske und Budrich.
Institut für Europäische Politik (1989) *'Comitology': Characteristics, Performance and Options*, Bonn: Preliminary Final Report.
Kingdon, J.W. (1984) *Agendas, Alternatives and Public Policies*, Boston: Little, Brown & Company.
Lowi, T.J. (1979) *The End of Liberalism* (2nd edition), New York: W.W. Norton & Co.
Ludlow, P. (1991) 'The European Commission', in Keohane and Hoffman (eds) *The New European Community: Decisionmaking and Institutional Change*, Boulder: Westview Press.
Majone, G. (1994) 'The rise of the regulatory state in Europe' *West European Politics* 17, 3: 77–101.

Majone, G. (1995) 'Independence and accountability: non-majoritarian institutions and democratic government in Europe' to be published in Weiler, Dehousse and Cassese (eds) (forthcoming) *Collected Courses of the Academy of European Law*, London: Kluwer Law International.

Milgrom, P. and Roberts, J. (1992) *Organization and Management*, Englewood Cliffs: Prentice-Hall International.

Moe, T. (1990) 'The politics of structural choice: toward a theory of public bureaucracy', in Williamson *Organization Theory – From Chester Barnard to the Present and Beyond*, New York: Oxford University Press.

Niskanen, W. (1971) *Bureaucracy and Representative Government*, Chicago: Aldine Press.

Peacock, A. (ed.) (1984) *The Regulation Game*, Oxford: Basil Blackwell.

Peters, G.B. (1992) 'Bureaucratic politics and the institutions of the European Community', in Sbragia (ed.), *Euro-politics*, Washington (DC): The Brookings Institution.

Rehbinder, E. and Stewart, R. (1985) *Environmental Protection Policy*, Berlin: de Gruyter.

Riker, W. (1986) *The Art of Political Manipulation*, New Haven (CT): Yale University Press.

Streeck, W. and Schmitter, P. (1991) 'From national corporatism to transnational pluralism: organized interests in the Single European Market', *Politics and Society* 19: 133–64.

Williamson, O. (1985) *The Economic Institutions of Capitalism*, New York: The Free Press.

Wilson, J.Q. (ed.) (1980) *The Politics of Regulation*, New York: Basic Books.

Part II
Regulations in practice

5 Regulatory legitimacy in the European context: the British Health and Safety Executive

Robert Baldwin

Regulators everywhere face problems in securing broad public support for their activities (see Baldwin and McCrudden 1987; Freedman 1978; Frug 1984; Mashaw 1983). Those who are controlled tend to resent the costs associated with regulatory compliance, politicians tend to vary in their support for regulation and the public is often uncertain as to the purposes of regulation and the effectiveness of the regulators in achieving it.

Problems of securing support – or legitimation – are difficult enough within the domestic context but, when a regulatory body acts within a Community of fifteen member states and domestic regulation has to be co-ordinated with Community controls, legitimation has an added dimension of difficulty.

This chapter considers the performance of the British Health and Safety Executive (HSE) within the framework of the European Community. It looks at the development of the British system of health and safety regulation and examines the position of the agency in the domestic political context. The question of legitimacy is introduced and the potential of the HSE to make effective claims to public support is assessed. Finally, the impact of EC health and safety regulation is analysed and the effect of such regulation on regulatory legitimacy assessed.

THE DEVELOPMENT OF A REGULATORY SYSTEM

It was the factories legislation of the nineteenth-century industrial revolution that laid the foundations for the modern system of British health and safety regulation (see the Factories Regulation Act 1833; Factories Amendment Act 1844; Factories and Workshops Act 1878; Baldwin and Daintith 1992; Dawson *et al.* 1988; Gunningham 1984; Bartrip and Fenn 1987; Carson 1974, 1979). A host of statutes and regulations was produced during the late nineteenth and first half of the twentieth centuries and eventually consolidated in the Factories Act 1961. These provisions were, however, narrowly directed towards factories. Certain other forms of premises were controlled by different statutory schemes (for example, coal mines and railways) and a series of occupations were unregulated. By the end of the 1960s the industrial accident rate had increased and there was considerable pressure for reform.

The Labour government, re-elected in 1966, responded to such pressure (notably from the Trades Union Congress) by appointing a committee of inquiry under Lord Robens (see Dawson *et al.* 1988), and it was the resultant Robens Report of 1972 that provided the blueprint for the present system of regulation (Safety and Health at Work, Report of Committee, Cmnd 5034, 1972 – hereafter referred to as Robens 1972).

The Robens findings and recommendations addressed three principal issues: the state of the law on health and safety at work; institutional structures for regulation; and the regulatory philosophy that was appropriate to the field.

On the state of the law, Robens discovered a highly complicated system of control in which nine separate groups of statutes were separately administered by five central government departments through seven separate inspectorates. It was concluded that there was too much law (apart from the statutes there were five hundred subordinate statutory instruments) and that this sheer mass of law was not only too narrow in its application but had become counter-productive in regulatory terms. It had an 'all pervasive psychological effect' (Robens 1972: 7) in which people came to see health and safety as an issue of detailed rules imposed by external agencies rather than as a matter for which they should assume direct responsibility. The recommended solution was to produce one 'framework' statute that would replace the existing complex laws and at the same time would broaden the application of health and safety controls so that all types of workplace were regulated.

On the institutional structure for regulation, Robens again recommended rationalization since it was considered confusing to operate through various enforcement bodies with overlapping jurisdictions. The way forward was seen as giving control to a self-contained organization with both clear responsibility for the area and day-to-day governmental autonomy. Central to the Robens proposal was the idea that all of those involved in the field – employers, workers and the public – should share responsibility and have a role in operating the new institution. It was recommended that an agency should be set up outside the central government departments so that clear identity and responsibility would be ensured. The agency was thus to be a separate body with its own budget and staff but functioning under broad ministerial directives. Enforcement was to be carried out by means of a unified inspectorate controlled by the agency.

The regulatory philosophy espoused by Robens was highly consensualist and still exerts a strong influence. It stemmed from a belief that accidents were, in the main, caused by *apathy* rather than other causes (for example, unsafe systems of work). Incorporated in this view was the notion (since much criticized) that there was no substantial conflict of interest between workers and employers on health and safety issues (see, for example, Gunningham 1984: 270–1; Woolf 1973: 88). In a well-known statement,

Robens referred to the 'natural identity of interest' between workers and employers on health and safety matters (Robens 1972: 21).

Robens's philosophy was built on two main ideas. First, that the primary function of health and safety law was to establish a framework within which self-regulation could flourish so that industry itself could take responsibility for health and safety matters. Second, that there should be workforce involvement whereby health and safety would be the responsibility not only of employers and senior management but also of employees.

The Labour Party lost the 1970 general election but the incoming Conservative administration endorsed the Robens analysis and action followed on all of the fronts focused on by that Committee. As far as the law was concerned, there was, as Robens had hoped for, a movement 'away from fragmented and complex statutory rules towards a mixture of statutory regulations and voluntary codes' (Robens 1972: 40). A new framework statute, the Health and Safety at Work Act 1974 (HSWA) was passed and an approach to subsidiary rules adopted which was 'constructive rather then prohibitory' (Robens 1972: 40). This strategy favoured the use, where possible, of non-statutory codes of practice rather than statutory regulations. To this end, the HSWA equipped agency policy-makers with a variety of rule-types: general statutory duties (HSWA 1974: ss. 2–9); regulations to be made by the Secretary of State (HSWA 1974: s. 15); and approved codes of practice to be made by the agency. The latter were designed to offer 'practical guidance' to those regulated (HSWA 1974: s. 17) but did not, in themselves, create civil or criminal liabilities and had to be approved by the Secretary of State rather than laid before Parliament.

Robens's institutional reforms were put into effect with the creation of a statutory Health and Safety Commission (HSC) and Health and Safety Executive (HSE) in 1974 and 1975 respectively. Two bodies were set up because it was thought necessary to separate policy-making from enforcement functions. The HSE was given considerable powers to inspect, regulate and, if necessary, to sanction offending enterprises. Separating these functions from HSC policy-making was designed to limit conflicts of interest and enhance the HSC's reputation for impartiality.

The HSC consists of a chair, appointed by the Secretary of State plus three employers' representatives, nominated by the Confederation of British Industry (CBI); three employees' representatives nominated by the Trades Union Congress (TUC) and two local authority representatives. The HSC is thus a tripartite body based on the consensualist notion that the 'sides' of industry can, if given the opportunity, come to an agreement on how to regulate health and safety at work. (The local authority representatives are involved so as to represent the general interest of society.) The functions of the HSC are to set objectives, allocate resources and review priorities, normally on the basis of HSE advice. The HSE is the expert consultant to the HSC on policy matters and the institution responsible for enforcing health and safety legislation in accordance with the directions of the HSC proposals.

The HSE is a three-person statutory body, headed by a Director-General and operating through inspectorates dealing with factories, mines, agriculture and quarries, nuclear installations, offshore establishments and railways. Overall, the HSC and HSE (referred to jointly as the HSC/E), employ around four thousand staff with the largest inspectorate, the Factory Inspectorate, utilizing around 650 field inspectors.

The regulatory problems faced by the HSC/E are considerable and it is worth outlining major aspects of these before looking at the political context within which the agency works. A first difficulty is resources. The inspectorates of the HSE not only inspect work activities, they provide advice to employers, workers and public; investigate accidents and ill-health; consider complaints; develop initiatives and use a variety of strategies to seek to achieve compliance (notably prosecutions, administrative notices, persuasion and negotiation, advice, education, promotion and encouragement, see Baldwin 1990: 16). The Factory Inspectorate, for example, has to deal with nearly half a million establishments, many of which have multiple or transient sites and, accordingly, the frequency of inspections cannot be high – many workplaces will not see an inspector for several years (HSE *Director General's Report 1979/80*: 16). Prosecuting offenders is highly resource-intensive and this, as a result, is not a compliance-seeking strategy that can be used routinely (see Fenn and Veljanovski 1988). More frequent resort is made to administrative responses in the form of Improvement Notices and Prohibition Notices. (These are formal orders issuable by inspectors that, respectively allow a specific time period for removing a hazard, or order work to be stopped pending removal of a hazard. Contravention of either form of Notice involves a criminal offence.) In 1989/90, for example, 2,651 prosecutions were instituted but 7,589 Improvement Notices and 4,501 Prohibition Notices were served. HSE staff devote considerable attention both to establishing priorities for inspection visits and to prosecuting only where this is absolutely necessary. To this end, the Factory Inspectorate has established a standard series of factors by which frequency of inspection visits is governed. These factors include: the present standards of health and safety in the premises; the nature of the potentially worst problem liable to arise; management's ability and attitudes; and the possibility of changes in hazards between visits (HSC 1985/6: 20).

The consensual scheme of regulation that is now operated by the HSE owes a great deal to Robens but it is arguable that the level of resourcing enjoyed by the HSE makes only one basic method of compliance-seeking possible – that is, advising, negotiating and persuading (see Fenn and Veljanovski 1988; Baldwin 1990; Nichols and Armstrong 1973). Such a strategy may prove to be appropriate in the case of large numbers of well-organized and well-intentioned employers but when hazard-creators are ill-intentioned and ill-informed the consensual approach may prove frustrating to field inspectors and may result in low levels of compliance (for different types of employer and regulatory strategies see Baldwin 1990).

A second major difficulty faced by the HSC/E is that of producing rules of a kind that will be consistent with the compliance-seeking strategies that have to be adopted by inspectors. Robens was clear that the old laws and regulations were too complex and legalistic and proposed a movement towards rules, regulations and codes that were constructive in nature (Robens 1972: 40). As has been noted, moreover, the Committee argued that action by means of non-statutory codes of practice should generally be preferred to the use of statutory controls.

The HSC/E has made extensive resort to codes of practice and, in developing rules in new areas, it now tends to produce 'packages' of rules comprising statutory regulations, approved codes of practice and (sometimes) informal guidance notes. Robens was perhaps too optimistic concerning the ability of a regulator to produce simple, intelligible rules that would have the requisite coverage and would be enforceable. For the HSE, life has been more complex. Not only has the enforceability and political acceptability of rules to be considered, but their scope, transparency, accessibility and justiciability also. Within the Factory Inspectorate there has tended to be a feeling on the part of some inspectors that the rules do not lend themselves particularly well to enforcement (Baldwin 1990). Field enforcers tend to want rules that are precise, easily prosecuted and contained in intelligible packages. The rule-makers tend to produce rules that are imprecise (imposing duties on employers couched in such terms as 'so far as is reasonably practicable'); that are, as a result, not easy to prosecute; and which make up packages of rules that are of daunting complexity. HSE policy-makers might want to design rules that take on board such factors as the kinds of employers likely to be causing the hazards at issue and the kinds of sanction that are necessary to produce compliance from such employers – they have to cope, however, with a number of factors which, together, tend to produce ineffective rules (Baldwin 1990: 332–7). These factors are principally: a tendency on the part of policy-makers to adopt a 'top-down' approach to rules in which 'superiors' assume enforcement to be unproblematic and in which feedback on enforceability is not given high priority; a tendency by rule-makers to underestimate the processes whereby rules grow in complexity during consultation processes (as different applications and compromises are embraced) and so become unwieldy; and a tendency to underestimate the distortions that will be produced by political pressures both internal and external to the agency.

A third major regulatory issue facing the HSC/E is the balance to be adopted between regulating health and regulating safety matters. In recent years the HSC has discerned a growing public concern about long-term health hazards due to the increasing industrial use of substances that are known to be carcinogenic or toxic. The trade unions have also pressed the HSC to respond more fully to health hazards. Such hazards do, however, present particular problems for regulators. The harms at issue are often hidden rather than manifest and establishing the causal connection between diseases and occupations is often problematic. Not infrequently there is a time-lag between exposure and effect which compounds such difficulties. A further uncertainty is the progressive discovery of adverse health effects arising out of new materials and substances. Problems of uncertainty do arise in relation to safety but generally on a lesser scale. In the past the HSC has been criticized for being slow off the mark in developing, for example, research into the relationships between diseases and occupations (see House of Lords Select Committee on Science and Technology Report 1983/4: 99 I, para. 54; evidence of TUC and of and General, Municipal, Boilermakers and Allied Trades Union). Calls have been made by the trade unions *inter alia* for large-scale surveying of occupational illnesses, for an improved system of reporting links between occupation and illnesses and for a statutory duty requiring employers to report ill-health that is occupationally related. The HSC has responded to such pressures by indicating that it will shift resources from safety to health regulation but this does pose newly acute problems for enforcers. Seeking compliance in relation to health hazards often involves relying on data of a highly specialized and sometimes contentious nature. Enforcement will mainly be of the 'advice and assistance' kind but employers will tend to be resistant to persuasion where expensive remedial steps are urged on the basis of evidence concerning hazards that is not cut and dried. Obtaining consent will thus become more difficult as the shift from safety to health takes place. Such a shift also demands that the agency moves towards a more pro-active strategy, seeking to identify new hazards and taking preventive steps. This may lead to regulation of a more politically contentious nature so that life becomes more difficult for the agency.

THE DOMESTIC POLITICAL CONTEXT

As noted above, the HSC is a tripartite body and its structure reflects Robens's consensualism. Shared responsibility provides the foundation for the operation of the HSWA. In the early 1970s a number of other important governmental bodies were established on tripartite lines (for example, the Manpower Services Commission (MSC), and the Advisory, Conciliation and Arbitration Service (ACAS)), but the effectiveness of tripartism as a regulatory structure was untried. Such tripartism is not merely encountered at the HSC level: it infuses the regulatory structure as set up by the HSWA. Many HSE committees are tripartite, and the 1974 Act involves both sides of industry in controlling health and safety. Employers were given certain general safety duties but also a duty to provide written safety policies and to provide adequate information, training and instruction (HSWA 1974: s. 2). The trade unions were given a regulatory role through the innovatory system of safety representatives and safety committees. The HSWA provided for recognized trade unions to be given the right to appoint safety representatives from amongst employees and obliged the employer to consult such representatives. Safety representatives were given the right to call for the creation of a safety committee and they have the functions: of investigating complaints, potential hazards, dangerous occurrences and accidents; of making representations to employers; and of inspecting the workplace. The safety committees task is to review health and safety matters and report on these to management.

Does the use of tripartite structures lead to effective regulation? As far as the policy-making process is concerned, tripartism feeds into this at all stages, not least through the consultative processes which involve numbers of tripartite committees (see Baldwin and McCrudden 1987: 137–40). It can be argued, however, that tripartism does not necessarily lead to accountable or effective regulation. There are limits to the representativeness of HSE committees and it is liable to be argued that large, organized firms or groups tend to be well represented in tripartite policy-making, rather than smaller firms; that this leads, in turn, to systems of control that are not attuned to the needs of smaller operators. Tripartism is perhaps weakest in representing the interest of particular sectors of the public. Thus, such a sector, affected by a specific hazard, must rely on local authority representatives to argue its case in HSC/E policy-making – there may be no pressure group to give them more direct access.

Turning to the way that a tripartite agency responds to external political forces, it should be noted, first, that tripartism is unlikely to produce regulatory policies of a radical nature. A system built on consensus gives those who are unsatisfied a veto – for example, employers' representatives who are concerned at the compliance costs involved in an initiative may more effectively veto that initiative under tripartism than when dealing with an agency established on more traditional lines. Conservatism is thus built into the tripartite structure.

Second, it is clear that the tripartite agency is as vulnerable to attacks on regulation (or regulators) as any other kind of agency. During the Thatcher years of the 1980s there were sustained attempts to reduce the burdens of regulatory compliance, particularly for small businesses, and the Department of Trade and Industry's 1985 Report, *Burdens on Business* advocated the simplification and rationalization of health and safety provisions (see also the White Papers Cmnd 9571/1985; Cmnd 9794/1986 and 512/1988). More recently John Major announced, on 2 February 1993, an attack on governmental red tape, and once again health and safety featured prominently – a complete review of health and safety legislation was promised with the object of reducing burdens on small businesses. The resource problems of the HSC/E have not been tackled materially in the last fifteen years – significantly to increase the weight of HSC/E regulation would sit uneasily with the Conservative government's emphasis on reducing compliance costs. The HSC/E, accordingly, has had to regulate, like many other agencies, in a generally inhospitable political climate. What may be true of tripartism, however, is that its inherent conservatism has proved effective in reducing the danger that one side of industry will mount a concerted attack on the agency. The HSC has for some time seen itself as involved in negotiation, not 'a crusade' (Locke 1981: 34) and the opportunities that management and unions have to participate in policy-making may militate against full-frontal attacks aimed at abolishing the agency.

A third, and final, point on the tripartite agency's subjection to outside pressure relates to the nature of the activity regulated. Health and safety at work is not a sector affected by sweeping policy changes. Labour and Conservative governments may differ as to emphasis but even the Thatcher administration made cuts in resources rather than effecting wholesale reforms. The HSC is perhaps high on the list of those regulatory bodies best able to make policy on long-term issues free from devastating ministerial interference.

REGULATORY LEGITIMACY AND THE HSC/E

As noted at the start of this chapter, nearly all regulators face problems in securing broad public support for their activities. It can be argued that regulators, in attempting to secure that support, may invoke five types of argument to invoke legitimacy (see Baldwin and McCrudden 1987), rather than making constitutional, legal, moral or aesthetic claims. They can be summarized as follows:

- *the legislative rationale*: claims support on the basis of a mandate from a democratically established parliament
- *the accountability rationale*: derives legitimacy from the assent of the people as expressed through control by means of representative groupings
- *the due process rationale*: urges support on the ground that fair procedures are used
- *the expertise rationale*: claims support on the basis that expert judgements are being made and experts can be trusted to act in the public interest
- *the efficiency rationale*: urges that the mandate is being pursued effectively or (in the alternative, where the mandate is very vague) that efficient action is being taken

Legitimacy-claiming is problematic because claims under each of the above headings are to a greater or lesser extent inherently flawed. Thus, a legislative rationale claim suffers because statutory mandates are rarely, if ever, specific or uncontentious; accountability claims are suspect because the representativeness of those holding the regulators to account is liable to attack; due process claims are fraught with risk because the extent to which fairness in procedures should be traded-off against efficiency is contentious; expertise claims are suspect because the average person distrusts experts, and fails to see why judgements cannot be explained; and efficiency claims are undermined by doubts as to the mandate that is supposedly being pursued efficiently. In spite of such problems, however, regulators, like other officials, may achieve different levels of public support by cumulating different kinds of claim – by making up for weaknesses under some rationales with strengths under others. (Weakness on all fronts may signify a lack of legitimacy.)

How, then, can support for HSC regulation be assessed? Taking the mandate and efficiency arguments together (the latter being viewable as a subset of the former), the HSC/E may argue that British regulation has produced results that compare favourably with those in the rest of Western Europe. Thus, in 1991, the HSE published a study of regulatory arrangements in France, West Germany, Italy, Spain and the United Kingdom (HSE 1991) and concluded that British fatal accident rates were 'substantially lower', both for individual industrial sectors and for all industries combined, than in France, Italy and Spain (apart from agriculture) and 'somewhat lower' than in West Germany in some sectors (HSE 1991: 1). This constitutes an efficiency claim of some weight but it is tempered by acknowledged problems of commensurability. There are significant differences in the way that individual countries define and record accidents and diseases, and a series of social, economic, and political, rather than regulatory, factors affects accident rates. Claims of such a statistical nature must, accordingly, be treated with some care. Critics of the HSC/E may counter by questioning whether other countries can be assumed to be regulating adequately and by pointing to a number of features of HSC/E regulation that might be improved. A first point relates to resources – the objective observer might question the efficiency claims of an agency operating with around 650 factory inspectors when there are nearly half a million premises to be controlled. In response, the HSC/E may point out that an elected government has chosen to fund only a limited number of enforcers and that the HSC/E has made the best use of such resources in difficult circumstances.

On the issue of how the HSC/E operates, it is possible to suggest ways to improve regulatory rule-making (as has been done above) and, as noted, critics on the trade union side may urge that the mandate has for years been skewed towards safety rather than health. The HSC/E has, however, shown that it is willing to consider and adjust its regulatory methods (*inter alia* commissioning research from academics – the Centre for Socio-legal Studies at Oxford University conducted an interdisciplinary study of regulatory methods in the years 1983–6), and may point to that responsiveness. It, nevertheless, has a residual criticism to face – that the HSC/E espouses consensual regulation, which relies to a large extent on the self-regulatory capacity of employers. Such a system works best when optimal safety conditions coincide with optimal profit-maximizing conditions and when aimed at the well-intentioned, well-organized and informed employer. Such consensual regulation may fail, however, in situations where employers and employees' interests conflict or where the latter are ill-informed and/or badly organized.

The HSE is aware of this problem (HSC 1985/6, para. 108), but, given present resourcing levels, it is extremely difficult, for instance, to offer a highly effective response to the activities of a certain group of employers. In so far as the HSC/E moves its focus from safety to health, it will, moreover, be moving into a field where it is yet more difficult to demonstrate effectiveness.

Turning to the accountability of the HSC/E, the limits of tripartism as an accounting mechanism have been noted. The HSC is not an elected body and, although the policy-making processes of the HSC/E involve extensive periods of consultation, the criticism that there are 'insiders' and (less well resourced) 'outsiders' is liable to be made. The quality of HSC/E accountability depends to a large extent on the communications networks created by the trade unions and employers' organizations. Where these bodies are well developed in a particular industry, the HSC/E policy-making processes work successfully as information is widely disseminated and inputs into policy and rule-making are broadly based. Where employers or workers are badly organized or, because of the nature of the industry, fragmented, such information lines are unlikely to exist and consultations will be more narrow in character.

In terms of the broad public interest, the HSC/E's accountability is limited in a way common to many other agencies. It is the Secretary of State that issues new regulations and it is he or she who accounts to Parliament for these. The Secretary of State possesses powers in relation to the Commission, notably to modify regulations or refuse consent to a code of practice. The HSC must submit particulars of its proposals and an annual report and accounts to the Secretary of State and the latter may give the HSC general directions regarding its functions. These provisions are familiar in the case of regulatory agencies and are not a product of the HSC's tripartism – cumulatively they mean that, although the Secretary of State for Trade will account to Parliament for such matters as the general directions given to the HSC/E on the broad thrust of regulations that have been approved, there is no accountability to Parliament for matters of day-to-day regulation.

Is the HSC/E accountable to other bodies such as courts or pressure groups? In the case of courts, the HSC/E is liable to judicial review like any other body exercising public functions but there is no judicial appeal body to whom recourse can be made in challenging the agency's decisions. Pressure groups, for their part, play a very limited role in relation to the HSC/E since the tripartite machinery offers a more established route to participation. Overall it can be summarized that the HSC/E scores well on accountability to certain interests in society but it performs far less well in relation to other interests.

The essence of a claim to support on a due process rationale is that individuals' interests have been dealt with fairly and with respect. In so far as the participatory processes of the HSC/E favour the better organized, it could be argued that this is unfair to the interests of other employers and workers. The HSC/E can, however, argue that it favours broad publication of its proposals and, to some extent, those who fail to organize and participate have merely forgone an opportunity – they have not been dealt with unfairly.

As to the fairness of HSE enforcement, the HSE approach is one in which only the most extreme offenders are prosecuted and in which other employers tend to be given opportunities to make good their defects before they are sanctioned. The HSE can fairly claim, therefore, that it does not operate with a heavy prosecutorial hand. Around 85 per cent of prosecutions lead to a conviction and, again, the HSE can claim that this reflects a considered approach.

The system of enforcement employed by the HSE is one that, necessarily, incorporates large elements of field-enforcer discretion. It might be argued that such use of discretion is conducive to discriminatory treatment, but the HSE's preference for non-prosecutorial compliance-seeking serves to defuse this contention – it might also be pointed out that any decision to prosecute will necessarily involve more than one level in the HSE hierarchy and that systems of structuring and checking do control prosecutorial discretions to a marked degree. Overall, it seems the HSE/E is in a position to make reasonably convincing claims under the due process heading.

On the question of expertise, the HSC/E is again in a position to make reasonably strong claims. The agency's reputation within Europe is high and it can point to an impressive accumulation of information on all aspects of health and safety. This is not to deny that the agency has been criticized for collecting too little information an occupational health matters or that its reputation may vary from industry to industry, from employer-type to employer-type. Some health and safety specialists in some large companies may feel themselves more skilled than the inspectors they deal with but, in response to the need for particular bodies of knowledge, the HSE has developed specialist inspectors in a wide range of fields and, in general, HSE and its inspectorates are respected by industry. To the extent that the HSE engages in extensive consultations and programmes of public information, it is less easy for critics to argue that the agency fails to explain its policies.

To summarise on general HSC/E legitimation within Britain, the agency's strongest claims relate to its fairness and expertise. It is perhaps on less secure ground on the issues of effectiveness and accountability.

THE EUROPEAN CONTEXT

British health and safety regulation has been radically affected by developments at Community level – so much so that the HSC Chairman was prompted to comment in 1989, 'The [Single European] Act in effect paved the way for a shift from national to EC primacy in policymaking in the area' (HSC/E 1988/9: 17). In order to assess the effect of Community action on British regulation it is necessary to look at the growth of Community initiatives in this sector before describing the impact of such initiatives on HSC/E regulation.

Community initiatives on health and safety at work

The Community has shown a concern for health and safety issues since the 1960s (Nielson and Szyszczak 1992). A major step was taken in the following decade when a Community Advisory Committee on Safety, Hygiene and Health Protection at Work was set up in 1974. This Committee constituted a response to perceptions that new problems were arising out of technological developments and the use of dangerous substances; and an awareness that protection against occupational accidents and diseases was an objective of the EEC Treaty. A Social Action Programme was adopted in 1978 (OJ 1978 C.165) and was followed by a second in 1984 (OJ 1984 C.67) which added new concerns with such matters as training, information and research. During the period of the two action programmes a number of directives were issued to deal with specific hazards such as vinyl chloride monomers (Directive 78/610, OJ 1978 L.197), lead (Directive 82/605, OJ 1982 L.247), and asbestos (Directive 83/447, OJ 1983 L.263).

Community action in the health and safety field has stemmed not merely from a social protection rationale but also from a market-completing base. Thus, steps taken to complete the internal market have impinged on health and safety in its product standards aspect. Under the 'new approach' to technical harmonization (see Commission White Paper 1985 COM.(85) 310 final, June 1985; Burrows 1990; Pelkmans 1986/7; Majone 1992), legislative harmonization in the form of Council directives based on Article 100 is restricted to 'essential health and safety requirements which will be obligatory in all member states'. European product standards under the approach are developed by private European standard-setting organizations (CEN and CENELEC) and these standards give a presumptive conformity to essential requirements in directives. A number of directives relevant to health and safety have been issued under Article 100A on such matters as toy and machinery safety. Although the primary purpose of such measures is to remove trade barriers, compliance with such standards does yield health and safety benefits on a Community-wide basis and Article 100A(3) states that Commission proposals will 'take as a base a high level of protection'. Market-completing directives under Article 100A may thus encourage the 'designing-out' of hazards by manufacturers, and noteworthy in this respect is the Machinery Directive of 1989 (Directive 89/392) which demands that machinery be designed so as to avoid risks due to gases, liquids, dust, vapours and other wastes produced.

The Single European Act 1986 (SEA) constituted a major advance in actions based on the social protection rationale. This introduced Article 118A to the EC Treaty to state:

- that member states should pay particular attention to encouraging improvements, especially in the working environment, as regards the health and safety of workers, and should set as an objective the harmonization of conditions whilst maintaining improvements made
- that, to such ends, the Council, acting on a qualified majority on a proposal from the Commission, in co-operation with the European Parliament, should adopt, by means of directives, minimum requirements for gradual

implementation, having regard to the conditions and technical rules obtaining in each of the member states. Such directives should avoid imposing administrative, financial and legal constraints in a way which would hold back the creation and development of small and medium-sized undertakings
• member states would be free to maintain or introduce more stringent measures for protecting working conditions

The Commission instituted a third Action Programme in 1987 and a series of directives followed on such matters as: use of plant and machinery; personal protective equipment; and safety in construction. Between 1987 and 1989, the Commission developed proposals for a framework directive and further specific directives to be made under Article 118A. In a further major advance, the framework directive (Framework Directives for the Introduction of Measures to Encourage Improvements in Safety and Health of Workers, Directive 89/391, OJ 1989 L.183) was adopted in June 1989. According to one commentator, it constituted 'the most radical measure so far to emerge from the social provisions of the Treaty of Rome since their revision by the SEA' (Neal 1990).

The framework directive marked a change in method on the part of the Community from adopting directives on specific hazards or sectors to using an overall directive in combination with a series of more specific 'daughter' directives.

The framework directive covers all sectors of activity, both public and private, and member states are instructed to take the necessary steps to ensure that employers, workers and workers' representatives are subject to the legal provisions necessary to implement the directive (Framework Directive, Article 4(1)). The obligations imposed on employers are extensive and, *inter alia* require that they ensure the health and safety of workers in every respect related to work (Framework Directive, Article 5(1)); that they develop an overall health and safety policy; record risks and preventive measure taken; consult workers on all health and safety matters; provide job-specific health and safety training; and designate workers to carry out health surveillance on workers. Workers, in turn, are to be given a set of rights, responsibilities and duties, *inter alia* the right to make proposals on health and safety; the right to stop work if in serious danger; and the duty to report potential dangers.

A series of 'daughter' directives has followed the framework directive (Baldwin and Daintith 1992: 10–11) and the impact of such Community controls on health and safety regulation across the member states has been considerable (for a review across a number of member states see the papers collected in volume 6 of the *International Journal of Comparative Labour Law and Industrial Relations*). Although the framework directive imposes 'minimum requirements', the standards of behaviour imposed on employers and workers can be construed as affording protections of a very high level. Articles 5 and 6, for instance, instruct that employers shall have duties to ensure health and safety in every aspect related to work and shall introduce systems of risk assessment – there is no hint of a gradual approach. The framework directive is not, however, a regulation (its contribution to improving working conditions can be seen as a form of harmonization of objectives rather than detailed legal rules); being a directive, member states' own domestic authorities are given freedom as to choice of form and method of achieving designated objectives. The degree of improvement of conditions that should follow in any member state is thus left indeterminate for a number of reasons. First, a degree of discretion is left to member states as to the achievement of the various goals set out in the framework directive. Second, member states are likely to implement the directive in different ways, reflecting considerable differences in organizing national health and safety control regimes, in enforcing institutions, types of legal concept and sanctions employed on health and safety offenders (for a detailed analysis of regulatory variables across a number of member states, see Baldwin and Daintith 1992). Third, the doctrine of the direct effect of directives may have an impact that varies across member states in so far as national regulatory systems relying on direct relationships between state and employers (for example, through social security schemes) are more likely to be affected by litigation appealing to the direct effect of directives than those in which employer–employee relations have greater significance (see *Francovich and Bonifaci* v. *Italy* [1992] IRLR 84).

The impact of the framework directive on British regulation

By 1990 the HSC Chairman was publicly conceding that the Community had to be regarded as 'the principal engine of health and safety law affecting Britain, not just in worker safety but in major hazards and most environmental matters' (HSC/E 1989: viii; see also Neal 1990; Baldwin and Daintith 1992). In 1989 the HSE committed an estimated forty-nine staff-years to work in pursuance of Community-generated health and safety provisions as not only daughter directives were produced but harmonizing directives on technical standards were emerging. The breadth and organization of the HSC/E's international work is represented in Table 5.1. Overall, the effect of Community legislation has been marked. New British legislation is now introduced only where significant risks are identified for the first time or where existing controls are clearly inadequate. On such issues as noise hazards, European developments have superseded domestic regulatory initiatives.

How have domestic regulators responded? A general reaction has been to seek to ensure that Community proposals, as far as possible, take British law as a starting point (HSC/E 1988/9: 20; see also HSC 1991: 21). Not only that but the HSC/E has put forward elements of its own regulatory strategies as models for broader adoption. It has, for instance, presented its own approach to the cost-benefit assessment of new proposals as an example for community legislators to follow. The HSC/E has also fought, where possible, to preserve

Table 5.1 The international work of the HSC/E

European Commission Directorate Generals			
III	V	XI	XII
Product Directives (Safety aspects)	*Framework Directive and daughters*	*Directive* (under Treaty of Rome and Euratom Treaty)	*Safety Related Research*
	Social Action Programme	Major Accident Hazards (Seveso) Radiation Chemicals CPL Bio-releases Pesticides (non-agricultural) Nuclear	Including major technical hazards programme, and nuclear

CEN/CENELEC Production of European Standards in support of product directives

ILO Conventions Recommendations Major hazards programme

OECD Chemical assessments Major accident hazards Nuclear Energy Agency	HSC/E

UN Major accident hazards Transport of explosives

IAEA Nuclear • safety standards • regulatory practices

Source: reproduced from HSC/E *Annual Report* 1989/90

its discretion to choose modes of implementation. In its *Plan of Work for 1990/1 and Beyond* the HSC/E resolved to seek to ensure that directives were expressed in terms of general principles, with subordinate detail to be decided nationally. The agency has, however, voiced a number of concerns during the process of bringing domestic regulation into line with Community requirements. First, British regulators have commented on the timescales imposed by Community legislation. Before the Single European Act was passed, the process of securing agreement in the Council of Ministers was relatively slow. Under qualified majority voting conditions post-SEA the European Commission is placed in a more powerful position in relation to domestic governments and regulators. Individual member states can no longer veto proposals and the overall effect is to increase the pressure on the domestic regulator to follow the Community lead and to do so without delay. The HSC Chairman has expressed doubts that domestic regulations can be adjusted to such tight deadlines and has spoken of the 'simultaneous and somewhat headlong negotiation on a very large number of directives and programmes' (HSC/E 1988/9: 15).

A second concern is that differences between British and continental legal systems pose particular difficulties for domestic regulators. British health and safety legislation recognizes the impossibility of eliminating all hazards and imposes duties in a highly selective manner. Many duties, moreover, are phrased not in absolute terms but are qualified by the requirement that actions be taken 'so far as is reasonably practical' (all of the general duties under the HSWA are subject to such qualification). The framework directive speaks of imposing duties in absolute terms and this goes against the British tradition of literal statutory interpretation, which is, moreover, inconsistent with implying reasonableness tests where duties are phrased in absolute terms. For British regulators, accordingly, there is considerable tension between the precise and absolute approach to duties that emanates from the Community and the flexible, reasonableness testing, strategy that is central to British regulation. This is seen as a difficulty peculiar to Britain because other member states may enact absolute duties knowing that their courts will not interpret literally and, unlike those of Britain, will exercise flexibility in interpreting seemingly absolute legal duties so that in general those on whom the duties lie are expected to approximate towards the stated legal objective (HSC/E 1988/9: 15). The framework directive made some concession to British worries by allowing member states to qualify implementation so as to avoid holding back the development of small and medium-sized under-takings but the HSC has not seen this as a wholly satisfactory solution to the problem of drafting duties in adequate terms (HSC/E 1988/9: 15).

A further and major concern of British regulators has been the degree of rigour with which health and safety provisions are enforced across the Community. Since the SEA was passed, the HSC/E has consistently pressed the European Commission to pay closer attention to the practical enforcement of Community legislation and has argued: 'Unless adequate, consistent standards are achieved, not only are the Treaty's social aims frustrated but countries (including Britain) with relatively high standards will be competitively disadvantaged' (HSC/E 1988/9: 21). Observers from other member states may, perhaps, see an irony here in so far as fears of social dumping are forthcoming from a member state which has refused to accept the Social Chapter of the Maastricht Treaty. Such a position may, however, reflect a divergence between agency and governmental policies. The HSC/E has stressed that a 'major effort' is required to secure workable legislation that is enforceable in an even-handed way. To this end, the HSC/E instituted in 1989 a series of comparative studies of enforcement practice in typical industrial settings across Europe, and the 1991 HSE publication *Workplace Health and Safety in Europe*, with its study of regulatory arrangements in France, West Germany, Italy, Spain and Britain was a contribution to this endeavour (see also Baldwin and Daintith 1992). The HSC has, moreover, supported the Commission's Social Action Programme proposal for a Community Institute for Safety and Health at Work – a body whose functions would include the co-ordination and auditing of enforcement practices.

To summarize on the impact of Community controls: the HSC/E has to a large extent been compelled to yield the legislative lead to the European Commission; it has had to respond to Community stimuli under the pressure of tight schedules; it has been faced with tensions between British and Community approaches to legislating and it has had to press for consistency of standards, implementation and enforcement across the Community. How such factors impinge on the legitimacy of health and safety regulation is an issue for final consideration.

LEGITIMACY IN THE EUROPEAN CONTEXT

Is the Europeanization of health and safety regulation likely to enhance or detract from public support for such regulation? As far as claims under the mandate and efficiency headings are concerned, the Community influence may prove a negative factor. The regulatory mandate is likely to derive increasingly from an agenda established through Community policy-making procedures rather than originating in the domestic parliament or agency. It could be argued, therefore, that a diminution of democratic legitimacy is potentially involved in this movement. The European Parliament neither possesses legislative power nor controls the legislative acts of the unelected Community organs and so the strands of legitimation are likely to remain weak in relation to Community directives. As for the efficiency of the regulators in achieving mandated ends, a serious concern must be the resource costs involved in co-ordinating domestic and community control regimes. It may be arguable that there is a *general* efficiency gain deriving from membership of the Community – one that extends across all industrial activities – but, looked at from the narrower perspective of health and safety regulation, it is difficult to avoid the conclusion that there is a diseconomy of scale involved in Europeanization.

Were it to be the case that, within a particular member state, standards of safety and health were noticeably raised as a result of pressures from the Community, it might be possible to claim improved regulatory effectiveness: but British regulators would be slow to argue this point and would suggest its relevance to other member states with traditionally more lax health and safety regimes. If, however, increased efforts are made to compare regulation across the Community, it may be possible for regulators who perform well in such exercises to claim success with a conviction not possible formerly.

Where Community rules are not implemented evenly there is a danger that national regulators may become frustrated and attempts to regulate effectively may be reduced. Thus, one study of efforts by the Community to harmonize competitive conditions between road and transport operators across member states found that a great deal of unevenness had resulted on the ground with different enforcement practices and variations in penalties in member states. An efficiency loss was the result: 'This unequal treatment of offences is a source of friction between operators and enforcement agencies and a disincentive to enforce the regulations generally' (Siedentopf and Ziller 1988: 14). The message for health and safety regulation is clear: unless the issue of evenness in applying Community directives is responded to in a satisfactory manner, regulators making claims to support on the basis of their effectiveness may be on increasingly uncertain ground.

As far as the accountability of regulators is concerned, Community legislation may again present problems. It might be argued that the European Parliament (EP) offers a means of holding regulatory rule-makers to account – particularly when (as in the case with Article 118A) co-operation procedure is used. This procedure demands that EP views be given serious consideration by the Commission in a process whereby the three Community legislative organs aim to find a common position. Against the view that the EP is a strong legitimating force, however, it can be responded that there is a democratic deficit in Community legislative processes and a gap between powers conferred to the Community and the controls of the elected Parliament (see Williams 1990; Harlow 1992; Snyder 1993). As for access to and the openness of the participatory process generally, the criticism made in relation to domestic rule-making – that it is attuned to the large-scale, well-resourced enterprise rather than to the small or medium-sized employer – applies all the more so on the Community stage.

Legitimacy claims urging that health and safety regulation deals with affected parties fairly and with due process are on no more secure a footing than the claims already discussed. As indicated, European level regulation involves the special problem of convincing affected parties that they are being dealt with fairly in relation to their Community competitors. Unevenness in either legal transposition or practical implementation tends to produce resentment. The study of (*inter alia*) road transport sector regulation already referred to (Siedentopf and Ziller 1988), noted German and British concerns at unequal application of social regulations. German employers and trade unions were said to 'feel abused and disadvantaged' by inequalities (Siedentopf and Ziller 1988: 228), and in Britain it was commented of the regulations on drivers' hours: 'It is strongly felt that there is no point in having common regulation through the EEC unless there are also common enforcement policies and common penalties' (Siedentopf and Ziller 1988:

700). Such concerns, the study went on to argue, were not ill founded – there was strong evidence that national governments were seeking to implement Community legislation to their domestic advantage.

The problem of unevenness in legal and practical implementation is one to which there is no easy response (see generally Baldwin and Daintith 1992, Chapter 8). A first difficulty is *measuring* the degree of implementation that has occurred. Judging whether a member state has *legally* implemented a directive is a time-consuming matter and it is this issue that tends to occupy most of the Commission's attention when dealing with enforcement (Siedentopf and Ziller 1988: 665). Assessing the rigour with which a member state seeks to achieve *practical* compliance is a hugely more complex task and one with which the Community has yet to come to grips (see Snyder 1993). A daunting series of variables affects such rigour (see Siedentopf and Ziller 1988, vol. I; Baldwin and Daintith 1992, Chapter 8), notable differences across member states include: legal systems and governmental frameworks; organizations used for implementation; areas of law employed; legal standards and modes of proof; and enforcement processes, sanctions and penalties. The most promising way to compare regulation is not to measure the costs of compliance that are imposed on industry or the efforts of regulators but to assess outputs in the form of either working conditions on the ground or accident and disease rates across member states. The former kind of assessment can be carried out by, for example, inspecting 'sample' workplaces in different countries but positing equivalence of workplaces is problematic. As for comparing accident and disease rates, this is, as noted above (see HSE 1991), a complex and difficult task that has to make allowances *inter alia* for industrial profiles, different patterns of diseases and injuries and different recording methods. A series of social and economic (rather than regulatory) factors may, furthermore, influence rates of accidents and diseases – for instance: the level of economic activity; the overtime worked; the extent of the 'black economy'; the degree of mechanization; the level of training; the rate of staff turnover and the social emphasis on safety and health. Measuring regulatory rigour by looking to outputs necessarily calls for contentious decisions to be made on commensurability or on the relevance of different factors. The resources and skills required for such an exercise are considerable. Suspicions of unfairness and uneven regulation can, however, only be allayed and legitimacy fostered if benchmarks for regulatory even-handedness can be established.

Assuming that problems of measurement are overcome, fair treatment still demands that steps be taken to ensure that even-handed regulation occurs. One broad means to exert such control is *centrally* – by using the main Community institutions to oversee implementation. At present, however, the Community central institutions are notable for their weakness on this front and commentators have stressed the Community's reliance on member states' organs for executive action; the lack of central enforcement agencies in the Community; and the primarily legislative roles of the Council and

Commission (see Cappelletti, Seccombe and Weiler 1986: 60, 68, 86, 88, 307). The Commission may bring infringement proceedings under Article 169 EC but there are limits to the effectiveness of such steps – notably the restricted resources of the Commission and the European Court of Justice and the heavy informational demands of infringement proceedings. The Commission could not monitor practical implementation on a routine basis and, even if it had the necessary resources, it would not be able to act through the European Court of Justice without imposing an impossible burden on that court (Gaja, Hay and Rotunda in Cappelletti, Seccombe and Weiler 1986: 67, 129).

Even where the Commission relies on reasoned opinions and reports rather than full-scale court actions, there are severe informational burdens. Member states can be required to send implementation reports to the Commission for collation (as with the original Community social regulations), but even so, informational gaps, delays and differences in the quality and quantity of statistical data create considerable difficulties (see for example, the European Commission 1987).

The Commission might act to strengthen central control of practical implementation without resort to court action. It might co-ordinate inspection procedures, enforcement methods and sanctions as well as act as a source of information exchange for enforcers. Such functions could be carried out by a specialist agency or, in a modest way, by a standing committee of experts (see Hepple 1990: 643, 654), but the remit of the European Agency for Safety and Health at Work (OJ no. L216/1 of 18 July 1994, Article 3) exemplifies the Council's unwillingness to give to agencies functions moving beyond information dissemination into monitoring and co-ordination. For its part, the Council might encourage implementation by, for example, adopting Resolutions as is the practice in the environmental sector (see OJ 1987 C.289/3). These Resolutions may even be used to set performance targets – as has been the case in the energy field (see the Council Resolution on Community energy policy objectives for 1995, OJ 1986 C.241/1).

The resourcing problems of centralized control could be avoided by adopting a decentralized system – one that facilitates proceedings before national courts in order to enforce compliance with Community law. Where necessary, ECJ preliminary rulings could be employed to guide such decisions. The Commission is encouraging decentralized enforcement in the context of the single market, and commentators have argued that greater effect could be given to social policy laws by giving interest groups powers to galvanize the Commission to take enforcement action (see Nielson and Szyszczak 1992: 219). More radically, it can be argued that, since controlling enforcement in highly disparate regimes is fraught with difficulty, some consistency of approach to practical enforcement should be designed into new health and safety rules, and procedures for monitoring and assessing enforcement should be agreed before legislation in promulgated at the Community level.

To summarize, then, there are severe problems in making claims that, at the Community level, health and safety regulation is legitimated by its fair treatment of affected parties. Problems of defining and measuring evenness of regulation undermine such claims and a series of potential steps are yet to be taken to ensure that practical as well as legal enforcement is even-handed.

Dealing briefly with legitimacy claims under the expertise heading, a problem at the Community level lies in the assumption that collecting the views of national experts during rule-making processes produces a cumulative expertise. Given the highly divergent approaches and strategies adopted in different member states it may be the case that a collection of contradictory proposals is amassed. Resolving such contradictions may not always be possible or uncontentious or seen as the exercise of an expert judgement (as opposed, for example, to the production of a political compromise). Broad consultative processes, conducted across member states, may serve to expose this problem rather than to solve it.

CONCLUSION

How, then, does regulating within the Community context affect HSC/E legitimacy claims? The above analysis indicates that on nearly all fronts it is more difficult to claim support when operating in tandem with the Community than when operating purely domestically. To some extent increased difficulties of legitimation may be seen as a worthwhile price to pay for being part of a broad Community of member states. Regulators may, however, have cause for concern since problems of legitimation have a generally undermining effect. The lesson to be learnt is that where steps can be taken to improve potential legitimation, particularly at the Community level, such opportunities should be grasped. To this end, the broad problems of the 'democratic deficit' in the Community should be addressed by such measures as making Community processes more open and further increasing the role of national parliaments and the European Parliament. Such steps would improve opportunities for legitimation in the health and safety field, as in others. More specifically in relation to the health and safety sector, the urgent problem is that of practical enforcement. Present arrangements for both measuring and ensuring the effective and even application of Community rules are manifestly inadequate. Until the enforcement nettle is grasped it will be impossible for regulators to make any legitimacy claims with confidence.

REFERENCES

Baldwin, R. (1990) 'Why don't rules work', *Modern Law Review* 53: 321.
Baldwin, R. and Daintith, T. (eds) (1992) *Harmonization and Hazard: Regulating Workplace Health and Safety in the European Community*, London: Graham & Trotman.
Baldwin, R. and McCrudden, C. (1987) *Regulation and Public Law*, London: Weidenfeld & Nicolson.

Bartrip, P. and Fenn, P. (1987) 'The administration of safety: the enforcement policy of the early Factory Inspectorate 1844–1864', *Public Administration* 58: 87–102.

Burrows, N. (1990) 'Harmonization of technical standards: Reculer pour mieux sauter?', *Modern Law Review* 53: 597.

Cappelletti, M., Seccombe, M. and Weiler, J. (eds) (1986) *Integration through Law*, vol. 1, book 2, Berlin: de Gruyter.

Carson, W.G. (1974) 'Symbolic and instrumental dimensions of early factory legislation', in Hood (ed.), *Crime, Criminology and Public Policy*, London: Heinemann Educational.

Carson, W.G. (1979) 'The conventionalization of early factory crime', *International Journal of the Sociology of Law* 7: 37–60.

Dawson, S., Willman, P., Banford, M. and Clinton, A. (1988) *Safety at Work: The Limits of Self-Regulation*, Cambridge: Cambridge University Press.

Department of Trade and Industry (DOTI) (1985) *Burdens on Business*, London: Department of Trade and Industry.

European Commission (1987) *Fourteenth Report on the Implementation of Council Regulation* (EEC) 543/69 of 25 March 1969. Com. (87) 389 of 11 September 1987.

Factories Amendment Act (1844), London: HMSO.

Factories Regulation Act (1833), London: HMSO.

Factories and Workshops Act (1878), London: HMSO.

Fenn, P. and Veljanovski, C. (1988) 'A positive economic theory of regulatory enforcement', *Economic Journal* 98: 1055–70.

Freedman, J.O. (1978) *Crisis and Legitimacy*, Cambridge: Cambridge University Press.

Frug, G.E. (1984) 'The ideology of bureaucracy in American law', *Harvard Law Review*, 1277–388.

Gunningham, N. (1984) *Safeguarding the Worker*, Sydney: Law Book Company.

Harlow, C. (1992) 'A Community of interests? Making the most of European law', *Modern Law Review* 55: 331–50.

Hepple, B. (1990) 'The implementation of the Community charter of fundamental social rights', *Modern Law Review* 53: 643–54.

House of Lords (1984) *Select Committee on Science and Technology Report 1983/84*, London: HMSO.

HSC (1985/6) *Plan of Work 85/86*, London: HMSO.

HSC (1991) *Plan of Work 1991/92 and Beyond*, London: HMSO.

HSC/E (1988/9) *Annual Report*, London: HMSO.

HSC/E (1989) *Plan of Work for 1990/91 and Beyond*, London: HMSO.

HSE (1979/80) *Director General's Report*, London: HMSO.

HSE (1991) *Workplace Health and Safety in Europe*, London: HMSO.

HSWA (Health and Safety at Work Act) (1974), London: HMSO.

Locke, J. (1981) 'The politics of health and safety', The Alexander Redgrave Memorial Lecture.

Majone, G. (1992) 'Market integration and regulation: Europe after 1992', *Metroeconomica* 43: 131–56.

Mashaw, J. (1983) *Bureaucratic Justice – Managing Social Security Disability Claims*, New Haven (CT): Yale University Press.

Neal, A. (1990) 'The European framework directive on the health and safety of workers: challenges for the United Kingdom', *International Journal of Comparative Labour Law and Industrial Relations* 6: 80–117.

Nichols, T. and Armstrong, P. (1973) *Safety or Profits: Industrial Accidents and the Conventional Wisdom*, Bristol: Falling Wall Press.

Nielson, R. and Szyszczak, E. (1992) *The Social Dimension of the European Community* (2nd edition), Copenhagen: Mandelshojskolens Forlag.

Pelkmans, J. (1986/87) 'The new approach to technical harmonization and standardization', *Journal of Common Market Studies* 25, 3: 249–69.

Robens, Lord (1972) *Safety and Health at Work, Report of Committee*, London: HMSO, Cmnd 5034.

Siedentopf, H. and Ziller, J. (eds) (1988) *Making European Policies Work: the Implementation of Community Legislation in the Member States*, vol. II, London: Sage Publications.

Snyder, F. (1993) 'The effectiveness of European Community law: institutions, processes, tools and techniques', *Modern Law Review* 56: 19–54.

White Paper (1985) *Lifting the Burden*, London: HMSO, Cmnd 9571.

White Paper (1986) *Building Business, Not Barriers*, London: HMSO, Cmnd 9794.

White Paper (1988) *Releasing Enterprise*, London: HMSO, Cmnd 512.

Williams, S. (1990) 'Sovereignty and accountability in the European Community', *Political Quarterly* 61: 299–317.

Woolf, A.D. (1973) 'Robens Report – the wrong approach', *Independent Law Journal* 2: 88.

6 Environmental regulation and administrative reform in Britain

Albert Weale

During the 1980s, Britain, in common with many other countries in the developed world, underwent a series of changes in its environmental politics and policies. New issues came on to the policy agenda, including acidification, the control of toxic substances, nitrate pollution, ozone depletion and the threat of global climate change. The locus of decision-making on environmental policy increasingly shifted from national and sub-national actors to international bodies like the European Community (EC) or the Conference of North Sea Ministers. New interest was shown in the development of innovative policy instruments, such as environmental impact assessments and the uses of taxes and charges to control pollution, and there was a general upsurge of public interest, symbolized by the Green Party's 15 per cent share of the vote in 1989 European elections and the increase in the membership and prominence of environmental organizations such as Greenpeace and Friends of the Earth.

The most visible form of change was, however, in the reform of the institutional structure responsible for the formulation and implementation of standards for environmental regulation. The Industrial Air Pollution Inspectorate, heir to the Alkali Inspectorate (the world's oldest national pollution control body), was amalgamated with other bodies to provide a unified approach to pollution control. The regulation of rivers and fresh waters was shifted from organizations with responsibility for managing the hydrological cycle to a body with the specific responsibility for water quality and pollution control. There were new specifications and standards for air pollution control and solid waste disposal, along with consequential changes in the responsibilities and competences of local authorities. There was an attempt to change the administrative style of environmental regulation, with a greater stress on due process and public access. And legislation was introduced to extend the scope and stringency of pollution control standards. Legislation adopted by Parliament in 1995 established a Unified Environmental Agency in April 1996, and may be seen as the culmination of these changes.

This chapter attempts to describe the reforms that have taken place so far, assess their origins and examine their implications for the conduct of environmental regulation in Britain. In this context, environmental regulation is understood in Selznick's sense of sustained and focused control exercised by a public agency over socially valued activities (Selznick 1985: 364–5). The stress in this definition is upon the fact that the activity being regulated is valuable in itself, and it is only in respect of its secondary or incidental effects that it needs to be controlled. Within environmental regulation this point can be observed in the fact that pollution is typically a by-product of otherwise legitimate economic activities like farming, industry and transport (Underdal 1980). Social regulation shares with regulation in general the objective of correcting for market failures, in particular the existence of negative externalities, and has been the traditional rationale for environmental regulation.

In examining the institutional evolution of environmental regulation in Britain in the 1980s the scope of this chapter is limited in a variety of ways. The term 'environmental protection' is a broad one in Britain and includes not only pollution control but also countryside protection and management, the protection of flora and fauna, the control of releases for genetically modified organisms and the protection of the built environment through planning controls and restrictions on change of use. In this chapter environmental protection will be considered exclusively in relation to pollution control, that is the control of substances or emissions given off from production processes which either damage or carry the risk of damaging human health or well-being, the built environment or the natural environment. Even within this demarcated field the focus will be narrower than would be implied by a comprehensive examination of pollution control, since attention will be restricted to *stationary* sources of pollution.

There is also a geographical limitation. The internal administrative and governmental relations of the United Kingdom are complex. Separate administrative arrangements in respect of environmental policy exist for England and Wales on the one hand, and Scotland and Northern Ireland on the other. Neither Scotland nor Northern Ireland has undergone the range of reforms and changes dealt with here. Hence the focus of this chapter will be on England and Wales, Britain as it may be conveniently designated.

These limitations of scope and coverage help focus the story, but should be seen to a large extent as analytic devices rather than as reflections of the politics of administrative reform within environmental policy in Britain. Thus, the exclusion of Scotland and Northern Ireland from the reforms that have taken place in Britain has been the subject of parliamentary questions and reports.

The chapter describes the institutional background to pollution control in Britain, the broad institutional background to pollution control policy, and provides an account of the main reforms in pollution control in the 1980s. It goes on to identify the character of the processes involved in those reforms. The concluding section seeks to identify the principal features and policy issues of the emerging system of pollution control in Britain.

INSTITUTIONAL BACKGROUND

The ministry primarily responsible for environmental protection and pollution control is the Department of the Environment and in its present form is the successor to a number of public bodies concerned with environmental health, going back to the Local Government Board of the nineteenth century.

The Local Government Board was established in 1871 to oversee local authorities concerned with the tasks of sanitation and slum clearance in English cities, and its powers were extended in 1875 (Ensor 1936: 23, 127). These health-related functions were consolidated in 1919 with the transformation of the Local Government Board into the Ministry of Health, the association of health and housing in the same ministry being 'a hangover from Victorian sanitarianism' (Webster 1988: 166). With the establishment of the National Health Service in 1948, the administration of health care ceased to be a matter of liaising with primarily local schemes and became instead a matter of administering a nationally controlled system of medical care. The gap between the local government wing of the department's work and the health wing became increasingly wide, and in January 1951 the ministry was split into two component parts, with local government functions, including responsibility for pollution control inspections, going to the newly created Ministry of Local Government and Planning, renamed the Ministry of Housing and Local Government on the Conservatives' accession to power later that year.

Edward Heath, well known for his interest in questions concerned with the machinery of government and Prime Minister in 1970, transformed the Ministry of Housing and Local Government into the predecessor of the present department. The Department of the Environment created in 1970 combined the Ministry of Housing and Local Government with the Ministry of Transport, the theory being that the institutional brigading of the various functions contained within these ministries would make possible a more comprehensive assessment of the needs of the environment. In 1974, with the accession of a Labour government, this mega-ministry was broken up, with transport acquiring its own department once again.

Despite its name the present Department of the Environment is not a ministry whose sole, or even primary, purpose is the protection of the environment. Much of its work is concerned with local government finance, a function that became particularly important in the late 1980s with the politically mismanaged reform of local government finance introduced under Margaret Thatcher. Nevertheless, the department does have responsibility both for pollution control and for nature and countryside protection. Junior ministers within the department, below the level of the Secretary of State who sits in Cabinet, have traditionally been assigned specialist functions, in which environmental protection in general and pollution control in particular are included.

The Department of the Environment shares its responsibilities for pollution control with three other departments of state: the Ministry of Agriculture, Fisheries and Food, which has responsibility for marine dumping of wastes, the Scottish Office and the Northern Ireland Office, the latter two being the territorial ministries responsible for environmental regulation within their sphere of competence. Despite this rather untidy set of relationships, the political focus of pollution control policy is centred within the Department of the Environment.

Two other sets of actors, not themselves directly involved in pollution control regulation, have considerable influence on the evolution of policy and thinking about regulatory structure. The first of these is the Royal Commission on Environmental Pollution. Established in 1970, this is a standing body whose task is to offer high-level scientific and expert advice to the government of the day on matters concerned with environmental protection. Its views on the appropriate organization of pollution control have at times been important in the evolution of administrative arrangements and structures.

The second group of actors comprises parliamentary committees, three of which have been particularly important in the development of institutional thinking about environmental protection: the House of Lords Select Committee on Science and Technology; the Environment Sub-Committee of the House of Lords Select Committee on the European Communities; and the House of Commons Select Committee on the Environment.

The present system of regulation in Britain stems from the Water Act 1989, consolidated within the Water Industry Act 1991, and the Environmental Protection Act 1990. These acts were the culmination of many reform processes that reached their full tide in the late 1980s. The 1989 Water Act established the statutory responsibilities of the National Rivers Authority (NRA), whereas the 1990 Environmental Protection Act defined the powers and principles of Her Majesty's Inspectorate of Pollution (HMIP), and the local authorities responsible for the implementation of some environmental regulation. Table 6.1 (see p. 110) summarizes, for each of the relevant bodies, their status, powers, focus and the policy instruments available for their work.

There is by and large a consistent assignment of functions to the various bodies, in the sense that no two bodies have overlapping responsibilities for controlling similar processes or pollutants (see Table 6.1). (There is an exception to this rule in relation to industrial discharges to water, where the National Rivers Authority and Her Majesty's Inspectorate of Pollution overlap).

In April 1996 the government introduced an integrated Environment Agency for England and Wales (along with a sister agency for Scotland, the Scottish Environmental Protection Agency). This will combine HMIP and the NRA together with personnel from the local authorities with responsibility for pollution control. The Agency will be a non-departmental public body, run by an appointed board. As such it will realize the ambition of many in the British environmental policy community, but its mode of working and

Table 6.1 Outline structure of pollution control institutions (prior to the establishment of the Unified Environmental Agency)

Body	HMIP councils	NRA councils	County	District
Type	ministry	non-departmental public body	local authority	local authority
Level	national government	national government	sub-national government	sub-national government
Main focus	discharges to air, waters and land from prescribed processes	rivers, estuaries and coastal waters	solid waste disposal to land	air pollution for prescribed processes
Operating principles	best available technology not entailing excessive cost	water quality objectives	duty of care	best available technology not entailing excessive cost

operation is likely to be influenced by the evolution of the bodies that constitute it. And it is on that process of evolution that this chapter will focus.

THE EVOLUTION OF REGULATORY BODIES

Her Majesty's Inspectorate of Pollution

Her Majesty's Inspectorate of Pollution (HMIP) was established in April 1987, but the history of some of its component parts goes back, in the most important case, to the nineteenth century. The four component parts of HMIP when it was founded were the Industrial Air Pollution Inspectorate, the Radiochemicals Inspectorate, the Hazardous Waste Inspectorate and the fledgling Water Quality Inspectorate. Of these, the most important in status and influence upon the administrative style of HMIP was the Industrial Air Pollution Inspectorate (IAPI). To understand the development of environmental regulation under HMIP, we need to place it in historical context, both the long-term story of air pollution control in Britain and the more immediate history surrounding the creation of HMIP itself.

IAPI was the successor body to the Alkali Inspectorate, established in 1863 by the Alkali Act and responsible for regulating a limited range of industrial processes that emitted hydrochloric acid. Although it had originally been established in the Board of Trade, the Alkali Inspectorate was moved to the Local Government Board in 1872. The Alkali Inspectorate occupied a key role in the British system of pollution control and by virtue of its position managed to establish four important features of British air pollution control which were to have influence in the 1980s reforms. These features were: the operating principle of regulation; the scope of regulation; the style of regulation; and the locus of responsibility for regulation.

In terms of the operating principle of regulation for air pollution control the key idea has been that of 'best practicable means' (BPM). The principle of best practicable means had been incorporated into early, nineteenth-century local authority legislation concerned with protection from smoke. For some time it had provided a defence in the courts from criminal liability from prosecution under smoke control legislation, since if manufacturers could show that they were using best practicable means in their processes, then they could avoid conviction as well as having a defence to a common law action for nuisance.

Over the life of the Alkali Inspectorate the principle of best practicable means came to have a definite meaning. In particular, it came to be understood as involving three elements: a technical engineering judgement about the possibility of abatement or control for a polluting process; an economic judgement about the costs of control, and especially a judgement about the financial implications for a plant operator of the Inspectorate requiring a particular technique of control; and an environmental judgement about the capacity of the atmosphere in the vicinity of a plant to absorb pollutants. In deciding whether a process within a plant was being operated in accordance with best practicable means, the air inspectorate referred to 'presumptive limits', that is, emission limit values for particular processes and specified substances. These presumptive limits were set by the inspectorate nationally and the assumption was that they would be tightened over time as engineering technology improved and new techniques of abatement became available. A plant operator whose processes met these presumptive limits could assume that no more stringent standards would be applied, although a plant where the processes failed to meet the presumptive limits might well be licensed to operate because the inspector responsible for granting the licence had the discretion to judge that the receiving environment could absorb the excess pollution or that the extra costs to the firm would not be warranted by the gain in environmental quality that would be secured. The operating principles of control therefore allowed considerable discretion to individual public officials. As Ashby and Anderson said, in summarizing the experience of the Alkali Inspectorate, its task was not to minimize pollution but to optimize it (Ashby and Anderson 1981: 131).

In addition to the principle of regulation, the experience of air pollution has also been important in defining the scope of regulation. One defining aspect of the traditional system of air pollution control is the idea that regulation should focus not on the plant or the operator, but upon the process responsible for potentially harmful atmospheric emissions. The term used to designate those plants that contained specific processes was 'scheduled works' and the idea was that the national inspectorate should focus only upon processes that were especially complex or hazardous in their operation.

The third element in the traditional system of air pollution regulation was the style developed by the Alkali Inspectorate. Two features of this style stand out. The first was its consensual character. The first Chief Inspector, Angus Smith, thought that the best way to secure progressive improvements with industry was to work with it rather than against it. In the language of contemporary regulation theory, he therefore pursued a compliance rather than an enforcement strategy, in which negotiation and discussion played an important role in the relationship between inspectors and plant operators. The use of formal and legal remedies was traditionally infrequent, to the point at which by the early 1970s some commentators on the work of the Alkali Inspectorate began to criticize its style in terms of regulatory capture (Bugler 1972; Frankel 1974).

The second point of administrative style relates to the discretion available to inspectors (Vogel 1986: 70). Operating within the framework of the principles of best practicable means and presumptive limits, there was a lack of formality and due process both in terms of the derivation of the standards and in terms of the latitude of their implementation. British regulatory practice has not operated under the close eye of the courts, who have typically been deferential when scrutinizing administrative action, thus leaving scope for lack of rules and standardization in the treatment of issues. Moreover, since air pollution control has not operated with the idea of ambient air quality standards, the optimization of pollution that Ashby and Anderson saw as the essence of the inspector's work has always had an implicit rather than explicit character, with no publicly accountable procedures by which the appropriateness of the judgements in particular cases could be assessed. Public access to information on compliance has been low because of fears of breaches of commercial confidentiality, and public access to standard-setting procedures was traditionally non-existent, thus reinforcing the absence of due process and formality in the style of air pollution regulation.

Throughout its history the Alkali Inspectorate remained a small technical branch of central government. Hence, it might be thought to have little general interest. However, its traditional style of regulation was to be felt more broadly in Britsh regulatory thinking, for example in the deliberations of the Robens Committee set up to examine the regulation of occupational health and safety (see Committee on Health and Safety at Work 1972). The Robens Committee's recommendations on the organization of occupational health and safety had direct consequences for the structure of environmental regulation in Britain, but also reflected the esteem with which the consensual style of regulation associated with the Alkali Inspectorate was held (see Chapter 5 above).

The legislation of 1974 implementing the Robens proposals created two related bodies. One was the Health and Safety Commission, an independent body established by statute with representatives from industry and the trade unions, and responsible for the development of policy. The second was the Health and Safety Executive, comprising the civil servants and professionals responsible for the operational tasks of health and safety regulation, which reported to the Commission. The desire of Robens to rationalize the *ad hoc* accumulation of inspectorates resulted in their all being placed in the Health and Safety Executive, including the Alkali Inspectorate. The brigading of the Alkali Inspectorate with the other inspectorates responsible for health and safety caused a high-level 'turf' dispute between the Department of Employment, which had responsibility for occupation health and safety, and the Department of the Environment, which hitherto had had responsibility for the Alkali Inspectorate. Eventually the Department of the Environment conceded the Alkali Inspectorate to the Health and Safety Executive, although in some ways this could be seen as a purely Pyrrhic victory for the Department of Employment, since during the whole time that IAPI spent in the Health and Safety Executive it never physically left its premises in the Department of Employment in Marsham Street.

Almost as soon as the new organization of regulation had been formed it came under attack. In 1974 the Royal Commission on Environmental Pollution was invited by the Secretary of State for the Environment to review the efficacy of the methods of control of air pollution from domestic and industrial sources, to consider the relationship between the relevant authorities and to make appropriate recommendations. Part of the background to this request had been an attack on the methods of working of IAPI by Social Audit, an independent public interest group specializing in issues of worker health and safety and environmental protection. Social Audit attacked the air pollution inspectorate for its preference for confidentiality, its unwillingness to prosecute and its insensitivity to public concern.

Thus, when the Royal Commission reported in January 1976 it was against the background of the incorporation of the Alkali Inspectorate into the Health and Safety Executive, consequent upon the recommendations of the Robens Committee. The Royal Commission was strongly critical of the move of the Inspectorate to the Health and Safety Executive, particularly as it had its own proposals for strengthening environmental inspection (Royal Commission on Environmental Pollution 1976: 72).

In making this point the Royal Commission was doing more than taking sides in the turf dispute between Employment and Environment that had gone on over the recommendations of the Robens Committee. In a manner parallel to Robens, it was seeking to rework in an incremental and evolutionary way the principles and practice that had underlain the history of air pollution control in Britain.

Although the request from the Secretary of State had been motivated by criticisms of the elitist elements of the Alkali Inspectorate's style, the Royal Commission did not make its most radical recommendations in respect of that style (Royal Commission on Environmental Pollution 1976: 56). The Royal

Commission was supportive of the Alkali Inspectorate's collaborative relationship with industry, arguing, rather in the way that Robens had, that this
enabled them to understand the technical problems of pollution control better.
It reserved its most radical proposals for its treatment of the difficulties
inherent in regulating for environmental protection in one receiving medium
only, without paying due attention to the effects of regulatory decisions upon
possible deteriorations of quality in other receiving media.

In fact, the solution to one pollution problem may well be a displacement
of pollution effects in another receiving medium. The Royal Commission was
sensitive to this problem and argued that the problem of cross-media transfers
was the most important challenge that the regulation of pollution faced and
the main burden of its 1976 report was the need to move from a discharge
control regime based on the idea of single-medium control to one based on
the idea of multi-media control. This principle of environmental regulation
became known as integrated pollution control (IPC).

There were two assumptions built into the Royal Commission's proposals
that were crucial to the manner in which they sought to accomplish this
reform. The first was the need to separate the organization of environmental
protection from that of occupational health and safety. This was the reason
why the Royal Commission supported the desire of the air pollution
inspectorate not to be incorporated into the Health and Safety Executive. The
second assumption reflected the incremental mode of reform favoured by the
Royal Commission. Its aim was not to replace the traditional principles and
standard operating procedures of traditional air pollution control, but to adapt
them in the light of the new understanding of the multi-media problem. Thus,
in rejecting the radical attacks on the discretion and secrecy surrounding the
work of the air pollution inspectorate, the Royal Commission endorsed a
continuity with past practice in its recommendations for reform.

The specific form in which the adaptation of pollution control was to be
worked out, according to the Royal Commission, would be a new inspectorate
whose title would be 'Her Majesty's Pollution Inspectorate'. This new body
would fill the gap created by the fact that no public body had the statutory
responsibility to take a total view of any one pollution problem. To overcome
the problem of partial responsibility, the Royal Commission proposed that
the new inspectorate should operate under an adapted version of the principle
of best practicable means which it termed the principle of 'best practicable
environmental option' (BPEO). This principle of BPEO would allow the new
inspectorate to optimize pollution discharges into the whole environment and
not simply into the air.

It was still assumed by the Royal Commission that the new inspectorate
would regulate only those processes that fell within the category of scheduled
works, and there was no suggestion that all discharges from a plant should
be controlled by one body. Moreover, the Royal Commission did not use the
fact of cross-media transfers to argue for the public development of clean
technologies, as the European Commission began to do in its successive

environmental action programmes. Instead, it took the problem of pollution as one generated by a fixed technology and sought the solution in the optimal level of discharges into different receiving media by that technology. Although it was clear to the Royal Commission that new legislative provision would be required to allow the scope of regulatory activity to be extended to cover all receiving media, it is clear that the Royal Commission did not see the need to change the style and operating practices of the air pollution inspectorate. It would still retain its ethos of a collaborative relationship to industry and its tasks would be to achieve policy objectives by means of the technical specification of production processes.

Despite the impeccable credentials of the Royal Commission, and the intellectual sophistication with which their views were advanced, it took two governments six years even to pen a reply to the Royal Commission's 1976 report. When the reply eventually did come, the then Conservative government, with Michael Heseltine as Secretary of State for the Environment, noted that the logic of the Royal Commission was unassailable, but, with a form of argument reminiscent of the Red Queen in *Alice in Wonderland*, it asserted 'there is little evidence that the present system is failing in terms of achieving a sensible balance in the control of pollution of different forms' (Department of the Environment 1982: 2; see also O'Riordan and Weale 1989; Weale, O'Riordan and Kramme 1991: 150–6).

In August 1986, the government announced the creation of Her Majesty's Inspectorate of Pollution (HMIP), a body that would formally come into existence in April 1987. It was to include the Alkali Inspectorate, which in 1982 had been renamed the Industrial Air Pollution Inspectorate, as well as the Radiochemicals Inspectorate, the Hazardous Waste Inspectorate and the Water Quality Inspectorate, all three of which were housed in the Department of the Environment.

The ten-year delay in the creation of HMIP and the circumstances of its creation meant that the development of the new inspectorate did not follow the incremental pattern that had been assumed by the Royal Commission in 1976. By the time that HMIP was formed, new issues and actors had emerged within the arena of environmental regulation which meant that traditional operating assumptions of pollution control were no longer feasible policy options. The first five years of HMIP saw the new body struggling to define its role and mode of operation in a sometimes hostile world.

One contingent, but none the less important, circumstance in the early days of HMIP was the government's policy of tightly controlling numbers in the civil service. Although the Thatcher government did not succeed in its general ambition of reducing public expenditure, it was relatively successful in reducing the number of civil servants employed by central government. Moreover, HMIP was established in a period of rapid growth in real employment incomes in Britain, and the professional skills upon which HMIP wished to draw were in high demand in industry and the economy at large. Consequently, in its first three years of life HMIP was constantly under its already small establishment of between 240 and 260 inspectors, sometimes by as many as thirty or forty people. This problem of under-recruitment in turn meant that inspection rates dropped and the technical work of revising pollution control standards slowed down (see the House of Commons Environment Committee in its 1989 report on the regulation of toxic waste).

However, the main reason why the development of HMIP departed from the expectations of the 1976 Royal Commission was the rise of the EC to prominence in the determination of Britain's pollution control practice. EC directives not only affected specific policy measures, requiring greater stringency of pollution control, they also affected the style of regulation and in particular precluded the incremental development of the principle of best practicable means along the lines envisaged by the 1976 Royal Commission. Whereas prior to the development of EC pollution control policies in the 1980s it had been possible to suppose that Britain could have maintained its flexible and discretionary style of regulation, such an expectation came increasingly under strain as the effect of EC directives began to work themselves out, not simply in the substance of specific policies, but also in the very mode by which policy was organized and conducted.

One element of the EC's influence is to be found in the preference within EC policy for uniform emission limits in terms of available technological possibilities, over environmental quality objectives in terms of the putative receiving capacities of the environment. By the mid-1980s this clash of approach had become serious as the British government sought to resist in a variety of proposed measures, not least the EC's draft Large Combustion Plant directive, the imposition of what were seen as inefficiently costly controls on sources of air pollution (see Boehmer-Christiansen and Skea 1991, especially Chapter 12). In its 1984 report the Royal Commission sought to defuse this clash of pollution control philosophies, when it argued that in practice the EC's emphasis upon 'best technical means available' could be read as coming close to the notion of 'best available technology' as used in the USA, but that in practice it 'appears to have acquired a meaning not unlike that of BPM' (Royal Commission on Environmental Pollution 1984: 46). But when one reads their arguments, it is difficult not to believe that the wish is really father to the thought. There was a genuine clash of approaches involved, as is partly revealed in the fact that a similar argument over the relative advantages of uniform emission limit regulation and regulation by reference to environmental quality objectives was occurring in the regime responsible for regulating the North Sea – a clash resolved only by the Paris and Oslo Commissions formally adopting both principles in their statement of operating practice.

These influences were to play themselves out in the development of the principles underlying the formulation and implementation of the 1990 Environmental Protection Act. The 1976 Royal Commission had foreseen the need for new legislation in order to expand the legal competence of the air pollution inspectorate to enable it to regulate in accordance with the principle of IPC. From the establishment of HMIP in 1987 legislative change had been promised by the government in order to create the legal framework for IPC. Originally promised for the 1988/9 session of parliament, the relevant legislation was not introduced until the 1989/90 session, because of the pressure of parliamentary business. In fact, the final impetus for the legislation came from the government's need to legislate in order to implement the EC's 1986 Framework Directive for air pollution control (84/360/EEC OJ L.188 of 16 July 1984; see Haigh 1989: 224–7). Indeed, much of the time and energy of the early months of HMIP was spent drafting proposals and consultation documents in connection with changes needed under the Framework Directive. Moreover, for a variety of reasons, the government was under pressure to reform the regulation of waste management, and so the 1990 Environmental Protection Act has a rather omnibus character, dealing not only with IPC and air pollution control, but also with solid waste disposal and a number of miscellaneous topics (litter, radioactive substances, genetically modified organisms and the organization of nature conservation, etc.).

In terms of HMIP the relevant aspect of the legislation is to be found in part 1 of the Act dealing with IPC and air pollution control by local authorities. The key regulatory device of the Act is the requirement for operators of 'prescribed processes' to obtain prior authorization from HMIP before they carry on their operation (Environmental Protection Act, 1990, s. 6). In granting such authorizations HMIP is supposed to operate with standards that may be specified in terms of either emission limits or environmental quality objectives. The objectives of the regulation are to ensure that in carrying on a prescribed process the 'best available technology not entailing excessive cost' (BATNEEC) is used for preventing the release of substances into any environmental medium (Environmental Protection Act, 1990, s. 7).

The basic principles of the Environmental Protection Act are therefore in part an adaptation of traditional modes of air pollution regulation to the demands of the new system of control required by the IPC regime, and in part the reflection of elements inspired by the principles of the European Community. Thus, the notion of a prescribed process takes over from the notion of scheduled works the idea that there are certain industrial processes that are sufficiently complex and potentially polluting to require regulation by a national inspectorate. The national inspectorate still has direct responsibility for the implementation of the standards it prescribes in respect of those processes governed by the IPC regime, unlike say Germany or the Netherlands where federal authorities draft regulations but sub-national authorities implement them. And the administrative instrument of regulation is an inspectorate located within a government ministry rather than a free-standing agency governed by its own board or commission with a general responsibility to pursue the cause of environmental protection. All these elements of legislation can be seen as continuous with the traditions of air pollution regulation over the last 130 years.

On the other hand, the 1990 legislation does introduce some genuinely novel elements. One of the these is the division of responsibility between HMIP and the local authorities in respect of those processes that cause air pollution but do not fall within the scope of IPC. Here the division between central standard-setting and local implementation is new. However, the most significant new element in the legislation is the specification of the principle of control in terms of BATNEEC. A case can be made for saying that this is not the principle of best practicable means brought up to date, still less the Royal Commission's principle of BPEO. Both BPM and BPEO are essentially based on the idea of optimizing pollution discharges from a given technology. BATNEEC carries the idea that operators of processes may be subject to 'technology-forcing' in that they have to change and adapt their technical processes to accord with the most feasible attainable standards. In this respect the principle of control comes closer to that favoured by Germany, the Netherlands and other environmental leaders in Europe than to the practice that has characterized the approach in terms of best practicable means.

The extent to which this legal change will produce a change in administrative and regulatory behaviour is open to question. For many years there have been influential voices urging that Britain should move away from its traditional style of co-operative regulation towards a more formal, and perhaps adversarial, style. Early experience of the legislation suggested that a more adversarial style was emerging. For example, in 1991 HMIP prosecuted successfully both the UK Atomic Energy Authority and British Nuclear Fuels for operations carried out without previous authorizations, despite its previous willingness to overlook such rule infractions by companies (*ENDS Report* 201, 1991: 10). However, by 1993 the Director of HMIP was reported as making the following statement in connection with the authorization of electricity-generating stations under integrated pollution control procedures: '[a]t the end of the day we are charged with getting these plants under authorization. . . . Most industries in this country do not have the capability to produce what the Environmental Protection Act requires, and to expect it overnight is unrealistic' (*ENDS Report* 219, 1993: 15). A clearer statement of the principles of co-operative regulation could not be found. It will be interesting to see how far this long-standing tradition carries over to the work of the new Environment Agency.

The National Rivers Authority

The National Rivers Authority (NRA) was established under the 1989 Water Act which privatized the previously nationalized water authorities, and its chief tasks are to regulate for environmental protection and to manage river resources. It thus monitors the quality of fresh waters, acts as the principal body controlling polluting discharges to water, and manages river and coastal functions like land drainage and flood defences. Unlike HMIP it is not part of the Department of the Environment, but is a non-departmental public body with its own board established by statute, although it discharges its accountability to Parliament through the Department of the Environment. Of the fifteen members of the board, two are appointed by the Ministry of Agriculture Fisheries and Food, one is appointed by the Secretary of State for Wales, and the remainder are appointed by the Secretary of State for the Environment. Although a new body with much less continuity with its predecessors than HMIP, the NRA has established itself as having a powerful presence in defining the newly emerging pattern of pollution control in Britain.

As with any other organization of government, the NRA did not inherit a clean sheet in the regulation of water pollution. Much that was characteristic of the British system of air pollution control in terms of its traditional style, principles and standard operating procedures also applied to water pollution control. For example, under public health and river pollution legislation of the 1870s, it was an offence to dump sewage or industrial or mining discharges into rivers, but it was allowable as a defence that an operator had used the best practicable means for reducing the pollution thus caused (Kinnersley 1988: 51). Moreover, the co-operative working arrangements that characterized air pollution inspection also characterized the working relationship between water pollution inspectors and those regulated (see, for example, Hawkins 1984).

Nineteenth-century legislation empowered local authorities to regulate pollution discharges, but in practice they turned out to be more interested in their functions as suppliers of water than in their function as environmental regulators (Kinnersley 1988: 66). Thus, although it was legally possible after 1888 for local authorities to establish interdepartmental boards for pollution control, only four such boards had been established by the 1920s. During the interwar period the Ministry of Agriculture and Fisheries (as it then was) established fisheries and land drainage boards to help manage rivers, responsibilities that were consolidated by legislation in 1948 and 1951 when River Boards, which merged the land drainage and fisheries functions, were created and given responsibility for pollution control. The boards were based on water catchment areas and their members were appointed by central government from interested parties and the lists of 'the great and the good'.

By contrast with the traditional system for air pollution regulation, which always lacked the idea of air quality objectives, the idea of water quality objectives underlay the practices of the river authorities in controlling water pollution. The 1951 legislation introduced the idea of water discharge consents, and the volume and quality of the consented discharge was supposed to be set in the light of the quality and use of the water discharge at that point. Water quality was defined in terms of a fourfold classification, and heavily polluting discharges, according to traditional regulatory principles, are not allowed where water quality is high or where there is a subsequent downstream use that requires protection. The converse of these principles of regulation is that where existing water quality is low or there are no subsequent downstream uses to be protected, the heavily polluting discharges may be allowed. The essence of the traditional system of water regulation was therefore to avoid national uniform emission standards and to set discharge consent levels in the light of the quality and use of the receiving medium. An influential argument among British policy-makers in this context has been that Britain is fortunate in having a large number of fast-flowing rivers that are capable of absorbing pollution. Hence, as with air pollution, there has been a resistance in the case of water pollution to imposing national uniform limits upon polluting sources.

The most important development in relation to the control of water pollution occurred in 1974 with the implementation of the 1973 Water Act. This act had been conceived within the context of the rationalizing ambitions of Heath's Conservative administration of 1970–4. Heath was unusually committed to improvements in the machinery of government as a way of securing improvements in public policy. During his period as Prime Minister government departments were restructured, including the creation of the Department of the Environment, local government was reformed and the National Health Service was reorganized. The reorganization of water supply and water pollution control needs to be understood against the background of these general trends. In particular, it should be seen as part of a broader attempt to improve the quality of public services by the creation of specialized forms of public enterprise.

The 1973 Water Act created Regional Water Authorities, all-purpose bodies, organized around river basins and designated with responsibility for the whole of the hydrological cycle; their functions thus combined those of water supplier, regulator and planner. In particular, they had responsibility not only for managing and controlling their own discharges, but also for issuing consents to other users. The idea of creating all-purpose authorities around river basins had a long history, but the 1973 Act was primarily the work of one civil servant, Jack Beddoe, who worked in the Water Division of the Department of the Environment, and who had become convinced of the value of all-round planning for water responsibilities (Kinnersley 1988: 94–7). With a sympathetic Secretary of State in Peter Walker, it was Beddoe who drafted the 1973 proposals which were to form the basis of the legislation. The creation of all-purpose water authorities marks one of the high points of the theory that state-organized enterprise could more effectively plan the rational use of natural resources than alternative forms of organization.

Just as the 1973 Act incorporated a particular view about the capacity of public institutions rationally to manage a resource like water, so the original impetus for change in manner of water pollution regulation came from a contrary vision of the superiority of private enterprise in the desire of Thatcher's government to privatize the water industry. Because the regional water authorities had combined the functions of river management, water supply and pollution regulator, it was simply assumed in the first version of the Conservative proposals for water privatization, issued when Kenneth Baker was Secretary of State for Privatization, that the regulatory function would be taken over by the newly privatized water companies. Not surprisingly, perhaps, this proposal ran into opposition from those private companies discharging to sewers and water courses who were not prepared to be regulated by other private companies. The proposal also met opposition in the House of Lords, which is generally well informed on matters to do with the environment. In consequence, revised versions of the original proposals separated the regulatory and river management functions of the water authorities on the one hand, from the functions of water supply on the other. It was these revised proposals that were to give birth to the NRA.

The NRA thus had a double independence. On the one hand, it was unlike HMIP in that it was a non-departmental public body with its own board and therefore at some length from direct ministerial control. On the other hand, the separation of the regulatory functions from the water supply functions meant that it was independent of the water companies. Almost from its inception, under its first Director-General, John Bowman, the NRA was keen to display its regulatory independence, initiating a successful prosecution against Shell for a pollution incident on the River Mersey, in which the company was fined £1 million. However, one of the main areas where the NRA had the opportunity to demonstrate its independence was in its treatment of the newly privatized water companies, particularly in respect of their sewage discharges.

The former water authorities had regulated their own sewage discharges with a rather light hand, particularly during the 1980s when Treasury-imposed expenditure limits made it difficult for the authorities to install expensive sewage treatment capital equipment. Consequently, it was not surprising when in early 1988, with national figures becoming available for the first time, over 20 per cent of sewage treatment works were in breach of the conditions for their own discharge consents (*ENDS Report* 159, 1988: 3). Moreover, in the run-up to the privatization of the water industry, the government extended the period within which the water companies could legally remain in breach of their consent discharges, in order to make the flotation of the shares more attractive to potential investors.

Against this background the NRA sought to demonstrate its independence. Even before it formally came into existence, Lord Crickhowell, the first chairman of the board, used the occasion of a debate in the House of Lords to identify the issue of management independence and identified policy towards sewage discharges as a particularly urgent matter. When it started operating, the NRA was able to use the existence of the EC bathing waters directive to put pressure on water companies to accelerate their timetables for compliance with water quality standards, and in 1990 it put forward a series of proposals to rationalize the system of discharge consents, measures that would have significant implications for sewage treatment works.

The working group that developed the proposals for the NRA took as their starting-point that uneven system of consent discharges that had operated under the former regional water authorities. Their recommendations were in line with the emerging philosophy of pollution control, under which the system was to become more formal. In particular, the idea was that the legal obligations of dischargers should be spelt out clearly and that operators discharging to water should be encouraged to take a closer interest in those obligations. Among the recommendations was the proposal that there should be absolute limits on effluent composition and flow from discharge sources which should not be exceeded at any time. This proposal, if carried forward, would not only have significant implication for sewage treatment works, but would mark a departure from policies followed from the mid-1980s, when regulators were prepared to countenance a small proportion of breaches of discharge consents as a routine feature of their operation (*ENDS Report* 186, 1990: 17–24).

Although the NRA sought to establish an independent stance in terms of regulation, and quickly acquired a positive image among environmental groups, it is clear that there are limits to this trend. Clean-up of sewage and other discharges involves significant increases in capital expenditure and this incurs opposition not only from industries affected but also from those bodies responsible for utility price regulation. Moreover, despite the formal separa-tion of the NRA from the Department of the Environment, there can still be political pressure placed on the NRA not to pursue particular cases with vigour. Indeed, the first Director-General of the NRA, John Bowman, resigned in June 1991, and sceptical observers alleged that one crucial issue in his decision was political pressure from a minister in the Department seeking to persuade the NRA not to impose a stringent discharge consent on a textile firm near the minister's own constituency (*ENDS Report* 196, 1991: 6). Within the new system the limits of independence have still to be determined.

Solid waste disposal

The disposal of solid waste has emerged as a significant pollution control issue in many countries, not least because of its implications for the quality of underground water supplies. Until the 1990 Environmental Protection Act, the regulation of solid waste disposal was controlled under the 1974 Control of Pollution Act. This legislation gave primary responsibility for the disposal of solid wastes to county councils, who not only acted as the regulators but also managed their own sites. The implicit theory was therefore akin to that of the regional water authorities, namely that an effective system of control would involve bringing together the functions of regulator and operator. By the beginning of the 1980s, however, concern began to be expressed in various quarters about the efficiency and effectiveness with which county councils were carrying out their tasks.

In 1981 the House of Lords Committee on Science and Technology conducted an enquiry into hazardous waste management, which identified shortcomings in the effectiveness of the local authority system (House of Lords Select Committee on Science and Technology 1981). As a result, a small advisory unit was established in the Department of the Environment and brigaded with HMIP in 1987, with the task of providing high-level expert advice to county council authorities on difficult waste management problems. The routine management of waste disposal remained poor, however. Thus, when the House of Commons Select Committee on the Environment conducted an enquiry into toxic waste in 1988, it emerged that 70 per cent of local authorities had not submitted waste disposal plans to the Department of the Environment in line with the 1974 legislation (these plans being a key policy instrument of the act), and that there was no mechanism operated by either the Department or the Association of County Councils to reduce the variability in the standards of performance by different local authorities (see two amusing, if rather bad-tempered, exchanges in House of Commons Environment Committee 1988/9: 26, 223).

When the government came to legislate on solid waste disposal as part of the 1990 Environmental Protection Act there was a general sense within the relevant policy community that changes would be required in the regulation of solid waste disposal in order to improve the efficiency and effectiveness of the system. The principle adopted by the government was to separate the functions of service provider from those of regulator. County councils were required to establish their functions as waste regulatory bodies from their functions as waste disposal authorities, with the aim of privatizing the latter. In effect, county councils were required to become environmental regulators for a particular receiving medium, namely soil. This approach is one example of a policy increasingly pursued by the Conservative government in the late 1980s across many policy sectors. As with health care, where the intention was to make health authorities purchasers rather than providers of services, and personal social services, where the idea was that local authorities should be responsible for providing care by contractual arrangements with other suppliers, the principle in the case of pollution control was to withdraw the state from the management and supply of particular services (for the changes in health and related services, see Weale 1990). In this instance, therefore, we can see a direct effect of a particular view about state–society relations.

The emerging pattern of regulation

It is clear that the present system is not the result of a synoptic process. Nor is it just one part of a process by which the British state ceases to be a provider of services and becomes a regulator of economic activity. Indeed, no single general conception of the role of the state in relation to the economy, industry and environmental regulation informed the views of those responsible for bringing the present system into being. There was nothing corresponding, for example, to the Robens review of occupational health and safety, which was both comprehensive in its scope and motivated by a conception of co-operative self-regulation as being of the essence of successful policy.

The reason why the process of evolution has been so slow and tortuous certainly cannot be lack of influential friends. Indeed, in many ways, the notion of an independent environmental protection agency has been one of the pet projects of the British pollution control policy community for a number of years. Not only did the Royal Commission on Environmental Pollution advocate it, in both its 1976 and its 1984 reports, but it was known to be a favourite idea of William Waldgrave when he was a junior minister in the Department of the Environment in the 1980s. The House of Commons Select Committee on the Environment has advocated the proposal in various reports, and Lord Cranbrook introduced a bill in the House of Lords in December 1990 that, had it proceeded, would have established such an agency. David Trippier, as Minister of State, suggested in June 1991 that such an agency was on the cards. And John Major's first speech as Prime Minister in July 1992 seemed to favour the plan. Yet, despite this heavy-weight support, there appears to have been no powerful political impetus to produce the change.

In one way this is not surprising. British government is party government, and if an issue is not a priority for a governing party then it will not be given legislative time. The Conservative Party, in government since 1979, has given priority to traditional economic aims of growth and the expansion of trade, effectively pushing environmental regulation legislation to the bottom of the agenda. Indeed, the legislation introducing the Agency was only passed in a year when, for internal party political reasons, the government sought to keep the volume of (its own) legislation as low as possible, thus giving the environmental legislation a chance to get through.

If we cannot account for the emergence of the present system of environmental regulation in terms of the application of a unified and synoptic theory of state–society relations, how are we to understand the processes at work? I conjecture that we are seeing the merging of two quite distinct strands of reform. On the one hand, there is the creation of HMIP and its associated regime of IPC, which owes its origins to a critique internal to the British environmental policy community of traditional air pollution control practices and the influence of the EC's Framework Directive. On the other hand, there is the creation of the NRA and the county councils as waste disposal authorities which can be seen as the expression of the view that the state should be less involved as a supplier of services and assume more the role of regulator.

Even if the latter motivation is stressed in the process of reform, it should be borne in mind that the separation of the functions of supply and regulator came almost as an afterthought to the primary desire to privatize the water industry. Thus, in the early days of the plans for privatization it was clear that the government wanted the NRA to be as small as possible, presumably intending it to play little more than a residual function (*ENDS Report* 155, 1987: 20). During the early 1980s the Thatcher government was hostile to regulation as such, and the Department of Trade and Industry under Lord Young had a unit whose task was to search for opportunities for deregulation. It was only in the late 1980s after the wave of privatizations that both social and economic regulation came to be seen in a positive light (compare Veljanovski 1990: 297). Indeed, the positive role assigned to regulation could be used in the case of water privatization with some rhetorical force to bolster the case for selling off the water companies on the grounds of separating the polluting poacher and the environmental gamekeeper.

So the origins of the new, and undoubtedly transitory, system are to be found in the convergence of a rather disparate set of trends, most notably the desire of the Royal Commission to move towards integrated pollution control, the influence of the EC, the consequences of privatization and the articulation of an emerging ideology of the enabling and regulatory state as opposed to the service and supply state. These trends formed powerful strands of reform, but they were never strong enough, either singly or together, to create the momentum for fully comprehensive reform leading to a national environmental protection agency. This does not mean that there were no common themes in the reform process. Indeed, the new structure itself is already revealing important tensions and contradictions, as well as common features, of its own. The final section seeks to document and analyse some of these common themes.

SOME COMMON THEMES

The previous sections have sought to show how the system of pollution control in Britain cannot be seen as the product of a synoptic process of reform but has instead to be seen as the outcome of a variety of processes, not all of which are consistent with one another. As the process of administrative consolidation unfolds, so these themes and conflicts, some of which are only latent, have become increasingly visible.

One of the most striking of these conflicts is that between social regulation in the form of environmental protection on the one hand, and economic regulation to prevent abuse of monopoly power over pricing from the newly privatized utilities on the other. Although the Conservative government of the 1980s was unsympathetic to many of the traditional arguments for public ownership of utilities, it could not avoid facing the problem of monopoly power, particularly as its privatization programme by and large failed to produce a competitive structure for the industries concerned (Veljanovski 1990: 299). Gas remained a national monopoly, electricity became a duopoly and water supply and services are in effect regional monopolies. To overcome this problem of the potential abuse of monopoly power the government put in place a series of regulatory agencies that would be responsible for controlling the pricing of utility supplies. The regulatory bodies established by the Conservative government were provided with the powers to control price directly. The formula adopted was the so-called 'RPI-X' principle. According to this formula, the price increases allowed to the privatized utilities would be equal to the rise in the Retail Price Index (RPI), the most widely used measure of inflation, less a percentage rate (X) to be determined by negotiation between the regulator and the industry and supposedly to hold in place for a number of years (Centre for the Study of Regulated Industries and Price Waterhouse 1992: 6–10).

The application of this formula can be modified in those cases where the industry is likely to incur costs that are outside its control. In these circumstances a cost-plus component or 'Y' factor may be added to the formula to allow a substantial proportion of these costs to be passed on to the consumer in final prices (Centre for the Study of Regulated Industries and Price Waterhouse 1992: 10). In the case of the water industry it was recognized at the time of privatization that the under-investment in waste water treatment of the 1980s would have to be made good and the X and Y components of the formula are effectively combined so that the pricing control formula becomes RPI + K (capital) (where K = X + Y).

This tension first emerged clearly in 1991, when the pricing regulatory body for water, the Office of Water Services (Ofwat), made it clear that it considers the water companies' profitability since privatization to have been excessive and called for voluntary reductions in planned charges for the following year. The NRA, by contrast, does not concern itself explicitly with the costs of its regulation to the water companies, and particularly in respect of the clean-up costs for sewage treatment plants it became clear that the NRA and Ofwat were imposing potentially conflicting requirements (Evans 1991: 12). Indeed, the water companies have argued that a high rate of return is needed on investment in order to finance the investment necessary under EC directives, and some reports suggest that water bills would have to double in real terms in order to meet the costs of enforcing the directives (Maddox 1992: 14).

However, the relationship between economic and environmental regulation is not a simple one of antagonism. In the case of electricity, the Office of Electricity Regulation (Offer) has imposed an environmental levy on energy production earmarked for a fund devoted to investment in energy conservation. The levy is a small one, and there are conflicting views on whether social and economic regulation should be combined in this way. Whatever one's views on this matter, it is clear that any system of pollution control regulation will have to establish a satisfactory working relationship with the system of environmental regulation. So far the terms of this relationship have not been formally and explicitly developed, although it is clear that the decisions of each type of regulatory body have an effect upon the work of the other.

As well as seeking to determine the terms of their relationship to other regulators, one of the primary tasks of the new regulatory system will be to establish the terms of the relationship with industry and with the general public. It is clear from the trends discussed in the previous section that there is now a greater stress upon formality and due process. The greater willingness to prosecute those in breach of consent or permit conditions by the NRA and HMIP, the increased caution about informal discussions with industry setting of standards, and the establishment of statutory water quality objectives all indicate a trend towards an emphasis upon formality and due process previously absent from Britain's generally co-operative system of regulation.

On the other hand, it is clearly possible to overstate the force and speed of these changes. Co-operative regulation, it may be argued, is implicit in the regulatory relationship – a point of view clearly articulated in the Robens philosophy. British courts lack the powers of their North American counterparts to scrutinize obligations imposed through administrative action, and, although there has been a growth in judicial review of administrative action during the 1980s, it is clear that its development is haphazard and subject to swings of judicial interest. Moreover, in terms of relationships with the public, there has been no hint of the British system of pollution control seeking to establish systems of 'regulatory negotiation', involving representatives of public interest groups in the setting of regulatory standards, of the type experimented with in the United States and Canada (see Amy 1990: 59–79; Susskind and McMahon 1985: 133–65; Doern 1990: 89–110). In this sense one could say that the system of pollution control has failed to adapt itself to the demands for more formalized rule-making.

Another source of uncertainty and tension is the division of labour – between functions of pollution control to be carried out centrally and those to be carried out locally – which constitutes one of the main structural sources of tension in any system of pollution control. Since rules are always open-textured, their application to particular cases is never a mechanical matter but requires interpretation and judgement, both of which rest upon substantial local or context-specific knowledge if they are to be exercised intelligently. Moreover, the process of implementation is one that can provide opportunities for policy learning, provided that there is an adequate feedback loop built into the system of administration. Hence, it can be argued that the relationship between central and local elements within the administrative system is the essence of successful regulatory design or reform.

In the British case, the long-established institutions of pollution control have constrained the design of the relationship between the centre and the locality. Since Sir John Simon lost the battle to have the Alkali Inspectorate as an advisory body to the local government inspection of polluting processes in 1872, the distinction between central air pollution inspection responsibilities and local ones has been one of the type of processes being regulated rather than the policy stage involved in the regulation. This division of responsibilities has precluded a distinction, for example, between the central formulation of regulations and their local implementation. The arrangements under the 1990 Environmental Protection Act run against this historical preference, however, at least in respect of non-prescribed processes, where the local authorities will be seeking to implement standards that have in part been determined by HMIP. However, this is clearly only a partial development towards a system in which there is a central formulation of standards which are then implemented locally.

The issue of redesigning the central–local relations of pollution control regulation has been complicated in Britain during the 1980s by the lack of good working relations between local government and successive Conservative governments. One consequence of this has been an unwillingness of Conservative administrations to give increased powers and functions to local authorities – indeed, the tendency has been to withdraw many functions. In 1992 the newly elected Conservative government established a Local Government Commission, with a brief to examine the functions of local government locality by locality on a rolling review basis. Pollution control is not a central part of the work of local authorities, and it is likely that much of the reform of local government will be based on issues that will be seen as higher priority. The lack of consistency that has characterized local authority pollution control functions hitherto is likely to remain a persisting feature of British environmental regulation.

The final tension that is likely to become more and more significant is that between the functional independence of an effective pollution control body and the requirements of political accountability. The issue of political accountability dominated the parliamentary debates about the establishment of the Health and Safety Commission, with many parliamentarians worried about the distance between the work of the Commission and the formal responsibility of government ministers to Parliament. In practice, the concern over accountability at the time has not been reflected in subsequent appraisals of the work of the Commission, although someone could argue that the ability of the Commission to resist the strong lead given in the direction of deregulation in the early 1980s by Norman Tebbitt as Secretary of State for Employment shows the dangers of lack of political accountability.

Similar issues about accountability are likely to be at the forefront of debates over environmental regulatory reform in Britain in the next few years. The more pressing a public issue pollution control becomes, the less willing ministers are likely to be to allow significant policy decisions to be made by an agency with statutory independence from ministers, with all the political embarrassment there is likely to be in seeking to override their decisions should there be a clash of view between the two parties. Moreover, the system of parliamentary committees, reformed by Norman St John Stevas in 1979, has worked well in the case of environmental policy, and government ministers are bound to feel wary of establishing a system in which an independent commission could receive the support of parliamentary committees against the preferred policy of the government. Hence, whether Britain will be able to reform once again its system of environmental regulation to move it towards a structure in which there is an independent integrated pollution control agency akin to the American EPA (Environmental Protection Agency) is something that only time will tell.

REFERENCES

Amy, D. (1990) 'Decision techniques for environmental policy: A critique', in Paelke and Togerson (eds) *Managing Leviathan*, Peterbrough, Ontario: Broadview Press.

Ashby, E. and Anderson, M. (1981) *The Politics of Clean Air*, Oxford: Clarendon Press.

Boehmer-Christiansen, S.A. and Skea, J. (1991) *Acid Politics – Environmental Policies in Britain and Germany*, London and New York: Belhaven Press.

Bugler, J. (1972) *Polluting Britain*, Harmondsworth: Penguin.

Carney, M. (1992) 'The cost of compliance with ever higher water quality standards', in Gilland (ed.) *The Changing Water Business*, London: Centre for the Study of Regulated Industries.

Centre for Study of Regulated Industries and Price Waterhouse (1992) *Regulated Industries: The UK Framework*, London: Centre for the Study of Regulated Industries and Price Waterhouse.

Committee on Health and Safety at Work (1972) *Report*, London: HMSO, Cmnd 5034.

Department of the Environment (1982) *Pollution Paper no. 1*, London: HMSO.

Doern, G.B. (1990) 'Regulations and incentives: the NO-VOCs case', in Doern (ed.) *Getting it Green: Case Studies in Canadian Environmental Regulation*, Ottawa, Ontario: C.D. Howe Institute.

ENDS (various years) *Report*, London: Environmental Data Services.

Ensor, R.C.K. (1936) *England 1870–1914*, Oxford: Clarendon Press.

Evans, R. (1991) 'An uneasy relationship', *The Financial Times*, 18 December 1991.

Frankel, M. (1974) *The Alkali Inspectorate: The Control of Industrial Air Pollution*, London: Social Audit Ltd.

Haigh, N. (1989) *EEC Environmental Policy and Britain* (2nd edition), Harlow: Longman.

Hawkins, K. (1984) *Enforcement and Environment*, Oxford: Clarendon Press.

House of Commons Environment Committee (1989) *Toxic Waste: Second Report*, vol. II, session 1988/9, London: HMSO.

House of Lords Select Committee on Science and Technology (1981) *Hazardous Waste Disposal: First Report*, London: HMSO.

Kinnersley, D. (1988) *Troubled Water*, London: Hilary Shipman.

Maddox, B. (1992) 'Water quality costs set to rise', *Financial Times*, 7 August 1992.

O'Riordan, T. and Weale, A. (1989) 'Administrative reorganization and policy changes: The case of Her Majesty's Inspectorate of Pollution', *Public Administration* 67, 3: 277–94.

Royal Commission on Environmental Pollution (1976) *Air Pollution Control: An Integrated Approach*, Fifth Report, London: HMSO.

Royal Commission on Environmental Pollution (1984) *Tackling Pollution: Experience and Prospects*, Tenth Report, London: HMSO, Cmnd 9149.

Selznick, P. (1985) 'Focussing organizational research on regulation', in Noll (ed.) *Regulatory Policy and the Social Sciences*, Berkeley and Los Angeles: University of California Press.

Susskind, L. and McMahon, G. (1985) 'The theory and practice of negotiated rulemaking', *Yale Journal of Regulation* 3: 133–65.

Underdal, A. (1980) 'Integrated marine policy – what? why? how?', *Marine Policy* 4, 3: 159–69.

Veljanovski, C. (1990) 'The political economy of regulation', in Dunleavy, Gamble and Peele (eds) *Developments in British Politics 3*, Basingstoke: Macmillan.

Vogel, D. (1986) *National Styles of Regulation*, Ithaca and London: Cornell University Press.

Weale, A. (1990) 'Social policy', in Dunleavy, Gamble and Peele (eds) *Developments in British Politics 3*, Basingstoke: Macmillan.

Weale, A., O'Riordan, T. and Kramme, L. (1991) *Controlling Pollution in the Round*, London: Anglo-German Foundation.

Webster, C. (1988) *The Health Services since the War*, London: HMSO.

The law and policy of competition in Germany

Pio Baake and Oliver Perschau

With the enactment of the German Constitution in 1949, the concept of the social market economy became the basis for both competition and general economic policy. The most important piece of legislation for the protection of competition in Germany is the Gesetz gegen Wettbewerbsbeschränkungen, GWB (1957), hereafter referred to as the Cartel Law.

This chapter examines the development of German competition law in general (Sturm and Ortwein 1993), the substantive legal provisions of the Cartel Law and its application, and the development of the Federal Cartel Office (McGowan 1993).

THE DEVELOPMENT OF COMPETITION LAW

The introduction of legislation

In 1897, the Imperial Court ruled that cartel agreements constituted an integral part of general competitive freedom and thereby effectively blocked any development of restrictive regulations until the First World War, when we witness the integration of numerous cartel organizations into state economic planning. During the Weimar Republic, economic policy focused on the restriction of cartel power and the reduction of the impact of anti-competitive agreements, starting with the Regulation on the Abuse of Economic Power in 1923. Cartels were not declared illegal as such, but the Minister of Economics was empowered to suspend cartel agreements where these had a negative impact upon supply, pricing or general economic freedom within the national economy. The influence of such regulations was marginal, however, and at the end of the Weimar Republic the estimated number of cartels still stood at around three to four thousand (Schmidt 1990: 150).

From 1933 until the end of the Second World War large sections of the German economy were progressively brought under state control, with the government making use of existing cartels and creating new ones where this facilitated the process of state intervention. In 1947, the Allies passed legislation to abolish cartels altogether in order to usher in free competition in Germany and to reduce the political and military might of its economy. At the end of the 1940s, in the course of the gradual re-establishment of German sovereignty, new regulations oriented towards the model of perfect competition, and to a large extent inspired by the tenets of structural neo-liberalism, were formulated by the Josten Committee (Robert 1976). The control of economic power was to be the cornerstone of a new social order, not only guaranteeing individual freedom, but avoiding the negative social consequences of a competitive economy by virtue of structural policies. More specifically, and in addition to the outright ban on cartels, the proposals contained provisions on the dismantling of concentrations of economic power by transforming them into individual, independent enterprises.

The Josten Committee's proposals largely reflected the concern of the American occupation authorities, but the government of the Federal Republic and German industrial associations considered that their adoption would endanger economic growth and future competitiveness in world markets. The German Cabinet thus agreed, under pressure from the Minister of Economics, Erhard, to accept the general ban on cartels and the negative supervision of dominant market enterprises, on the understanding that the former would be softened by the introduction of sectoral exemptions. Subsequently, the Allied Control Commission, then responsible for competition legislation in the Federal Republic, put pressure on Germany to include provisions for merger control in the draft legislation. Contrary to the wishes of the Allies, however, no provision was made for the compulsory dismantling of concentrations of economic power.

The first draft of the law was thus designed to create a social market economy with competition – guaranteed by the state. In line with the principles of structural neo-liberalism, competition was considered the best instrument to achieve economic growth, but, in order to satisfy the concept of the social market economy, it had to be supplemented by an active state-led social policy, thus pushing state operations beyond the merely structural policies demanded by neo-liberalism.

The first draft thus heralded a shift in competition policy towards the promotion of economic productivity, and away from notions of structural neo-liberalism aimed at the reform of society. Neither the draft, nor Erhard's concept of the social market economy contained a clear set of rules against the build-up of concentrations of economic power. Cartels and economically powerful enterprises were to be tolerated where they promoted economic productivity. In doing so, Erhard underestimated the dangers which large and economically powerful enterprises pose to competition. This misconception is clear in the degree of trust he placed in the power of market forces to determine the optimal size of businesses. Thus, the draft legislation lacked legal provisions on the dismantling of large combines, and on merger control, and contained no clear definition of 'competition', other than as a kind of 'perfect competition', or as a reliance on dynamic market interactions.

Notwithstanding the stark difference between the original proposals of the Josten Committee and the draft legislation, sections of the government were still deeply critical of Erhard's ideas, and of the principle of anti-competitive economic conduct contained in the draft. The Cartel Working Group of the Christian Democratic Party (CDU), for example, concluded that the principle of anti-competitive conduct would allow the state to intervene in the market and lead, *paradoxically*, to the creation of illegal cartels (Robert 1976: 190).

Similarly, the German Confederation of Industry (BDI), and the Conference of German Industry and Commerce (DIHT), took issue with the government's proposals. Using their influence within the coalition parties, the CDU and the Liberal Party (FDP) secured important exceptions to the general principle of anti-competitive conduct during the preparatory stages of the legislation. Moreover, other economic sectors sought to limit the sphere of application of the law in their favour, most notably the insurance and finance industries which exerted pressure on the relevant federal ministers. As a result, the latter – who feared that the proposed legislation would lead to a reduction or overlapping of their competences – proposed that the federal and individual state (*Land*) Cartel Offices responsible for the application of the law, be responsible to the federal and *Land* ministries of economics.

Thus, internal political opposition effectively blocked the parliamentary draft, despite the fact that it had – through the intervention of Erhard – become the linchpin of the entire concept of the social market economy.

In 1956, with the ratification of the Treaty of Paris, the Federal Republic achieved full sovereignty in the matter of competition policy, and thus the danger receded of the imposition of an allied decree on competition law embodying the principles of American antitrust legislation. In this changed political climate, the BDI and many members of the Bundestag – most notably the CDU and FDP – were more favourably disposed towards the unchanged draft. This was again presented to the Bundestag and eventually passed shortly before the general elections in 1957 (effective as of 1 January 1958). This followed intensive work on the draft by the Ministry of Economics in co-operation with the newly created BDI Cartel Working Group, together with the personal intervention of Chancellor Adenauer. In the course of consultation with representatives from industry, however, the law was further watered down: merger control, for example, was removed altogether.

The industrial interest groupings had been successful. Not only had the gradual establishment of national sovereignty allowed the development of a considerably milder law than that envisaged by either Josten or the original draft, but political pressure on the government to enact the law had risen dramatically with the approaching elections. In stark contrast to the coalition partners, the Social Democratic Party (SPD), the largest opposition party – firmly committed to the social market economy – made clear their support for the draft in the course of its passage through the Bundestag. Yet another failure to enact the law, due to disagreement among the coalition partners, could have severely damaged the credibility of the ruling coalition, and above all that of its Minister of Economics, Erhard.

The first version of the law

Apart from a general ban on cartels, the original version of the Cartel Law contained derogations for all rationalization and export cartels not having an effect on the domestic market. Rationalization and export cartels having a domestic effect had to be registered with the cartel authorities which would grant authorization subject to conditions laid down in the Law. Even where legal conditions in relation to structural crisis and import cartels were satisfied, however, the cartel authorities retained discretionary powers regarding authorization.

The Minister of Economics retained the right to grant an authorization even should none of the legal derogations be applicable. In such cases the Law merely detailed that 'anti-competitive measures [need be justified] with reference to their effects on the entire economy and the common good' (Article 8), or by the need to combat dangers which might place the continued existence of a substantial part of the enterprise in danger. Despite the broad formulation of this provision – which was in any case interpreted very narrowly – it was to have very little practical significance.

In relation to the negative supervision of dominant enterprises, the cartel authorities were authorized to intervene in cases of a vertical misuse of market power. Such competences were nevertheless restricted to those instances where excessive pricing, impossible conditions or tie-in deals were imposed.

The price-fixing of brand-named goods was in general allowed, but was subject to the negative supervision of the cartel authorities. All proposed mergers were permitted, but had to be registered with the Federal Cartel Office (Bundeskartellamt) where those involved might subsequently attain or exceed a given market share of 20 per cent. Registration was also required where one of the parties already possessed such a market share.

From the very beginning, the field of application of the law was limited by the exclusion of the sectors of transport, farming and energy, insurance and credit industries.

In addition to substantive legal stipulations, the law also contained provisions on the creation of the cartel authorities responsible for its application, and their legal status. The Federal Cartel Office was an independent federal agency, under the supervision of the Minister of Economics and bound to follow the Minister's general political directions, but autonomous in cases of individual decision-making. Each federal state or *Land* had its own cartel office, responsible to the *Land* Minister of Economics.

All those agreements requiring registration or authorization which had an effect across *Länder* fell under the competences of the Federal Cartel Office. It was, in addition, responsible for all structural crisis, export and import cartels, as well as for the negative supervision of dominant enterprises and price-fixing of brandnames. The *Land* cartel offices were responsible where cartel agreements had an effect within the *Land*.

The amendments

When applying the law the cartel authorities were constantly faced by a series of unclear legal provisions which required firm legal interpretation (Jäckering 1977), in particular the discrepancy between the ban on cartels and the total lack of merger control policy. At the beginning of the 1960s, the SPD proposed amendments to take account of merger control. The government did not, however, act on these proposals, but instead attempted to place the problem of economic power concentrations in the context of the larger markets arising from European integration. At the same time, the emphasis was placed on the possibility that SMEs (small and medium-sized enterprises) might overcome their structural disadvantages *vis-à-vis* large concerns through co-operation. Thus, the Ministry of Economics produced a 'co-operation manual' for SMEs in 1963 which was designed to receive legal recognition in the first planned amendment to the law. The concept of cooperation, introduced into the discussion by the BDI, was now to be adopted by government and contrasted to the concept of the cartels.

The first amendment in 1965 expanded the law to include the notion of countervailing power. The amendment was designed to foster co-operation among SMEs by allowing for specialization cartels and contained procedural short cuts for their authorization. The negative supervision of economically dominant concerns was strengthened with the introduction of a general (catch-all) paragraph. Open oral proceedings were introduced for the examination of abusive practices. Finally, the law included more detailed provisions on the supervision of price-fixing agreements.

The provisions contained in the first amendment did not solve the problem of the systematic increase in power concentrations in the marketplace. Instead, the government attempted to compensate for the unfair advantage which the law gave to large concerns through its failure to take account of merger control, by easing the way for joint action on the part of SMEs. The underlying design of perfect competition was thus further restricted by competition policies oriented towards real market practices, without, however, being replaced by a new theory. The demand by the opposition, that the law be tightened up, was rejected.

The late 1960s saw an economic upturn and a change in government, with the Conservative and Liberal coalition being replaced the CDU–SPD grand coalition in 1966. This in turn led to the active promotion of policies to minimize economic fluctuations and to champion economic growth, policies which were given a legal base by the 1967 Law for the Encouragement of the Stability and Growth of the Economy. In the context of general economic policy, competition measures were now to partner global management and structural policy as a mechanism to guarantee price stability and economic growth.

The job of developing a relevant theoretical basis for competition policy was given to the Cartel Working Group of the Ministry of Economics, founded in 1967. This working group contrasted the model of perfect competition with that of *functional* competition. Thus it was able to justify an active structural policy on the part of the state within the market and at the same time to expand the state's room for manoeuvre. The optimal market structure was no longer that of perfect competition but that of extensive oligopoly with its interdependence between concerns, its partial market transparency and its narrow product homogeneity (Kartte 1969). The competences of the cartel authorities were redefined to the extent that measures designed to create a market structure fostering general economic efficiency and growth might be accommodated within state-led global management.

The second amendment (1973) made functional understanding of competition and the new theoretical interdependence of market structure and market results a part of competition law with its enactment under the Socialist–Liberal coalition in 1973. It also contained provisions which facilitated co-operation between SMEs and which tightened up the negative supervision of dominant businesses. In addition, concrete presumptions detailing market dominance and a ban on particular forms of behaviour were introduced, in order to reduce the danger of a circumvention of the general ban on cartels. The government hoped that the abolition of vertical price-fixing for brand-named goods, in favour of non-binding price recommendations – initially subject to the negative supervision of the Federal Cartel Office – might encourage greater flexibility in pricing and with this put the brakes on persistent price increases.

The eventual inclusion of merger control within the Cartel Law was the most important element of the second amendment. One of the largest gaps in the law was therefore finally bridged. The reaction to preventative merger control was positive, not only by the Federal Cartel Office, but also by the European Commission and the Competition Committee of the OECD.

The Federal Cartel Office, which had examined the model of functional competition as early as 1965 in its Annual Report (Tätigkeitsbericht 1965: 8), drew support from American studies. Accordingly, neither efficiency nor research and development activities might be clearly correlated with the size of firms. In addition, the Federal Cartel Office thought that action should concentrate upon the erection of a competitive market structure and not on the *ex post* correction of market distortions (Tätigkeitsbericht 1967: 13). Two overwhelmingly decisive factors explain the stance taken by the Office. First, the possibility that abusive practices might effectively be pursued by them did not exist prior to 1967. Second, the danger arose that, in its role of pursuing abusive practices, the Cartel Office could be perceived as being dictatorial regarding free market forces. This might lead to conflict between the Cartel Offices and firms over the concrete circumstances of cases of abusive practice.

Amongst those supportive of the amendment there was disagreement as to the character of individual legal provisions. The Federal Cartel Office, which was responsible for merger control, did not limit its demand to that of independence from the general direction of the Minister of Economics, but was also opposed to Article 24, para. 3, promoted by the government, which would allow the Minister to authorize individual mergers against the wishes of the Cartel Office. In contrast the CDU/CSU, which dropped its opposition to merger control following the electoral defeat in 1973, supported the creation of a new body, independent of the Ministry of Economics, to be entrusted with the power to judge the authorization of individual mergers.

The ruling coalition nevertheless won the day. It emphasized that the Minister should allow mergers of major public interest, and highlighted the need for political control over authorizations, a control which might thus ensure the instrumental character of competition.

Despite this, agreement was reached that Article 24b should provide for the creation of an independent Monopoly Commission, with the statutory function to assess the present state and foreseeable future development of economic power concentrations. Moreover, the Commission was given the right to produce reports on current questions of competition policy, and proposals for amendments to the legal provisions of the Cartel Law. These rules furnished the Commission with the opportunity to give an opinion in those cases where the Minister issued an authorization against the wishes of the Cartel Office.

The independence of the Commission was guaranteed by the legal requirements laid down in Article 24, para. 2. Its members – appointed at the request of the government – could not be members of federal or state bodies, representatives of economic associations, employers or associates of employers organizations. The only civil servants eligible were to be university professors or staff of academic institutions.

The third amendment (1976) contained supplementary provisions on mergers between newspapers and made no fundamental changes to the law.

The fourth amendment (1980), however, attempted to combat the ever more powerful trend towards concentration in the German industry (Kartte and Holtschneider 1981). Article 23(a) represented such a wide-ranging expansion of the provisions on merger control that vertical mergers and mergers within conglomerates could now be more easily supervised. In addition, the circumvention of merger control was further obstructed, whilst the examination of mergers between large firms and SMEs was to be facilitated. The legislation particularly aimed at stopping the penetration of large firms into markets where SMEs were the dominant actors.

The new provision covering the protection of small enterprises from unfair obstruction was designed to promote economic productivity, as were changes made to the law to bring about a better formulation of the abuse of selling power. Finally, rules on abusive practices were tightened up in so far as the preconditions for abusive obstruction and abusive exploitation were more precisely formulated and the duty to pay damages was extended.

The fifth amendment (1990) mainly affected those parts of the law dealing with commerce and with derogations from the Cartel Law (Schmidt 1990:

154). Merger control was strengthened through the adoption of specific sales criteria, and the control of market behaviour was reinforced. The law also took more account of the concept of functional competition, with a derogation now to be allowed for purchasing agreements between SMEs in so far as they were designed to promote parity with larger competitors.

The fifth amendment also changed the status of the transport sector under the Cartel Law. While the sector is still exempt from the central provisions of the law it is now subject to the principle of negative supervision. Cartels between insurance companies and banks were now no longer to be subject to the principle of negative supervision, but were instead to be brought within the ambit of the principle of forbidden conduct.

THE SUBSTANTIVE LEGAL PROVISIONS OF THE GERMAN CARTEL LAW

The provisions of the law are grouped according to the particular contractual or other form of association between the enterprises in question (Rittner 1989: 136ff.), and fall into two broad categories: anti-competitive behaviour which is based on contractual relations, and anti-competitive behaviour which is not.

Concerning the former, the law covers both horizontal and vertical contracts. The prohibition of the former rules that contracts or decisions between enterprises or groups of enterprises are void if they are '[c]apable of influencing the manufacture or marketing of goods or commercial services, through the restriction of competition' (Article 1). Where enterprises disregard the void nature of such contracts, they are acting illegally. Vertical contracts are prohibited '[i]n so far as one of the parties to the contract is restricted in his freedom to determine prices or conditions, in the case of contracts made by him with third parties concerning goods thus supplied, or other goods or commercial services' (Article 15). The competition rules are designed to promote patterns of conduct amongst enterprises conducive to fair and productive competition. Exclusivity agreements and linking agreements are forbidden when they limit the freedom of competition for a large number of combines, unfairly limit the market entry of other enterprises or seriously impede competition.

The Cartel Office and the judiciary interpret the law so that it applies to all contracts designed to limit competition, but the efficacy of the law is heavily compromised by the number of exemptions. The latter are partly a result of political conflict over the nature of the Cartel Law and its five amendments, and partly due to the re-orientation of the law, away from the concept of *perfect competition* to that of *workable competition*. Exemptions are primarily introduced when the legislator judged these to be beneficial in terms of market results.

The first group of provisions deals with cases where SMEs co-operate in order to strengthen their competitiveness or reduce structural competitive disadvantages in relation to large-scale competitors. Such agreements are acceptable only if they do not have a serious impact upon general market relations. As legal exemptions, such agreements need not be registered with the Cartel Office, but are subject to its negative supervision. Similarly, contracts made between SMEs, designed to rationalize economic processes and thus increase competitiveness, are given an extra chance to improve their market position, above and beyond the rules on exemptions accorded to rationalization and specialization cartels.

Also exempt are arrangements between enterprises, irrespective of size, which intensify competition by increasing market transparency.

Finally, the legislator exempts cartels which promote an increase in economic production that could not be achieved by the competition process alone (structural crises cartels, standardization and formalization cartels, rationalization cartels, import and export cartels).

The law also empowers the Minister of Economics to authorize individual cartels which do not satisfy any of those exemptions laid down in law. These provisions are, however, subject to a very strict interpretation, and few cartels have been authorized in this way.

The second amendment introduced provisions on the application of competition rules to facilitate fair and productive forms of competition. These may be formulated by business or professional associations and optionally registered with the Cartel Office. The Office must consult with all those enterprises operating at the same economic level but not involved in the agreement, and hear the views of all suppliers and clients affected by the agreement prior to granting an authorization.

Concerning anti-competitive behaviour not based upon legal contractual relations, the law applies to all enterprises and prohibits all actions by firms which may lead to the circumvention of legal bans made on particular forms of conduct, or by a regulation of the Cartel Office, in order to prevent the use of economic threats to enforce unspoken cartel agreements and vertical price-fixing, or to ensure that non-binding recommendations are in fact applied. The law also prohibits any attempt to force firms to join specific forms of association, to adopt a homogeneous form of anti-competitive conduct, or to accede to a merger. It prohibits any encouragement in obstructing supplies or purchases with the aim of unfairly disadvantaging other firms.

Finally, it empowers the Cartel Office to force an economic or professional association to accept a firm into their ranks, where its exclusion would lead to unjust discrimination or unfair trading or production disadvantages.

In addition to the measures cited above, dominant enterprises, or groups of firms, are subject to a form of negative supervision. The law covers both the vertical and horizontal relations of a single firm or a group of firms. It aims to offset the lack of control of competition through the intervention of the Cartel Office. A firm is deemed dominant if 'it has no competitors or is not involved in competition to a significant degree ... or, in relation to its competitors, has an overwhelmingly commanding market position'

(Article 22). The law lays down a series of specific criteria to assess a dominant market position (size of market share, financial strength, access to raw materials and complementary markets, strength of existing entry barriers and so forth). Additional factors in the decision-making process are the flexibility of market partners in readjusting their operations, and their potential to turn to other suppliers or clients – in other words, substitutional competition, seen from the perspective of the firms. Furthermore, the law gives concrete examples of dominant market shares for firms or groups of firms. Where such figures are surpassed, there is a presumption of dominance. The delineation of a particular market, necessary for the calculation of dominance, is carried out in accordance with the principle of market demand. In an alternative formulation, all products considered interchangeable by the consumer are deemed to belong to one market.

The law distinguishes between two forms of unfair conduct: unfair enrichment, when enterprises increase their profits through the imposition of increased prices or unusual conditions; and unfair restrictive practice, when the enterprise employs its dominant position 'to restrict the competitive opportunities of other firms, significantly affecting the market without a substantively justifiable reason' (Article 22, para. 4, s. 2, no. 1).

The ban on discrimination applies to firms which engage in price-fixing, legalized cartels and dominant enterprises. The law states that dominance occurs where market partners do not have sufficient opportunity to deal with other suppliers or clients.

The fourth amendment to the Cartel Law introduced a legal presumption of market dominance. Clients would stand in a dominant position in relation to their suppliers, if the latter regularly offered them discounts over and above normal price reductions. Suppliers may be in a dominant position in relation to their clients where, for example, the products concerned are well-known brand-name goods.

Dominant enterprises with a strong market position, may not, 'in a form of business dealing, normally accessible to all comparable firms, unfairly restrict any firm, either directly or indirectly', and neither may they, 'directly or indirectly, discriminate against comparable firms, without a substantive justification'. These provisions are only valid in the case of firms with a strong market position to the extent that they discriminate against SMEs.

The law covers cases of a refusal to supply, and cases of price discrimination where firms thus affected experience those consequences cited in the law. It is designed to protect individuals as well as the institution of competition as a whole. Both goals might be simultaneously achieved as, in the process of balancing the interests of both market partners, a duty to contract or the removal of discriminatory provisions might be enforced if the protection of competition demands it.

In cases of a refusal to supply or any other restrictive practice carried out by a dominant enterprise, the primary point for consideration is the justifiable interest of the firm in the control of its business methods. It was the previous practice of the Cartel Office, and above all of the Federal Court to ascribe a higher value to the protection of the supplier than to the process of competition on the lower economic level. The Federal Court, for example, overturned a ruling by the Cartel Office which prohibited a large car manufacturer from obliging its subsidiaries and workshops to fit only original spare parts on the grounds that the process of weighing up interests should take note of the close relationship between the car manufacturer, the spare-parts market and service provision for consumers. Thus, the interest of the car manufacturer in ensuring the homogeneous quality of spare parts should take precedence over the interests of firms thus restricted.

As regards price discrimination, that is, discrimination which goes beyond what occurs under normal competitive conditions, horizontal price discrimination occurs when the direct competitors of a firm in a dominant market position are damaged (legal action has above all concentrated on the protection of the institution of competition), and vertical price discrimination covers all restrictions of competition for upstream and downstream firms.

Since the fourth amendment the law has prohibited any demands by the client, which have no substantive justification, for preferential conditions. This rule thus forbids any price discrimination by clients against upstream firms, irrespective of competitive consequences. Prior to the fourth amendment, the provision of additional price reductions to clients, on their demand, constituted an indirect discrimination against their competitors and was thus a prohibited restriction of competition.

The Cartel Office includes within its definition of discriminatory conduct on the part of the client demands for the payment of subsidies for advertising costs, and for special discounts, reductions or bonuses (Tätigkeitsbericht 1983/4: 24ff.).

The problem of proof is apparent in proceedings to prohibit that form of discrimination which arises at the demand of the client. This explains why the Cartel Office has only reached one formal decision in the recent past, when it prohibited a large business firm from requiring that their suppliers pay them a fee to accept new products amongst the selection normally ordered and to open new branches. As this decision was not given legal force on the grounds of too restrictive a definition of the market in determining whether the firm was in fact dominant, there are still no valid precedents on the case of market discrimination by a strong client.

Any attempt to judge the legal provisions and their practical application by the Cartel Office, and by the Federal Court in the case of anti-competitive behaviour not based on contractual relations, will primarily focus upon those difficulties in providing proof which regularly crop up when distinguishing discriminatory practices from competitive actions. This applies both to the identification of discriminatory pricing on the basis of the concept of the comparable market, and to the interpretation of restrictive business strategies.

In the past, the Federal Court has valued the protection of the individual over that of competition, and consequently has a very restricted notion of abuse. Thus – as in the legal and practical treatment of anti-competitive behaviour based upon contractual relations – the protection of competition has yet to be achieved to a sufficient degree (Schmidt 1990: 248ff.).

Merger control

Prior to the introduction of merger control with the second amendment in 1973, it was possible to attain a dominant market position through mergers. From 1973, however, merger control has been subject to supervision. The law must be considered with these provisions as it contains definitions of a dominant enterprise and thus is indispensable to the examination of the merger.

Theoretical distinctions made between different types of merger give rise to different consequences when mergers are dealt with by the Cartel Office. A horizontal merger is between enterprises previously active within the same substantive and spatial market. This is the dominant form of merger, on both domestic and foreign markets. The effects are easy to identify. An increasing horizontal concentration which restricts the number of independent firms leads, once a certain limit is exceeded, to the restriction of competition.

Vertical mergers take place between buyers and sellers, that is, where one of the enterprises was active at a higher or a lower level than the other. Such mergers may improve efficiency where vertical integration leads to a reduction in transaction costs and to technical advantages. Nevertheless, they may also restrict competition where such a merger strengthens barriers to market entry, whilst a dominant market position on one economic level may be utilized, through restrictive practices and/or threats made against non-vertically integrated competitors, on other economic levels.

Mergers involving enterprises from different market sectors are referred to as conglomerates or diagonal mergers, where one firm serves a variety of markets. This and other advantages (for example, finance and advertising) increase the likelihood of cross-subsidizing, the financing of pressurizing strategies, and for reciprocal dealing (Berg 1985: 282ff.).

The Cartel Law contains a basic prohibition of all mergers between enterprises when it is assumed these will create or strengthen a dominant position. This is presumed to be the case when a large-scale producer: enters a market structured for medium-sized concerns; intends to merge with a dominant small producer; or where firms with a turnover in billions of DM merge or join together in the leading group of an oligopoly.

Mergers must be registered with the Cartel Office where the criteria laid down on the type of merger (Emmerich 1988: 337ff.) have been satisfied and where the absolute and relative criteria of the law (Article 23, para. 1) have been met. Prior to the fifth amendment in 1990 of the law these criteria included a market share of at least 20 per cent, or alternatively one thousand employees or a turnover of at least DM500 million. The amended Cartel Law (20 February 1990) dispenses with the first two criteria, leaving only the last, that of a turnover of DM500 million, to be applied.

In addition, enterprises are required to register a merger where one of the parties has a turnover of at least DM2 billion, at least two of the parties have turnovers of at least DM1 billion each. Merger control is, however, only applicable to such mergers should the 'threshold clause' cited below have been overstepped. This clause is designed to restrict the scope of merger control to mergers which may affect the entire economy. Intervention thus only occurs once those firms involved, or in some cases the market concerned, satisfies certain minimum criteria. Thus the Cartel Office will not investigate a merger if:

- the combined turnover of the firms involved, in the year prior to that merger, did not exceed DM500 million. (In the case of newspaper publishers this sum is DM25 million)
- the merger involves an independent small or medium-sized concern (the turnover must be less than DM50 million), which wishes to merge with a large-scale concern. Where the large-scale concern has a turnover in billions, the turnover of the concern to be subsumed must not exceed the maximum of DM4 million. This merger clause is not, however, applicable (per Article 24, para. 9), 'in so far as the merger [restricts] competition in the publishing, printing and distribution of newspapers and magazines'
- when the *de minimis* clause (trifling mergers) is relevant, allowing those mergers in which all those markets affected have had for at least five preceding years a total turnover in goods or services of less than DM10 million. The five-year stipulation means that markets still in a developmental stage are not excluded from merger control. This *de minimis* clause relates to those markets in which a merger occurs giving rise to or strengthening an existing dominant market position

Where a merger does not satisfy the terms of the threshold clause, the law obliges the Cartel Office to prohibit the merger where this is expected to create or strengthen an existing dominant market position (Emmerich 1988: 362). The Cartel Office will not prohibit the merger if the firms can demonstrate that it will lead to an improvement in competitive conditions such as to outweigh the disadvantages of market dominance.

As regards market dominance, in addition, the presumptive criteria to be applied only in the case of merger control must be considered. The judgement of market dominance is primarily based on long-term investigation. In addition to the consideration of market shares, a further list of particular features influence the decision of the Cartel Office. These include: the market shares of the next most powerful competitor; the distribution of other market shares; the reserve capacities of competitors; substitutional competition; as well as the existence of potential competitors. A central characteristic to feature in the decision is the financial power of the new concern. In practice, the Cartel Office deals mostly with cases where an existing dominant position is strengthened. This is because mergers generally take place only between firms who already possess market power. The prevention of the strengthening of dominance serves to protect the remaining existing competition on the market (Emmerich 1988: 369ff.). A merger may therefore be prohibited on the simple grounds that actual or potential competition will be disadvantaged.

In practice, horizontal mergers present far fewer problems than their vertical or conglomerate counterparts. In the first case, the Cartel Office largely bases its decision as to market dominance upon the market share of the firm. Recently it has also taken increased note of the financial power of the enterprise. The Cartel Office, however, has more problems in finding a basis for judgement in the case of vertical mergers. The only factor that could be investigated here is whether from the standpoint of competitors the merger has increased the room for manoeuvre of the merged concern (Emmerich 1988: 377ff.). Has it for example, increased its hold on raw material and supplementary markets, or has its defensive and aggressive potential increased? Conglomerate mergers are particularly problematic as there is little empirical evidence on which to base, first, an exact prognosis on how future market relations will develop and, second, general rules on the treatment of such mergers.

The Cartel Office must also take account of the exemption clause mentioned above, which allows the Office to weigh up the advantages and disadvantages of a merger. Three conditions must be satisfied before this clause can be applied: the merger must improve competitive conditions; there must be a causal link between the merger and any advantages; and the advantages must outweigh the disadvantages. Any such decision must, above all, take account of the impact upon competitors.

This balancing of interests hinges on whether the merger will increase competitive conditions for actual or potential competitors. A merger attracts the attention of competition law only when it leads to the creation or strengthening of market structures such as to endanger the competitive process. If the Cartel Office decides that a merger is likely to lead to the creation or strengthening of a dominant position (and the exemption clause is not applicable), it will not issue an authorization. In such situations firms may apply to the Minister of Economics for an authorization. Such authorizations may be granted on the grounds that the advantages for the entire economy outweigh the anti-competitive impact, or in individual cases where for reasons of overwhelming public interest the merger may be justified. In the past (until 1992), the Ministry of Economics has been less than generous with such authorizations: six such mergers have been authorized. Of these, four were granted in the 1970s and two in the 1980s (one being the Daimler-Benz–MBB merger). Four were subject to conditions, in comparison with the fifteen applications made under Article 24 (authorization by the Minister of Economics), and a further 101 applications were rejected by the Cartel Office (Tätigkeitsbericht 1991/2: 10).

A ministerial authorization is issued only when the general economic advantages outweigh the anti-competitive impact of the creation or strengthening of market dominance. Considerations of the public interest therefore have priority over the strict protection of competition. The federal government's concrete formulation of the public interest may take precedence over competition policy, as was the case in the 1970s, when mergers between energy producers were accepted for political reasons.

The ministerial authorization was conceived with individual cases in mind, and consequently there are no precise rules for its application. In other words, a successful competition policy may be negated by referring to the mention in the law of the need to maintain the international competitiveness of German enterprises. With this notion much of that which the Cartel Office would consider against the interests of competition may be justified. Similarly, a concern for job creation may put pressure on those with political responsibility for such decisions who may, with an eye to the electorate, issue an authorization (Herdzina 1987: 218).

In making a decision, the Minister of Economics evaluates both the advantages and disadvantages of a merger. This evaluation is based on the judgement of the Cartel Office regarding the possible anti-competitive impact, set against the possible general economic advantages. Moreover, the Monopoly Commission gives an opinion on the proposed merger which it submits to the Minister of Economics.

In cases where the Minister of Economics refuses to issue an authorization, those concerns affected have the right to contest the validity of this administrative action before the High Court. The Court, however, investigates only how exhaustive the Minister's formulation of the public interest has been (Emmerich 1988: 369).

The Daimler-Benz–MBB merger

In 1989, Daimler-Benz AG decided to purchase a majority holding of just over 50 per cent in Messerschmitt-Bölkow-Blohm (MBB). MBB were involved in the production of military technology and aircraft, and Daimler-Benz wished to restructure their entire business. Thus, in addition to a holding company, to be called Daimler-Benz AG, several subsidiaries were to be created: Mercedes-Benz were to be responsible for the lucrative private cars and industrial vehicles sector; AEG – purchased earlier – were to take charge of the electrical and electronics sector; and the restructuring would also lead to the creation of Deutsche Aerospace AG, which would incorporate MBB. As a result of the merger with MBB, Daimler-Benz AG would have control of 80 per cent of the Deutschen Airbus GmbH, which itself had a 37.9 per cent stake in the European Airbus project. With the acquisition of MBB, Daimler-Benz AG would now also play a role in the production of the highly subsidized European Airbus project. As those characteristics which triggered the duty to register were present, both firms concerned informed the Cartel Office of their intentions.

Following a comprehensive examination, the Cartel Office prohibited the merger for the following reasons:

- dominant positions would be created in the military technology and equipment for military aircraft sectors, whilst a dominant position would be strengthened in the military aircraft, helicopter, guided missile and power plant markets
- a dominant position would be created in the space technology, non-commercial orbiting and carriage systems and scientific satellite markets
- the powerful market position of Daimler-Benz in relation to the area of civilian road haulage would be greatly enhanced

The Cartel Office also examined – on the basis of the exemption clause – whether improvements in the competitiveness of civil spacecraft markets were likely to occur, and whether these would outweigh disadvantages created by the increased dominance. The Office investigated the indirect involvement of Daimler-Benz in the European Airbus industry, following which it decided that the merger would not increase the competitiveness of the European Airbus industry on the world aircraft market, and accordingly the merger was prohibited.

Daimler-Benz and MBB petitioned the Minister of Economics for a ministerial authorization. The Minister in turn commissioned an opinion from the Monopoly Commission which, after having weighed up the possible benefits to the public interest against the potential anti-competitive impact, concluded that the merger of Daimler-Benz with MBB would leave only one supplier on the German market for military production. This, in the opinion of the Office, would lead to a bilateral monopoly between the supplier, Daimler-Benz, and its client, the Ministry of Defence. Each of the monopolists would be politically dependent upon the other.

Those restrictions in competition which may arise in markets notwithstanding, and despite the possibly difficult relationship between the Ministry for Defence and Daimler-Benz in the sector of military production, the majority of the Monopoly Commission felt the merger could be allowed under certain conditions. These were an increase in benefits to the public interest and/or a reduction in particular competitive disadvantages. The majority of the Commission felt that this could be achieved with the attachment of certain conditions to the merger authorization. The majority of members felt that these conditions should include the purchase by Daimler-Benz of the outstanding stake in Deutschen Airbus, the forced sale of the military engine sector, or the exclusion from the deal of the major part of the military technology sector. The President of the Commission, Immenga, disagreed with this opinion, and refused to support it even if the Daimler-Benz were to fulfil these conditions. The majority, however, urged the Minister to authorize the merger under the terms of the conditions, whereupon Immenga promptly resigned.

On the basis of this opinion the Minister of Economics issued a conditional authorization (some military technology firms had to be sold off and the remaining 20 per cent of Deutschen Airbus purchased). The Minister justified this decision on the grounds of the overwhelming advantages to the economy and the great common interest in such a merger. The advantage was to be found in Daimler-Benz's assumption of the entrepreneurial risk in relation to the Airbus project, the state being relieved of such a hazard. The Minister pointed to the advantages arising from the combination of the air and space transport sectors and improvements in the internationally relevant area of high technology research.

Exceptions to the Cartel Law: a selective examination

The fourth section of the substantive legal provisions of the Cartel Law stipulate the limits to its applicability. A large number of economic sectors of vital importance for the entire economy are completely or partially exempt. Mostly, exemptions are from those provisions governing cartels, those dealing with individual co-operation agreements and those covering recommendations. Total exemptions are extended to sectors which, for example, exercise public-service functions and have public-service competences (Deutsche Bundesbank, Kreditanstalt für Wiederaufbau, Deutsche Bundespost). Partial exemptions are given to coal and steel producers and to those areas of agriculture and forestry regulated by several pieces of legislation. Similarly, the utilities sector, comprising electricity, gas and water, enjoys partial exemptions. The remaining areas of agriculture and forestry, together with the credit and insurance sectors, also enjoy partial exemptions.

The fifth amendment of the Cartel Law in 1990 did away with the exemption which dealt with those areas where the state regulated prices and conditions, or required that prices be authorized by the state (for example, post and telecommunications). In addition shipping and air transport in the European Community are subject only to European competition law.

The fifth amendment extensively exempted the transport sector from the jurisdiction of the most important part of the law, dealing with the invalid nature of anti-competitive contracts and agreements, and was justified on the grounds of its public-service characteristics, best guaranteed by state intervention rather than by an exclusive reliance on market forces or competition (Emmerich 1988: 422). The main reason for exemption was the fear of ruinous competition, presumed to arise where the free market holds sway in transport services.

Until the enactment of the fifth amendment, insurance and credit institutions were also exempted from the part of the law dealing with the anti-competitive nature of contracts. These provisions were not applicable to the contracts of insurers, credit institutions or their association. Firms in this sector were, however, liable to the negative supervision of the Cartel Office. This extraordinary position was traced back to a conflict between the federal government and the Bundesrat. Whilst government had desired the inclusion of this sector within the supervisory ambit of the Cartel Law, the Bundesrat (supported by vested interests) supported the total exclusion of the two industries (Schmidt 1990: 164). The representatives of the banks and insurers produced arguments to support their exemption, based above all upon the need to provide comprehensive protection for investors and insurance consumers.

As a consequence, a compromise was introduced whereby insurers and banks became subject to most of the law's provisions, but were exempted from the most important areas of the law and were required to submit to a (largely ineffective) form of negative supervision through the Cartel Office (Emmerich 1988: 249). Similarly, insurers and bankers were subject to comprehensive supervision by sectoral regulatory authorities (the Bundes-aufsichtsamt für das Versicherungswesen – insurers, and the Bundes-aufsichtsamt für Kredit- und Bausparwesen – banks) which aimed to provide for any lacking investor protection to secure the solvency of insurers (see Chapter 10 below). The fifth amendment rescinded the power of veto which these two regulatory authorities had had regarding decisions of the Cartel Office. In addition negative supervision was replaced by the prohibition principle.

In addition to those exempted sectors already dealt with, the utilities sector is similarly in receipt of significant exemptions. All other areas of the law are fully applicable. Under certain conditions, utilities enterprises may conclude demarcation, concessionary, price-fixing and co-operation contracts. (These written contracts must be registered with the Cartel Office.) The exceptional status for utilities is justified on the grounds that they constitute natural monopolies (Schmidt 1990: 164). Historically, German utilities have for many years been charactererized by a strong and inter-dependent system of monopolies. When the Cartel Law was being drafted, this exemption was regarded as a temporary measure, and in the following years federal governments made a concerted effort to re-regulate this sector. Such attempts, however, failed in the face of strong opposition from coalitions of utilities enterprises and local authorities. In 1975, federal government gave up reform plans, stating that, in its opinion, the character-istics of the utilities sector (for example, in the case of electricity, the dependence upon particular power lines and the impossibility of substitution) meant that a competitive structure was unsuited to this industry.

In the most recent amendment to the law, the introduction of a time limit for contracts protecting particular supplies in one area ensured that de-marcation contracts could no longer block a change in the supplier of utilities once a concession had expired. Competition between utilities for the control of any one area is now possible. Competition within that area, however, remains impossible.

In all cases of exemption, the exclusion of the paragraphs named above does not preclude supervision through the remaining parts of the Cartel Law. Supplementary provisions are found in each sector-specific law. Those areas with partial exemptions are liable to negative supervision by the Cartel Office.

THE FEDERAL CARTEL OFFICE

Historical and organizational features

The 1957 law envisaged the creation of a Federal Cartel Office, established in January 1959 by the Minister of Economics, Erhard. Prior to the enactment of the law, cases had been examined under the terms of the allied de-concentration provisions. With the founding of the first investigative division, the Federal Cartel Office undertook those duties accorded it by the Cartel Law, and was empowered to decide on the creation and dissolution of cartels, and applications for approval and registration.

The Office was initially staffed by seventeen lawyers and economists from the Cartel and Monopoly Office of the Ministry of Economics, later complemented by a staff of thirty-six personnel responsible for the expansion of the Office, and civil servants seconded from the public administration. In 1959–60, the number of employees rose to the point where further investigative divisions could be created (two in 1959, and two in 1960). In 1989, the Office employed about 230 persons, of whom 106 are senior civil servants (lawyers and economists), and handled a budget of DM17 million. For a clearer picture of the current organization of the Federal Cartel Office see Figure 7.1 on p. 150).

The sections of the Research Department prepare opinions on the general economic interest of a case, and monitor the activities of the investigative divisions in order to avoid discrepancies between their decisions. The potential danger that the independent decisions of the investigative departments will lead to different results in the same circumstances should be reduced with the aid of basic principles of economic science.

The Legal Department represents the Federal Cartel Office before the courts in cases of legal conflict arising out of the provisions of the Cartel Law. Moreover, it helps in the direction of the Office, providing co-ordinating and administrative services.

The examination and evaluation of the development of international competition law based on the analysis of legislation, court proceedings, the press and specialized literature is carried out by the Department for European and International Cartel Law. This is divided into three sections dealing respectively with European Cartel Law, International Competition Issues and International Merger Control (the latter deals with the topical question of merger control within the European Community).

Finally, the Administrative Department is responsible for personnel and organizational questions within the Federal Cartel Office, and for a number of external units which carry out tasks on behalf of the Office.

The Office is the decisive institution as regards the application of the 1957 Cartel Law. The Ministry of Economics and each individual *Land* Cartel Office (Landeskartellamt) has certain competences in the sphere of competition regulation.

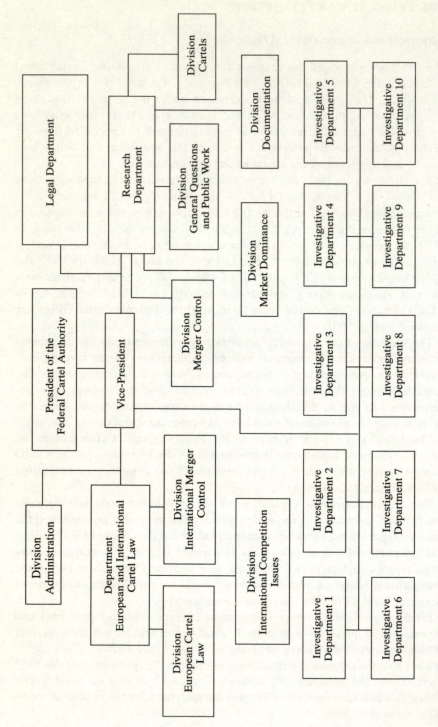

Figure 7.1 Organization of the Federal Cartel Office

The Federal Cartel Office is competent in the following instances:

- in cases of structural, export and import cartels. It can issue and revoke authorizations, impose restrictions and conditions and negative super-vision
- in cases of price-fixing contracts and recommended prices for brand-name goods
- in merger cases – here the duties of the Office include the registration of mergers and intervention in those cases where the dominant market position of the new company is strengthened
- when the impact of anti-competitive or discriminatory practices extend beyond the boundaries of a single *Land*. Thus, the *Länder* are responsible for all restrictions which do not fall under the duties of the Federal Office or the Federal Ministry of Economics. The danger that the single *Land* and the Federal government may pursue different competition policies is lessened as the Federal Cartel Office is always involved in proceedings undertaken at the *Land* level. Moreover, both *Land* cartel offices and the Federal Cartel Office are obliged to maintain reciprocal channels of information in the case of investigations or proceedings (Müller, Giessler and Scholz 1981: 289)

Where the Federal Cartel Office takes decisions within the sphere of its competences, the law gives the decisive role to the ten investigative divisions, each responsible for a particular sector (see Figure 7.1).

Investigative divisions are designed in accordance with the wishes of the Federal Minister of Economics. On average, five to six lawyers and econom-ists work in each division, directed by a chairman. In particular decisions, the law requires that a committee be constituted, comprising the chairman and two members. This body of rules which details individual competences is designed to prevent the manipulation of individual responsibilities within each division (Markert 1988: 6).

Each investigative division is bound by competence rules in both their investigations and decision-making process. There is therefore no organ-izational distinction between the investigation of a concrete case and the final decision, both being undertaken by the same division (Markert 1988: 18–19). Where the personnel of an individual investigative division does not possess the relevant skills for a particular case, additional members are co-opted from among civil servants seconded to the Federal Cartel Office. The President of the Office, on the contrary, is empowered to decide on the individual mix of personnel in each division. The President decides on the jurisdiction of the investigative divisions and is responsible in all those cases not involving competences in individual concrete proceedings cases. He or she thus represents the Cartel Office in court. The divisions are nevertheless very active in legal proceedings such as cases which come before the Berlin High Court, which mostly review the investigation and evaluation of particular facts. Finally, it falls within the competences of the President to decide whether to appeal against the Berlin High Court's decision, partially or completely overturning the direction of an investigative division, before the Federal Court in Karlsruhe.

The co-ordination of the investigative divisions, each with its own decisional competence, is of particular importance as the general administrative co-ordination is not sufficiently foolproof. As the Cartel Law does not contain explicit rules on the co-ordination of the application of the law, communication between the divisions is vitally important. A co-ordination committee, consisting of the president and vice-president and the chairmen of all the investigative divisions exists to ensure a sufficient degree of co-ordination. The conclusions which this committee reaches, although not formally binding on the individual decisions of the divisions, have in the past prevented serious discrepancies between the divisions' interpretation of individual legal concepts and the use of their discretionary powers (Markert 1988: 18–19).

The legal status of the Federal Cartel Office

The Federal Cartel Office is an independent federal agency under the supervision of the Ministry of Economics, governed by the Constitution which empowers the government to establish federal agencies in general for activities within its ambit. These agencies are placed under the supervision of the relevant federal ministry. Thus the term 'independent' extends only to the organizational independence of the agency *vis-à-vis* its ministry.

The Office is legally required to take account of the policy views of the Federal Ministry of Economics, to which it is responsible and to whose undefined power it is subject. Its activities must be in accordance with the basic principles of the competition policy of the federal government. The Federal Ministry possesses a series of powers of intervention, including the right to play a part in determining the composition of the investigative divisions and in drafting the annual Report of the Federal Cartel Office. It also issues a series of directions relating to the Cartel Office's use of its powers.

There is, nevertheless, much controversy as to whether the Ministry of Economics may direct the actions of the Cartel Office in individual cases. Some feel that the Constitution supports this (Müller, Giesser and Scholz 1981: 304–5), in so far as it requires that in addition to legal control, or the legal review of administrative conduct, each administrative act must be subject to parliamentary supervision. The Constitution would therefore contradict the notion of independence in relation to individual decisions, as in such cases the federal government would no longer be subject to parliamentary control. Consequently, it is felt that the Minister of Economics might direct the Federal Cartel Office in individual cases. This school of thought also holds that such control would extend to the investigative divisions of the Office.

Another school of thought sees the legal and factual boundaries of this right to direct in the transfer of decision-making competences from the Office to the investigative divisions (Langen *et al*. 1981: 1136–8; Markert 1988: 16ff.). The law transfers to the investigative divisions the competence to take decisions in individual cases. Accordingly, not even the chairman of an investigative division may instruct fellow committee members in individual cases. This school of thought similarly identifies further restrictions on the power of the Minister.

The principle of collegial decision-making contains a similar restriction. Thus, in relation to the decisions of the investigative divisions, there must be a limit to the power to direct decisions. Were this not the case, each individual member of the decision-making committee could be directed to reach a certain decision by the President of the Cartel Office, who might be acting in his or her own interests or those of the Minister of Economics. It follows that the Minister of Economics must recognize the quasi-judicial position of the investigative divisions. Neither the Minister nor the President of the Federal Cartel Office is allowed to influence the action of the investigative divisions in particular cases. Such divisions make decisions based on the German Cartel Law alone, and which are subject to comprehensive judicial review.

In conclusion, one may state that specific directions in ongoing cases are not admissible. One indicator of this is the quasi-judicial nature of decision-making proceedings prescribed by the law. The investigative division – in a manner reminiscent of a collegial court – decides in each case. This should guarantee an exhaustive and substantive investigation of each case (Emmerich 1988: 468). One can therefore presume that contradictory instructions issued by the Minister of Economics would have no status in any subsequent legal proceedings.

The Minister of Economics, however, may opt to use his powers to remove the investigation of a case from the competences of one particular investigative division by changing the general division of labour. He may also prohibit the carrying out of an investigation or demand that proceedings be initiated. The Minister has, however, made sparing use of these directive powers.

In summary, the likelihood of the Federal Cartel Office being directly influenced in its decisions is slight. Until the early 1990s, only one individual direction has been issued, when the Minister of Economics instructed the Cartel Office to stop investigations of the self-regulation of the mineral oil sector (Kartte 1976: 55).

In practice, in order to satisfy the principle of parliamentary control, both institutions, the Ministry and the Cartel Office, continually provide reports on the status of ongoing proceedings. In addition, the President of the Office or the deputy attends weekly meetings of the heads of department of the Ministry of Economics. The Ministry is informed in writing of any final proceedings under way at the Cartel Office.

Sanctions and legal provisions

The Federal Cartel Office has a series of legal powers of intervention. It may impose fines or prohibit actions. Moreover, sanctions, including orders to pay compensation and injunctions, may be imposed under civil law.

The law declares a series of contracts (for example, cartel and vertical price and condition-fixing contracts), and other legal relations (for example, mergers prohibited by law), to be either void or unenforceable under civil law. Civil judges have jurisdiction not only in these cases, but also in all others relating to legally prohibited conduct. In such cases, the civil courts are obliged to apply prohibitions or other legal consequences laid down in the Cartel Law. Similarly, judges have the power to demand payment of compensation and to impose injunctions.

Most of the sanctions specified in the Cartel Law are administrative legal sanctions. The Office is empowered to impose decisions on enterprises or associations of firms, including the prohibition of void or unenforceable contracts and the misuse of a dominant market position. A decision may also forbid a firm from carrying out a planned merger, or require it to discontinue a *de facto* one. Contracts may be declared unenforceable and conditions inadmissible. Conditions can be imposed on cartels and mergers, and later be discontinued should the reasons for their imposition cease to apply.

Federal Cartel Office actions may be challenged in the Berlin High Court. Disputing such an action in the first instance initially had a postponing effect. The Cartel Office was not able to pursue the action and firms were not required to abide by its decision. This would in effect have neutralized the actions of the Office, whilst firms would have been able to continue their anti-competitive conduct. Therefore, prior to the second amendment of the law, temporary injunctions were used to offset this danger. With this amendment, the postponing effect of a claim before the *Land* supreme courts or the Berlin High Court was set aside as actions of the Office are immediately binding. In all cases, however, supreme courts may suspend the Office's action until legal proceedings are complete.

As regards administrative violations, the law lists the circumstances which qualify as such and for which fines of DM1 million, or a sum equal to three times the profit made as a result of the violation, may be imposed. In practice, there have been problems in assessing profit made, and the fourth amendment therefore empowered the Cartel Office to make this calculation.

Cartel authorities responsible for a concrete case are regarded as the first instance in relation to administrative violations, and may impose a fine for an administrative violation if it is in the general interest to pursue the case. Fines may be challenged in the cartel division of the relevant *Land* supreme court. These decisions may in turn be challenged in the cartel division of the Federal Court.

In investigating the substantive facts of a case, the responsible investigative division first decides upon the composition of those investigative competences which it possesses. Administrative proceedings generally start with an informal investigation. A formal investigation takes place where the informal request is refused or where there are doubts about the accuracy of the information provided. In contrast, administrative violations start with formal investigative proceedings, which may for example include the examination of business premises.

The investigative division may examine the files of a business only with the agreement of the President of the Federal Cartel Office. The department will suspend proceedings should the investigation find no proof of an abuse, or should there be no public interest in further action. If, however, the department feels that there are sufficient grounds for it to take action, it must give the firms involved the opportunity to state their view. This refers particularly to those affected by the action of the Office. In general, such persons are provided with a written copy of the content of the decision and the substantive and legal justifications for the action. Those affected are also entitled to examine files relating to the proceedings. The department must deliver its decision, together with a justification, to those affected by it.

CONCLUSION

The first draft of the 1958 German Cartel Law not only lacked any form of merger control but also contained many loopholes in the form of exemptions. The first two amendments to the law increased the number of exemptions in favour of SMEs and introduced merger control. The final three amendments focused on the intensification of the negative supervision of dominant enterprises and improvements in the protection of SMEs, and tightened up provisions regarding exempted sectors.

The Federal Cartel Office, as an independent federal agency, applies the law. The decisions of its ten investigative divisions, whose competences are determined by the Federal Minister of Economics, cannot be disputed by either the President of the Office or the Minister of Economics, and the latter has the power only to direct the general actions of the Federal Cartel Office.

The basic philosophy of the German Cartel Law follows the American pattern, namely that free competition is in the public interest. The law enumerates the types of restraints on competition which can be prohibited by the Federal Cartel Office. Furthermore, the exemptions of the law are mainly driven by the desire to strengthen competition. However, the Minister may allow cartels and mergers in spite of a negative decision by the Cartel Office if there is an overwhelming public interest. This is the only exemption from the basic principle of the law to safeguard free competition.

In judging the efficiency of the German Cartel Law, one should consider not only the large number of exemptions, but also the practical actions of the Federal Cartel Office, the Federal Court and the Minister of Economics. In particular, the difficulties experienced by the Office in gathering proof on the abusive manipulation of prices or conditions led the Federal Court to overturn many of the Office's decisions. The result has been a virtual protection of firms using anti-competitive practices, instead of the protection of competition in general. If one considers all exemptions from the prohibition of mergers and cartels granted by the Minister of Economics, one is led to the conclusion that they deal almost exclusively with large firms. Clearly, such exemptions are driven by political considerations, mainly the protection of domestic employment, rather than by general efficiency considerations.

REFERENCES

Berg, H. (1985) 'Wettbewerbspolitik', in Bender (ed.) *Vahlens Kompendium der Wirtschaftstheorie und Wirtschaftspolitik*, vol. 2, Munich: Vahlen.

Emmerich, V. (1988) *Kartellrecht* (5th edition), Munich: Beck.

Herdzina, K. (1987) *Wettbewerbspolitik* (2nd edition), Stuttgart: Fischer.

Jäckering, W. (1977) *Die politischen Auseinandersetzungen um die Novellierung des Gesetzes gegen Wettbewerbeschränkung (GWB)*, Berlin: Duncker & Humblot.

Kartte, W. (1969) 'Ein neues Leitbild für die Wettbewerbspolitik', in *FIW–Schriftenreihe*, vol. 49, Cologne: Heymann.

Kartte, W. (1976) 'Wettbewerbspolitik im Spannungsfeld zwischen Bundeswirtschaftsministerium und Bundeskartellamt', in Gutzler, Herion and Kaiser (eds) *Wettbewerb im Wandel*, Baden-Baden: Nomos.

Kartte, W. and Holtschneider, R. (1981) 'Konzeptionelle Ansätze und Anwendungsprinzipien in Gesetz zur Wettbewerbsbeschränkungen–Zur Geschichte des GWB', in Cox, Markert and Jens (eds) *Handbuch des Wettbewerbs*, Munich: Vahlen.

Langen, E., Niederleithinge, E., Rittner, L. and Schmidt, U. (1981) *Kommentar zum Kartellgesetz* (6th edition), Neuwied-Darmstadt: Luchterhand.

McGowan, L. (1993) 'The evolution of German competition policy – the Bundeskartellamt, its role and competence', RUSEL Working Paper no. 14, University of Exeter: Research Unit for the Study of Economic Liberalization and its Social and Political Implications.

Markert, K. (1988) 'Die Rolle des Bundeskartellamtes bei der Durchsetzung des Wettbewerbsrechts in der Bundesrepublik Deutschland', in Blaurock (ed.) *Institutionen und Grundfragen des Wettbewerbsrecht*, Frankfurt: Metzner.

Müller, H., Giesser, P. and Scholtz, U. (1981) *Kommentar zum Gesetz gegen Wettbewerbsbeschränkungen, Kartellgesetz* (4th edition), vol. 2, Frankfurt: Deutscher Fachverlag.

Rittner, F. (1989) *Wettbewerbs- und Kartellrecht: Eine systematische Darstellung für Studium und Praxis* (3rd edition), Heidelberg: Müller.

Robert, R. (1976) *Konzentrationspolitik in der Bundesrepublik – Das Beispiel der Entstehung des Gesetzes gegen Wettbewerbsbeschränkungen*, Berlin: Duncker & Humblot.

Schmidt, I. (1990) *Wettbewerbspolitik und Kartellrecht* (3rd edition), Stuttgart: Fischer.

Sturm, R. and Ortwein, E. (1993) 'The normative and legal framework of German competition policy – a political science perspective', RUSEL Working Paper no. 15, University of Exeter: Research Unit for the Study of Economic Liberalization and its Social and Political Implications.

Tätigkeitsbericht (various years) *Annual Report of the Bundeskartellamt*, Berlin: Bundestagesdrucksache.

WuW (various years) *Wirtschaft und Wettbewerb – Zeitschrift für Kartellrecht, Wettbewerbsrecht, Marktorganisation*, Düsseldorf: Handelsblatt GmbH.

8 Independent administrative authorities in France and the case of the French Council for Competition

Fabrice Demarigny

Two factors have helped reduce the economic powers of the state built up during the Second World War: the internationalization of the economy; and the need for enterprises to develop more flexible strategies. In France the end of the Gaullist era witnessed the birth of new institutions which transcended the classical demarcation between public and private spheres, and occupied a position mid-way between the centralized administration of the state and civil society.

French independent administrative authorities have been created in those areas of extreme sensitivity, where the intervention of the state is vital in order for the latter to establish control and effectively exercise its regulatory duties. At the same time, however, direct state intervention in such spheres constitutes a potential threat to civil and economic liberties. The installation of intermediary institutions is a measure which helps overcome this apparent contradiction and which reconciles these two viewpoints.

The interposition of more neutral and objective bodies between the state and civil society is to avoid the situation whereby the intervention of one leads to the alienation of the other, so that:

> Independent administrative authorities ... are an instrument of state action in that they direct civil society, but at the same time they open the door of state structures to civil society. They clearly straddle the line of demarcation between the private and the public. ... their unequivocal insertion into the public sphere creates a fixed demarcation between that sphere and the private domain and prevents a true osmosis between the two.
>
> (Chevalier 1986: 7)

This general reflection perhaps does not apply to all independent administrative authorities and there must be variations in the mode of their operation owing to their relative ages. Some have slowly but surely confirmed their role and become institutionalized, whilst others have never attained this status.

This chapter deals in turn with the emergence of new forms of regulation in the shape of independent administrative authorities, with particular reference to three sectors: information and communication; citizens and their relations with the public administration; and the economic and financial sector. Finally, in order to illustrate the process of affirmation of this type of institution – mid-way between the state and civil society – we will focus on one of the most important administrative authorities in the economic and financial sector which has been responsible for the control of competition since 1953, and the way in which it has secured its own 'reserved domain' within the general area of public regulation of the economy, that is, the Council for Competition (Conseil de la Concurrence).

A NEW FORM OF REGULATION

Built upon the ruins of the welfare state?

Two ideas gave birth to independent administrative authorities in France. The first was the rediscovery of the central importance accorded to the judiciary in the classical tripartite apparatus of state powers. In addition to being a means whereby power might be exercised, the state is an arena for the resolution of conflicts between economic and social interests; it is also the forum for the administration of justice, the reformulation of state tasks, and, as a consequence, the reform of administrative institutions. The second idea is the re-evaluation of the economic functions of the state amidst the ruins of the welfare state. As the grand theories of the state and the neoclassical and Keynesian techniques of control broke down under the pressure of economic complexity, the concept of a less ambitious and less comprehensive role of technical arbitration was to emerge hand-in-hand with that of a more modest state (Mény and Thoenig 1989: 25–199; Rosanvallon 1990: 243–80).

If the state no longer sees itself as the unique locus of power, administrative pragmatism re-emerges as a determining force. The diminishing ardour with which the aims of successive national 'plans' were pursued opened up the field for the 'prudence of the wise'. In other words, different perceptions, linked with practical knowledge and experience, were not slow to secure for themselves a visible place within the administrative structures and in the way in which power was exercised.

As Winckler (1988: 76–86) explained, the development of independent authorities was accompanied and favoured by the decline of the dominant postwar theories of political economy: planning, industrial and financial policy, and the centralized and contractual management of economic production.

One must, however, take care not to establish too close an inverse causal link between these two movements. The American example indeed contradicts such an approach. Thus, the most important regulatory agencies did not see the light of day, as in France, as a result of an 'excess of state apparatus'. Quite the reverse: they were born out of a crisis of *laissez-faire* liberalism. Some of the great American independent agencies emerged with the New Deal – that is, in the context of an intense period of government intervention in the wake of the Depression – and were part of that same movement which gave birth to the concept of the American welfare state.

The obsolescence of French national planning

Chronologically, the Technical Commission for Co-operation Agreements and Dominant Positions (La Commission Technique des Ententes et des Positions Dominantes) was born in 1953 towards the end of the period of the system of national planning, initiated by Jean Monnet. The Commission's judicial approach gained in importance as the importance of national planning declined. In the 1970s, the first revival of a competition authority was accompanied by a further decline in the substantive notion of planning. Lastly, the establishment of an effective Council for Competition in 1986 followed the final attempt to reactivate national planning by the first socialist government in 1981.

We shall see that the decline of the 'Plan' was accompanied by the successive failures of the great programmes of industrial policy of the 1970s, such as the Plan Calcul (Zysman 1983), and of the sectoral policies of the early 1980s, as well as the closure of large-scale iron and steel production plants and the dockyards. These grand designs were unable to adapt themselves to the ever increasing complexity of markets, now open to international competition.

In addition, since the 1970s France has witnessed the progressive dissolution of traditional corporatist structures in the economy. It is evident that the system of national planning had favoured the emergence of this form of concerted regulation, and as a consequence had exposed itself to the power demands of corporatist organizations. The plan had supported the proliferation of sectors protected from competition and structured as reserved domains. In effect, it had created a dense tissue of interdependence between sectoral associations and the state. This final factor was augmented by rigorous political control of prices. Concerted intervention, however, was unable to overcome chronic inadequacies in resource allocation and only aggravated market disfunctions.

This situation was upset by several factors. The expansion of the competitive sector, which was increasingly exposed to international competition, the entry of France into a European Community concerned with the free movement of goods and services, and the difficulties encountered by the corporatist system in the face of crises, prompted the relaunching of the debate on the mode of economic regulation to be employed by the state.

It is true that France increasingly had no choice but to opt for the free market system. During the 1980s a conception of a different form of state intervention emerged which combined the pragmatic need to escape from a sharp juxtaposition of state versus market with the need for a more modest form of state (Crozier 1987).

A change in the source of initiative

The appearance of intermediary institutions represents the practical translation of this conceptual change in approach to the role of the state. In reality,
the greatest upheaval of the two preceding decades had been the relocation
of the source of initiative. During the finest hours of the 'Plan', initiative
was in the hands of the state, or, more precisely phrased, in those of the
'guardian state'. Since that time, the market had rediscovered its rights and
the initiative had passed back into its domain. The state was to intervene
solely as a regulator of a market which referred only to itself. The state was
now to play the part of arbitrator and regulator, and not that of entrepreneur
or economic actor.

In addition, however, as Minc (1990: 185–93) has argued, the state no
longer appears able to execute its role, either alone or directly. Increasingly,
independent commissions and agencies have come into being which are
no longer imprisoned within traditional notions of sovereign functions.
Such bodies have an autonomous status and are increasingly being brought
within the sphere of judicial review. The decisions made by these semi-
administrative, semi-judicial, intermediary institutions play the role of
signals given to the market rather than edicts handed down from above.

Additionally, and as a direct consequence of their greater flexibility, such
intermediary institutions are better placed to comprehend the increasing
complexity of the market – a market upon which the state is no longer able
to impose its will, and to which it appears that the courts do not possess the
technical competences necessary to regulate it. Specialization inexorably
imposes itself upon society.

This evolution is without doubt gradual. The state is beginning to admit a
reduction in its role, either because it realizes the risks of political interference, or because of a willingness to refer to authorities less likely to be
contested than itself. This involves an extraordinary admission as 'the state'
has now recognized that it does not always possess sufficient credibility and
that certain persons or institutions are better equipped to resolve conflict.

To take an example from outside the economic sphere, the National
Committee of Ethics, comprised of prestigious medical researchers, members
of the clergy, moral philosophers and senior civil servants, determines the
allowable limits to be placed upon genetic technology. Whilst the Committee
has no formal place within the general administration (the final word in such
matters rests with the law), it does have practical authority because of its
moral weight. With this, the state has recognized that morality and ethics do
not lie within its domain and that it cannot determine such principles with
the same degree of assurance with which its sets, for example, motorway
speed limits.

As this example suggests, it is striking that it is often the extremely
sensitive character of the issue at hand which leads the state to delegate. This
might concern the extreme moral sensitivity inherent in medical affairs, the

political sensitivities regarding the freedom of information, cultural and political sensibilities in the area of radio and television broadcasting or, lastly, the sensitivity of market valuations in the sphere of economics or finance. In France, as we shall see in our case study, whilst the state transfers its powers in a very gradual manner, it simultaneously attempts to ensure that powers thus abandoned will continue to lie somewhere within its sphere of influence. The way in which the members of the new independent administrative authorities are appointed, the definition of their powers, the allocation of their human and financial resources, still leave the executive power a considerable margin of influence, which is, however, difficult to define precisely.

In addition and in stark contrast to the American example, some of these bodies do not come under the authority of Parliament, nor are they answerable to it. Today, their composition does not require the approval of the National Assembly, which would usually, in the case of rule-setting organizations, seem to be the most natural procedure.

Clearly, these independent administrative authorities were initially set up as auxiliaries to state power. There is, however, no doubt that these authorities are developing a life of their own, and as a consequence desire full recognition of their independent existence in order that they might fully enter into their roles.

Finally, the expansion of these intermediary institutions is in part due to the increasing recognition of the role of the Constitutional Council. This Council, introduced by the Constitution of 1958, was originally conceived as a functional organ, responsible for the technical monitoring of the respective domains of the legislative and executive powers (Stone 1992). There was no intention to usher in the development of a legal order superior to Parliament. In 1971, a Council decision which rejected a bill dealing with associations was to alter its role radically and opened up an immense sphere of competence for itself, which it has occupied ever since. The extension of the range of those cases in which the Council might give judgement enabled the Council to escape from its original quasi-administrative role. Thus, for the first time an institution independent of the executive power possesses legitimate force and may enforce its rules. This legitimacy is in essence based upon 'wisdom'. In the same way but at a more modest level, the independent bodies take their inspiration from the example of the Constitutional Council in order to establish their legitimacy and explicate their activity in the framework of a more modest state.

A new separation of powers?

Gentôt (1991: 41–5), puts forward a different explanation for the rapid development of independent administrative authorities. He argues that this is due not to the inability of the administration to manage economic and social change, but to the existence of a new form of the separation of powers within the administration itself. A distinction is to be made between the function of the formulation of impersonal norms (preparation of bills and regulations), true executive functions (the application of norms in particular cases) and the arbitration of disputes (litigation and administrative adjudication). He notes that there are few organic links between these different functions and as a consequence, a consistent adaptation to changing situations has been impeded. All too often, purely legal conceptions determine the definition of the meaning of a norm while the efficacy of the administrative law suffers as a result of excessive delays in the settlement of cases. Similarly, the ability of the state and its agents to formulate the general interest, to extricate themselves from the dominance of political power and to free themselves from the clutches of a technocracy which is less than fully understanding of the daily lives of citizens, are all greatly hindered.

In order to remedy this situation, the argument goes, the state has created intermediary institutions. Such institutions perform tasks which are an extension of each of these three functions – rule-setting, execution and adjudication – independent of, but co-existing alongside, the central adminis-tration and hierarchy.

The other striking feature of these administrative authorities is the extensive publicity given to their regulatory activities, which is in stark contrast to the marked preference of the administration for secrecy.

In addition, they constitute instances in which disputes may be debated and which, by virtue of their collegial mode of operation and composition and competences, form a part of the general political equilibrium, often including the representation of the affected interests.

We will now turn to a more concrete description of the true place of the independent administrative authorities. This situation transcends the classical demarcation between the public and private domains of power and decision-making.

The duality of the independent administrative authorities

In France, as elsewhere, the economic and political debate has traditionally maintained a strict division between the public and private sectors. This distinction was based upon three differentiations. The first of these was wholly symbolic in nature, and juxtaposes a public sphere which embodies the 'general interest', against a private domain made up of individual or particularistic interests. The second differentiation is a legal one, and follows from the first – that is, the application of particular rules peculiar to the public sector, and of derogations from the rules of private law. The third and final distinction is organic – the state is conceived of as a structure and entity with relatively well defined contours operating according to a sole tenet, namely, the public interest. The decisional autonomy and coherence of this public domain are guaranteed by its unitary structure.

From the practical point of view, this Weberian perspective of the unitary state is guaranteed by powerful hierarchical structures, which are themselves based upon various relations of subordination and notions of tutelage. Ideally, this scheme should be centralized. We have nevertheless witnessed the appearance of new institutions, situated outside the hierarchy, which are able to evade the hierarchical chain of command and, increasingly, of state control. Such institutions have similarly conquered for themselves a sphere of free action, also protected by the law. The arrival of these independent administrative authorities, which have blurred the neat distinctions between public and private, is not, as we have seen, merely a chance development. This new symbolic, legal and organic category is, however, difficult to characterize given the wide range of situations in which it arises, and the non-homogeneous nature of the functions of these institutions.

According to Chevalier (1986), two distinct formulations can be identified: the first offers a definition of true independent administrative agencies, strictly limited to those which exercise a real decision-making power and which have been accorded some measure of independence, guaranteed by precise and clear rules on their composition; the second possible definition is wider as it conceives of the notion of a regulatory agency in a more extensive manner (which concerns the exertion of moral authority or a power of influence upon certain decisional procedures). This is based upon less constraining legal categories (decision, recommendation or simple advice), in which case the rules governing its internal organization are less rigorously formulated and often very varied. One might cite seven or eight French independent administrative authorities as falling into the first category, and more than twenty in the second.

Whatever the reason, it is clear that this rapid expansion of independent administrative authorities reflects a new approach to the relations between the state and civil society. Today, these authorities are present in three areas of regulation: information and communication; relations between the administration and addressees of its action and protection against bureaucratic excesses; and economic and financial activities.

Independent administrative authorities in the sector of information and communication

The creation of a commission to control the sphere of information and communication is based on the principle that all individuals have the right to full information across the spectrum of opinion. This information must not be falsified and must be freely produced according to certain ground rules. Respect for these simple principles, which have been clearly enunciated only recently, is guaranteed by certain specific institutions.

The High Council for Broadcasting (Le Conseil Supérieur de l'Audio-visuel), first established in 1981, is responsible for matters of radio and television broadcasting, while the High Council of the official press agency, France-Presse, founded in 1957, and the Joint Representative Commission for Publications and Press Agencies (La Commission Paritaire des Publications et des Agences de Presse), dating from 1950, are responsible for the press. Similarly, it has become necessary to verify the quality of that information indispensable to the proper functioning of democracy, and this is done by the Opinion Polls Commission (Commission des Sondages), set up in 1971, the Commission for Financial Transparency in Political Affairs (La Commission de la Transparence Financière de la Vie Politique), and the National Commission for the Regulation of Campaign Contributions (La Commission Nationale des Comptes de Campagne), which date from 1991.

Without going into too much detail, I will present a closer examination of certain aspects of the life of one of the most important independent administrative authorities in this area in order to provide a concrete example of the problems faced by such institutions.

For a long time, the use of broadcasting means of communication was under the control, and even the direct influence, of governmental authority, and for a long period the state had a monopoly of the use of the airwaves. The management of this monopoly was conferred upon a single body, which in 1964 was named the French Office for Radiobroadcasting and Television (Office de Radiodiffusion et Télévision Français). In 1974 this office split into seven independent offices in competition with each other. Eventually, the state was to cede this monopoly and allow the co-existence, in the area of radio as well as in that of television, of a public and a private sector. In these circumstances a decision was taken in 1981, following the victory of François Mitterand in the presidential elections, to 'install an intermediary body between government and the operators, designed to prevent any direct relations and similarly to end the traditional context of dependence' (Chevalier 1989). The High Authority for Broadcasting Communications (La Haute Autorité de la Communication Audiovisuelle) was thus founded.

As Gentôt (1991: 119–25) has stressed, however, these institutions were quickly paralysed by their lack of competences and enforcement powers, and their consequent inability to force private operators to respect the assignment of radio frequencies or the allocation of private network television channels. Likewise, the large degree of consensus which had initially given them force did not survive the political changes following the 1986 elections. The government of J. Chirac requested its new parliamentary majority to replace this 'too partisan to the state' model, with a new more 'liberal' authority, the National Commission for Communication and Liberties (La Commission Nationale de la Communication et des Libertés, CNCL).

Nevertheless, and despite the improvements which it was able to secure, the CNCL was unable to deflect political criticism and was to suffer badly from the effects of a declaration made by the President of the Republic to the weekly *Le Point*, during his campaign for re-election. François Mitterand declared that 'the CNCL has to date done nothing which might merit that sentiment which we term respect'. Following his re-election he was to modify the law and create a new body, the High Council for Broadcasting (Conseil Supérieur de l'Audiovisuel, CSA).

The new government supported the idea of providing constitutional protection for the independent authority in order to insulate it from political pressures. The requisite degree of political consensus in Parliament, however, is likely to be insufficient to secure for the authority this privileged status. For instance, the way in which its members are appointed is identical to that of the defunct High Council. All members are nominated by the three principal political authorities: the President of the Republic; the National Assembly; and the Senate. Similarly, the CSA appears to have fewer powers at its disposal than the CNCL and its general governing principles emanate, through the law, from the government.

The example of the traditionally politically sensitive area of broadcasting demonstrates the difficulty of firmly installing an independent institution in a world where the temptation to exercise control is strong, particularly where successive bodies of this type lack a clear definition of themselves. Quite apart from this, it is clear that for well over a decade the need has generally been recognized for some form of independent public regulation of an activity that cannot be completely left to the logic of the market.

Independent administrative authorities regulating relations between the citizen and the public administration

In another sensitive area, that of the regulation of relations between the public administration and those under its jurisdiction, intermediary institutions were created partly to diffuse the power of interest groups, and in part to combat the dominance of political power.

Thus 1978 saw the creation of the already mentioned National Commission for Information and Civil Liberties (La Commission Nationale de l'Informatique et des Libértes, CNIL), to preserve transparency in the use of files containing information in accordance with fundamental civil liberties. The same year witnessed the founding of the Commission for Access to Administrative Documents (La Commission d'Accès aux Documents Administratifs, CADA). This second body was initially to give decisive impetus to the movement towards administrative transparency in conferring on all individuals the right to obtain documents of an administrative character, and ever more frequently so by informing the citizens about the existence of certain documents which it then makes available. Although there is no formally defined 'informational' jurisdiction, the 12,000 suggestions and recommendations which the latter body has made constitute a veritable body of 'case law' in this area.

Likewise, two other bodies were created. In 1977, the Commission for Fiscal Information (La Commission des Informations Fiscales), was founded with a view to providing certain procedural safeguards and to limit arbitrary use of the powers of the tax authority in criminal sanctions. The second, the

National Commission for the Control of Security Interceptions (La Commission Nationale de Contrôle des Interceptions de Sécurité), was given a pivotal role in the regulation of 'electronic eavesdropping' in 1991, when the regime was for the first time organized on a solid legal basis.

Finally, the Ombudsman (Le Médiateur de la République) was installed as an independent authority by Article 69 of the Law of the 13 January 1989. It is important to note the absence of the term 'administrative' because, as Lagatte stated in his report of April 1990 on the Ombudsman, 'such a qualification is incompatible with the exercise of a mission which demands total independence from the administration' (cited in Gentôt 1991: 142).

The Ombudsman is responsible by law for the remedy of those disfunctions in the administration which are reported to him. He is required in such cases to make recommendations which appear to him to be best suited to regulate the difficulties he has identified. Alternately, he might propose ways in which the effects of the actions of the organization concerned might be ameliorated. He is not merely to be satisfied with the purely legal responses of institutions to his recommendations, and might also intervene in equity by imposing any restrictions which seem to him to be opportune (in other words he might require an administrative body to depart from the letter of the text, which it is generally constrained to implement). Of all the independent authorities, the Ombudsman is without doubt the one which deals with the greatest number of cases: in 1990, 23,000 complaints were received and twenty-two reforms proposed.

Administrative authorities in the economic and financial sector

Finally, the third category of independent administrative authorities comprises those institutions which have as their object the regulation of economic and financial activities. Increasing freedom in financial and commercial transactions has necessitated the intensified regulation of such activities and the creation of a form of supervision better adapted to market realities. These new institutions facilitate the protection of investors, shareholders, depositors, the insured and consumers.

For this reason the Stock Exchange Commission (La Commission des Opérations de Bourse, COB) was created in 1967. It was, however, 1989 before this body gained any concrete powers. Its principal objectives are: first, to improve the dissemination of high-quality financial information; second, to safeguard the transparent functioning of the market; third, to safeguard public interests; and finally, to sanction transgressions of the norms of transparency and fairness in the market, on the basis of its rules. Its independence is guaranteed by the manner of the appointment of its President and board members and by its financial autonomy.

In common with all the other authorities, the Stock Exchange Commission formulates recommendations. In addition, however, it exercises an extremely original power, that of advising market actors who ask its opinion whether the operation which they envisage performing conforms to its rules. The communication differs from a simple suggestion or advice because it implies that the Commission will check whether those targeted have in fact and in good faith respected the rules.

The need to regulate the activities of banks, and thus to offer guarantees to depositors, prompted the creation of the very first independent administrative authority, the Commission for the Control of Banks (La Commission de Contrôle des Banques) in 1941. The banking law of 1984 redistributed banking regulation functions and created the Banking Commission (Commission Bancaire), which inherited a part of the earlier authority's attributions.

The Banking Commission is responsible for ensuring that credit institutions abide by those legislative and regulatory provisions applicable to them and with sanctioning any offences committed. Similarly, the Commission exercises extensive oversight with regard to the respect of the professional rules of good conduct. Its general duties of regulation and control are exercised with reference to its character as an administrative authority. In relation to any possible breaches, however, it is allowed to take on state responsibilities. The Commission is nevertheless less concerned with applying sanctions than with formulating measures which might redress such situations, and with preventing the occurrence of any circumstances which endanger the interests of depositors. In a word, it safeguards the solvency of credit institutions.

Finally, one of the most important administrative authorities in the economic and financial sector is the Council for Competition, which we will now examine.

THE COUNCIL FOR COMPETITION

The staking-out of a reserved domain

The present Council for Competition (Conseil de la Concurrence) witnessed an extension of its powers with the Regulation of 1 December 1986. Nevertheless, certain domains remain the competence of the executive, and to date there has been only a partial attainment of the balance necessary to ensure the effective functioning of an independent administrative authority.

The increase in the power of the Council for Competition falls into three distinct phases. The first found its origins in the 1953 Law on Agreements. The second, which for the first time was to see the installment of an independent administrative authority, did not commence until 1977, at the very end of the Gaullist period. The third era is that of the present Council for Competition, instituted by the law of 1 December 1986.

The beginnings

The process of the evolution of a legal competence to regulate relations between economic operators, as well as the abuse of a dominant market position, dates from the 1810 Chapelier Law prohibiting guilds and any other type of associations. Its greatest impetus, however, derives from the 1945 law on price fixing (modified many times). All these texts, however, and the mode of their application relate almost exclusively to the state's role as an economic police officer. The inspiration for them lies in times of shortage, crisis and fear of inflation. Their principal objective was to prevent possible speculation, or the concentration of economic power in a very few hands. The period of development, however, which followed on from the first era of shortages, increasingly led the state to withdraw from its role as police officer on the basis of pricing. For this reason the need for a new type of authority, following new procedures, emerged as an issue.

Chronologically, the power of the centralized state was transferred to a 'satellite' authority in two stages in the wake of a long period of uncertainty, beginning in 1945. From 1953 onwards the state was to make a distinction between its policing powers (investigation and sanctions), which were exercised by the Pricing Office (Direction des Prix) of the Ministry for Economics and Finance, and its functions of economic analysis. A Commission for Agreements was created. It was, however, merely a consultative body.

As stressed by Dumez and Jeunemaître (1991: 74), this move was very timid. This was due to the fact that at the heart of French tradition lay the perception that agreement or collaboration between enterprises was altogether positive. This was particularly the case if such agreements were designed to protect French firms against foreign competition. The 1953 Law did not impose a blanket prohibition on such agreements, but instead preferred to subject them to the so-called 'economic balance' procedure (*bilan économique*). In other words, if an agreement were found to exist, the enterprises concerned would be required to show that the result of the agreement was to the economic benefit of consumers or the economy at large. Put another way, they were compelled to prove that the agreement served economic progress.

As Winckler (1988: 76–86) points out, this was the basis upon which the Commission was to exceed its simple role as adviser to government, as it fell to this administrative body to judge upon the character of any possible harmful restrictions of competition.

In addition, a double movement took shape which in certain respects heralded the reforms to come. Primarily, the technical 'advice' given by the Commission became so precise and so decisive that the initial distinction drawn between an administrative decision-making authority and a 'consultative' council rapidly lost any meaning. Second, the rapid growth in the commercial sector was not only to make the political process of decision-making more difficult, but was above all to upset the effective application of sanctions. In effect, this satellite authority constituted a perfect means whereby the state might disengage itself from delicate arbitrational tasks.

Laying the foundations

It was in 1977 (Law of 19 July 1977), owing to the impetus of Raymond Barre, that the authority responsible for the regulation of competition was able to conquer the domain previously reserved to the administration. It was an independent administrative authority to the extent that it was equipped with sufficient powers to escape from the structure of the administrative hierarchy. It had its own personnel, the ability to initiate cases independently from the administration, the power to set up adversarial proceedings and, in some cases, the power to take effective decisions.

Dumez and Jeunemaître (1991: 77–83) have highlighted the most decisive innovations incorporated within the Commission for Competition. The Minister for Economics was no longer the sole person possessing the power to call the Commission into action. From 1977, producer or consumer organizations were free to petition the Commission directly. Even more significantly, the Commission itself had the power to act. This last power was, by virtue of the weak powers assigned to the Commission, a symbolic gesture more than anything else, but nevertheless represented considerable progress.

The same law also authorized the Commission to propose that the Minister should issue injunctions against agreements already under way. It was to be for the Commission to impose amendments on agreements, to promulgate precise decisions taken against firms and to publish such decisions. That the final decision lay with the Minister was evidently a restriction; the Commission was not allowed to impose penalties.

The legislature had restricted the power of this body to prevent it from rivalling the central administration. The procedures were carefully designed to avoid any danger of this. The provision did not require firms contemplating a merger to inform the Commission. If they were to omit to do this, however, they would run the risk of an *ex post* examination which might, in turn, lead to the break-up of the completed merger. In contrast, if they did inform the Commission of the proposed merger, and it were judged acceptable, they would benefit from a form of absolute judicial guarantee. As Dumez and Jeunemaître (1991: 79–80) have stressed, the system provided incentives for all firms proposing a merger to inform themselves on the content of the law and to correct any potential violations. In effect, if there were such a risk it was to be expected that the firms concerned would decisively opt for 'judicial security'. It was therefore likely that, even in the absence of a formal obligation to do so, only those operations which posed a risk would be notified to the Commission, whilst the overwhelming majority, which posed no risk, would not burden the system. The only possible dangers in this mechanism were those financial and economic difficulties which might arise during such an *a posteriori* breaking up of a merged enterprise. In nine years of existence, however, this occurred only once, and the decision was subsequently annulled by the State Council (Conseil d'Etat).

The French thus chose a 'soft' institution, which was not to be staffed by civil servants. It was instead to comprise business people and a law professor, and was to be presided over by an extremely neutral State Counsellor (Conseiller d'Etat). The absence of economists is striking. This was not the first time that France appeared to be happy with this form of exclusion, inspired by the example of Clemenceau who had declared in relation to the army that: 'war is too serious a matter to be assigned to the military'. Within the Council for Competition, economists were victims of such a form of scepticism.

This Commission nevertheless was more successful than its creators had ever imagined. This was largely due to the nomination of two economists as rapporteurs. As the members of the Commission were often occupied with other functions, the position and influence of the rapporteurs became increasingly decisive. Even though the rapporteurs had no decision-making power of their own, it was their conception of the 'politics of competition' which played a fundamental role in the slow but steady process of legitimizing competition policy in France.

One of these men, the Rapporteur Général, Fréderic Jenny (1990: 74), has distinguished three main themes in the 1977 law which have led to a reinforcement of the competition control mechanism. First the law represented a complete break with the kind of industrial policies encouraged under Gaullism which were based on the notion that the extreme concentration of firms allowed the maximization of efficiency and competitiveness. Abandoning this philosophy, the 1977 law placed the concept of free competition at the very foundation of economic policy. In other words, it re-established the idea that the greater the number of firms, the greater the level of economic efficiency. In addition, this law favoured acceptance of the notion that vertical concentration which limits free competition has negative consequences for economic welfare.

Second, the Minister of Economics was empowered to impose administrative sanctions of up to 5 per cent of the current turnover of a firm, or 5 million francs for non-firm participants to anti-competitive practices.

Finally, the powers of the Commission to instigate proceedings against firms were extended.

Although these powers constituted a great improvement on the earlier law, Jenny has nevertheless detected certain weaknesses which harmed the efficacy of the structure put in place by the 1977 law.

The main weakness was clearly the placing of the final decision-making power in the hands of the Minister for Economics. Once the Commission had undertaken an economic analysis and had measured the effects upon competition, it formulated a recommendation upon the sanctions which the Minister might impose. Firms, however, retained the right to defend their position before the Minister, who similarly retained the right to agree to a reduction of the penalty imposed.

As a result, the dissuasive effects of the procedure were to lose their force.

The Commission itself was to exercise a degree of self-censure in the levying of sanctions proposed in order to render its recommendations more acceptable from the political point of view. Additionally, the notion of arbitration was inevitably to become prominent in the final treatment of cases submitted to the Commission for consideration.

From the point of view of sanctions, the final decisions tended to depend more on the institutional weight of the firms concerned than on the seriousness of the offences committed. Finally, the central role of the Minister for Economics in the matter of the repression of anti-competitive practices, especially as the latter is responsible for price regulation, gave rise to a political impression that competition policies were merely a supplement to price control, which they were in fact supposed to replace.

These shortcomings were accentuated with the increase in the number of cases which the Commission was called upon to judge. It was only in 1986 when a new law was introduced, prompted by far more liberal considerations, which led to the partial easing of such difficulties.

The present Council for Competition

The Regulation of 1 December 1986 transferred the decision-making power in cases of anti-competitive practices to the Council for Competition, an independent body with powers greater than those possessed by the Commission for Competition. If the birth of the Commission marked a rupture with traditional industrial policy in favour of a new competition policy, then the founding of the Council for Competition heralded a re-orientation towards 'competition law'.

Today, intervention by the Council may be instigated by firms themselves. This is important for two reasons. First, it implies that the majority of the cases which the Council has to deal with are not only those which the Minister wishes to refer to it. In this sense, the creation of the Council for Competition constitutes a further development in the direction of a truly independent regulatory body. Second, it modifies the relationship between firms and the market. The previous structure had not imposed the notion of competition within the management and strategic planning of firms sufficiently firmly to deter a flagrant abuse of the rules.

The burden of proof has now been reversed. A firm may use provisions in force to condemn the illicit practices of its competitors, suppliers or clients. It is for the latter to prove their innocence. The rapid success of this form of instigating proceedings is demonstrated by the large number of firms who have taken note of the benefit which they might derive from initiating action under the competition law.

In order to reinforce this guiding principle, a fundamental modification was introduced. Following numerous debates it was decided that appeals against the decisions of the Council would no longer be referred to the Council of State but to the Court of Appeal in Paris.

From an organizational point of view, the legislature sought to counter-balance the executive power assumed by the permanent rapporteurs and the General Rapporteur in the former Commission. For this reason they decided to re-apportion the power in favour of the members of the new Council. A permanent structure was thus created, comprising a president and two vice-presidents.

Jenny (1990: 74–6) who, with good reason, was confirmed as General Rapporteur of the new Council for Competition, has recognized the core importance of three major merits in the modifications which the law of 1986 introduced.

Of greatest importance, provisions relating to the control of abuse of a dominant position were amended. Prior to 1986, the activities of an enterprise or group of enterprises holding a dominant position in the domestic market (or a substantial part of that market) were prohibited if they might damage the normal functioning of the market. This was amended to prohibit those activities which had as their object or consequence the prevention, restriction or distortion of competition.

This slight terminological modification is not without importance. The rather vague notion of damage to the normal functioning of the market, which is difficult to establish, was replaced by the more precise concept of damage to competition. This modification confirmed the desire to institute a true competition law in the place of a case-by-case analysis. The Council, however, retains the right not to impose a blanket prohibition on dominant positions and does not forbid such competitive strategies where they are not in fact abusive.

We should note that the former Commission did not condemn dominant positions as such, but that it took this stance as it considered such positions as 'handicaps', destined to facilitate the competitive possibilities of competitors. It is, however, true that the Commission had adopted an extensive interpretation of what it considered to be an abnormal functioning of the market, from which it construed the existence of a dominant position.

The second important modification introduced by the 1986 law concerned the addition of a prohibition of abuse by an exploitative enterprise of 'the state of economic dominance in which it finds itself, as regards its relations with a client firm or supplier not in a similar situation' (Article 8 of the law). This concept, inspired by the German example, is directly aimed at large distributors or sales centres. It has as its object the re-establishment of an equilibrium between producers and distributors.

The third and final amendment was an alteration of the exemptions from prohibitions on anti-competitive practices. Two exemptions were envisaged in this legal scheme of prohibition of anti-competitive practices. The first comprises practices which derive from legislation or regulation, while the second covers practices which the actors prove to be conducive to the development of economic progress, most notably an increase in productivity.

As regards the first exemption, the former Commission for Competition had adopted a very restrictive interpretation requiring that the texts relied upon an unequivocal approval of practices which might be condemned *a priori*. As a consequence the chances of exemption were very low.

Regarding exemptions by virtue of the possible economic benefits of anti-competitive behaviour, the former Commission allowed such immunity only where two conditions were satisfied. First, enterprises were required to demonstrate that the economic benefits put forward as a justification were a direct result of the anti-competitive practices. Second, they were compelled to establish that these benefits could not have been achieved through other, less anti-competitive, means.

Under the 1986 law, the already restricted ability of a firm to avoid the prohibition as regards agreements and the abuse of dominant positions was further restricted. In addition to the former conditions, it imposed two additional requirements. First, the condemned practice must not lead to the elimination of competition with regard to a substantial portion of the products concerned. Second, an equitable part of the profits deriving from such practices must be reserved for the benefit of the users of such products (Article 85 of the Treaty of Rome).

The ambiguous position of the Council for Competition – an incomplete reform?

The various stages of development described above did not come about without some degree of tension between the authority responsible for competition and the political powers of the day.

For example, one of the first cases to be addressed by the Council for Competition was the dissolution of the exclusive right of chemists to sell certain products which could equally well be sold by other retailers. The chemists' association immediately brought pressure to bear upon politicians. Clientelistic considerations prevailed, and the Liberal government, which would normally have been expected to support free competition, concluded the affair by introducing those regulations necessary to reinstate the monopoly of the chemists over the products concerned, such as cosmetics and baby milk, not already covered by law.

Moreover, the executive power has preserved certain of its prerogatives. This is certainly the case, for example, in relation to the power of investigation. Whilst regulators in Brussels or Berlin themselves undertake an investigation into anti-competitive practices, in France this power remains in the hands of the central administration, and has not been transferred to the Council for Competition. It is apparent that the political power wished to retain important prerogatives which it might use in negotiations with economic interests, deploying the 'competition weapon', such as the power to instigate investigations, as an element of dissuasion.

More importantly, however, the 1986 law reinforced the powers of the Minister for Economics in relation to economic concentrations. The exemptions described above allow the executive power to 'preserve' certain practices which it judges to be beneficial to the economy. In this way, the power to manage issues of a more political character falls to the Minister. In the final analysis, this power concerns the evaluation of the 'structural' evolution of the market. Thus, the Minister remains the master in mergers and acquisitions.

This distinction between those affairs which touch upon the 'structural domain' and those which concern the 'functioning' of the market is very vague and lacking in any firm theoretical foundation. For example, the establishment of a joint venture is both a merger and an agreement in the classical sense. Thus, this form of distinction does not provide a clear separation of tasks between the different authorities. From a practical point of view, it merely means that important affairs (the transfer of capital ownership in large industrial and commercial concerns) are the business of the executive. On the other hand, the day-to-day management of the market is delegated to the independent authority responsible for competition. Paradoxically, it is the authoritative policing of the market which is transferred from the state to the Council, whilst the power of shaping of economic structures rests in the hands of the executive. It is likewise true that such policing powers are the least popular of the two.

This form of separation of powers differs in particular from the German example. The main attribute of the Bundeskartellamt is precisely that of the regulation of mergers. It is clear, however, that the French executive did not want to forfeit this power which enables it to re-establish a certain degree of that coercive force which it has lost by virtue of European Community regulations.

The texts, however, are insufficiently clear to ensure that conflict between the two competences might be averted. The political power, if it wishes to avoid such a clash, should emphasize its powers of influence and not its guardianship. It is not to be doubted that the 'sociological' proximity of the members of the Council to the administration, as well as the desire of that Council not to be marginalized within the administrative system, are together sufficient to ensure this power of influence.

This discretionary approach to the practical management of anti-competitive practices is inconvenient for firms and economic agents in general. This case by case policy might thus prove hazardous and diminish the legal certainty vital to a true competition law.

Even more seriously, however, this uncertainty endangers the *development* of a 'competition policy', firmly based upon law, which has been clearly delineated and democratically adopted. By contrast, in Germany competition law is extremely detailed and subject to regular amendment, subject to debate in the Bundestag. On this basis, legal reforms are taken note of by all parties concerned, and the criteria upon which regulators may base their opposition to an operation are known in advance. It is for the elected political executive or legislators to determine new parameters (such as nationality of ownership, the degree of concentration, consideration of technological progress, and so forth), in the regulation of anti-competitive practices. It is for the authority responsible for competition to interpret the statutes, and to give shape to them in accordance with proper secondary norms of application. Finally, it falls to the courts to govern the application of these laws and norms and to create a body of case law on the matter.

It is in this sense that reforms introduced by the 1986 law are incomplete. The law thus fails to take its own logic to its ultimate conclusion, preserving instead a margin of arbitration for the executive.

The practical difficulties arising from the legal loopholes in the definition of the functions of the Council for Competition, which make its insertion into the fabric of the state even more complex, derive from a double contradiction in French law. In effect, the ultimate goal of this reform was not clearly determined: was it to ensure the free functioning of the market? Or did it instead seek to favour economic development? In other words, must the Council restrict itself to a simple arbitrational function, or should it attempt to be the representative of the general interest?

If its role is that of a simple arbitrator, then in this case the rules must be formulated more precisely and the possible restrictions must be reinforced with a power of sanction. If its role is to represent the general interest, the formulation of norms must be complemented by a mode of composition and mediation which ensures that the general welfare or the efficient functioning of the market is not harmed by particular interests.

The present system lies somewhere between the two models, as it preserves the system of *a posteriori* sanctions without conferring the power to judge the effect of such operations on general economic interest.

The definition of balanced regulation

The various historical stages of regulation, and the present uncertainty which weighs upon the separation of competences between the different authorities responsible for the regulation of competition, demonstrate the problematic nature of the regulatory role of the state in the economic sphere. Clearly, this function must be exercised on the basis of certain balances or equilibria.

As has been shown, the true *political objectives* of this form of economic regulation are diverse, sometimes vague and quite often contradictory. The clash between a political logic on the one hand, and an economic logic on the other, might itself rest upon a contradiction in emphasis. It is in effect vital to the political power that those institutions which regulate the market be independent and responsible for difficult decisions and delicate arbitration. In this way, the political power may dissociate itself from those cases which are politically and administratively explosive. It is, however, equally important to this same political power to preserve some degree of control over the manner in which these independent institutions address these cases, to exert some measure of influence over decisions taken and, on some occasions, to be able to rectify them. The final point is vital to the political power, as it is on this basis that it is able to organize its relations with the most powerful economic forces. Competition policy is thus both a threat and an aid in negotiations with economic actors and their representatives.

Finally, and from a purely political point of view, this power might be used as a bargaining device to ensure that emphasis is laid on those economic advantages which accrue to consumers, small producers or small commercial ventures.

In order to avoid this clientelistic kind of competition policy, a true economic regulation of competition must reconcile a certain number of equilibria (Guillou and Padioleau 1988), which, if attained, will ensure a differentiation between true and symbolic policies.

The first equilibrium is that between economic analysis and political and administrative decision-making. Those institutions which regulate the markets have important decisions to take, prohibitions to define and, in some cases, sanctions to impose. This decision-making function must be based upon well-defined and valid analyses. For example, the creation of a central purchasing centre, which is a form of concentration, may have a favourable impact on the end-consumer, as it makes possible a reduction in prices. The centre, however, may often act in a manner prejudicial to free competition. In this context the efficiency of a competition norm is directly linked to its own rigorous definition.

In this sense, a concerted effort with the major economic actors involved is a great aid to the definition of the norm and to its ultimate efficiency. Nothing is less serviceable than a norm which is theoretically coherent but practically inapplicable. In such a case it loses all deterrent effect and sanctions effect little or no change.

It is for this reason that the authorities responsible for the regulation of the market must favour the path of co-operation and concerted action with economic agents as a means of putting effective rules applicable to the economy into action. At the same time they must continue to survey the actions of these same agents, sometimes even resorting to the imposition of penalties. In the last instance, the efficacy of regulation depends upon the balance drawn between these two functions.

It is equally true that those important pressures which work upon the regulator, such as the need to take decisions rapidly and confidentially, also limit the depth of the analysis of any given situation.

The various competition authorities in France often pay insufficient attention to the definition of their rules. The different authorities which regulate competition give the overall impression of having been forced to adopt, rather than of having chosen, their regulatory scheme.

The second equilibrium, which has been examined on numerous occasions in this chapter, is that of the necessary independence of those authorities responsible for economic regulation, and the no lesser need to retain some degree of control over them. The means to assure this equilibrium are organizational and, for the most part, very practical. Many apparently trivial details have a symbolic and practical importance: for example, the mode of the nomination of the President of the Council, the possibility of impeachment, the agreement on the latter's powers in the matter of the nomination of his or her collaborators and, finally, the means of financing the institution. On these different points, the successive institutions responsible for the regulation of competition in France have become more independent over time.

Similarly, there is the problem of the manner in which such an authority conducts its investigations. Clearly, an institution which lacks investigatory powers will remain blind to the functioning of the market which it must control. In order to procure the necessary information, the burden of proof is a crucial element. We have seen that in the present French structure this power rests with the executive.

One might equally lay emphasis upon the importance of the rules governing the treatment of cases. For instance, the possibility that the authority responsible for the control of competition might itself choose to initiate proceedings is significant. Its competence to select freely those cases which it considers important, and not only those which the government considers suitable for treatment, implies that its independence has increased in this respect as well.

A further important aspect is that of the power to impose penalties. It has been shown that in France considerable progress has been made with each successive reform. It is also true, however, that for the moment the Minister for the Economy retains the final decision-making power in the matter of imposing sanctions.

CONCLUSION

It is thus clear that the organizational structure of a regulatory institution covers many different spheres. In these different spheres, a measure of progress, in the sense of the attainment of a greater degree of independence, has been accomplished even though the steps taken have often been very timid. A form of political control still exists and tends to be applied more to the decisions of the Council for Competition than to that body itself (the executive power reserves the right to overrule a decision of the regulatory body as well as insisting on the hegemony in the 'structural' domain).

The establishment of the independence of a regulatory body, based on a balance drawn between autonomy and control, rests not only upon organizational questions but also upon practical experience and technical expertise, which is formed slowly and in a gradual process of adaptation.

To this list of equilibria, Dumez and Jeunemaître (1991: 87–8) have added the equilibrium between legal considerations and economic concepts. They note that the lawyer pays greater attention to the general balance of power in society, to the control of the accumulation of power and to the uniform application of legal norms. The economist, on the other hand, focuses on economic developments relating to decisions in competition matters, often neglecting their distributional consequences over and above the fact that they may maximize 'aggregate welfare'.

To obtain equilibrium between these two distinct points of view it is necessary to reconcile two basic organizational elements. The authority responsible for the regulation of the markets must escape from restrictive civil service rules of personnel recruitment in order to benefit from diverse abilities and increase its permeability to change in economic theory and in the world of business. The second stage consists of not turning the institution into a series of 'expertise ghettos', which might sometimes be antagonistic towards each other and which might take extremely narrow viewpoints.

On this final point, the French system is sufficiently original to the extent that these two types of competence have been ranked in a hierarchical power structure, with lawyers at the top, but with economists playing a decisive role in terms of the influence they wield.

The example of the Council for Competition demonstrates the difficulty of installing an independent administrative authority in a country such as France, where the state has centralized power to varying degrees since the reign of Louis XIV. Although there was at the very beginning no doubt that these bodies were administrative, they have been able to affirm their status as authorities only slowly and after much conflict. It is in relation to their independence that fundamental progress has been made.

However defined, the crisis of the welfare state has undeniably favoured the emergence of such bodies and it is to be expected that with the passage of time the Council for Competition, for example, will be able to extend the boundaries of its 'reserved domain' so as to affirm a new mode of economic regulation.

REFERENCES

Chevalier, J. (1986) 'Reflexion sur l'institutions des autorités administratives indépendantes', *Semaine Juridique* 3254.
Chevalier, J. (1989) 'Les instances de régulation de l'audiovisuel', *Regards sur l'actualité*, March.
Crozier, M. (1987) *Etat modeste, Etat moderne*, Paris: Fayard.
Dumez, H. and Jeunemaître, A. (1991) *La concurrence en Europe: de nouvelles règles du jeu pour les entreprises*, Paris: Editions du Seuil.
Gentôt, M. (ed.) (1991) *Les autorités administratives indépendantes*, Montchrestien: E.J.A.
Guillou, B. and Padioleau, J.-G. (1988) *La régulation de la télévision*, Paris: La Documentation Française.
Jenny, F. (1990) 'Concurrence: la Nouvelle règle du jeu', *Revue Française de Gestion*, November–December.
Mény, Y. and Thoenig, J.C. (1989) *Politiques publiques*, Paris: PUF.
Minc, A. (1990) *L'argent fou*, Paris: Grasset.
Rosanvallon, P. (1990) *L'état en France de 1789 à nos jours*, Paris: Le Seuil.

Stone, A. (1992) *The Birth of Judicial Politics in Europe: The Constitutional Council in Comparative Perspective*, Oxford: Oxford University Press.
Winckler, A. (1988) 'Conseil de la concurrence et concurrence des autorités', *Le Debat* 52: 76–86.
Zysman, J. (1983) *Governments, Markets and Growth: Financial Systems and the Politics of Industrial Change*, Oxford: Martin Robertson.

9 Competition law and policy in Spain: implementation in an interventionist tradition

Lluís Cases

Until recently, competition law in Spain placed virtually no limitations on firms' behaviour, as the first Spanish competition law, enacted in 1963 and in effect until 1988, was never actually enforced. However, the enactment of the 1978 Spanish Constitution and Spain's accession to the European Community in 1986 generated a process of economic liberalization and a gradual drop in state intervention in the market. Since 1989, when a new competition law was enacted, the enforcement of competition law has become increasingly important.

This law was substantially similar to European Community competition law, and created an independent administrative body, the Competition Tribunal (Tribunal de Defensa de la Competencia, TDC) empowered to establish competition policy.

This chapter analyses the 1963 law and its lack of enforcement, the impact of the 1978 Constitution – and of European integration – on Spanish competition law enforcement, and finally the law currently in force and the role played by the competition law enforcement agencies.

THE LAW ON THE PROHIBITION OF ANTI-COMPETITIVE PRACTICES

The introduction of competition law in Spain

The first attempt to establish a system to protect market competition was Law 110/63 (Ley de Represión de Prácticas Restrictivas de la Competencia) which prohibited anti-competitive practices. It was largely unsuccessful owing to the interventionist economic regime which existed at the time of its enactment, and the fact that it was simply not applied.

The 1963 law was a political response to external pressures, which required a liberalization of the Spanish economy. It was enacted at the time when a protectionist, interventionist and centralized economic system existed and was to a certain extent imposed by foreign policy requirements (Tribunal 1989: 11).

One such external pressure was an agreement between the United States and Spain pertaining to competition law which obliged the Spanish government to discourage monopolistic or protectionist arrangements, and to promote competition, productivity and the conditions necessary for the development of international commerce. A second external pressure was constituted by the signing of the Treaty of Rome in 1957 (see section dealing with the impact of EC law below).

The need for an instrument to discourage anti-competitive practices finally led to the enactment of the 1963 Competition Law. Its form was clearly influenced by competition laws in effect at the time in other countries, especially since the Royal Decree of 29 November 1962 instructed the Minister of Commerce to design a law in line with OECD standards. The law's preamble states that

> [t]he state, through the vehicle of economic policy, seeks to create the conditions which will allow enterprises to act freely ... through the elimination of administrative interventions which, although justified in the past, could today obstruct the functioning of the market, and by the creation of an adequate institutional framework, which should allow greater flexibility for the entire economic system.
>
> (1963 Competition Law, Preamble, para. II)

The 1963 Law responded to real, structural needs of the Spanish economy. The elimination of administrative interventions was accompanied by the introduction of mechanisms designed to eliminate private actions having the same negative effects on economic liberalization, and in particular, on economic development and consumer interests.

The law was designed to protect both the economy and enterprises against the excesses of a free market by prohibiting enterprises from abusing their economic power (Manzanedo 1970: 647), and ensuring that any benefit that accrues to the individual enterprise as a result of the exercise of its freedom of contract should lead to an overall benefit to the economy.

Substantive provisions of the 1963 Competition Law

The 1963 law comprised three basic elements. First, it established the general prohibition of anti-competitive practices and the prohibition of the abuse of a dominant market position, and listed specific prohibited practices. The statute provided for the application of economic sanctions on enterprises which had engaged in prohibited practices.

Second, the 1963 law established exceptions to these prohibited practices: the most important being anti-competitive practices resulting from the exercise of legally sanctioned administrative powers. Government restrictions on competition already in existence at the time the law came into effect could be eliminated or modified by the government by applying to the Competition Tribunal or the Ministry of Commerce's jurisprudence.

Third, the 1963 law provided for the authorization of practices by private parties which infringed the law's prohibitions, where such practices brought about an improvement in the production or distribution of goods or services, or promoted technical or economic progress. Such practices were required to be registered in the Competition Register (Registro de Prácticas Restrictivas de la Competencia).

It is worth noting, however, that mergers of enterprises were *not* covered. The law required only mergers – representing 30 per cent or more of the national market for a particular good or service, or when one of the enterprises involved already held this percentage of the market – to be listed in the Competition Register.

State agencies responsible for the administration of the 1963 law

The 1963 Competition Law was to be implemented by the Competition Tribunal (Tribunal de Defensa de la Competencia, TDC), the Competition Office (Servicio de Defensa de la Competencia, SDC), and the Council for Competition (Consejo de Defensa de la Competencia, CDC), with intervention also by the Council of Ministers. The first two institutions were responsible for ensuring that private enterprises acted in accordance with the law.

The Competition Tribunal (TDC)

The Tribunal was the main agency responsible for the enforcement of the 1963 Law, and was established as an agency within the Ministry of Commerce. Although it was conceived with a full and absolute independence in the performance of its functions, in practice it has not worked as such an independent body.

It was created to allow important decisions regarding the economy to remain within the ambit of the Ministry of Commerce, though pretending that such decisions were being made by an independent court with special expertise.

The Tribunal was composed of a president, designated by the head of state, and eight members, nominated by decree of the Ministry of Commerce. The law specified that members could be selected from among judges or civil servants in the financial administration.

To ensure the independence of the Tribunal, its members could not be dismissed, suspended or declared incompetent except in cases specified by the law (the law did not specify the duration of their appointment, implying that they could remain in office until retirement). In cases of removal, it was the responsibility of the Tribunal itself to make such declaration to the president or members.

It administered the extraordinarily demanding rules regarding conflict of interest applicable to its members, and also took the oath of those designated as members of the Tribunal. Thus, once appointed, its members were no longer under the control of the Ministry of Commerce.

The Tribunal had the following functions: to declare the existence of anti-competitive practices; to authorize otherwise prohibited conduct; and to issue opinions. We shall deal with each in turn.

Declaration of anti-competitive practices

By law, the Tribunal was the sole institution empowered to declare the existence of anti-competitive practices. In this sense, the 1963 Competition Law attempted to make such decisions uniform. It provided that declarations made by the Tribunal in this regard were not subject to judicial review (this ceased after the enactment of the Constitution in 1978). Accordingly, declarations made by the Tribunal were presumed legally and automatically binding.

The Tribunal was also empowered to notify the responsible parties to refrain from engaging in such practices and to require them to suspend them, and to publish such notification in the *Official Journal* (*Boletín Oficial del Estado, BOE*). Failure to comply after notification would subject the responsible parties to criminal penalties and civil sanctions ranging from 1,000 to 5,000 pesetas for each day the conduct continued.

The 1963 law did not, however, empower the Tribunal to impose such sanctions: the only sanctions which it could impose directly were fines ranging from 5,000 to 100,000 pesetas for engaging in an anti-competitive practice covered by the exceptions (Article 4) without prior registration, or for failure to notify a concentration to the Competition Register when such notification was required.

Once the Tribunal had declared the existence of an anti-competitive practice, the government could impose two types of administrative sanctions. However, it was within the power of the Tribunal to request their imposition, a power which 'was not exercised by the Tribunal for decades' (Tribunal, *Memoria 1990*, 1991: 29). The first type of sanction was an economic fine. In deciding the size of the fine, the government had to take into consideration the damage caused to the national economy. The second type of sanction was disgorgement, that is, the taking away of ill-gotten gains: when the Tribunal determined that the prohibited practices had allowed the responsible party to obtain benefits beyond those which it would have obtained in a competitive regime, it could propose to the government, through the Ministry of Finance, the disgorgement of such benefits through taxes. Firms could appeal against such government-imposed sanctions.

Authorization of possibly prohibited practices

This constitutes an *a priori* control, exercised before the execution of the acts. When the responsible parties anticipated that their conduct could be covered by the prohibitions of the law, they were required to apply to the Tribunal for authorization.

Logically, the trigger for a Tribunal decision was the petition of the party soliciting authorization. Other parties with a legitimate, personal and direct interest in the matter could intervene in the proceedings, as could the Trade Union Federation. The decision of the Tribunal had to be made within six months of the date the petition was filed, to be published in the *Official Journal* and registered in the Competition Register. Moreover, the Tribunal could also impose conditions to render the agreement acceptable, including supervision by the Competition Office.

The issuing of opinions

Various provisions of the 1963 law empowered the Tribunal to issue opinions on competition issues. Such opinions could potentially become part of the framework of competition law. As already stated, anti-competitive practices resulting from the exercise of legally sanctioned administrative powers were excluded from the 1963 law. By means of opinions, however, the Tribunal could propose to reduce, modify, or suppress such exclusions. The 1963 law provided that new restrictions on competition had to be approved by the courts, which were in turn obliged to obtain the opinion of the Tribunal prior to making a ruling.

Finally, the 1963 law required the Tribunal to publish an annual report containing detailed explanations of its activities in the application of the law (Article 35).

The Competition Office

The 1963 law established the Competition Office within the Ministry of Commerce, but not organizationally linked to the Tribunal.

The 1963 law required the Office to perform the following functions: the preparation of cases for resolution by the Tribunal; the enforcement of the Tribunal's decisions and the maintenance of the Competition Register; and the analysis and provision of information regarding the state of competition.

Under the legal framework created by the 1963 law, it was essential to have an institution with a special jurisdiction to initiate proceedings to be resolved by the Tribunal. The Competition Office was the initiator of proceedings against anti-competitive practices.

The Office was also responsible for maintaining the Competition Register, which consisted of two sections: a confidential provisional register which listed agreements or acts provisionally authorized by the Tribunal within thirty days of the date of such an authorization; and a final public register which listed cases of definitive authorization by the Tribunal.

The third main function of the Office was to prepare studies, opinions and assessments. Accordingly, it was required to study international competition legislation, in order to integrate the national legislation and practices with the international trends; to analyse potentially anti-competitive practices which could be considered as anti-competitive from both an economic and legal perspective in order to control, and in some cases to neutralize and reduce forces which disturb the political or economic system of the market; to maintain relations with other national and international organizations; to prepare opinions pursuant to the 1963 law (Article 4); to help in the preparation of studies by competent authorities; and to collaborate with other national departments or international authorities to facilitate the collection of relevant information.

The Council for Competition

The 1963 law established the Council for Competition within the Competition Office to perform consultative functions on behalf of the Ministry of Commerce. This goal was reflected in the composition of the Council for Competition, which included members of the public administration, a representative for each of the Ministries of Finance, Public Works, Agriculture, Industry, Labour and Commerce, and six representatives of the Trade Union Federation.

The Council for Competition was able to influence the competition law system, even though it did not have the power to either institute or resolve proceedings. Its functions were:

• to provide opinions on all acts implementing the 1963 law
• to provide opinions according to the sectoral rules of competition submitted to the government by the Trade Union Federation for approval
• to study the distinct economic sectors analysing the situation and the degree of competition of each and the existence of administrative measures which protect commercial restrictions, and to propose legal measures leading to the removal of such obstacles to competition
• to propose to the Competition Office the initiation of remedial proceedings
• to be informed about proceedings negotiated by the Competition Office before referring them to the Tribunal

Thus, these provisions allowed the Council for Competition to play an important role in the application and development of competition law through its role as liaison between the Tribunal and society. It was not limited to act as a simple consultative body.

The ineffectiveness of the 1963 Competition Law: lack of enforcement

The 1963 law is unanimously perceived to have been ineffective for various reasons. First, the public authorities were not committed to having an effective competition law. Without this commitment, the system could not function. The interventionist regime of the time and the public administration continued to intervene to protect specific restrictive practices. The Tribunal itself pointed out that

[t]he combination of a series of factors (interventionism, corporatism, . . .) strangled the expectations to utilize the free market mechanism. The political will that could have been used at the time of the promulgation of Law 110/1963 to achieve its objectives, making it one of the legal pillars of economic policy, was exhausted at the same time.

(Tribunal 1989: 12)

Second, the dysfunctionality of the established organizational framework of the Tribunal contributed to the ineffectiveness of the 1963 law. Briefly, three elements undermined the strength of the Tribunal: it could not supervise the actions of the Competition Office, which was fundamental for the full operation of its functions; it could not control the implementation of its decisions, because it could not impose sanctions for infractions or supervise the implementation of its notifications; and its power to issue opinions was concurrent with the power of the Competition Office to do the same.

Third, the public authorities responsible for the application of the law lacked the means to do so. The Tribunal complained:

What could be expected from a body with three or four civil servants in its technical unit, who were not specialists in competition law, working in an indifferent if not hostile, political and administrative environment, giving the sensation of walking over a glass ceiling?

(Tribunal 1989: 13)

Similarly, the Tribunal's evaluation of itself as an institution underlines its weak operation:

The Tribunal has been characterized as a body to which one gained entry at a relatively advanced age and which one left only once all possible job renewals had been exhausted, at the age of seventy-five. This feature of the Tribunal shaped its nature, and without doubt, affected the attitude it adopted in how its responsibilities were performed.

(Tribunal 1989: 14)

These considerations are clearly reflected in the research done regarding application of the 1963 law. In the period 1965–85, the average number of annual decisions of the Tribunal was fourteen. In contrast, the Tribunal issued sixty-six decisions in 1990, fifty-four in 1991 and sixty-two in 1992 (see Figure 9.1).

Fourth, the decisions made by the Tribunal resolved issues of little importance. The Tribunal itself later stated:

the number of decisions would have had little importance if the decisions made had addressed matters of significance, concerning prominent sectors of the national economy. But it is enough to look at the compilations of the Tribunal's decisions made every five years to notice that this occurred only exceptionally.

(Tribunal 1989: 14–15)

Fifth, for the first twenty-five years of its existence, not a single economic sanction was imposed for violations of the law. It was not until 1988 that the first economic sanction was imposed.

Finally, as the Tribunal itself states: 'the deterrent effect of the existence of the Tribunal on anti-competitive conduct is practically nil' (Tribunal 1989: 15).

Given that the inspection function was ineffective, and the sanctioning power was not used, few enterprises felt any compunction to apply for authorization of their anti-competitive conduct. The law and the complex organizational framework it created constituted a lone exception to the interventionist and controlling order that ruled corporate conduct in the market.

CURRENT COMPETITION LAW

The Constitution of 1978, Spanish accession to the EC and the revision of Spanish competition law

Given the ineffectiveness of the 1963 Competition Law, Spanish competition law was completely revised with the enactment of the 1989 Competition Law (Ley de Defensa de la Competencia).

The 1989 law prohibits agreements, decisions, recommendations, mergers, concerted practices or conscious parallelism designed to impede, restrict or distort competition in all, or part of, the national market. It also prohibits abuse of a dominant market position (Articles 85/86 of the Treaty of Rome), and declares the nullity of contracts or agreements in violation of the law.

The law also endows the Tribunal with jurisdiction over acts of unfair competition that distort free trade in an appreciable manner in all, or part of, the national market, and which affect the public interest, and the prohibition of abuse of a dominant position applies to monopolies established by law. The obligations created by the 1989 law apply to both private and public enterprises.

This revision was especially induced by two major events: enactment of the 1978 Constitution and accession of Spain to the European Community in 1986.

The 1978 Spanish Constitution

The 1978 Constitution established the framework for a free market economy and made the public powers responsible for guaranteeing the protection of this system (Spanish Constitution 1978, Article 38). Accordingly, it conceived of competition law enforcement as a public function.

Competition law enforcement is one of the essential instruments for achieving a free market economy. This concept was enshrined in the 1989 Law when it stated that

[c]ompetition, as a strict principle of the entire market economy, represents an essential element to the model of economic organization of our society and constitutes, in the realm of individual freedoms, the first and most important form in which the freedom of enterprise is exercised.

(1989 Competition Law, Preamble, para. 1)

In this sense, the Constitutional Court considered competition law enforcement as one of the necessary activities of the state for the existence and maintenance of a market economy, and stated that

The recognition of the market economy by the Constitution as a framework required for free enterprise, and the commitment to have it protected by the state (Article 38.2), imply the need of an action specifically designed to aid in achievement of those constitutional goals. And one of the actions that may be needed is that which eliminates those practices that can affect or seriously damage an element so decisive in the market economy as competition among enterprises. It appears, then, that competition law enforcement is a necessary protection, not a restriction, of the freedom of enterprise and of the market economy, which could be threatened by the absence of control of its natural tendencies.

(Constitutional Court, Decision 88 of 1 July 1986)

The Constitutional Court insisted that competition law enforcement was a form of state intervention in the regulation of the market, the terms of which are derived from Article 38 of the Constitution. The development of a market economy requires an action of public powers designed to ensure the maintenance of an adequate regime of competition in the market. As stated by the Tribunal:

[t]he state is to act as a counterweight to the free market, for the benefit of enterprises and consumers; far from any interventionist task, the role that the public powers have to play is just the opposite. The limited intervention of the state should strive to avoid the replacement of a market managed by the administration, with other control by more powerful economic agents, since it is known that the spontaneous action from competitive forces in the market may end with the substantial reduction, if not removal, of competition.

(Tribunal 1989: 16)

The Constitution required the revision of the organizational framework established by the 1963 law to meet the new constitutional parameters.

Spanish accession to the European Community

Spain's accession to the European Community also inspired the revision of national competition law. A 1985 law (Law 47 of 27 December 1985) regarding the delegation to the Spanish government of responsibility to apply the law of the European Community made express mention of the 1963 Competition Law as one of the areas in need of revision.

The revision of Spanish competition law was heavily influenced by Community competition law, which Spain adopted almost in its entirety. This influence is evident in the entire legal corpus. For example, the Royal Decree 157 of 21 February 1992, on which the implementation of the 1989 law is based, makes constant reference to European norms such as for the interpretation of terms regarding exemptions by category, and individual authorizations.

Administrative bodies responsible for the application of the 1989 law

As shown above, the 1989 law was based on a conception of competition as a governing principle of the entire market economy. It constituted an important element of the model of economic organization established in the Constitution of 1978.

To accomplish its objectives, the law establishes a complex administrative structure, partly inherited from the 1963 Competition Law, based on the existence of the Tribunal and the Competition Office. The law also attributes important functions to the administration – the most significant of these being the control of mergers.

The Competition Tribunal: an independent administrative body?

The Tribunal, originally established, as we saw, under the 1963 law, was maintained by the 1989 law, although its nature and functions were modified. Its competence extends throughout Spain and its functions basically consist of resolving proceedings initiated by the Competition Office and preparing various types of proposals and opinions. The 1989 law grants complete independence to the Tribunal. As Article 20 states, the Tribunal 'exercises its functions with complete independence and only defers to the judicial order'.

The law emphasises the need 'to endow the system with the necessary independence from government' (1989 Competition Law, Preamble). This implies that decisions regarding its enforcement are not made by the administration, which is headed by a political executive. In general, 'through independent agencies, one is able to guarantee that ordinary political conflicts do not control how a given sector is governed' (Lopez Ramon 1991: 190). Thus, the 1989 law attributes the task of defining the public interest to an administrative body which is hierarchically independent of the Ministry of Economics and Finance.

Various elements are designed to ensure this independence. The Tribunal is composed of a president and eight members recommended by the Ministry of Economics and Finance and appointed by the government, from among lawyers, economists and other experts with more than fifteen years' professional experience. Accordingly, this constitutes a pure system of governmental appointment, which eliminates intervention by other bodies, such as the Parliament, in the process. However, the president and members do not have a staff to work with them in the exercise of their functions.

Tribunal members are appointed for a six-year term, renewable for three years. This is potentially significant for the independence of the Tribunal, since it implies that the term of its officials could last beyond the term of the government that has appointed them. Thus, this provision could cause a break of the bond which results from appointment of Tribunal officials by the government. Indeed, it is possible that the bond will never be formed because the Tribunal operating at a given time is not appointed by the government in power at that time.

The members of the Tribunal cannot be suspended or dismissed by the government that has appointed them. Article 23 of the 1989 law establishes the ways in which a Tribunal official's term may come to an end: retirement, expiry of the term of office, conflict of interest, conviction of a fraudulent offence, permanent incapacity and serious lack of performance of duties based on the vote of three-quarters of the Tribunal. The most open clause is the last, and it is significant that it is the Tribunal, and not the government, that makes this assessment. For this reason, Article 27 of the 1989 law lists making such assessment among the functions of the Tribunal.

Accordingly, after nominating members of the Tribunal, the government loses control over them, and since it cannot revoke the nomination the independence of the members of the Tribunal is theoretically guaranteed.

The members of the Tribunal have the status of senior civil servants under the 1989 law. In this way, the law attempts to attribute to the institution a high degree of importance. Officials must exercise their function with absolute dedication. It should be emphasized that any controversies with regard to challenges or conflicts pertaining to Tribunal officials are resolved by the Tribunal itself.

Pursuant to Article 27(a) of the 1989 law, it is the responsibility of the Tribunal to promulgate national regulations in its area of competence. Through these regulations the Tribunal must define its administrative functioning and the organization of its services. The Tribunal contains two technical units: the Subdirectorate for Research, which is responsible for carrying out studies in the field of competition for use by the Tribunal in the performance of its functions; and the Subdirectorate for Mergers, Acquisitions and State Aids, which is responsible for gathering information on mergers.

Together, these provisions are designed to ensure that the Tribunal will operate independently of the government. Accordingly, the European Court of Justice, in its decision of 16 July 1992, ruled that the Tribunal constitutes a 'jurisdictional body' under Article 177 of the Treaty of Rome. However, as shown in Figure 9.1, the Spanish administrative system does not allow the Tribunal truly to manage competition policy.

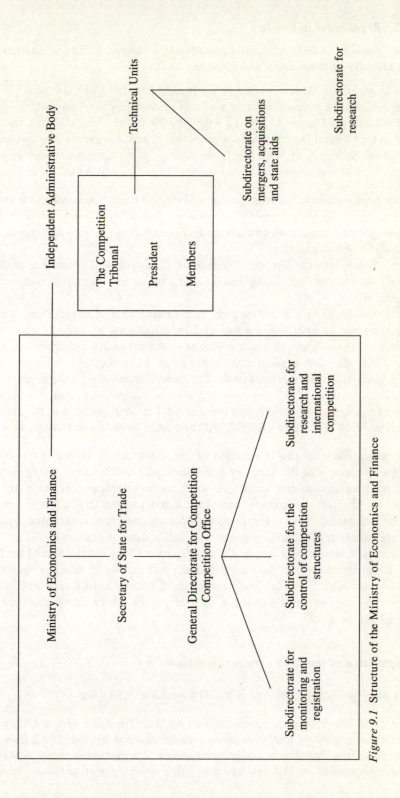

Figure 9.1 Structure of the Ministry of Economics and Finance

The Competition Office: an administrative body hierarchically integrated into the Ministry of Economics and Finance

The Competition Office is cited in the Preamble to the 1989 law as the body that initiates the proceedings that are later resolved by the Tribunal.

Under Royal Decree 177 of 19 February 1990, the Competition Office is part of the General Directorate for Competition, which organizationally comes under the Secretary of State for Trade, who is, in turn, organizationally part of the Ministry of Economics and Finance. The Competition Office includes:

- the Subdirectorate for Monitoring and Registration, responsible for sanction proceedings for prohibited conduct, authorization proceedings, investigation, inspection, and advice and proposal in the area of agreements and prohibited practices
- the Subdirectorate for the Control of Competition Structures, mainly responsible for controlling and advising on issues regarding mergers of enterprises
- the Subdirectorate for Research and International Competition, which carries out competition studies and investigations of various economic sectors. In particular, it gives evidence in the necessary collaboration with the European Commission in the application of Community competition law in Spain, it attends meetings of the European Community for the preparation and elaboration of EC norms in the area of competition, and co-operates with foreign organizations and international institutions such as the special committees of the OECD, UNCTAD and other international institutions

The significance of the integration of the Competition Office in the hierarchical structure of the Ministry must be emphasized because, being part of the ministerial administration, and with no hierarchical relation with the Tribunal, the Tribunal cannot control the activity of the Office (an exception being complaints filed by private citizens against acts committed by the Office, which the Tribunal is sometimes called upon to resolve).

Finally, it should be noted that this delegation of the application of the law to administrative bodies does not affect the jurisdiction of the civil courts, as is the case with European competition law. Rather, civil courts retain the power to impose civil penalties on companies which have engaged in prohibited conduct.

Application of the 1989 Competition Law

The basic procedural powers of the Tribunal and the Office

The 1989 law entrusts its enforcement to the Tribunal and the Office by establishing powers and procedures, supplemented by the 1992 Law on Administrative Procedures and judicial review. It requires the public administration to provide the Tribunal and the Office with information requested, and regulates the confidentiality of proceedings, data and documentation. Moreover, it requires a preliminary judgement for criminal offences: 'criminal proceedings before a court of justice will suspend the resolution of the administrative proceeding which is based on the same facts'. The 1989 law requires that a party wishing to bring an action for damages must *a priori* obtain an administrative decision declaring the existence of conduct prohibited by the 1989 law. This gives rise to jurisdiction of the courts in actions for the recovery of damages and injuries caused by this conduct. The Tribunal is empowered to impose 'precautionary measures' (such as a prohibition) which may be modified, revoked or renewed, but which must not cause irreparable damage to the firm nor cause a 'violation of fundamental rights'. These measures are backed up by fines ranging from 10,000 to 150,000 pesetas, which can be re-imposed periodically if the violation continues.

Authorization of restrictive practices

One of the fundamental characteristics of Spanish competition law is that it is not a rigid and immovable framework and that anti-competitive conduct may be authorized under some circumstances, either by a government exemption or by the Tribunal.

The Tribunal gives only a non-binding opinion on the government exemptions and, consequently, a fundamental element for the development of competition policy is beyond its control. This is not compensated for by the fact that, under certain circumstances, the Tribunal may waive a general exemption.

The Tribunal can also authorize otherwise prohibited conduct which leads to the improvement in production or the commercialization of goods and services, or promotes technical progress, provided that consumers also benefit. Such conduct may be authorized when justified by the general economic situation and the public interest, when it promotes or protects exports, when it revives a flagging market, discourages unprofitable excess production capacity or leads to an increase in the social or economic standards in depressed areas and so forth.

Authorization proceedings, like sanction proceedings, take place in two phases: the first before the Office, and the second before the Tribunal.

As regards the Tribunal's power of final authorization, however, such authorizations are temporary, and thus the Tribunal has discretionary power to determine their duration. The Tribunal also has the power to impose conditions or obligations, or make modifications, regarding the conduct authorized.

Control of mergers of enterprises

The principal characteristic of the regulation of mergers under the 1989 Competition Law is that the government, not the Tribunal, has been delegated the main power to control them.

Royal Decree 1080 of 11 September 1992, promulgated pursuant to the 1989 law, specifies the proceedings to be followed by competition law authorities regarding mergers, and the form and content of voluntary notification.

The regulation governing mergers can be summarized in five points:

- a merger is not subject to prior administrative authorization and need not be registered
- the public administration reserves the power to control those mergers which may seriously affect free competition
- the government is delegated the power to authorize or prohibit a merger
- the government may base its decision not only on competition considerations, but also on general public policy concerns
- the role of the Tribunal is relegated to that of providing a technical opinion based primarily, but not exclusively, on the effects that the merger will have on maintenance of effective competition in the relevant market

(see Alonso Soto 1990: 3)

The Ministry for Economics and Finance can officially institute proceedings with respect to a merger when a 25 per cent share of the entire national market for a given good or service, or a substantial part of that market, is reached or exceeded as a result of the transaction, or when total global sales of the merged enterprise exceeds 20,000 million pesetas in the last accounting period.

Although prior notification is not required, enterprises may voluntarily notify the Ministry of a merger in order to obtain authorization. This may be done before the transaction is finalized or up to three months afterwards. One month after a proposed transaction is correctly notified, authorization of the transaction will be tacit, even if the Tribunal has no knowledge of the notification.

Whether proceedings are initiated with or without voluntary notification by the parties, the Ministry will submit the information to the Tribunal where it considers that the merger could impede effective market competition.

Therefore, the Tribunal's knowledge of the merger depends on the judgement of the Ministry. If the latter decides that the merger cannot possibly impede effective competition, or simply does not consider it proper for the Tribunal to know of the particular transaction, it may decide not to inform the Tribunal about the merger and its possible impact on market competition.

In cases where it receives the files, the Tribunal must issue an opinion concerning the merger. It may request information necessary from other administrative bodies, or from any person, natural or legal. It may hear from enterprises that may be affected and from the Consumers' Association Council, and convoke the participants in the merger. The Tribunal is required to let the participants know of all the information or allegations that have been presented by other enterprises, individuals or consumers.

The Tribunal's opinion is not limited to the competitive aspects of the merger, but will be based on an analysis of the restrictive effects, potential or actual, of the merger, focusing on the definition of the particular market, its structure, the possibility to choose suppliers, distributors and consumers, the economic and financial power of the enterprises, the evolution of the transaction and foreign competition. On the other hand, the Tribunal can analyse whether any anti-competitive effects resulting from the merger are offset by improved production or commercialization, the promotion of technical and economic progress, the international competitiveness of the national industry or the interests of consumers or users.

The Tribunal will give an opinion on the merger, including recommended conditions under which approval should be given, and the appropriate means to re-establish effective competition.

After receiving the Tribunal's opinion, the government has three months in which to complete the final resolution of the proceedings. The government can decide not to oppose the merger, to approve it if certain conditions are satisfied or to oppose it. In all cases, the decision must be registered in the Competition Register and published in the *Official Journal*.

When the government opposes a proposed merger, it can order the finalization not to take place. If it is already finalized, the government can order the appropriate means for establishing effective competition, including dismantling the merger.

In summary, the Tribunal does not play a central role in the regulation of mergers, since it simply provides an opinion to the Ministry. The opinion is not binding on the Council of Ministers which has the competence to make final decisions on mergers.

The regulation of state aid to industry

The 1989 law contains a provision on the regulation of state aid to enterprises. However, this provision, described in parliamentary debate as 'very timid' and 'ineffective', grants the Tribunal minimal powers to act.

The regulation provides that the Minister of Economics and Finance will require the Tribunal to give an opinion on the competitive effects of specific state aid to enterprises – the consultative powers of the Tribunal allow it to prepare opinions on specified programmes of state aid to enterprises.

The Minister of Economics and Finance, with knowledge of the Tribunal opinion, may propose to the state the termination or modification of a state aid programme so as to maintain or re-establish competition.

The law does not require an analysis of the effect on market competition to be taken into account in decisions relative to state aid programmes. The latter may be adopted without evaluation either of their effects on competition or of whether the possible benefits are outweighed by the damage they cause.

Study of market competition issues

The Tribunal is responsible for examining issues of market competition that may not be of immediate importance, but which have an impact in the medium or long term. Thus it is the focal point for research and information on matters of free market competition (Rossignoli Just 1987: 10).

This function is apparent from many of the provisions of the 1989 law already discussed, such as those requiring it to prepare opinions on mergers and state aid to enterprises. Moreover, the law empowers the Tribunal to prepare other opinions. For instance, it can propose the modification or suppression of anti-competitive practices established in accordance with legal norms. This has already been the source of important opinions such as that dealing with the free exercise of entrepreneurial activity. The Tribunal must also prepare the rules of exemption by category for government approval.

Together with these concrete provisions, the 1989 law regards the Tribunal as a consultative body and attributes it, more generally, with the task of examining competition matters, including the following:

- participation in the preparation of first drafts of laws affecting competition; such drafts must reflect the Tribunal's input regarding effect on competition – in this way, its input should assure that the final decision takes into account the effect that the proposed legislation may have on competition
- the direction of opinions to any public body and the conducting of studies; the Tribunal may explain to the public body its opinion on the effect of the action in question on market competition
- the preparation of opinions on specified subjects at the request of the Parliament, government or individual ministries, the Autonomous Regions, local government and organizations of enterprises and consumers
- the preparation of a public annual report (*Memoria*)
- the possibility for the Tribunal to act as arbitrator in private disputes – this provision, however, needs further legislative development before it can be implemented

In summary, these functions, many of which may be executed by the Tribunal on its own initiative, allow it to play a prominent role in the implementation of competition law.

There is an overlap of competences between the Tribunal and the Office, as the 1989 law attributes functions of study and deliberation to the Office, and thus these activities of the two bodies must be co-ordinated. The attribution of the principal role to the Tribunal in the Spanish competition law system implies that the tasks of the Office must be developed in accordance with the guidelines or criteria of the Tribunal.

AN EVALUATION OF THE 1989 COMPETITION LAW

Will political intervention block the 1989 law?

An unprecedented process of economic liberalization in Spain has begun, especially since its accession to the European Community. Important ministerial interventions, however, still persist, limiting that liberalization and impeding effective application of competition law.

The law excludes conduct permitted by some other law or regulation from the ambit of competition law (Article 2.1). It provides that competition law is not the only mechanism available for controlling the conduct of enterprises in the market. Thus, the state can intervene in the economy disregarding the rules of the competition regime. For example, the legislature can regulate a market sector in a way which is not consistent with competition law. In such cases, the 1989 law will not apply. Such an exception must be strictly interpreted, however, in order to guarantee that it was truly the legislature which opted to waive competition rules.

Similarly, Article 2 provides that competition law enforcement is not an absolute. The system itself incorporates its own adjustments in order to avoid the universal imposition of competition law, to the exclusion of other policy objectives.

Thus, the Parliament or government may adopt legislation allowing anti-competitive practises. In these areas, the Tribunal may not exert control, such as exercising its sanction power or its power to order a party to cease and desist from certain conduct.

All such laws in existence before the 1989 Competition Law was enacted continue in effect. With regard to these, the Tribunal may only propose the modification or suppression of the restrictions on competition created by such norms.

A restrictive interpretation of this provision of the 1989 law is necessary in two respects. First, the exclusion must be based on a law (or regulation promulgated pursuant to a law) for which the intent of the legislature was to create an exclusion from application of the competition law. However, the government may not, through regulatory norms which are not based on a law for which the legislature intended to create such exclusion, allow anti-competitive conduct.

Second, the requirement of a link between the restrictive practice and the legal norm must be strictly interpreted. An express indication in the law is not required, but one must be able clearly to infer that the legislature intended to allow restrictive practices which could not be revised to satisfy the requirements of competition law.

Finally, as discussed above, through regulations of exemption by category, the government may authorize an entire set of practices and the Tribunal may adopt particular authorizations. It is logical that the legislature should be able to enact a law which allows specific practices, given that the government may authorize such practices in specific cases. However, the two situations are not identical, and the 1989 Law does not address the differences. In particular, when the Tribunal considers an authorization application, it may weigh the harm to competition against the benefits derived from permitting the practice. However, this does not always happen in the legislative process. The 1989 law does not limit legislative power by providing that the effect on competition of proposed legislation must be taken into consideration. Rather, the decision to make such evaluation is at the discretion of the legislature.

The failure of the established system to guarantee the full operation of the Competition Tribunal

Although Spanish competition law attributes important functions to the Tribunal, this system has various deficiencies which, in reality, prevent the latter from operating effectively.

The principal deficiency is the separation of functions between the Competition Tribunal and the Competition Office – some reside in the independent administrative body, the Tribunal, and others in the administrative body hierarchically integrated into the Ministry of Economics and Finance, the Competition Office. This separation was derived from the organizational system created by the 1963 law. This separation was needed under the 1963 law because it created the Tribunal as a quasi-judicial body. At present, the Tribunal is an administrative body whose decisions are subject to appeal. Thus, the basis for the separation no longer exists. The maintenance of the separation implies that proceedings go through three distinct steps: proceedings before the Office, administrative resolutions before the Tribunal and administrative appeal. This leads to a significant duplication of effort and delay in the final resolution of cases.

Moreover, the separation of functions generates a loss of control by the Tribunal:

> [c]ertainly, the functional independence of the Tribunal will be strengthened if steps were taken to attribute it with the power to open and conduct proceedings and to convert the Competition Office into one of the Competition Tribunal's components.
>
> (Tribunal 1989: 27)

The 1989 law attempted, through various provisions, to provide the Tribunal with more powers to control the proceedings which it must resolve. But these provisions are simple corrections, and do not accomplish a more general revision providing the Tribunal with the responsibility to conduct the proceedings.

The separation makes the Tribunal dependent on the Competition Office: if the latter does not perform its functions properly, the former will not be able to do so.

In addition, as indicated above, the Office is hierarchically integrated into the Ministry of Economics and Finance. Thus, the activity of the Tribunal depends to a significant degree on the action of a ministerial body, thus impeding its independence.

Moreover, the separation between the proceeding phase and the resolution phase established in the 1989 law is not required by the Constitution.

The distortion established by the separation of functions between the

Tribunal and the Office is illustrated by the marked increase in appeals brought against the Office in 1992. In 1991, resolution of such appeals accounted for about 13 per cent of Tribunal resolutions, and about 34 per cent in 1992. Thus, revising and correcting the acts of the Office has become one of the significant functions of the Tribunal. Clearly, this impedes the Tribunal's efforts to accomplish more important goals. This problem could be corrected if the proceedings were the responsibility of the Tribunal.

The Tribunal is also prevented from playing a central role in competition law enforcement in Spain because the government's power to create exemptions by categories implies the loss of control for the Tribunal in this area: its only role in this process is to prepare an opinion for the government.

Second, the entire system of competition law could be impeded by government intervention in the market, that, by virtue of the 1989 law (Article 2.1), can protect anti-competitive behaviour. A broad interpretation of this provision, allowing it to operate by virtue of regulatory norms, would imply attribution to the administration of the power to displace the application of the 1989 law.

In the same way, an interpretation which does not require a clear link between the legislative intent of the law and actual conduct may imply the displacement of the application of the 1989 law to many kinds of anti-competitive acts. Therefore, a strict interpretation of the exemptions, requiring them to be derived in all cases from the legislative intent, is necessary. This will introduce a regulatory system conducive to competition.

The Tribunal plays a minor role in the regime of control of concentrations of enterprises, an area of great importance for the scheme of competition law. In this area, the decisive functions are attributed to the government, not to the Tribunal. Moreover, its input is not even guaranteed because it depends on the will of the Minister of Economics and Finance.

Similarly, regarding the regulation of state aid to enterprises, the Tribunal's power is limited to giving an opinion regarding particular regimes of aid at the request of the Minister of Economics and Finance. The Tribunal may be cut off from other fundamental aspects of the protection of free competition. Nor does the 1989 law require protection of fair competition to be considered in the granting of state aid to enterprises.

All of these shortcomings make it difficult for the Tribunal to play a leading role in the protection of free competition. It has thus not been given sufficient powers as an independent administrative body to perform fully the tasks for which it was created.

The impact of EC law on Spanish competition law

As stated, the accession of Spain to the European Community in January 1986 is one of the fundamental reasons for the revision of competition law, to the effect that the role of competition regulators has become more important.

Community law, and, in particular, the role of the European Commission in prosecuting prohibited conduct, has significantly influenced this process.

This influence can be appreciated from three perspectives. First, it is evident in the substantive law of competition. As the Minister of Economics and Finance said in 1987 in the Spanish Parliament:

> [t]he new Spanish law must by definition, be absolutely consistent with, and derived from, the Community norm. I believe that no one intends to establish its own norm, *sui generis*, independent of the Community norm, because we have a sort of judicial interpenetration in the area of Community competence and the internal norm evidently must be consistent.
>
> (Joint Committee on the European Community 1987)

In fact, the definition of prohibited practices, abuse of a dominant market position and the stipulation of exemptions established under the 1989 law are totally consistent with the provisions of Community law.

Second, the influence of Community law is clear in the regulation of the powers of the administration to acknowledge the existence of prohibited practices. Although differences exist in the administrative organizations, parallelism in the powers attributed to them to control illicit conduct is apparent.

This parallelism demonstrates the evolution towards harmonization of procedural law of the European Union (Alonso García 1989). Moreover, because of this parallelism, decisions of the European Court of Justice sustaining the powers of the Commission to determine the existence of prohibited conduct may find direct application in the Spanish legal system.

Third, Community influence may be seen from the effect of potential action by the Commission on the diligence of the Spanish administration. The possible intervention of the Community for conduct occurring within Spain, but which affects commerce between member states, implies that the Spanish administration will be more diligent in its action to avoid situations where it appears inoperative or ineffective. The Spanish government would certainly do its best to avoid being unaware of events which occur within Spain and which later become the subject of Commission proceedings.

There is then a contradiction between the system designed to protect competition as a whole, which is strongly influenced by EC law, and its actual operating capacity within the legal context as a whole.

REFERENCES

Alonso García, R. (1989) *Derecho comunitario, derecho nacionales y derecho común europeo*, Madrid: Civitas.

Alonso Soto, R. (1990) 'El control de les concentraciónes de empreses en la nueva ley española de defensa de la competencia', *OJEC*, b-57, October.

Joint Committee on the European Community (1987) *Diario de Sesiónes del Congreso de los Diputados, III Legislatura 1987*, no. 153, session of 10 September 1987.

Lopez Ramon, L. (1991) 'El consejo de seguridad nuclear: Un ejemplo de administración independiente', *Revista de Administración Pública* 126.

Manzanedo, J.A. (1970) 'Defensa de la competencia', in Manzanedo, Hernando and Gomez Reino (eds) *Curso de derecho administrativo económico*, Madrid: Instituto de Estudios de Administración Local.

Rossignoli Just, J.A. (1987) 'Hacia una nueva aproximación al derecho de la competencia en España', *Información Comercial Española*, October.

Tribunal de Defensa de la Competencia (1989) *La Libre Competencia in España 1986–1988*, Madrid.

Tribunal de Defensa de la Competencia (1991) *Memoria*, Madrid.

10 The German Federal Supervisory Authority for Insurance

Michelle Everson

A dearth of European study on the political economy of regulation in the classic American sense has been attributed to the historically 'interventionist' rather than 'regulatory' nature of European states (Majone 1989). Thus, the argument continues, the reluctance of European countries to entrust regulation to 'specialized, single-purpose commissions or administrative agencies' is reflected by the high degree of nationalization of public-utility industries.

This point is in the main undoubtedly correct. Specialized agencies have, however, been in existence – albeit in a limited form – in parts of Europe for almost a century, one of the oldest being the Federal Supervisory Authority for Insurance in Germany originally founded in 1901. As such it is ripe for study in the 'American' regulatory sense, as an independent, specialized commission seeking to control the behaviour of 'an activity valued by the public' (Selznick quoted in Majone 1989).

A note of caution must, however, be sounded. The lack of historical adherence to 'pure' specialized regulation in Europe becomes apparent in the 'dual' nature of the German Supervisory Authority. Historically, insurance regulation in Germany did not merely focus on the correction of inefficiencies in one particular market, but constituted one element in a general policy of social and economic development.

As part of its drive towards completion of the internal market, the Community has turned its attention to the state of insurance supervision in the member states. In stark contrast to the traditional approach within the Federal Republic of Germany, it favours a distinctly liberal form of regulation in these markets, which appear to be prompting a radical re-alignment in insurance regulation in Germany. Consequently, this chapter is divided into two sections: the first concentrating upon the historical development of the dual, regulatory and interventionist role of the Federal Supervisory Authority; the second examining how the interventionist elements of this role are now increasingly being called into question.

THE PRESSURE TO REGULATE AND THE REGULATORY RESPONSE

The pressures on governments to regulate insurance industries are immense, the impetus for regulation being provided by two factors: the interests bound up in insurance, and the nature of the product itself.

Insurance is thus the focus of attention by governments, national industries and financial markets, and the general public. Government has a vested interest in such markets (Von der Schulenburg 1989) as state income may be raised indirectly by the imposition of investment requirements on insurance funds and used to further general economic policy. National industries and financial markets also rely heavily upon the investments made from insurance funds. And the general public is dependent upon private insurance for social support not provided by the state.

How do regulators react to the conflict of interests centred around the insurance industry? A brief description of the interests centred on the industry, and the nature of the insurance mechanism itself, indicates the need to address this question on three levels. First, how do regulators respond to the desires of the various groupings with interests in insurance? Second, how does the agency perceive the workings of the insurance market, or, more precisely, to which economic theory of market efficiency does it adhere? And third, how can governmental interests in the market be identified? These seem to extend beyond a desire to see the efficient regulation of one sector of the economy. Where the talk is of the use of insurance investment funds to promote domestic economic growth, the boundaries of 'sectoral' industrial policy appear to have been overreached. The regulation of one industry may in fact encompass macroeconomic policy. If this is so, how does the regulator respond to the administration of what is no longer 'regulation', but has become 'macro' industrial policy?

The Federal Supervisory Authority for Insurance

The German Federal Supervisory Authority for Insurance in its latest incarnation as the Bundesaufsichtsamt für das Versicherungswesen (BAV, hereafter referred to as 'the Authority') was established in 1951. It is the direct successor of a series of agencies with much the same internal character and external functions. The functions of the authority and the nature of insurance regulation were laid down in the Insurance Supervisory Law (Versicherungsaufsichtgesetz, VAG) of 1901, which, with major amendments in 1931, remains largely unchanged and in force to the present day. Under the traditional terms of the law, the Federal Supervisory Authority has until recently presided over some of the most restrictive industry regulations in Europe. Not only was (and is) the Authority an entry-controlling and, to some extent, a rate-controlling agency, but it was also a product-controlling and process controlling agency with interventionist powers relating to almost all aspects of an insurer's daily business.

In summary, the main powers of the Authority, prior to recent European developments, were to supervise the following: state control of premiums and/or strict guidelines for the calculation of premiums; compulsory notification of changes in premiums; approval of the wording of contracts; compulsory notification of price agreements or contractual conditions; standardization of clauses; and compulsory specialization of insurance business.

The Authority traditionally responded eagerly to its role in administering such a restrictive regulatory code and is at present continuing to endeavour to protect certain aspects of its interventionist role against European Community reforms. An examination of the history of the Federal Insurance Supervisory Authority, however, shows how the homogenous nature of the authority and its response to its regulatory role was largely preserved by a set balance of interests, including those of governmental macro-industrial policy, which dictated the shape of the regulation it was required to apply. Similarly it becomes apparent that the philosophy of the regulatory response owed much to the prevalence of one economic theory.

THE HISTORY OF THE AUTHORITY

The Federal Supervisory Law of 1901

The coming of age of commercial companies providing mass-market insurance came late in German economic development and coincided with the huge increase in disposable income brought about by the industrial revolution. Thus from the 1850s onwards rapid expansion initiated a period of intense competition. The relative youthfulness of such a highly technical industry meant that inexperience together with opportunistic business practices led to a large number of insurance collapses. Several German states introduced their own regulatory provisions and we witness the creation of low-level rate-setting and product-term dictating cartels (Hollenders 1985: 21). In this way the nascent industry hoped to reduce pressure upon itself. Into this mix of competing state regulation and a form of anti-competitive self-regulation came demands that the new Reich should introduce one comprehensive regulation for the whole of Germany focusing on the need to protect the mass policy-holder from the detrimental effects of the collapse of insurers. However, a more detailed examination of the period between the first government proposal for federal legislation in 1879 (Büchner 1952: 10, 12) and subsequent enactments of 1901 reveals that a balance was drawn between several sets of interests which did not necessarily focus solely on the policy-holder and which determined the nature of supervision up until the 1990s.

The law of 1901 'recognized that insurance differed from all other forms of commercial activity and that competition should be restricted to ensure its stability' (Büchner 1952: 16). A federal authority would be created with powers to restrict entry and allow for interventionist supervision. The interest of the federal government in the creation of such regulation was first signalled in its proposal of 1879. With Bismarck's social legislation, the state became involved in the provision of social insurance. Whilst social factors may explain the entrance of the state into regulatory matters, the federal and restrictive nature of that legislation was dictated by economic factors. A common system would allow for integrated growth and central control would facilitate the restriction of foreign penetration into the German market (Hollenders 1985: 23). The choice of a restrictive regime of supervision was made with a controlled growth of the German economy in mind. Once again the preamble to the Supervisory Law emphasized the importance of the role of insurance capital in the general growth of the German economy.

A final political-economic factor of major importance in the decision to create the central interventionist Authority was the opportunity this gave to the federal government to raise direct income on insurance policies. At this time the federal government relied solely upon indirect taxation for its finances. Before the arrival of the Supervisory Law those individual states which maintained insurance supervision were the recipients of any such fiscal advantages.

Contrary to general expectations, the insurance industry did not at first welcome the regulatory proposals. In their response to the plan the insurers rejected the idea of a central office to assess the applications for entry into the market, preferring instead the concept of entry on the simple fulfilment of legal requirements. Similarly, they deemed the interventionist powers of a supervisory authority to be damaging to the prospects for a sustained growth of the industry (Arps 1965: 61). Instead it appears that the insurers felt themselves to be capable of controlling their own activities. The desire of insurers to 'put their own house in order' is of major importance to this day, and, once enmity towards a central authority had been replaced by an air of co-operation between the authority and the insurers, the industry's role in advising and co-operating with that authority became decisive.

The industry was thus to welcome the introduction of the Insurance Authority in 1901 for various reasons. The insurers shared the concern of the federal government that the proliferation of regulations in the *Länder* was damaging the integrated growth of the industry. Similarly, the lack of public confidence in the market, as a result of the increasing numbers of insolvencies, was crippling to an industry which trades in trust. Finally, for the first time they faced government competition. Insurers were concerned not only that the new state-run health insurers would take business from the private market, but that government would extend the nationalization into other lines of insurance. When Bismarck displayed an eagerness towards proposals for the state running of life assurance (Arps 1965), insurers began to ask themselves whether fire insurance would follow. The answer to these dilemmas seemed to be a form of co-operation with the state which would ensure a united market and re-enforce public confidence and place a strictly controlled private insurance industry in the front line, should further social welfare plans call for further social insurance.

The technical nature of the insurance instrument meant that much attention was paid to the role of economic theory when regulation was drawn up. Market failure, relating to the difficulty of maintaining adequate solvency margins in the face of competition, was identified as the main danger against which to guard. This restriction of competition, by requiring not only that entry into the industry should be limited, but that business conduct should be strictly controlled, was prevalent in Germany (Finsinger, Tapp and Hammond 1985: 50). Government interests were well served by such an approach. Arguably, their major economic aim, that the vast capital reserves generated by the industry should be deployed to the benefit of the emergent German market, was facilitated by such regulation. Similarly, in the social sphere a co-ordinated growth of welfare provision through private insurance was aided by such an approach.

The character of the Federal Supervisory Authority

The law of 1901 laid down the basic character of the Federal Supervisory Authority, which remains substantially unchanged to this day. The first point of interest was the placing of responsibility for the agency in the hands of the Department for Financial and Fiscal Affairs within the Ministry for Economic Affairs. This department, although now a part of the Finance Ministry, was and is responsible for the direction and political orientation of the Federal Supervisory Authority. The law envisaged that Insurance Authority would be responsible for the day-to-day supervision of insurers. The use of sectoral regulation to further general economic goals would be a matter for government. The administrative structure of the agency, however, ensured the primary importance of the leading figures of Authority. The arrangement of the authority as a body with a small highly qualified technical staff led by a president assisted by a vice-president, gave the person in charge a decisive role in the formulation and direction of policy. This central role has often proved to be at odds with perceived governmental political control, and powerful presidents often drawn from industry have continuously asserted the independence of the agency.

The staff of the agency had administrative and legal powers, and the agency had a large degree of discretion as regards its interventionary powers to allow for the sustained growth of a young industry.

In the parliamentary debates which accompanied the creation of the Federal Supervisory Authority doubts were raised as to the ability of bureaucrats to understand the technical nature of insurance and to maintain their independence in the face of powerful corporations. It was, however, generally felt that the creation of such an agency would constitute a significant control on the activities of the industry. The questions of competence raised in the Bundestag, however, are somewhat misleading.

Rather than a classic process whereby government introduced legislation to curb the activities of a hostile industry which in turn sought to 'capture' the regulatory agency, the run-up to the enactment of Insurance Supervisory Law showed that a spirit of co-operation between the industry and the agency was, in fact, inherent to the regulatory functions of the Insurance Authority. An unusual feature of the activities of the agency remains its partnership with industry, not designed to ensure the dominance of industry interests but promoted by the regulatory agency as a vital aspect of the regulatory mechanism.

In this context, the question to be asked of the new authority is how its relationship to the interests which had dictated the creation of regulation was now to develop. The administrative make-up of the new authority engendered close co-operation between its staff and both government and industry. Whilst the main public aim of the authority was to ensure the protection of the policy-holder, close ties with industry ensured that the latter's voice was heard. The control of the agency by the Finance and Fiscal Department, its location in Berlin close to the seat of government and the drawing of its members from traditional bureaucratic ranks ensured that government policy would be closely pursued. The history of the Federal Supervisory Authority for Insurance from its inception to the intervention of the EC is one of a balancing act between sectoral industrial policy and macro-industrial policy.

The first period (1901–31) – limited agency supervision

During this period the Federal Supervisory Authority restricted itself to the supervision of market entry, solvency and investment. It gradually made inroads into the control of product terms with the development of a comprehensive set of policy conditions and with its involvement in the preparation of a new Insurance Contract Law (Versicherungsvertragsgesetz, 1908). Government interests were easily satiated. The close watch kept on the entry of new insurers ensured that collapses due to fraudulent or speculative behaviour were eradicated. A ban on the investment of insurance funds abroad maintained the presence in Germany of large amounts of capital vital to domestic economic development. Industry too – in particular the cartels – was pleased by developments, having been delegated responsibility for the maintenance of reduced competition through rate-setting. The task of the cartels had been facilitated by the entry conditions created by the Federal Supervisory Authority.

This period of stability did not last, as during the period of hyper-inflation in Germany and the worldwide economic collapse of 1929, the Federal Supervisory Authority appeared to falter, reacting too late to changing circumstances. Similarly, in the renewed onslaught of competition brought about by the change in world capital markets, the industry found the pressures on the cartel system too great and pricing arrangements collapsed.

On the part of the industry, the cartels were proving to be somewhat unstable. A shift in their attitude became apparent. They began to look towards binding premium calculation administered by the Insurance Authority as the way to reduce competition. Thus in 1924 the association of life insurers lobbied the Authority for premium calculation regulation (Finsinger, Tapp and Hammond 1985: 51). Though rejected at this time, such an approach was to become the norm in the 1930s. The Authority had its own problems. It was the recipient of much criticism as the 1923 relaxation of the ban on the investment of insurance funds in fixed property came too late to offset the virtual decimation of market resources by inflation. Here the nature of the mandate of the agency to protect the policy-holder was to have a decisive effect. The regulatory regime had been introduced in a welter of publicity about its function in defending the well-being of the populace. Where the Authority failed to avert a crisis it was seen as failing in its duty to protect the public as a whole. The pressure to act was enormous, the agency took corresponding steps. At this stage a change in legislation was not felt necessary and instead the wide degree of discretion given to the agency enabled a tightening of control to be achieved through a change in administrative methods. Members of the agency 'who had failed to live up to their functions' were replaced (Starke 1952: 29). Interestingly such members had little experience of the industry and this may in turn have strengthened the policy of the agency to recruit members with industry backgrounds. Extra aid was given to the cartels themselves, the authority becoming increasingly active in the negotiation of price agreements. In the matter of protection of the policy-holder, supervisory functions were extended. In pursuit of the provision of fair information to clients, the agency even intervened in the relationship between insurers and their agents (Büchner 1952: 30).

Whilst it survived the period of hyper-inflation with a change in its working practices, the economic collapse of 1929 dealt a severe blow to the agency providing the impetus for the regulatory changes of 1931. The single most important event of this period was the collapse of the Frankfurter Allgemeinen in 1929. That this is the only German insurer to have collapsed since the inception of central regulation is a measure of the success of the Supervisory Authority. It is also, however, a pointer to the devastating impact of any such occurrence upon the agency. Market failure had become a spectacular reality. Pressure for a traditional response, the strengthening of regulation to correct market inefficiencies, grew.

In response to the difficulties experienced by the industry in this period the amendment law of 1931 heralded the most restrictive period of regulation.

The second period (1931–51) – strict control

The law of 1931 placed a duty on the agency to supervise all areas of business. A move was slowly made away from industry control of regulatory rates to legally binding price norms administered by the agency. Thus in 1933 the same tariff for all automobile insurers was introduced and had become legally binding in the form of the 'unitary tariff' by 1938. The health of industry cartels, however, was also fostered. Although their main function – the setting of rates – was now undertaken by the Authority, they remained a vital regulatory partner, organizing the collection and distribution of statistics across the industry (see Hollenders 1985: 20ff.). As such they had direct input into the decision-making process regarding the calculation of rates. Supervision of the daily work of insurers similarly increased as companies were subjected to ever greater reporting requirements.

An unusual step to take in relation to a regulatory agency, was the removal of the power of the courts to review administrative decisions taken in the course of the Federal Supervisory Authority's work (Änderungsgesetz, 30 March 1932). The preamble to the Amendment Law makes specific reference to a series of judgements of the Reichsgericht (Supreme Court) which had overturned several agency decisions. These decisions struck at the core of supervision, reversing the designation of several concerns as insurers. Thus the agency was unable to decide for itself over whom it should exercise control. There is a clear indication that the Authority considered that courts were incapable of understanding the technical difficulties associated with insurance and, as a consequence of the application of 'too formal a legal approach' (Büchner 1952: 28) to Insurance Supervisory Law, had damaged the effectiveness of insurance regulation. Although this provision did not survive the re-creation of the Authority in 1951, its inclusion in the 1931 law reflects an important part of the philosophy of the regulatory agency. The feeling that the agency is a body set apart by its specialist knowledge of an intricate industry persists to this day.

For the Insurance Supervisory Authority the Third Reich heralded a period of almost intrusive government interference in its affairs. Although governmental measures remained within the general tenor of the promotion of government interests which had led to the enactment of Insurance Supervisory Law, these interests were now pushed to an extreme. Changes made to regulatory laws damaged the interests of other parties, most notably policy-holders, thus upsetting the balance struck between interest groups at the inception of regulation. The use of insurance regulation as a macro-industrial policy tool contradicted the reason for its existence – the sectoral regulation of an inefficient market for the benefit of consumers.

The power of insurance supervision as a general economic policy tool was furthered by a law of 1937, requiring the regulatory agency to take account of the 'general economic' climate before endorsing the licensing of new insurers. The agency was thus given a political-economic role which would seem to conflict with pure bureaucratic functions. In the postwar period the agency complained that the attempt of government to deploy insurance for its own political goals meant that even trivial decisions had had to be submitted to the Reich's Economics Ministry for approval (Starke 1952: 35). Similarly, government desires to raise revenue directly from the industry were taken to damaging extremes. Insurers were first encouraged, and later forced, to invest most of their portfolios in government bonds. The destructive nature of such a policy was revealed only in the postwar years when severe losses of policy-holder income were revealed (Finsinger, Tapp and Hammond 1985: 56).

With the collapse of the Third Reich the Insurance Supervisory Authority ceased to exist. During the period 1945–51 a form of supervision was established in each of the three Allied zones and in Berlin. A single Insurance Supervisory Authority was re-established in the Federal Republic of Germany in July 1951 (Bundesgesetz, 31 July 1951).

The third period – dichotomy in the German political economy

The Federal Supervisory Authority re-established at this time is the 'modern' Insurance Supervisory Authority. The 'modernity' of the agency seemed, however, only to extend to its name. The continuity of restrictive supervision was in fact preserved and with it the homogeneity of the agency.

The power of the balance of interests, established at the turn of the century, and the continued dominance of restrictive economic theory proved all the more remarkable as they survived a sea-change in Germany's political economy. The creation of the Federal Republic brought with it a radical change in economic philosophy (Finsinger, Tapp and Hammond 1985: 52). Ludwig Erhard, Minister for Economic Affairs, led the movement for a liberal economy, inspired by competition and pluralism.

Insurance, as ever, was the exception. Although attempts were made to introduce regulatory reforms (Erhard lobbied for the inclusion of insurance within the regime introduced by the 1958 Cartel Law: see Chapter 7), these were resisted by the industry. The Authority was re-established with much the same restrictive powers of supervision. Some changes were made as the more extreme measures of the foregoing years were abandoned. The licensing of insurers was no longer dependent upon the general economic climate. Investment restrictions were eased: insurance funds were now committed to any purpose which would guarantee a safe return. In general, however, supervision remained as restrictive and as anti-competitive as ever.

On the administrative level, the powers of the courts to review the decisions of the Authority were re-established after objections had been raised about the dual administrative and judicial nature of the agency (Starke 1952: 52).

An interesting consequence of the period of government intervention in the agency was a subtle shift in the attitudes of that body to their influence. Some demands were made for the agency to be given specific constitutional guarantees of independence much in the manner of the Bundesbank. Although this was not to be the case, there was a definite cooling in relations between the federal government and the agency. The latter remained in Berlin away from the new seat of federal power in Bonn. The attitude of the Authority towards its political masters, already strained by virtue of its administrative structure, became increasingly antagonistic. The importance of this was shown as the Authority displayed hostility to the new economic attitudes of a government which called for the introduction of competition in the insurance markets. In the eyes of the agency these moves may have appeared remarkably similar to those of the national socialist regime. The agency became increasingly isolated from modern economic developments, instead drawing heavily upon the older economic philosophy, which had shaped its creation.

Attempts to liberalize the insurance markets were intense. Led by Erhard himself, the attack was two-pronged. A direct attempt was made to reform the supervisory practices of the agency, whilst an indirect assault on the use of industry cartels to dampen competition was undertaken.

The attack on supervisory practice slowly gathered momentum. The unitary tariff for motor insurance, for example, continued to be imposed until 1962 (Finsinger, Tapp and Hammond 1985: 53). At this time the Ministry of Economic Affairs intervened, forcing a change to a form of premium calculation mechanism. This attempt at reform was only partially successful. Whilst it allowed for a certain degree of price competition, uniform calculations ensured that premium levels remained above their costs. The Ministry continued to press for changes but with limited success. Although premium calculations were finally abolished in 1980, the Authority continued to allow the use of a uniform calculation clause in all contracts negating any attempts to stimulate competition. Similarly the authority continued to exercise control over the terms of contracts, solvency margins and the day-to-day business practices of insurers.

The second attempt at reform centred on the industry cartels. The centrepiece of Erhard's new economic strategy was the Cartel Law introduced in 1958 (see Chapter 7; see also McGowan 1993 and Sturm and Ortwein 1993) which ruled that all private agreements between German concerns having an anti-competitive impact were deemed illegal. The Federal Cartel Office was established to oversee the administration of this provision. The new law would have brought an end to the high profile of industry cartels in setting the terms and provisions of insurance contracts. The industry, supported by the Federal Supervisory Authority, was, however, to ensure the exemption of insurance from the new law on the basis that anti-competitive behaviour was to be permitted where it could be shown to be in the public interest. The economic argument that market stability could only be achieved through the restriction of competition prevailed above the arguments of Erhard. All agreements relating to the supervision of insurance within the ambit of the Authority were exempted.

The concept of insurance regulation in Germany had come into conflict with powerful government-led forces and survived. The agency and the industry had undoubtedly offered stern opposition. Industry pressure groupings played a prominent role in the Bundestag during debates on an exemption for the insurance sector, but was this the only factor which led to their success? Had simple consumer protection and economic theory arguments prevailed over opposing liberal sentiments? Was this merely a case of re-establishing the postwar relevance of the historical approach to sectoral regulation? At this stage a re-examination of the use of insurance capital to build up the German economy in the early years of the century proves useful. Much the same situation existed in postwar Germany. With little pressure from foreign competition, insurers were free to invest their premium income in the German market. Similarly, indirect taxation on what was to become the third largest insurance market in the world gave government a vital source of income. This seems to point to a possible dichotomy in the postwar political economy. The continued relevance of one perception of historical sectoral policy was not the only issue under consideration. Instead, two divergent attitudes towards economic development had emerged. In the form of insurance regulation, an aspect of prewar economic policy was left to co-exist with new postwar economic liberalism.

The present-day structure of the Federal Supervisory Authority for Insurance

In the more recent past, the character of insurance regulation in Germany has been much altered owing to the intervention of the European Community. Such intercession, however, has largely been directed at black-and-white regulatory provisions and has as a consequence had a lesser effect upon the administrative make-up of the Authority itself. Although the appointment in the early 1990s of a new, apparently more pro-European, president, Hohfeld, may finally lead to changes in the day-to-day workings of the Authority, this is as yet unapparent to the casual observer. Therefore, it is still possible to link the current operations of the agency directly with its historical role.

The Insurance Supervisory Authority recently stated that its role 'is to safeguard proposers, policy-holders, beneficiaries and any other third party interested in the due performance of the contract'. To this end, it deems it imperative 'that the insurance concerns conduct their business properly and remain solvent and that the contracts conform to the law'. The authority guarantees this state of affairs through the exercise of 'constant oversight over insurance concerns' (OECD 1984).

With the removal of the Department for Financial and Fiscal Affairs to the Finance Ministry in 1972, the Authority now finds itself subject to the political control of a different governmental department. The Authority, however, continues to be headed by a president assisted by a vice-president, and whilst members of the Department continue to assert their political will over the actions of the agency, the pivotal role of the president and the Authority's continued determination to preserve its own political identity remains apparent. The penultimate president, August Angerer, in particular, through numerous publications and a tough personal style, reflected the independent nature of the agency.

A small number of highly qualified technical staff are organized in seven divisions, each dealing with a particular type of insurance business. These staff perform all agency functions, including on-site inspections of insurers. The position of the president remains of primary importance. Decisions are taken by the president, by means of an 'order'. Important orders, such as a decision to refuse the licensing of a new insurer, or to revoke the licence of a practising insurer, must be taken by the Beschlusskammer, a body made up of three members of the Federal Supervisory Authority and two members of the Insurance Advisory Council (Versicherungsbeirat), which has sixty members drawn from insurers, 'competent' policy-holders from all sectors of industry and commerce, the professions, civil servants and members of trade unions, as well as insurance agents and staff members of insurance companies and professional actuaries. The role of the Insurance Advisory Council is 'to help in the preparation of important decisions'. Thus actions of the Authority are subject to a wide degree of consultation. The nature of those persons consulted, however, betrays an overemphasis on the importance of industrial figures. The agency consults only those policy-holders deemed to be 'competent'. The policy-holder body, which sits on the Advisory Council and is cited by the Authority as the main consumer organization, is the Deutscher Versicherungs-Schutzverband. This large and well-staffed body is financed by large industrial clients and contrasts strongly with the position of the mass-market consumer, whose interests are protected by the small Bund der Versicherten. To characterize the Schutzverband as an industry pressure group may be to go too far. Its continued presence, however, as the main policy-holder body points to an important aspect of the Authority's traditional philosophy. The mass policy-holder, deemed to be unable to make an informed choice on the nature of an insurance policy, is likewise deemed to be unable to understand the decisions of the regulators. Whilst a certain amount of representation may be apparent for various kinds of insurance through such bodies as the automobile association, small-scale insurance consumers are, in the main, conspicuous by their absence.

The decisions of the Authority continue to be subject to the review of the German administrative courts. There is, however, much evidence of continued agency ambivalence towards such supervision. Once again the outspoken Angerer, defending an agency action, offered a stern critique of the action of the courts in overturning many such terms, stating that judges had a habit 'of construing the law in a manner other than that envisaged by the law-maker' (Angerer 1975).

To the extent that the agency might continue to determine policy rates and conditions, the relationship between the Federal Supervisory Authority and the cartels retains a position at the core of supervisory activities. The cartels continue to act in concert with the agency in the all-important matter of the approval of policy terms and the calculation of premiums. Initiatives in this area are largely based upon statistics gathered by the cartels from their members. The agency mostly works directly with the cartels, who then disseminate information and decisions further to their membership.

THE PRESSURE FOR CHANGE

The preceding section demonstrates the traditionally restrictive nature of the regime of insurance supervision in the Federal Republic, and shows how the Federal Supervisory Authority has, over the whole of the twentieth century, played a pivotal role in maintaining a consistent balance between the interests of those groups centred on the German insurance industry.

The regime of insurance regulation in general, however, and the role of the supervisory agency in particular, are now under attack from many sources. The prime mover for change is clearly the European Community. Supervisory practice in Germany, substantially more restrictive than that of some of its Community partners, has proved to be a barrier to the unification of the European insurance market. It has consequently attracted the intense and particular attention not only of the European law-maker, but also of Community strategists. Such concerns with the German market are, however, complemented by and encouraging of varying forces within Germany itself. Community action has thus highlighted the underlying tensions between the liberal, pluralist nature of many of the country's economic principles and the restrictive nature of insurance supervision.

The consequences of this new movement are manifest within the present process of the disintegration of the long-established equilibrium maintained between the various actors within the 'regulatory network'. A quieter debate is also under way focusing on undermining the economic principles which form the basis for supervision. Similarly, consumer interests have been liberated by EC actions, and the voice of the insurance client, long subordinate to the 'paternalistic' character of insurance regulation, has at last been heard. These emergent forms of expression are now placing increasing strain upon the old network. Similarly, members of the coalition of interests which form the backdrop to regulation are finding that they are forced to withdraw from the network. Industry, for example, under pressure from its European competitors and encouraged to follow new paths by the Community, has had to change its business practices and has thus found itself increasingly isolated from the Supervisory Authority.

In brief, the three forces for change may be identified as traditional economic dichotomies, initiatives of the EC and consequential strains placed upon the network by those internal and external to it. A definitive demarcation between these three is elusive, but a distinction might be drawn between those due largely to internal pressures and those stemming from the Community. Internal, purely technical economic pressures, despite EC competition law having furnished them their greatest opportunity yet to assert themselves, have hardly dented the old network. Commission and European Court of

Justice advances, on the contrary, appear to have had a forceful 'dissolving' impact upon the traditional constellation of interests.

'Pure' internal pressures

The attack of economic theorists

It has often been noted that the 'insularity' of regulatory agencies, prompted by a combination of political factors, tradition or sheer ignorance of technical economics, exasperates economists (Behan 1980: 77). Arguments demonstrating how regulatory aims may best be served by 'working with the market' rather than imposing 'rules from above' are often ignored. Where the emphasis of a regulatory agency has shifted and 'pure' economic arguments have been taken into account, radical changes in regulatory policies have ensued (see Chapter 1).

German regulation in general and the Federal Supervisory Authority in particular are no strangers to such attacks. The last ten years in particular, have seen a sustained offensive by economists who have tested the regulatory practices of the Authority against its own stated aim, as formulated by Angerer himself: 'the protection of the trust placed by concerned citizens in an insurance industry which functions well' (Angerer 1975: 197). A significant argument states that the interests of the consumer are poorly served, as limitations in the product range and poor servicing of contracts are commensurate with anti-competitive conduct (Von der Schulenburg and Finsinger 1985). Moreover, the claim made by the Authority that the insurance market is an exception to the general rule that 'competition is good for the consumer' has been countered by influential studies which show: that standard product terms may be discarded, problems of product transparency being eased by the creation of a class of independent financial advisers; that calculations for tariffs need not include supplements for solvency purposes, guarantee funds being an adequate safeguard against the collapse of insurers; and, finally, that the easing of investment restrictions would cause no serious financial difficulties for insurers (Finsinger, Tapp and Hammond 1985).

Whilst the Authority has responded to such criticisms, these responses have largely consisted of a repetition of the economic arguments advanced at the turn of the century, with little contemporary evidence to show their continued relevance. The necessity for such a reply from the Authority would seem, however, to be limited. Such arguments as have been advanced are rooted in modern technical economics. As such they perceive insurance regulation to be a mere matter of problem-solving. Accordingly, they undertake to investigate this conundrum with reference to the industry alone. As such they fail to broach those wider economic policy concerns which seem to condition the nature of insurance regulation in Germany. Until such time as economists challenge the 'hidden agenda' of the regulator, the relevance of efficiency arguments remains questionable.

The limited direct effect of such arguments upon the Supervisory Authority notwithstanding, such 'pure' economic arguments have gained a more powerful entrée into the debate by virtue of Community competition law activities. The case of the Association of German Fire Insurers (Sachverband der deutschen Feuerversicherer) was thus noticeable as it spawned an intense debate within the Federal Republic on the importance of competition in insurance markets.

The case of the Association of German Fire Insurers

When seen through the eyes of the Federal Supervisory Authority, the case of the Association of German Fire Insurers, heard by the European Court of Justice in 1987 is disturbing indeed.

The Association was, and is, a classic insurance 'cartel', which, on the basis of statistics gathered from its members, recommends premiums to be charged for fire insurance. It is a traditional regulatory partner to the Federal Supervisory Authority, with a seat on the Insurance Advisory Council, and thus is to be regarded not only as a private actor, but also as a partner to the Supervisory Authority in the matter of regulation.

The early 1980s, however, saw the Association undertake certain activities which led it to Luxembourg, the seat of the European Court of Justice (ECJ). At the time of Court proceedings all fire insurers authorized to conduct business in Germany were members of the cartel. Importantly, foreign insurers were included within its ranks. In 1982, the Association issued a non-binding recommendation to its members to make across-the-board increases in gross premiums of up to 30 per cent. This was the usual response of a private cartel, acting with the full blessing of the Authority, in accordance with an exemption under German competition law, to a dramatic fall in average fire insurance premiums. A drop of 50 per cent in premiums had been experienced between 1973 and 1979, giving rise to a sectoral deficit whereby the premiums received would not suffice to offset the total losses indemnified.

Significantly, it was argued that the danger of market failure was met by the industry, not in a private capacity but in its role as a regulatory partner to the Authority. The European Commission nevertheless refused to allow an exemption to the cartel, instead bringing proceedings against it as a private market actor in contravention of Community Competition rules (Article 85 of the Treaty of Rome). The ECJ confirmed the Commission's view, holding the recommendations of the Association to be anti-competitive and damaging to the free flow of trade across Community borders. In purely competition terms this was clearly a fully justifiable response. The use of *gross* premiums as a basis for the calculation of rates would appear to be an abusive response to sectoral crisis. A problem, however, arose in that the ECJ not only disapproved of the 'gross premium' element within the recommendation of the cartel, but also called the activities of this body into question in their entirety. That is, the right of the Association to make any recommendation whatsoever was now doubted.

In refusing to recognize the historically accepted regulatory role of the Association, and in finding its recommendations, in their entirety, to be those of a private cartel and therefore anti-competitive and damaging to the free flow of trade across Community borders, the ECJ at one stroke upset an intricate regulatory arrangement. Viewed from the standpoint of the Authority, this was a fine example of 'rarefied' law upsetting practical historical accommodations. To cite the most striking phrases within the judgement, the core German objection to the application of Article 85 EEC in this case had been: 'no provision of the Treaty authorizes the institutions of the Community to contest . . . the choice of national governments to use cartels as an instrument of regulation and thereby to . . . compromise the conduct of national economic policy'. The apparent inability of the ECJ to address such concerns within the legal framework of the EC Treaty, however, merely brought a simple conclusion that such an argument could not be accepted, as 'Community law does not make the implementation of [competition policy] dependent upon the manner in which the supervision of certain areas of economic activity is organized by national legislation'. Therefore, competition law, freed from the political restraints which would delimit its application in any national context, was to cut swathes through established German supervisory perceptions. In a slightly more complex formulation, 'pure' competition policy was deployed to upset general, contextual economic strategies. The use of cartels to maintain market stability may well have been a restrictive form of regulation, but it was restrictive for a definite purpose: historically in relation to the insurance sector at least, market stagnation was seen as a good thing, an aid to general economic growth.

Whilst the Commission was quick to act to defuse political conflict, introducing a block exemption to free insurers from the exhaustive application of competition policy (Council Regulation (EEC) no. 1534/91 of 31 May 1991), this process of Community 're-regulation' has brought with it further phantoms for the Authority. Whilst theoretically at least, such bodies as the Association might persevere in their quasi-regulatory functions, they will always be required to satisfy both European and national competition policy. A historical consideration of insurance regulation in Germany, however, clearly demonstrated just how great a role the Supervisory Authority had played in mediating between different actors, thus ensuring continuity in supervisory policy. Lying at the centre of the web of interests, with a great deal of influence over the national legislative process, the Authority was able to oversee the actions of many market players, being able to offer concessions in return. This then is the crux of the problem now facing the Authority. Such inducements are no longer its alone to give. It must now reckon with the active involvement of the European Commission, and will itself be forced to negotiate anything it wishes to do with an organization extraneous to the body politic of the Federal Republic. In other words, now active within the network of interests in Germany is a party (the Commission) which has no historical ties to the balance of interests maintained there and which furthermore may have goals quite different from those traditionally pursued by national actors.

Leaving aside such long-term disturbances to the interest network in Germany, the case of the Association of German Fire Insurers also caused a more immediate disruption of the German regulatory regime. The findings of the ECJ were to place the exemption of the insurance industry from German competition law in doubt. The case thus prompted yet another reappraisal of Article 102 of the Cartel Law. This was potentially the economic theorists' finest hour. In the matter of competition law at least, their arguments and credentials would appear to be impeccable. Interestingly enough, however, they failed to make full use of this initiative. This can only indicate that, even in recent years, the balance of interests set in place at the turn of the century remained remarkably strong.

The reform of German competition law

Large-scale concentration in the distribution industry in the 1980s prompted a reform of national competition law. Community involvement with the Association of German Fire Insurers ensured that the insurance industry would also be subject to this revision.

Article 102 has been the traditional battlefield where the forces of 'free competition', the Federal Cartel Office, have confronted the forces of 'restraint', the Insurance Supervisory Office, and this conflict has undoubtedly been heightened in more recent years by the control of the two agencies by different government departments. Article 102, being the exemption of the insurance industry from competition law, allowed the continuance of the creation by the cartels of joint product and rate agreements, providing these were for the purposes of insurance supervision and registered with the Cartel Office. This arrangement had long been the focal point of the earlier identified dichotomy in the postwar German political economy. The Cartel Office is the child of Erhard, and as such it is imbued with the pluralist, liberal economic philosophy of the postwar period. In its dealings with the Authority it was to clash with an agency whose philosophy was of an earlier age. As might be expected, the philosophical clash is mirrored by administrative conflict. The two agencies are called upon to co-operate in the administration and supervision of insurance cartels. The Federal Supervisory Authority, jealous of its competence to regulate the industry and suspicious of the aims of the Cartel Office, has often tried to circumvent the provisions requiring co-operation. In 1987, the Federal Monopoly Commission, an independent body of experts producing policy reports on concentrations and mergers and reporting directly to the federal government, complained bitterly of the designation of the insurance cartels by the Authority as mere 'agents of insurance supervision'. In this manner, agreements between insurers would be concluded together with the agency and as such be characterized as agency decisions, not requiring review by the

Cartel Office. In the words of the Monopoly Commission the 'arrogant' actions of the Authority had infringed upon the supervisory competences of the Cartel Office. A solution to the conflict was reached only after the Ministries of Finance and Economic Affairs, and the Authority agreed to discontinue the practice of joint agreements. The Monopoly Commission, however, pointed to the likely continuance of conflict should the Cartel Office's involvement depend upon the agreement of the Authority, an agreement which could be withdrawn for 'supervisory' purposes (Cartel Law, Article 102, point 4, prior to the reforms of 1989; see also Chapter 7 above).

Against this background a reform of Article 102 was included in the legislative changes made to competition law in late 1989. Whilst on the surface a fundamental re-alignment, the practical reform to the law was not in fact wide-ranging. Although insurance cartels were to come under the general *Verbotsprinzip*, cartel agreements made within the ambit of the activities of the Insurance Supervisory Office still retain certain of their immunities. All 'technical or organizational agreements', which, through the introduction of recommended policy terms, are designed to improve the performance of the contract are thus deemed to be acceptable; quite clearly such a broad formulation might be used to justify most existing cartel arrangements. In its explanation of the new proposal the German government stated that price agreements are also to be included in the notion of 'policy terms'. Some smaller changes were, however, made. An additional requirement, that no less anti-competitive measures should be available, was added to the law. Similarly, all such agreements are now registered with the Cartel Office. The requirement for the Authority to agree to such supervision was dropped, and instead the two agencies were called upon to work together (Cartel Law, Article 102).

The new formulation of the exemption fell far short of expectations. Both the Social Democratic Party and the Green Party had called in the Bundestag for the total removal of the exemption. The Monopoly Commission had focused upon economic arguments to back its call for the removal of Article 102, suggesting that the use of cartel agreements to offset the lack of market transparency and the dangers of insolvency in the industry could be replaced with other less anti-competitive measures. The Monopoly Commission had undertaken a wide review of Insurance Supervision as a whole, attacking not only the more extreme anti-competitive measures of cartels which could not be justified for the purposes of insurance supervision, but the concept of market stagnation in itself. In effect, the economic basis of sectoral regulation was challenged.

The new approach to the exemption, on the contrary, appeared less concerned with encouraging competition as with delineating more clearly the competences of the Insurance Supervisory Authority and the Cartel Office, thereby eradicating the more dubious practices of industry cartels. An immediate consequence of this move was noted even before the law was enacted. The Cartel Office reported in May 1989 that there had developed a closer form of co-operation between itself and the Authority. The first fruits of this collaboration had been the agreement by the Authority to outlaw the calculation of rates for most forms of insurance on the basis of gross premiums. Instead, net premiums were to be used. Similarly, the addition to premiums of an across-the-board flat fee for administrative and organizational costs was abandoned; such supplementary charges were to reflect the costs of individual insurers.

The governmental proposal for the reform to Article 102 clearly stated that examination of the old version of the law showed 'that the reasons for its justification, to a large degree, no longer existed'. In addition, introducing the reforms to the Bundestag, Wissmann, a member of parliament for the Christian Democrats, welcoming Community measures to stimulate competition, confirmed that privileges had been lifted in the banking and insurance sectors to 'accommodate the fresh winds of competition'. Why then did the Bundestag not seize the opportunity to alter radically the entire scheme of insurance supervision?

The answer to this question seems to lie in the interplay between competition policy, sectoral industrial policy and macro-industrial policy, which in turn reflects the conflict between the competitive economic spirit of the postwar period and the continued restrictive approach to the regulation of certain industries. 'Modern' domestic German competition policy is far from being a neutral economic instrument. Notwithstanding economic arguments which demonstrate the relevance of such a policy, it is employed *de facto* not by virtue of those arguments, but because it serves various social and economic ends.

It is the aim 'the greatest possible good for the people' and not the economic theory which is the guiding principle of competition policy. To this end it is deployed to restrict the concentration of industries in the private sector. In the government sector, however, other interests may intervene to dictate that this aim should be served in other ways. Trade-offs are commonplace. The consumer may be placed at a 'price disadvantage' in a restricted market, in order for political, social or even economic benefits to be reaped in other areas.

Those who based their critique of the actions of industry cartels on economic arguments were perhaps less than sensitive to their 'governmental' role. Since 1900 the cartels had been more than private actors, forming instead a vital regulatory partner to the Authority. As such their interests were prominent amongst those which had led to the enactment of regulation. In this context the use of economic efficiency as a 'rationality criteria' in the reform of the insurance exemption was, in a sense, superfluous.

The same governmental and industry interests had played a role in the reform process, the cartels having taken part in preliminary redrafting of the measure. As the interests which led to such restrictive legislation were not themselves challenged, the *status quo* was maintained. This failure to address the balance of interests was significant on two levels. In relation to sectoral

regulation, economic arguments may have exposed inefficiency but traditional attitudes towards the accommodation of interest groups were left
unchallenged. In addition, no attempt was made to challenge the economic
efficiency of the hidden policy agenda.

As a final point, a marked contrast emerges between the actions of the
European Court in the case of the Association of German Fire Insurers and
the subsequent German debate. The corrective legislation introduced to the
Bundestag two years later was prefaced by a series of trade-offs between the
(divergent) interests of government, the regulatory agency, industry and the
public. Central to the introduction of the reform to the Bundestag was the
philosophy that it is the end result, 'the greatest possible good of the people',
and not the economic rationale of competition policy, which is its essential.
Within the institutional constraints of a European court on the other hand, it
is the economic theory of competition policy which becomes the main
consideration. This process in turn disenfranchises national interest groups.

External pressure from the Community

Community actions

More recent forays by the European Community into matters 'regulatory'
have created a crisis within the ranks of the Supervisory Authority for
Insurance, challenging the intricate balance of interests masked by restrictive
German insurance regulation. The Authority is regarded as a 'tough negoti-
ator', often blocking Commission initiatives and failing to implement its
Directives properly.

Although the desire of the Community to see the creation of a form of pan-
European market in insurance is long-standing, tensions between the German
Supervisory Authority and the Community have surfaced only in the past few
years. The degree of concord between the two bodies at the inception of the
harmonization process owed much to the relatively modest aims of the EC.
This, in tandem with a traditional approach to the division of competences
between the Community and the member states, combined to avert crisis. The
primary Community goal was to open up 'channels of access' between
markets, through the realization of the right of establishment. The concept of
the open market was thus restricted. Insurers would be 'free' only inasmuch
as they should establish themselves in any European market on the basis of
rigorous solvency and administrative mores applied in common by all
member states. In this way the competence of the Authority to supervise all
insurance operations conducted within the Federal Republic was preserved.
Foreign insurers were still required to be authorized by the Authority and to
submit themselves to its regulatory requirements. Any harmonization of
regulatory provisions was confined to the monitoring of solvency. The
Authority was fortunate to find itself in a majority of national regulatory
agencies wishing to preserve their own restrictive regimes (within Europe the
British and the Dutch alone rely largely on the market and competition to

regulate insurers). Thus, vigorous lobbying by the Authority within the Community ensured that nations such as Britain were required to 'harmonize upwards' to German standards, rather than the other way round.

Latter-day moves by the EC to realize the freedom of services in the insurance sector and to bring the internal market to its conclusion have, however, upset this equilibrium. With the publication of its White Paper in 1985 (Com. (85) 310), the Commission signalled its intention to create a form of European insurance market where 'an insurer established in Cologne would note no legal differences were it to pursue business in Bavaria or in Scotland' (Sir Leon Brittan, 1990). The main plank in this campaign was to be the realization of the freedom to provide services contained in Article 59 of the EC Treaty. In other words, insurers with a main establishment in one European country should be free to offer their products throughout the EC, without being required to open additional branches.

Such an integration strategy, however, inevitably brings with it a blurring of distinctions between the regulatory sovereignty of the member states. Service provision, for example, does not merely entail the freedom to operate within a foreign territory, but relates to the ability to offer the domestic product in an unadulterated form on another market – that is, free from the exhaustive application of the regulatory provisions of the host state. To allow the sale of the unsullied 'foreign' product on the domestic market is to introduce the regulatory mores of a 'foreign' supervisory system into the home territory. As such norms are divorced from the domestic balance of interests, they cannot but place pressure upon it.

Community desires to see an open market in insurance services therefore present the Authority with an unprecedented, triple challenge to the supervisory constellation: the loss of domestic sovereignty; the consequential phantom of 'regulatory competition'; and the centralization of regulatory powers in the hands of the European Commission.

Some regulatory regimes of Germany's neighbours are significantly more liberal than its own. In particular, the entry of Great Britain into the Community in 1973 brought the spectre of a competitive regime which eschewed the correction of 'market failures' altogether. Were such Community insurers to be given free rein to operate on the German market under the terms of their own regulators, the power of the Authority to supervise the activities of such firms would be circumvented, in turn upsetting the delicate balance of interests, economic policy and sectoral regulation encompassed by federal regulation. Seen in this light, the case of the *Commission* v. *Germany* from 1986 becomes very significant (Case 205/84 ECR 1987, 3766ff.).

This hearing focused upon the realization of the right to provide services. The European Court of Justice concluded that Article 59 of the Treaty of Rome was to apply to insurance businesses. It therefore determined that certain categories of high-risk insurance business should be conducted across national frontiers largely on the basis of home control, that is, free from the interference of host regulators. Consequently, a German provision requiring all insurers transacting business in Germany to be established there was found to be incompatible with the Treaty.

The ECJ thus effectively dented traditional notions of sovereignty. Seen from the standpoint of a German regulator, however, what did this entail?

The freedom to provide services is what one might term a 'pure' economic freedom. The free flow of goods and services across national frontiers is designed to foster the wealth of the Community and is founded in liberal economic theory. The clash between this economic right and German supervisory provisions thus represented a collision between 'pure' economic theory and contextual economic policy fashioned in a national arena and suited to the interests of particular national actors.

In court, the German government explicitly argued that to allow the freedom of services would be to sidestep the jurisdiction of the Authority. Thus, it was maintained, the right of national governments to regulate in the best interests of the consumer should not be set aside without prior political agreement on consumer protection. Such a position, however, somewhat obscured the true political reason for German protest. To reiterate, inherent to German supervision was a set balance of interests and an element of macro-industrial policy; therefore the underlying thrust of the submission was that this balance should be negotiated away only within a political forum, and not displaced in pursuit of 'pure' supranational economic goals. Even had this rationale been made explicit, however, the ECJ would have been unable to address it, such a forum affording scant opportunity for transparent political debate of this kind. Although being political in its desire to execute the completion of the internal market, the ECJ is no stage for the balancing of national interests. Accordingly, it was able to approach the problem solely on the basis of 'pure' competition law. It thus appeared to answer the consumer protection concerns of Germany with its decision that only large-scale consumers should benefit from the provisions of Article 59. This distinction, however, based on technical consumer protection alone, left no room for the consideration of 'wider' contextual interests. In effect, in blurring regulatory competences and opening the door to British insurers to operate in the German market, it ushered in a degree of regulatory competition. Such competition should not be understood merely as a contest between technical supervisory provisions, but as the entry of other interests into the national network, interests which do not share the same national goals.

So much for the impact of 'rarefied' Community law on the balance of interests in the Federal Republic. Even in relation to 'negotiated' integration moves, Germany was not to fare much better. Initially, political negotiations following the case allowed the German regulatory regime to regain some lost ground. Thus, the Authority and the Finance Ministry were able to shore up the German position in discussions on the Second Non-Life and Life Insurance Directives, designed to elaborate upon the judgement of the ECJ.

Through the addition of a series of administrative restrictions upon the conduct of cross-border insurance services and a strict regime of control upon mass insurance business, including the prior approval of policy terms, they reasserted a degree of supremacy over transactions conducted in the Federal Republic. Community pressure for change, however, did not abate. Final agreement.has now been reached upon the third generation of directives (the framework directives, 'Third Council Directive on the Co-ordination of Laws, Regulations and Administrative Provisions Relating to Direct Assurance other than Life Assurance,' and 'Third Council Directive on the Co-ordination of Laws, Regulations and Administrative Provisions Relating to Direct Life Assurance' approved respectively by the Council on 18 June 1992 and 29 June 1992). These framework directives betray the rearguard nature of such tough negotiating stances, striking at the heart of some of the more fundamental aspects of the Authority's supervisory regime. Thus, for example, such requirements as the prior approval of foreign policy terms and conditions have been outlawed altogether. But by far the most disruptive element within these new provisions is the almost total abolition of host control over foreign insurers – with the introduction of a common insurance passport or single licence insurers will be free to ply their trade throughout Europe, overseen almost exclusively by their own regulators. Once this measure has been implemented, the remaining extent of host regulatory sovereignty will be negligible. In effect, the German regulator will find that large sections of those interests centred on the insurance business within the country are totally outside the regulator's sphere of influence. This can only upset the delicate balance of national interests, so tightly entwined with national economic policy.

The final challenge presented to the Authority by the Community is that the Commission is arguably moving towards a 'hands-on' approach to the supervision of European insurance business. With its total harmonization of prudential control mechanisms and the large degree of influence which it has accumulated in the matter of their adjustment, DG XV appears prepared to accept a degree of centralization of technical insurance regulation. Whether or not this is informed by a desire to ensure the efficient supervision of a pan-European industry, it entails an immense challenge to the competences of all national regulatory bodies. Another interesting facet of this tendency is the strategic use of general 'requirements' that there should be a unitary form of insurance regulation in Europe. The Commission has not been slow to highlight some of the problems which insurers and regulators face as a whole. For example, the most potent of these is undoubtedly the fear of extensive, or even unlimited, liability in relation to environmental risks. The European policy-makers have taken note of the problems which have beset the American market in this field, and the Commission has explicitly asserted its desire to play a part in tackling such issues (Brittan 1990: 754). This is undoubtedly a matter of strategy. In assuring the industry that it is willing to expend energy to avert the danger that they may find themselves hopelessly over-extended in relation to such international risks, the EC appears to be purchasing itself a degree of goodwill. Should it become embroiled in the technical regulation of such matters, however, the Community will find itself at the core of the intricate trade-off between interests which marks the relation of insurance to the needs of the economy as a whole.

It was earlier claimed that internal pressures on the network of interests in Germany had failed to alter significantly the relationship between the supervisory authority and the interests focused upon the national insurance market. Alternately formulated, the discussion of economic theory arguments in a national body, such as the Bundestag, enforced a trade-off between different positions and ensured that economic regulation was placed firmly in the context of (national) interests. It is furthermore asserted that Community actions, being divorced from such contextual checks, might upset such an interest equilibrium. Such an assumption requires proof. This is duly offered with a description of how the network is beginning to dissolve.

Consumer pressure

An obvious omission from the workings of the Authority in particular, and German regulation in general, has been any form of interaction with the mass-market consumer. The attitude of the Authority is plainly paternalistic. In the words of Angerer, competition in the terms of insurance contracts is a danger as the consumer 'runs the risk of choosing the wrong policy' (Angerer 1985: 221–38, 224). Consumers are unable to judge the workings of the industry, consequently the agency will take decisions for them. This paternalism extends to the internal organization of the agency. Whilst industrial consumers are consulted on most important decisions, mass consumers have little or no representation.

The consumer, however, has not been living in a vacuum, and arguments highlighting the disadvantaged position of German consumers in relation to their European neighbours have trickled down from academic debate, through Parliament to the mass media. Similarly, no consumer could possible miss the 'hype' of the Community with regard to the integrated markets of 1993. The intricate nature of a harmonization of national law not being given much prominence, recipients of such reports are left with the impression of an accessible international market without restraint. Expectations have arisen accordingly.

By the late 1980s, the ramifications of Community action became clear, as a loophole in Community law gave consumers in Germany the chance to act upon their 'expectations'. An insurance operation set up in Luxembourg. It did not require German authorization, nor was it subject to the supervision of the Authority. It advertised on German television offering British life assurance products at substantially lower premiums to German consumers, and took care to avoid the jurisdiction of the Authority, using no brokers within Germany. Instead, potential policy-holders applied by post or by travelling to Luxembourg.

Its popularity with German consumers was matched only by the displeasure of the regulatory agency. A combination of factors had combined to upset the traditional 'client politics' of German regulation. Until the intercession of the Community, the benefits of regulation were enjoyed by the few, and the costs were spread widely amongst policy-holders, whose opinions – in the absence of bodies designed to represent the mass-market – did not play a part in the regulatory process. With the introduction of foreign competition, consumers were given the chance to air their views rather than just 'voting with their feet' and leaving the marketplace. With the consumer free to seek the best price for a product outside the domestic market, the regulator is under pressure to bring practices into line with those of neighbours.

With increased Community intervention in the German market these pressures on the regulatory system can only increase. Similarly, consumer pressure has begun to tell upon the industry itself. The consumer, armed with an awareness of product terms and conditions enjoyed by his or her neighbours, has begun to bring pressure to bear upon the German industry to offer equally advantageous policies.

Pressure from industry

The German insurer has played a significant part within the balance of interests which has ensured the continuity of insurance supervision and the role of the Insurance Supervisory Authority in Germany for the past ninety-odd years. Recognized as a regulatory partner at the inception of interventionist supervision, the industry has, through the offices of the cartels, supported the position of the Authority.

Now, however, the intertwining of industry and supervisory agency appears to be under threat. The European Community has managed to dilute some of the barriers to entry which sheltered the native industry from foreign competition, and, in the area of large industrial insurance, better rates and terms offered by other European firms are now forcing German insurers to reassess their business practices. Similarly, Community strategists have shamelessly manipulated the commercial fears of the German industry, in the hope of accelerating this process. As such a long-standing regulatory partner to the Authority, the industry would clearly be somewhat hostile to EC advances. DG XV has not been slow to point out that the introduction of competition will help to overcome the long-term structural difficulties faced by the sector. Thus, the brewing distribution war between banks – freed from older regulatory constraints – and insurers is more likely to be settled in the insurers' favour (Brittan 1990). Similarly, the message that competition is a saviour is hammered home by the missive that new business structures, such as the mutuals, which are taking business from traditional insurers, might best be combated within such a competitive framework (Brittan 1990). Additionally, a measure of the Community's approval of the consequential change in the structure of the German market might be found in a gleeful announcement in the *European Bulletin* (18 June 1992), detailing a rise in premiums collected by the German market abroad from DM3.7 billion in 1985 to DM18.9 billion in 1989 (the German industry traditionally having been so inward-looking, this represents a sea-change in business practices).

Such constant touting has had its effect. The Gesamtverband der Deutschen Versicherungswirtschaft, a representative body for insurers, has noted a rift between the industry and the Authority. Where foreign competition has threatened the domestic market dominance of the German industry, insurers have responded by requesting the agency to approve less restrictive policy terms and conditions. The Authority, however, isolated from market realities and adhering to the old market philosophy, has refused to approve such requests. Such tension can only escalate.

CONCLUSION

To a certain degree, the Federal Supervisory Authority for Insurance remains a regulatory agency with a dual function. On the one hand, it is a purely regulatory body with a duty to oversee sectoral regulation. On the other, it appears to be an instrument of national industrial policy. The astounding continuity of the composition and actions of the agency is due to the stability of the network of interests which dictated the nature of its formation.

Today, however, both rarefied EC law and the more strategic manoeuvres by the Commission appear to have instigated the disintegration of the network of interests in Germany. New competitive realities appear to be undermining the network, at least between industry and the agency. Similarly, consumers have found a new voice with which to articulate their long disregarded dissatisfaction.

In relation to such growing fissures, the position of the government of the Federal Republic will now take centre stage. In the past, the Finance Ministry has undoubtedly supported the position of the Supervisory Authority when negotiating with the Commission and appearing before the European Court, but there is now an increasingly apparent probability that it too will become more antagonistic towards the agency. It is thus clear that the commitment of the Federal Republic to the Community is absolute, and should the government prize developments towards an integrated Europe above those of (an arguably outdated) internal economic policy, we may witness a complete collapse of the interest network.

In the light of such a scenario, the question to be asked is: what will the agency become? A key to the answer may be found in the nature of the economic philosophy of the Community. That this is of a liberal character is undoubted. Liberal economic philosophy would in turn seem to suggest that we may yet witness a transformation of the traditional European style of regulation to the American model. Were this the case, the Authority would indeed become a purely sectoral regulator, discarding its general economic role, but retaining its brief to exercise vigilance over the promotion of an activity valued by the public.

REFERENCES

Angerer, A. (1975) 'AVB unter Gesichtspunkten der Versicherungsaufsicht', *Zeitschrift für die gesamte Versicherungswissenschaft.*

Angerer, A. (1985) 'Wettbewerb auf den Versicherungsmärkten aus der Sicht der Versicherungsaufsichtsbehörde', *Zeitschrift für die gesamte Versicherungswissenschaft.*

Arps, L. (1965) *Auf sicheren Pfeilern: Deutsche Versicherungswirtschaft vor 1914*, Göttingen: van den Hoech & Ruprecht.

Behan, B. (1980) 'Civil Aeronautics Board', in Wilson (ed.) *The Politics of Regulation*, New York: Basic Books.

Brittan, L. (1990) 'Der Europäische Binnenmarkt der Versicherungen: was noch zu tun bleibt', speech delivered to the Gesamtverband der Deutschen Versicherungswirtschaft on 7 June 1990 in Cologne.

Büchner, F. (1952) 'Die Entwicklung der Deutschen Gesetzgebung über die Versicherungsaufsicht', in Rohrbeck (ed.) *Fünfzig Jahre Materielle Versicherungsaufsicht*, Berlin: Duncker & Humblot.

European Commission (1985) *European Commission Survey of Insurance in Europe*, Brussels: European Commission.

Finsinger, J., Tapp, J. and Hammond, E. (1985) *Competition or Regulation*, London: VVF.

Hollenders, C. (1985) *Die Bereichsausnahme für Versicherungen nach Article 102 GWB*, Baden Baden: Nomos.

McGowan, L. (1993) 'The evolution of German competition policy – the Bundeskartellamt, its role and competence', RUSEL Working Paper no. 14, University of Exeter: Research Unit for the Study of Economic Liberalization and its Social and Political Implications.

Majone, G. (1989) 'Regulating Europe: Problems and Perspectives', *Jahrbuch zur Staats- und Verwaltungswissenschaft*, vol. 3, Baden Baden.

OECD (1984) Report on *Insurance Supervision in the Federal Republic of Germany*, compiled by the Bundesaufsichtsamt für das Versicherungswesen, Berlin.

Starke, E. (1952) 'Die Entwicklung der Materiellen Staatsaufsicht der ersten Hälfte des 20. Jahrhunderts', in Rohrbeck (ed.) *Fünfzig Jahre Materielle Versicherungsaufsicht*, Berlin: Duncker & Humblot.

Sturm, R. and Ortwein, E. (1993) 'The normative and legal framework of German competition policy – a political science perspective', RUSEL Working Paper no. 15, University of Exeter: Research Unit for the Study of Economic Liberalization and its Social and Political Implications.

Von der Schulenburg, M. (1989) 'Regulation and Reregulation of Insurance Markets in the Federal Republic of Germany', Florence: EUI Working Paper 89/408.

Von der Schulenburg, M. and Finsinger, J. (1985) 'Nachfragerverhalten bei unvollständigen Preisinformation: Eine Marktanalyse am Beispiel der Kraftfahrzeugversicherung', BWZ, Discussion Papers.

11 The European Commission as regulator: the uncertain pursuit of the competitive market

Laraine Laudati

The founding fathers of the European Community recognized the importance of competitive markets for the achievement of an open and liberal economic union. To this end, they incorporated the notion of 'undistorted competition' into the Treaty of Rome as one of the fundamental objectives of the Community, together with basic competition rules as the means to achieve it. Antitrust enforcement has, however, always been uncertain in the Community, partly because the enforcement mechanism in the Treaty reflects many of the institutional flaws typical of the European regulatory tradition. The enforcing institution, the Commission, is a body of political appointees from each of the member states. Its substantive responsibilities cover the full range of areas in which the Community has been delegated power. It is not immune to political influence, both from the member states and within the Commission itself, and the degree of transparency in its decision-making is not sufficient to ensure public accountability. Moreover, most member states do not have a firmly rooted antitrust tradition. Rather, antitrust enforcement as a means of regulation is a relatively recent phenomenon through most of the Community. The old habits of direct government intervention in the economy, which remain from the era of nationalization, are evident in the Commission's enforcement of competition laws. Factors other than competition-related criteria, particularly those related to social and industrial policy, are frequently considered by the Commission in its application of the antitrust rules.

Pursuit of the competitive market in the Community is also hindered by the tension between centralized regulation at the Community level, which creates uniformity, and the subsidiarity principle, which promotes the preservation of regulatory diversity in the member states. Thus, largely as a result of pressure to conform with Community competition law, each member state enacted its own competition laws and created its own enforcement institutions. However, interpretation of the laws differs in important respects, largely as the result of the varied political, economic, social and legal traditions in the member states. Moreover, the institutions established to enforce those laws vary widely in terms of their degree of independence from political control, their size, experience, power, underlying philosophy and degree of acceptance of the market mechanism. None, however, has the same underlying goal as that of the Community: to create a competitive market throughout the European Union.

This chapter seeks to demonstrate that the Commission as regulator of competition in the Community has been obstructed in its ability to pursue 'undistorted competition' as a result of two main factors: its institutional characteristics, and the reluctance of the member states to accept its underlying policy goal. This chapter addresses in turn the lack of independence of the Community competition law enforcement mechanism from political and other influences, problems with its internal functioning, and the balance of power between the European competition regulators and national competition authorities. The chapter concludes that the conflicting forces placing pressure on the Community competition law system are likely to persist, but the existence of the system none the less has been a positive influence on the regulator of competition in Europe.

LACK OF INDEPENDENCE AND TRANSPARENCY IN THE EC COMPETITION LAW ENFORCEMENT MECHANISM

EC competition policy and law

The fundamental goals of Community competition law are to promote economic integration and effective competition throughout the Community. The predominance of the market integration goal in Community competition enforcement policy is evident in its development of competition rules. For instance, agreements which have the effect of segmenting markets along national boundaries constitute clear violations (Hawk 1992, supp.: 6). The Community also frequently takes account of social and political values in its decisions which often cause it to modify results based on pure competition analysis (Hawk 1992 supp.: 10).

These policy goals are based on provisions of the Treaty of Rome, as modified by the Maastricht Treaty. The original Treaty established the Community's primary objective of integration of the separate economies of the member states into a unified common market. It also listed among the fundamental activities of the Community 'a system ensuring that competition in the internal market is not distorted', and referred to social objectives related to employment and the treatment of Community workers.

Although the Maastricht Treaty leaves essentially unchanged the market integration and undistorted competition provisions, it places a new emphasis on social and industrial policy goals. It adds to the list of fundamental objectives an industrial policy clause, 'the strengthening of the competitiveness of Community industry', and sets forth specific objectives for industrial policy (accelerating industry's adjustment to structural change, encouraging an environment conducive to the development of enterprises and co-operation between them, and fostering better exploration of the fruits of research and development), and provides that 'the Community shall contribute to the achievement of the objectives [of industrial policy] through policies and activities it pursues under other provisions of this Treaty'. Moreover, reflecting the relatively high levels of unemployment throughout Europe in the early 1990s, it recognizes the need for social and employment protection (EC Treaty, Articles 2, 130). Accordingly, the Community's objectives with regard to competition policy constitute a subtle balance of economic and social concerns, with the latter taking on an increasingly important role after Maastricht.

Currently, the Community is moving into a new era in its development. Substantial progress has been made towards market integration and it is now necessary to provide direction to the large integrated market, and to reconsider competition policy objectives. The predominant concern must be identified among, for example, workable competition, contractual freedom of operators or competitiveness of industry even at the expense of the consumer. Commission officials consider that this choice falls within their discretionary powers, where the latter are not constrained by decisions of the European Court of Justice. They believe the Treaty's policy provisions to be sufficiently flexible to allow various emphases in competition enforcement policy.

The competition laws, set forth in Articles 85–94 of the Treaty of Rome, prohibit cartels and restrictive practices which may distort competition (Article 85), the abuse of a dominant position (Article 86) and state aid which threatens to distort competition (Article 92). In addition, a Merger Regulation was enacted in 1989 prohibiting mergers within the exclusive jurisdiction of the Community, determined by turnover thresholds of the enterprises involved, which create or strengthen a dominant position (Merger Regulation). The procedures for implementing Articles 85 and 86 are set down in Regulation 17 and those for the Merger Regulation in a separate procedural regulation (Merger Procedural Regulation, EEC 2367/90 of 25 July 1990).

Institutional independence

The degree of independence of an antitrust enforcement institution is determined by two elements: the structural independence from political authority, and separation of investigatory, prosecutorial and decision-making functions. The Community antitrust enforcement mechanism has a low level of independence in both respects.

The EC competition law enforcement mechanism

The Treaty of Rome endowed the Commission with independent powers to ensure the application of the competition laws (EC Treaty, Article 89). All final decisions in competition cases are reached through a vote of the Commission (Regulation 17, Article 9; Merger Regulation, Article 8). Thus, the ultimate decision-makers are the twenty Commissioners, who are political appointees of the governments of the member states (EC Treaty, Articles

157–8). The Treaty provides that they shall be 'completely independent in the performance of their duties', that they 'shall neither seek nor take instructions from any government nor any other body', and that '[e]ach member state undertakes to respect this principle and not to seek to influence the members of the Commission in the performance of their tasks' (EC Treaty, Article 157). Commissioners serve five-year renewable terms during which they cannot be dismissed, with limited exceptions, one of which is 'serious misconduct' (EC Treaty, Articles 158, 160).

One of the Commissioners is responsible for competition, and the others are responsible for the full array of areas within the competence of the Commission. Beginning in the 1980s, the Competition Commissioners have been strong figures who contributed greatly to the development of the Community's competition policy (Franciscus Andriessen, 1981–4; Peter Sutherland, 1985–8; Sir Leon Brittan, 1988–93; and Karel Van Miert since 1993).

Sir Leon Brittan increased the profile of competition policy in the Community through his strong will and independence, outspokenness and dedication to free market principles. During his term as Commissioner, he made more than four hundred speeches and took forceful positions on controversial issues. He pursued a hard line against cartels, state subsidies, anti-competitive mergers and national monopolies.

In January 1993, Karel Van Miert, a Belgian Socialist, was appointed as Brittan's successor. Formerly Commissioner for Transportation and Consumer Policy, Van Miert was expected to be less severe than Brittan in enforcing the antitrust laws, but has proved not to be. The change has been more one of style than of substance: he is more balanced, makes fewer speeches, is more open to dialogue and compromise, and insists that his personally appointed cabinet should also be open.

The Competition Commissioner presides over the Competition Directorate-General (DG IV), one of twenty-three Directorates-General. A change of Commissioner has little effect on the day-to-day operations of DG IV, since its personnel, as well as the law they enforce and the jurisprudence interpreting that law do not change with the appointment of a new Commissioner. This provides an element of stability to competition law in the Community.

DG IV is headed by a director-general, at the time of writing Claus Dieter Ehlermann (appointed in 1990), previously Director-General of the Commission's in-house counsel, the Legal Service. Like Van Miert, Ehlermann believes in openness and has made considerable efforts to improve transparency in DG IV procedures.

DG IV is subdivided into five directorates plus the Merger Task Force, each of which is headed by a Director. The staff of DG IV consists of 420 persons, all civil servants or *fonctionnaires*, of whom roughly half are professionals. An additional twenty-five professionals work with DG IV on temporary secondment from the competition authorities of the member states.

Staff-level professionals, or *rapporteurs* as they are known, are generally lawyers or economists. Their number has grown little over the years, other than through the addition of the Merger Task Force in 1989. It is not likely to increase significantly in years to come owing to budgetary constraints, although there will be some increase in connection with the accession of the three new member states. Critics claim that the professional staffing of DG IV is 'lawyer-heavy', with a ratio of approximately seven lawyers to one economist (House of Lords 1993: 209). DG IV officials acknowledge that more economists are needed.

The professional staffing of each of DG IV's directorates is as follows: Directorate A (general competition policy, international matters and co-ordination of competition decisions), approximately twenty-five; Directorates B, C and D (restrictive practices, abuse of dominant positions and other distortions of competition in the various sectors), approximately thirty each; Directorate E (state aids), approximately fifty; the Merger Task Force, approximately thirty; and the Director-General's office, approximately ten.

Although the staff size of DG IV has remained stable, its workload has steadily increased. For instance, the number of new cases under Articles 85 and 86 increased from 293 in 1981 to 399 in 1992 (House of Lords 1993: 110), and the backlog of unresolved cases under these articles numbered 1,231 cases at the end of 1993. Competition cases are based on the facts gathered by rapporteurs. In cases not involving a controversial policy issue, the rapporteur acts with considerable independence. Over its nearly forty-year history, DG IV has grown accustomed to using its extensive powers to great effect. This has created an ambience of power in DG IV. Some observers believe DG IV has developed a defensiveness and resistance to change as a result of that power.

An internal check on DG IV's decisions is provided by the Legal Service, the Commission's in-house counsel, which is organizationally situated directly under the President of the Commission. It must be consulted before the Commission adopts any act which is legally binding. It is heavily involved in the day-to-day decisions of DG IV because it is consulted on all Statements of Objection, draft decisions and final decisions. It attends oral hearings held by DG IV and meetings of the Member State Advisory Committee, which provides input from member states on competition decisions. It also may be involved in meetings between DG IV and private parties. The Legal Service represents DG IV before the two European Community courts, the Court of First Instance and the Court of Justice. It has eight lawyers handling antitrust matters.

Over time, the influence of the Legal Service on competition law enforcement has varied considerably, because of diverse political and other factors. The attitude of the Competition Commissioner towards the Legal Service is an important determinant of its degree of influence. For instance, its influence during Brittan's tenure was low, but has increased significantly under Van Miert, who consults with it frequently (House of Lords 1993: 70). The Legal Service and DG IV have at times had considerable difficulties in reaching agreement, in part owing to the different roles they play. The Director-General of DG IV actively pushes to implement competition policy, is willing to take risks to that end and is therefore result-oriented. In contrast, the Legal Service is less focused on achieving any given result, more cautious in its approach and more concerned with whether current policy fits within the existing legal framework (although this orientation may vary depending on the personalities involved) (House of Lords 1993: 150). In recent years the differences between the two have grown, largely owing to philosophical differences in antitrust policy of the individuals in charge. However, little ideological debate occurs between the two services, which instead focus on resolving issues raised in individual cases.

The Community's antitrust enforcement system is largely isolated from external organized critique of how it functions. Unlike the situation in the United States, where the American Bar Association's section on Antitrust Law is well organized to provide the private bar's continuous input on legislation, rules, court decisions and functioning of antitrust enforcement institutions, there is no comparable organization of antitrust lawyers in the Community. Informal groups of European competition lawyers meet occasionally, but are not organized to provide sophisticated professional advice and criticism on specific issues. DG IV's isolation from the outside world is magnified owing to the absence of a 'revolving door' tradition in Europe. Such a tradition exists in the United States, allowing lawyers to pass freely between the public sector and the private sector. This creates a commonality in the profession – unknown in Europe – which improves communication and enhances understanding by both sides of the other's concerns.

The European Parliament does not conduct investigations or hold hearings regarding the enforcement of Community competition laws, largely through lack of sufficient professional knowledge and training of its members, and time restraints. The most in-depth, professional investigation and critique of the competition law enforcement system was done by the House of Lords Select Committee on the European Communities during its 1993/4 session. The Select Committee received evidence and heard testimony from public and private sector witnesses, and issued a report with recommendations. However, the investigation was limited to procedural issues, and did not endeavour to cover the many controversial questions of substantive Community antitrust law.

Finally, a review of competition policy which focused on the concerns of business was carried out by the Confederation of British Industry, which issued a report with recommendations in January 1994 (*Financial Times*, 28 January 1994: 8).

Structural independence from political authority

Antitrust enforcement involves the application of law to facts, often requiring complex economic analysis of data to determine such issues as market definition, market concentration, barriers to entry and pricing policies. This process is best accomplished by lawyers and economists working without political interference. As Sir Brian Carsberg, Director-General of the UK Office of Fair Trading, observed: 'I see a very great part of the work in which I am engaged in administrating antitrust law as being . . . a professional or technical activity and which should not be subject to the kind of values and currency . . . of politics' (House of Lords 1993: 99). When the Community system was established, it was believed that placing the powers to execute the competition laws in the hands of the Commission would minimize political interference with enforcement by the member states. The Commission has, however, become a highly political body, and political considerations play a significant role in its competition enforcement decisions. National antitrust officials acknowledge that pressure from national governments may influence the Commission's decisions because the Commission must have the co-operation of national governments in order to fulfil its mission (see, for example, Antitrust & Trade Reg. Rep. (BNA), no. 63, at 118 (23 July 1992)). Thus, the Commission exerts considerable effort to reconcile national policies with Community policy.

Moreover, DG IV cannot act independently of the other DGs since final decisions are made by the full Commission. Political pressure from other DGs is felt constantly, owing to the broad economic implications of competition decisions. Such pressure, in general, runs against negative decisions by DG IV, particularly with regard to mergers. Moreover, it forces DG IV to take account of policy considerations other than competition policy. This is so even with regard to mergers, notwithstanding the Merger Regulation's emphasis on competition-based criteria for assessing the lawfulness of a merger (Merger Regulation, Article 2). This type of pressure has grown in recent years owing to the increasingly important role of competition law, and the economic recession and high levels of unemployment throughout the Community.

For instance, DG III (industrial policy) and DG V (social policy) frequently take positions at odds with those of DG IV. Other DGs likely to intervene regulate specific sectors of the economy, and tend to reflect the views of industry – for example, DG XIII (telecommunications) and DG XVII (energy). This does not mean that all communication among the DGs is contentious. Rather, collaboration and consultation regularly occur between rapporteurs of DG IV and those of other DGs, especially DG III, because of their familiarity with the various sectors. But if DG III staff believe that a merger should be cleared and their counterparts in DG IV believe the opposite, the staff members of each DG must convince their Commissioner of the merits of their position. Commissioners themselves then resolve the dispute.

Another fault of the system is that it requires Commissioners with no expertise in competition law and severe time constraints to apply complex laws and economic analysis to facts in all cases, then make the final decision.

It is doubtful whether all Commissioners are professionally qualified to perform this function. Critics point out that, in practice, most competition decisions are adopted with little or no debate, as written proposed decisions are circulated to the cabinet of each Commissioner and considered to be adopted if no objections are made within a limited period (House of Lords 1993: 219).

An additional problem results from a lack of clarity as to the standards being applied in deciding antitrust cases. As stated above, policy areas other than competition are considered, especially industrial and social policy. However, parties with competition matters before the Commission have no substantive or procedural rules to follow regarding the presentation of evidence on such policy issues, even though these matters could have significant impact on the outcome of their cases. This raises due process concerns.

Case study – the proposed DeHavilland merger

As stated above, in merger cases, Commission-level politics generally work to the advantage of the parties. If DG IV recommends a clearance, it is unlikely that any other DG will challenge it. Problems have arisen, however, in the two cases where DG IV has recommended a prohibition. In those cases, national politics have taken on an important role, and when DG III has concluded that the merger would be positive for the European companies involved, it opposed the prohibition. The most striking example of this was the proposed DeHavilland merger.

In the summer of 1991, ATR, a joint venture between Alenia, an Italian company, and Aerospatiale, a French company, notified the Commission of its intention to acquire DeHavilland, a Canadian aircraft manufacturer. In the weeks which followed the notification, the companies involved lobbied intensively in Brussels for a clearance.

Following the investigation, DG IV concluded that the merger would violate the Merger Regulation because it would create a dominant position in the market for commuter aircraft of twenty to seventy seats. Thus, Sir Leon Brittan, the Competition Commissioner, recommended to his colleagues in the Commission that the acquisition should be prohibited. A senior Commission official stated that during the Commission's deliberations on the case, 'Leon Brittan changed a lot of minds. He spent a lot of energy explaining to colleagues what the case was about and making them aware it was an important issue' (*Financial Times*, 4 October 1991: 22).

In October 1991, the Commission voted nine to six to prohibit the acquisition. The two Italian commissioners voted against prohibition, which some commentators interpreted as an expression of national sentiment. Of the two French commissioners, one was absent, and President Jacques Delors abstained. Delors was said to believe that opposing the DG IV recommendation would have been viewed as a nationalistic vote, undermining the credibility of the Commission's Merger Regulation (*Financial Times*, 4 October 1991: 22).

Thereafter, a fierce media battle ensued, illustrating the Commission's internal conflict between enforcing Community competition policy and underlying national considerations. French officials and industry representatives accused Sir Leon of attempting to block the acquisition because of his interest in protecting British Aerospace, which would have faced the dominant firm as a competitor and which was, at the time, known to be vulnerable to takeover (*The Independent*, 8 October 1991: 26).

Moreover, French Foreign Minister Roland Dumas officially complained about the decision, and arranged a meeting with senior Commission officials to determine whether the prohibition could be reversed. He said Community competition policy should be used 'to strengthen, not hinder, the competitiveness of European industry' (*Financial Times*, 7 October 1991: 1).

In France, a right-wing press campaign was initiated demanding the resignation of Jacques Delors from the Commission. Moreover, politicians from Delors' own Socialist Party criticized his actions and the Commission's vote. Former French Prime Minister Michel Rocard, interested in the Socialist Party presidential candidacy in 1995, called the prohibition a 'crime against Europe' (*Financial Times*, 11 October 1991: 2).

In response, Delors, thought at the time to have an interest in running as the Socialist party candidate for the French presidency in 1995, stated that he could not be held responsible for the Commission's decision, and could not have vetoed it. He stated that the attacks on him revealed France's 'schizophrenic attitude' towards EC institutions (*Financial Times*, 7 October 1991: 1). Political analysts suggested that Delors' actions may have damaged his chances of becoming the Socialist presidential candidate (*The Economist*, 12 October 1991: 18).

The DeHavilland prohibition also set off a public confrontation between DG IV and DG III. Martin Bangemann, the Commissioner of Industrial Policy, attacked the competition 'ayatollahs' in DG IV, arguing that they rule on merger cases without taking into account economic reality, and stating that the DeHavilland prohibition was 'completely wrong' (*Financial Times*, 11 February 1992: 2). Bangemann suggested that the consultation procedures within the Commission on competition matters were inadequate. In response, these rules were amended in February 1992, requiring DG IV to follow a detailed consultation procedure before making a decision on a merger (*The Economist*, 14 March 1992: 98, 101). Bangemann also attempted to remove the Competition Commissioner's authority to handle Community merger investigations up to the point when they come before the full Commission. However, this effort was not successful (*Financial Times*, 28 October 1991: 2). The DeHavilland prohibition ultimately remained in effect.

In contrast, in January 1994, the Commission voted to allow a merger between three European steel tube manufacturers (Vallourec from France, Ilva from Italy and Mannesmann from Germany), notwithstanding Commissioner Van Miert's and the Merger Task Force's recommendations that the merger should be prohibited (see *DMV*, European Report no. 1921, sec. IV:3 of 28 January 1993). Commentators suggested that this decision called into question the authority of the Merger Task Force and the personal reputation of Commissioner Van Miert, as it was the first time he was overruled by his colleagues in a competition case.

The separation of investigatory, prosecutorial and decision-making functions

A system which endows a single enforcement body with investigatory, prosecutorial and decision-making functions may find it difficult to provide an objective assessment of facts or to protect rights of parties. DG IV is responsible for all three functions, with no involvement of other Community institutions before the Commission reaches its final decision. A team of up to three rapporteurs is assigned to each matter under the Merger Regulation; a sole rapporteur is assigned to matters under all other provisions. Under the Merger Regulation, the rapporteurs conduct a one-month Phase 1 investigation, during which they check the information contained in the mandatory notification of the parties by contacting other market participants. The rapporteurs and their supervisors then decide whether this 'raises serious doubts as to [the merger's] compatibility with the common market' (Merger Regulation Article 6(1)(c)). If so, the rapporteurs conduct a Phase 2 investigation, which must be completed within four months, and then drafts a Statement of Objection. The undertakings concerned have the right to an oral hearing prior to a decision being taken in a case which has proceeded to Phase 2. If, after an oral hearing, the rapporteurs and their supervisors conclude that the merger violates the regulation, they draft the Commission's decision. The responsibilities are essentially the same under Articles 85 and 86, but there are no strict time limits for completion of the tasks.

The rapporteur exercises substantial discretion in performing these functions with some degree of oversight by his or her supervisors, the Head of Unit, the Director and the Director-General. However, no uniform written guidelines exist regarding, for example, what factors should be considered, how the fact-finding procedures should be conducted, what economic analysis should be performed and what elements should be included in an adequately drafted Statement of Objections. The statutes themselves are of little help, as they allow considerable discretion in determining what constitutes an offence. Case law provides some guidance in areas such as determining the relevant product and geographic markets and assessing joint dominance. Accordingly, the quality of analysis may vary considerably depending on which rapporteur has been assigned to the case (see *Flat Glass* (10 March 1992) and *Wood Pulp* (31 March 1993)). This shortcoming is particularly acute with regard to economic analysis, as reflected in Commission decisions (House of Lords 1993: 100, 209).

Aware of this problem, DG IV is in the process of developing guidelines regarding internal control, determination of whether a joint venture is covered by the merger regulation, determination of turnover levels under the merger regulation, and specific problems related to the banking and insurance sectors. Moreover, the Commission itself has indicated that it could improve transparency by issuing guidelines on application of the Merger Regulation, including assessment of concentration (Commission Merger Report 1993: 4). None of the forthcoming guidelines, however, addresses substantive issues of competition law.

In 1995, Director-General Ehlermann took the first steps in systematically considering the need for substantive modification of the law and improvement in the consistency of its application. He formed a working group headed by David Deacon, DG IV's senior in-house economist, and one official from each Directorate to prepare a Green Paper on updating the rules applied in analysing vertical restraints under Article 85. One major issue which the group is addressing is whether more economic analysis is needed when applying Article 85(1) and, if so, how such analysis can be made in a uniform manner in each case. The DG IV officials working on the Green Paper are seeking input from outside lawyers, economists and industry. This process may lead to the preparation of a White Paper with proposals for legislative modifications.

Dr Ehlermann also formed a working group composed of senior DG IV officials to reconsider the rules applicable to restrictions to competition more generally. The group met regularly early on in 1995, exchanging views on the economic and legal aspects of restrictions of competition, and has prepared a memorandum suggesting possible areas for additional consideration.

One check on the discretion of the rapporteur is the oral hearing at the end of the Phase 2 investigation for mergers and cases brought under Articles 85 and 86. Director-General Ehlermann believes this to be an important control, a decisive point where the parties can urge their interpretation of the evidence (House of Lords 1993: 109). The hearing is presided over by a hearing officer, a DG IV official who is separate from the operational directorates that handle the individual cases, and whose job is to ensure that the hearing is properly conducted.

Critics argue that the rapporteur assigned to the case should not also have responsibility for drafting the decision after the hearing. The notion that a single individual or institution can act initially as investigator, developing a case file and, often with it, a certain prosecutorial zeal, then subsequently act as objective decision-maker, seems doubtful (Roundtable Two 1993: 118; House of Lords 1993: 69–70). It requires great self-restraint and critical analysis, and is psychologically difficult to achieve. Thus, critics urge the reform of assigning different individuals to the case after the hearing to make and draft the decision. The House of Lords Select Committee considered this issue in its investigation of Community Competition rules, and concluded that separation of functions 'is not essential if procedure is fair and transparent and there is independent judicial control to guarantee this'.

Accordingly, the Report recommended other procedural changes to improve fairness and transparency of proceedings (House of Lords 1993: 48–50). In any event, DG IV is not currently prepared to make this reform owing to resource limitations.

One crucial factor which can assuage the lack of objectivity which may result from performing multiple functions is thorough judicial review, where both the facts in the administrative record and any new evidence which the parties offer are considered. In the Community system, judicial review is provided through the Court of First Instance and ultimately the Court of Justice. However, an extensive backlog of cases causes substantial delay in reaching a final decision.

Lack of transparency in Community competition law enforcement

Procedures under Community competition law have been criticized as insufficiently transparent, thus reducing public accountability and possibly allowing political influences unrelated to competition criteria to influence the Commission's decisions. A review of the procedures reveals this criticism to be well founded, but that it is not readily apparent how the system could be improved as the institutional arrangement does not lend itself to a high degree of transparency.

The discussion which follows focuses mainly on transparency problems related to merger procedures. The procedures under Articles 85 and 86, together with those governing state aids, are even less transparent than those for mergers.

Transparency vis-à-vis the member states

The Merger Regulation provides that the Commission shall keep 'in close and constant liaison' with member-state authorities when carrying out a merger investigation. Accordingly, it provides that they receive copies of all merger notifications and the most important related documents, and that they have a right to express their views 'at every stage of the procedure up to the adoption of a decision', and to be present at oral hearings held in Phase 2 proceedings (Merger Regulation, Article 19).

Draft decisions for all Phase 2 cases must be submitted to the Member State Advisory Committee after the oral hearing, which prepares its opinion for transmission to the Commission. The Commission must take 'utmost' account of the opinion of the Advisory Committee, and inform the Committee of the manner in which its opinion has been taken into account (Merger Regulation, Article 19).

Notwithstanding the safeguards, Commission officials recognize that improvements are needed in transparency *vis-à-vis* the member states. For instance, in most cases the Commission decides not to oppose a proposed merger during the first phase provided certain conditions are met by the parties, but such conditions are not first revealed to member-state authorities. This denies them the opportunity to comment on the settlement terms. In its recent review of implementation of the Merger Regulation, the Commission proposed a modification of procedures to allow member states to be fully informed of settlement terms. This would entail publication of proposed settlement terms and, if settlement proposals are submitted at a late date during the first phase, extension of the time limits in order to allow member states time to comment (Commission Merger Report 1993: 16–17). In the period before such an amendment is made to the Merger Regulation, the Commission is considering accepting only such settlement offers as are made early enough in the proceedings to allow concerned third parties to comment, but to date it has not done so (Commission Merger Report 1993: 23–4).

Member-state authorities also are concerned that they do not receive the draft decision sufficiently in advance of the Advisory Committee meeting to prepare their positions adequately. Drafts are issued only in English, French or occasionally German, and they believe they should be translated into all the official languages. Commission officials respond that the tight deadlines of the Merger Regulation and resource limitations make it impossible to meet these requests.

Transparency vis-à-vis the public

The Merger Regulation provides some safeguards of transparency with respect to the public. The fact of the notification must be published when the Commission finds that a notified concentration falls within the scope of the Regulation. Interested third parties may then participate in the proceedings by meeting Commission officials and expressing their views about the proposed transaction. However, a press release issued at the time proceedings are open is the only information published by the Commission until it takes a final decision (Merger Regulation, Articles 4, 20).

Commission officials contend that a sufficient level of publicity already exists as to the issues in a case under investigation. They assert that through newspaper reports, interested third parties such as competitors, distributors, unions and consumer groups are all aware of the issues and the fact of initiation of Phase 2 proceedings.

However, the depth of information which the press can provide is limited, primarily as a result of its restricted access to knowledgeable persons within DG IV. The media does not have access to the rapporteurs working on the case, but to a press secretary for the Competition Commissioner, whose level of knowledge about individual cases is limited. Moreover, although the media may follow closely the nuances of large, controversial cases, it is unlikely to do so with smaller cases. In addition, the Brussels press corps is not highly specialized in antitrust matters.

Information also reaches the public through leaks, often from the Commissioners themselves or members of their cabinets. This may include sensitive information about what happened during preparatory meetings, or what is the proposed disposition of a case.

Regulation 17 (which governs Articles 85 and 86 proceedings) provides that the opinion of the Advisory Committee 'shall not be made public'. Dr Ehlermann favours amending this to allow publication, but the Commission has not yet done so (House of Lords 1993: 109). However, this improvement in transparency of proceedings was made in the Merger Regulation, under which Advisory Committee reports are to be published together with the Commission's final decision, but only on completion of the proceedings, and only if the Advisory Committee so requests and the Commission concedes (Merger Regulation Article 19, para. 7). Thus, any disagreement of the Advisory Committee with the final outcome is revealed. The Commission has made a public commitment to publish all Advisory Committee opinions regarding mergers when the Commission's decision is announced (see Commission of the European Community, XXIst Report on Competition Policy 1991: 57, hereafter the XXI Competition Report). Moreover, in instances where the Commission decision departs from the Advisory Committee opinion, the Commission intends to explain the reason for the departure in its decision (Commission Merger Report 1993: 24, 28).

However, many aspects of the procedure remain opaque with respect to the public. For instance, as is the case with member states, the public may not be aware of conditions imposed for settling a merger case, which denies the possibility for comment. As stated above, the Commission itself has suggested that it could improve transparency by making proposed settlements known to interested third parties and publishing proposed commitments 'where appropriate' (Commission Merger Report 1993: 16–17; House of Lords 1993: 120). This, along with extension of time limits when settlement proposals are submitted at a late date, would give competitors and interested third parties the opportunity to comment.

In merger cases, final decisions of the Commission are published. Critics argue, however, that published decisions are not sufficiently detailed to provide a clear explanation of why the Commission voted as it did. Although they generally set forth detailed reasoning, national competition authorities complain that they provide only limited information about the parties and no summary of the evidence (House of Lords 1993: 48). The disposition of cases brought under Articles 85 and 86 is most often through 'comfort letters' which are non-binding decisions that contain no reasoning, and thus even less transparency than merger decisions. Director-General Ehlermann would like to have short, simple decisions issued after the comfort letters to improve transparency. Private competition lawyers believe this would be a very important improvement in transparency. However, Dr Ehlermann believes that the Commission's internal machine is incapable of producing this owing to resource restrictions, especially with regard to translation capacity (House of Lords 1993: 131).

Some have suggested that the Commission's draft decision in merger cases should be published, thus enabling the public to see the Merger Task Force position. They argue that this would be based on legal and economic analysis and free from the political influences that exist at the Commission level. However, publication of the draft decision is highly problematic under the Community's institutional framework. The Commission would oppose the idea that its final decisions should be compared and criticized on the basis of the work of its rapporteurs, who draft the decisions, and who have no legitimacy independent from the Commission. Moreover, it is doubtful that the independent judgement of the rapporteurs and their supervisors would be reflected in a published draft decision, as the Competition Commissioner ultimately determines what proposal will be put to the Commission and could instruct DG IV officials to draft the decision as he or she wants. Even without such instructions, rapporteurs may be inclined to focus on the likely outcome at the Commission level rather than the proper outcome based on legal and economic analysis were the decision to become public.

Finally, critics claim that the public does not have sufficient access to information regarding the Commission's method for establishing the level of fines (House of Lords 1993: 7).

Proposal for an independent European cartel office

The idea of creating an independent European cartel authority has been put forward by various sources in recent years, notably the German national authority and competition officials in Britain. Each has different reasons for advocating such a change. An independent authority would allow decisions to be made on the basis of competition criteria, and eliminate political interference. However, Director-General Ehlermann has argued that many problems exist with accomplishing this goal on a European level (House of Lords 1993: 134–6).

First, regarding the structure of such an office, it is unlikely that member states would want its decisions to be subject only to judicial review. Thus, some political body would have veto power, which raises the likelihood that political factors would be considered at that level, thereby defeating the purpose of the independent authority. Moreover, unlike the situation in Germany, it is doubtful that public opinion would run against a European reviewing body overturning a cartel authority decision which could result in a loss of jobs, in an economy with high and rising unemployment. The antitrust tradition is not so firmly rooted in most of the other member states. Thus, whatever Community body were delegated the final veto power would feel free to overrule the independent authority (Antitrust & Trade Regulation Rep. (BNA), no. 62 at 336 of 12 March 1992). These concerns could perhaps be met if the political authority had a limited veto power, enabling it to reverse the independent authority's decision only on specific grounds in a well-reasoned public decision which itself would be subject to judicial review.

Second, the structural separation created by an independent cartel authority would result in a higher level of transparency. If, however, the public does not consider that competition oriented criteria are the correct criteria, and instead believes that social and labour policy should also be considered, then overruling the cartel authority on the basis of such considerations would be viewed as a normal process. Thus, transparency would not pressure the reviewing body against considering such factors.

Third, an independent agency is in danger of being too separate, and its employees too single-minded. A problem with vertical compartmentalization already exists in the Commission, so that information is not readily shared. Moreover, in Europe there is already a separation of government from academia and business. Thus, the independent agency would risk being extremely isolated.

Fourth, setting up the independent agency probably would be highly political, with the allocation of representatives of the member states to positions in the hierarchy being highly contentious. However, an arrangement similar to that for the European Central Bank might resolve this problem.

Finally, the rest of the Commission may suffer from the loss of DG IV's influence in antitrust matters. Thus, there would be no powerful group within the Commission horizontally advocating competition-oriented ideas. For instance, DG VII handles what are often very important state aid cases in the transportation sector, and DG IV provides advice with regard to such cases. The independent cartel office could provide the Commission with policy advice, although DG IV officials assert that this would not be consistent with the Authority's independent status. If a small part of DG IV were to remain within the Commission, it would be substantially weakened through loss of expertise.

The House of Lords, which considered this proposal in its investigation, did not favour establishment of an independent authority. Its conclusion was based on the poor performance record of other agencies established by the member states in recent years and the unlikeliness that transfer of lawyers and economists from DG IV to a new agency would 'increase their objectivity [or] improve their morale' (House of Lords 1993: 37, para. 104).

Until the antitrust tradition becomes more firmly rooted in European culture, Commission officials believe it is best to leave the current structure in place, notwithstanding its many shortcomings.

THE SHIFTING BALANCE OF COMPETITION LAW ENFORCEMENT TO THE MEMBER STATES

Differences between Community and member-state policy goals

In contrast to the Community's policy goals, in the national context market integration plays little or no role in the enforcement of competition law. Rather, member states focus on promoting their individual economic interests using varying combinations of the market mechanism and dirigisme. Some member states, such as Germany, believe that the free market should generally be allowed to function on its own, with government intervention primarily to provide the framework for market activities. Thus, there is little conflict between competition policy and industrial policy. Other member states, such as France, view competition law enforcement as a means to promote economic progress, and balance industrial policy interests against those of protecting competition.

The harmonization of national competition law with EC competition law

It is beyond the scope of this chapter to describe the systems of the member states in detail. However, some broad observations will be made to provide an indication of the state of harmonization of national laws (Stockmann 1992: 441).

In a substantial portion of the European Community, antitrust legislation is a relatively new phenomenon. Of the original six founder members of the Community, only France and Germany had competition laws prior to 1957, but the integration process has placed increasing pressure on the member states to harmonize their national competition laws with Community law in order to create a level playing field for their enterprises (Stockmann 1992: 441). Following the entry into force of the rules on competition of the EEC Treaty in 1957, each member state enacted some form of competition law, or modified already existing laws.

The first wave of member states to do so, in the late 1950s and early 1960s, was Germany, the Netherlands and Belgium. The German law was enacted in 1958 in response to politically motivated external pressure from the United States, which insisted on the abolition of German cartels and monopolies, rather than by a desire to harmonize with EC law. The German law reflects the influence of American antitrust law (see Chapters 3 and 7). Similarly, Spain, which was not a member state at the time, enacted its original antitrust law in 1963 in response to external political pressure, primarily from the United States, and later from the European Community, with which Spain was determined to work closely (see Chapter 9).

The second wave of laws was enacted in the 1970s and early 1980s, by Luxembourg (1970), Ireland (1972), Greece (1977) and Portugal (1983). The laws in Greece and Portugal were modelled on Articles 85 and 86 of the Treaty of Rome, in anticipation of their imminent accession to the Community. In addition, France modified its already existing law in 1977 and again in 1986, each time bringing it closer to Community law (see Chapter 8). However, Britain enacted a restrictive practices law in 1976 which followed an approach in stark contrast to that of Article 85.

The third wave of laws was enacted in the 1990s, and is even more clearly inspired by Articles 85 and 86. A new law which closely tracks Community law was enacted by Italy in 1990. Earlier laws were replaced in Spain (1990), Ireland (1991), Belgium (1993) and Portugal (1993), all of which were motivated by a desire to follow Community law more closely. However, Denmark enacted a new law in 1990 which still differs considerably from Community law.

Thus, at present, seven member states (Belgium, France, Italy, Greece, Ireland, Portugal and Spain) have competition laws which substantially resemble those of the Community. German law differs from Community law in so far as it is even stricter in assessing restrictive practices than Article 85(1) (which the Commission has interpreted broadly), exempts whole sectors of the economy from coverage and subjects abuses of dominant positions to case-by-case analysis under the 'abuse control principle' rather than general prohibition under the 'prohibition principle' (Stockman 1992: 442). It is expected that German law will undergo changes so that it will conform more closely with Community law in the future. Luxembourg law is inspired by Community law, but subjects restrictive practices and abuses of dominant position only to abuse control exercised by the Minister of Economics. Dutch law is also based on abuse control, but modifications are under consideration to harmonize with Community law.

In Britain and Denmark, competition law still differs considerably from Community law. Both British and Danish law are still predominantly based on abuse control. The British system is a complex patchwork of diverse legislation which is weak, largely owing to ineffective remedies. British law does, however, cover some situations which would not be covered by EC law, such as in the area of abuse of a dominant position (House of Lords 1993: 52). In 1989, a British White Paper proposed to reconcile British competition law with Community law. While there is general agreement in Britain that this is needed, it has not occurred because the issue lacks political clout (Antitrust & Trade Regulation Rep. (BNA), no. 63 at 99 of 23 July 1992; but see also House of Lords 1993: 52–3).

A number of member states have adopted domestic merger control laws since the Community Merger Regulation took effect (House of Lords 1993: 102). However, merger control laws are less harmonized than laws prohibiting restrictive practices and abuses of dominant positions, mainly owing to conceptual differences. However, logically, the rules in smaller member states differ from those in larger ones, since mergers do not impose a similar threat in smaller countries. Moreover, national markets may disappear as the Community market evolves. Four member states – Denmark, Finland, Luxembourg and the Netherlands – still do not have merger control laws.

The last round of enlargement brought three new member states (Sweden, Finland and Austria) which traditionally are not competition-oriented. However, with the exception of Austria (which, like the Netherlands, has a corporatist tradition), all three have enacted competition statutes and set up competition authorities inspired by the Community system. They were members of the European Free Trade Area (EFTA), which entered an agreement with the Community to create a European Economic Area (EEA), effective in early 1994. Under the agreement, the EEA will have uniform competition rules based on the Community system. Also pursuant to the agreement, the EFTA countries have established the EFTA Surveillance Authority, with equivalent powers and similar functions to the Commission in the field of competition (XXIst Competition Report 1992: 51).

In summary, a high level of harmonization has occurred spontaneously in the member states, and DG IV officials do not favour imposing further harmonization in the classic sense through a directive, especially given the recent emphasis on subsidiarity.

Changes in the balance of enforcement between the Community and the member states

The Maastricht Treaty for the first time articulated the 'subsidiarity principle', which limits the Community's powers *vis-à-vis* the member states.

> In areas which do not fall within its exclusive competence the Community shall take action, in accordance with the principle of subsidiarity, only if and in so far as the objectives of the proposed action cannot be sufficiently achieved by the member states and can therefore . . . be better achieved by the Community.
>
> (EC Treaty, Article 3(b))

Commission officials believe that Community competition law incorporated strong elements of subsidiarity from the beginning. Sir Leon Brittan observed that subsidiarity 'has always been the central pillar upon which the jurisdictional divide between the Community and the member states in the field of competition policy is based' (Antitrust & Trade Regulation Rep. (BNA), no. 63 at 150 of 30 July 1992). Moreover, the subsidiarity principle does not eliminate the need for Community competition law because member-state law alone is not sufficient to meet the Community's competition policy objectives. Only Community law can create a level playing field (House of Lords 1993: 102, 113), and with it the likelihood that investment decisions will be based on operating efficiency rather than the most favourable national laws. Moreover, only the Commission has the procedural tools, including more extensive discovery powers than the national authorities, to review cross-border arrangements effectively. Finally, it is preferable for a single authority, rather than diverse national authorities, to examine such arrangements (House of Lords 1993: 113).

Combined with the new emphasis on subsidiarity, a dramatic change has occurred in recent years in competition law enforcement in the member states. Where national enforcement of competition law was virtually non-existent until 1958, at present a large number of member states have professional, competent, competition-oriented national authorities, structured to perform their functions with limited political interference – at least with respect to non-merger cases – and with a mandate to enforce the laws based on competition policy, relying on economic analysis, rather than protecting national champions. Most of them have the power to impose significant remedies, with the exception of Great Britain, where essentially no penalties exist for most infringements of competition rules until a second offence is committed, such as a second failure to register a registrable agreement or breach of an order prohibiting certain conduct (Ministerie van Economische Zaken, Directoraat-Generaal voor Economische Structuur, Implementation of Competition Policy, Part I, Amsterdam, March 1993).

This evolution of the national authorities, in conjunction with increased emphasis on the subsidiarity principle, is likely to change the structure of competition law enforcement in the European Community. Sir Leon Brittan anticipated that this evolution would lead to 'the achievement of the Community's objectives through a coordinated partnership involving regulation at the Community and national level' (Antitrust & Trade Reg. Rep. (BNA) no. 63 at 150 (30 July 1992)). Substantial efforts at co-ordination are already being made. For instance, officials of the UK Monopolies and Mergers Commission keep abreast of developments in Community competition law to avoid conflicts in cases where there may be a Community element, and consult the Commission for its views in various cases (House of Lords 1993: 49–50). However, arriving at a co-ordinated partnership may prove difficult, owing in large part to the basic philosophical differences among the member states and the resulting tentativeness of the Community's pursuit of competition principles. This could impede the creation and maintenance of a fully integrated market.

The tensions which exist between the Commission and the member states in regulating competition are illustrated in recent Commission decisions. The Commission's interest in maintaining control of Community competition policy and the desire of the member states both to limit the Commission's power and to broaden their own power are evident. Three areas have been selected to demonstrate these tensions: first, DG IV's enforcement decentralization project; second, the failure to reduce thresholds which determine exclusive Community jurisdiction over merger control; and third, control of state aid during privatization.

Enforcement decentralization project

Under the doctrine of direct effect, member-state competition authorities and courts are empowered to apply Community competition law (see *Van Gend*). However, this authority is limited: they may prohibit restrictive practices and abuses of a dominant position, pursuant to Articles 85(1) and 86, only as long as the Commission has not opened procedures covering the same offences. But they may not grant exemptions for restrictive practices that meet the requirement set forth in Article 85(3), which is that they 'contribute to improving the production or distribution of goods or to promoting technical or economic progress, while allowing consumers a fair share of the resulting benefit'; only the Commission can grant Article 85(3) exemptions (Regulation 17, Article 19).

Some member states, such as Germany, have argued that national authorities should have the power to grant Article 85(3) exemptions, controlled by appropriate procedures to determine competence and ensure uniform law enforcement (House of Lords 1993: 198, para. 4(a)). However, DG IV is not willing to relinquish its monopoly to grant exemptions under Article 85(3). This power 'forms the very heart of the Community's competition policy', and its exercise requires a 'qualified judgment as to the interests of the Community as a whole' (House of Lords 1993: 116). In applying Article 85(3), DG IV is able to 'ensure that the core of Community competition policy remains identical throughout the Community', thus preventing 'forum shopping and thus artificial distortions of capital flows' (House of Lords 1993: 116–17). Moreover, if the member states had this power, an exemption granted by one national court or national authority would have to be respected by all the others. Some private practitioners in the field believe these justifications for the Commission's Article 85(3) monopoly to be unpersuasive.

With this limitation, DG IV for years has encouraged national courts and national competition authorities to increase Community competition law enforcement. Specifically, it has urged them to bring actions against agreements and practices that affect trade between the member states, and therefore have an impact on the Community as a whole.

To this end, DG IV has recently initiated a 'decentralization' project, the long-term goal of which is to have one Community competition statute applied throughout the Community by a network of DG IV, national competition authorities and national courts. Each member state would also be free to impose additional requirements for strictly local phenomena.

Although the decentralization effort is partially motivated by subsidiarity, the main motivation is to improve efficiency in enforcement, given DG IV's limited resources. DG IV has a backlog of notifications under Articles 85 and 86 which have yet to be answered, and new notifications arriving continuously. If the member states were to take on some of these cases, it would alleviate the burden on DG IV, thereby freeing it to pursue more important matters. Some private practitioners urge a less rigid interpretation of Article 85(1) as a more effective way to cut DG IV's workload (see, for example, Forrester and Norall, 1983).

DG IV's decentralization project is addressed to both national courts and member-state competition authorities.

National courts

In 1992, the Court of First Instance affirmed the right of the Commission to decline complaints by private parties that raise no significant Community interest where adequate redress is available at the national level (*Automec* v. *Commission II, Judgement of the Court of First Instance*, 18 September

1992). Pursuant to this decision, DG IV will reject such complaints, which it expects will lead to a significant increase in the number of Community competition law actions filed by private parties in national courts (House of Lords 1993: 114). Accordingly, in 1993, DG IV issued its 'Notice on Cooperation Between National Courts and the Commission in Applying Articles 85 and 86 of the EEC Treaty' (Notice on Cooperation), to aid national courts in dealing with such cases. The notice was developed by a DG IV working group and reviewed by the Member State Advisory Committee. It sets forth a procedure to guide national courts in applying Community competition law.

The notice recognizes that national courts hold concurrent power with the Commission to apply Articles 85(1), 85(2) and 86 through the doctrine of direct effect. National courts may also apply the substantive provisions of exemptions granted by the Commission under Article 85(3), but may not themselves grant exemptions. Thus, the Notice states that 'individuals and companies have access to all procedural remedies provided for by national law on the same conditions as would apply if a comparable breach of national law were involved', including provisional remedies, injunctions and damages (Notice on Cooperation, para. 11). Such relief is not available under Community law, which allows only the imposition of fines.

National competition authorities

DG IV established a working group to explore ways in which national authorities could play a greater role in enforcing Community competition law. Its mission was to increase efficiency in the implementation of Articles 85 and 86, to determine whether decentralized enforcement is necessary and desirable to this end, and if so, to establish the means for decentralized enforcement. Its members were personal appointees of the Directors-General of each of the national competition authorities and of the Director-General of DG IV. In September 1994, the working group submitted a report to the Director-General of DG IV which contained various non-operational general conclusions. However, the report was not published because it discusses many issues not yet resolved among the member states.

The most controversial issue before the working group related to the power to grant exemptions under Article 85(3). Another problem related to differences in discovery powers (often weak or non-existent) across the member states and *vis-à-vis* the Community.

Moreover, national enabling legislation is required to allow national authorities to apply Articles 85 and 86, and to establish that national remedies apply. Six member states do not have such legislation (Denmark, Ireland, Italy, Luxembourg, the Netherlands and Britain). Remedies vary considerably among the member states, based on deeply rooted historical differences and cultural attitudes (House of Lords 1993: 132). Thus, the rights of parties would vary depending on the remedies offered by the member state in which the action is brought.

In the current situation, in areas where Community law and national law coincide, there is little benefit for a private party or national authority to raise claims under Community law. The remedies are the same for both, and are those provided by national legislation. Community law provides an advantage only when it prohibits acts which are not prohibited under national law, which is not the normal situation (see Bechtold 1993; Zekoll 1991).

Merger regulation threshold levels

Seventeen years of negotiation and much political compromise were required for passage of the Merger Regulation (see Chapter 4). One of the most controversial issues was deciding which cases would be handled by the Merger Task Force and which by national authorities. It was finally agreed that jurisdiction would be determined by threshold levels. Thus, the Merger Regulation establishes exclusive Community jurisdiction over all mergers with a 'Community Dimension': that is, where aggregate worldwide turnover of all the undertakings concerned is at least 5,000 million ECU; and Community-wide turnover of each of at least two of the undertakings concerned is more than 250 million ECU. Below these thresholds, mergers are subject only to national merger control, if it exists. However, under the 'two-thirds rule', if each of the undertakings concerned has achieved more than two-thirds of its aggregate Community-wide turnover within a single member state, then the merger does not fall within the Community's exclusive jurisdiction.

The thresholds were initially set very high. This was a victory for Germany and Britain, the two member states with the strongest national authorities and the most reluctant to cede power to the Commission. Some member states believed that the threshold levels should have been lower because they had little or no merger control of their own, and little experience in its implementation. As a compromise, when the Merger Regulation was enacted in 1989, it was agreed that the Commission would review the threshold levels before the end of 1993. It was expected that they would be lowered if the Merger Task Force was able to handle fifty to sixty cases a year (*Financial Times*, 19 January 1993: 14).

In the early 1990s, Sir Leon Brittan, then Competition Commissioner, stated that the thresholds were too high to cover all mergers with a Community-wide dimension, and advocated that they should be lowered (Antitrust & Trade Regulation Rep. (BNA), no. 63 at 737 of 10 December 1992).

Industry generally favoured the lowering of thresholds, because mergers which fell above them could benefit from a one-stop shop, and, in most cases, certainty of a clearance within one month. However, some observers believe that industry's preference for broader Community jurisdiction is based on the Commission's leniency in granting clearances. The probability of obtaining an unconditional clearance or a clearance with acceptable conditions is considered high if the case is within the Community's jurisdiction, and much lower if it is in the jurisdiction of some member states, particularly Germany. For instance, the Commission has permitted the creation of oligopolies in various mergers. In some instances, experts suggest that, under any reasonable antitrust analysis, some of these mergers should not have been permitted. The recent steel tubes merger illustrates this point: an oligopoly was created, with the merged company sharing 69 per cent of the market with one other manufacturer. In fact, since 1989, only the DeHavilland merger had been prohibited at the time of writing.

However, in 1993 the political climate changed owing to several factors. First, in conjunction with ratification of the Maastricht Treaty, the attitude of the member states towards the Community became less positive. Rather than supporting increases in Commission powers, the political climate fostered scepticism and an emphasis on subsidiarity. Second, the European economy was suffering from a recession. Finally, the new Competition Commissioner, Van Miert, had never expressed a position on threshold reduction.

In 1993, the Commission conducted a review of application of the Regulation and prepared a Report for the Council of Ministers regarding its implementation (Commission Merger Report 1993). It specifically addressed the threshold levels. The research conducted in preparation of the report indicated that the 250 million ECU Community-wide turnover was too high, especially for industries in a growth phase, and was preventing the Commission from controlling mergers in a number of sectors. A Community wide threshold of 100 million ECU was thought to be more appropriate.

Regarding the two-thirds rule, the report concluded that a substantial number of cases with a geographic market much wider than the member state concerned were being excluded. Based on its statistical study, it suggested that a three-quarters rule would be more appropriate for separating those cases having only a national dimension from those with a Community dimension (Commission Merger Report 1993: 11, para. 6).

The Report stated that the European Parliament and the Economic and Social Committee favoured the reduction of thresholds, as did many, but not all, industry representatives. However, a majority of the member states were satisfied with the current threshold levels. They stated that the regulation had been in effect for only three years, and more experience was needed before reducing the thresholds. Individual member states argued against reduction also for individual reasons: Britain, on the basis of subsidiarity; Germany, on the basis that an independent cartel office should first be established; France, on the basis that regional and social criteria should be considered in merger analysis. Opposition by these three member states alone was enough to defeat any proposal for threshold reduction.

Aware that it did not have a majority of member states in favour of threshold reduction, the Commission decided to postpone proposal of revisions to the regulation until 1996 (Commission Merger Report 1993: 2). Thus, at present, threshold levels are so high that most mergers in the

Community fall within the jurisdiction of the member states. To the extent that merger control policy shapes the structure of European industry, it is national rather than Community merger control policy which will perform this function.

Although DG IV officials acknowledge that thresholds are high, they maintain that they will be eroded over time through inflation and growth in the size of companies, and through the addition of turnover in the new member states following enlargement in 1995. However, the failure to modify the two-thirds rule is more problematic and will not be affected by these changed conditions.

Finally, the Report suggested a linkage between the frequency with which the Commission would utilize the 'referral back' provision of the regulation and threshold reduction. This provision states that the Commission will refer a merger meeting the threshold requirements back to a national authority which affects only a distinct market entirely within a single member state (Merger Regulation, Article 9, para. 2). Since the Regulation took effect, seven requests have been made by national authorities for a referral back, and two of those requests have been granted. German and British national authorities have complained that the Commission has not referred back more cases. The Report suggested that the standard for referrals would be made more flexible only in conjunction with a lowering of thresholds (Commission Merger Report 1993: 14–15, para. 14).

State aid and privatization
Control of state aid

State aid is financial intervention by public authorities (national, regional or local governments) to the benefit of individual public or private enterprises or sectors. It may take the form of debt write-offs, capital injections, loans or guarantees at better than normal market conditions. It constitutes an established and sizeable component of economic policy in all member states, which Commissioner Van Miert estimates to have exceeded 89,000 million ECU annually in the period 1988–90 (Ehlermann 1993).

Article 92 of the Treaty of Rome bans all state aid to public and private enterprises which 'distorts or threatens to distort competition'. All aid must be notified to the Commission before it is granted. In most instances under the EC Treaty, the Commission decides independently of other Community institutions whether aid is present and, if so, whether it is permissible under one of the exceptions listed in Article 92. Under the European Coal and Steel Community Treaty, Commission decisions in state aid cases require consultation with, and unanimous assent of, the Council of Ministers (ECSC Treaty, Articles 67, 95). This determination is made within two months (*Gebr. Lorenz* at 1481). Commission and Council decisions with respect to state aid are subject to review by the Court of Justice.

In 1990, the Court of Justice held that the Commission has power to order a suspension of the payment of aid pending a final decision on a notification, if it believes that a member state is planning to pay the aid prior to the Commission's final decision, and to provide the Commission with all information necessary to decide whether the aid is compatible (see *Boussac*). If the member state ignores a Commission order to provide requested information, the Commission may terminate the procedure and make its decision regarding compatibility based only on the information available to it (compare *Pleuger Worthington* at I-7). This provides the Commission with a powerful lever to encourage national governments to supply all requested information.

The Commission may permit state aid which promotes the 'common interest' of the Community, as provided in exceptions to the general prohibition set forth in the statutes (EC Treaty, Article 92(2), (3)). Various guidelines for determining common interest have been promulgated with regard to specific sectors, such as textiles, environment, motor vehicles, research and development, synthetic fibres and small and medium-sized enterprises. However, the Commission has broad discretion to make this determination, which can be highly political and involves consideration of economic and social factors. This function is of crucial importance because, as Commissioner Van Miert observed:

> [i]f aid which is prejudicial to competitors [in other member states] is not monitored by an independent body to see whether it is in the Community's interest, the political essence of the Treaty is in jeopardy. This is because the waiving of conventional protectionist measures such as trade restrictions and customs duties that was necessarily ... associated with the establishment of the common market can be demanded of the member states only if they can be sure that their firms do not have to compete against rival firms in other member countries that operate with the backing of massive financial support from state resources.
>
> (Van Miert 1993: para. 3)

If none of the exceptions provided in the statutes applies, aid can be allowed only through a 'decision of the Council acting by a qualified majority on a proposal from the Commission' (EC Treaty Article 92(3)(e)). This provision has been employed only once, for the shipbuilding industry directive.

In general, the Commission would like to end state aid (except in limited circumstances discussed below) because it distorts competition and may as such delay necessary restructuring of European industry and waste scarce resources. However, Commission officials believe that aid will continue to be necessary to equalize regional differences, to promote social and economic cohesion and to correct market failures.

Although national politicians may recognize the harmful effects of state aid, they prefer to phase it out gradually rather than cutting it off abruptly, especially in strategically important industries, in order to avoid plant closure and job losses (Van Miert 1993: para. 1). In reviewing state aid, the

Commission is often in conflict with national governments, and has difficulty resisting political pressures to allow aid. None the less, since the mid-1980s Competition Commissioners have taken an increasingly restrictive approach to aid, and have encouraged a shift away from supporting particular business sectors towards supporting needy regions (*Financial Times*, 28 January 1994: 8).

Member states have attempted to use state aid to prolong the life of their 'sunset industries', often with disastrous results. For instance, in the steel industry, massive injections of aid were granted throughout the 1980s and early 1990s rather than having the industry undergo drastic restructuring (for example, Italy provided 11,100 million francs (11,000 million ECU) to Ilva, the Italian steel group, and its corporate predecessor in the 1980s, and 6,600 million francs (6,000 million ECU) in 1993; Spain provided 8,000 million ECU to state-owned CSI; and Germany provided 428 million ECU to Ekostahl, the East German steel mill).

In December 1993, the Commission reached agreement with state steelmakers on a plan to restructure the industry, which provided 8,000 million ECU in aid to state-owned companies, mainly in Italy, Germany and Spain, in return for capacity cuts of more than 5 million tonnes. It also called upon private, non-aided companies voluntarily to reduce capacity by 25 million tonnes (*Financial Times*, 15 February 1994: 1). A 240 million ECU fund was created to ease layoffs. Private steelmakers opposed the plan, arguing that keeping inefficient public sector enterprises in business through aid depresses prices, and may lead to the closure of more efficient, private sector plants (*Financial Times*, 11 March 1994: 15). In October 1994, however, the Commission abandoned the plan, in response to the industry's refusal to make the required capacity cuts (*Financial Times*, 26 October 1994: 2).

Member states also have used state aid to protect national champions. For instance, in the *Groupe Bull* case, the French government argued that Europe should be self-sufficient in a strategically important industry such as computers. However, Europe consumes roughly fifty per cent of the world computer output, but produces only ten per cent. If state-owned Bull, which has been heavily in debt for years, were to fail, this negative balance would increase. Aid of 6,600 million francs was allowed in July 1992 but proved insufficient, and France was subsequently allowed to pay an additional 11,100 million francs in October 1994.

In recent years, the Commission has focused on the special problems associated with state aid to public enterprises. Under the 'neutrality principle', public undertakings receive the same treatment as private undertakings with respect to competition rules, including rules covering state aid (EC Treaty, Article 222). But decisions regarding state aid to public enterprises are often taken at the highest political levels owing to the impact of the decision on the member state involved.

Control of state aid to public enterprises poses specific problems because the financial relationship between the member states and their public enterprises is often lacking in transparency, with aid being paid without being notified (Ehlermann 1993: 4–5). Thus, in 1980 and 1985, the Community adopted directives obliging member states to keep financial relationships with their public enterprises fully transparent. However, studies in several sectors showed that these directives had not been effective in providing the Commission with the information it needed. In 1991, the Commission issued a communication establishing a broad annual reporting obligation applicable to all publicly controlled companies with a turnover in excess of 250 million ECU (State Aid Communication). Italy, Spain and France, all with substantial public sectors, expressed concern that the reporting system could lead to discrimination by the Commission against public enterprises, in violation of the neutrality principle. France challenged the Communication, and, in June 1993, the Court of Justice annulled it on the grounds that its legal basis was not correct (see *French Republic*). In July 1993, the reporting requirements were readopted as a directive (Transparency Directive). The member states their concerns of discrimination with respect to the directive, perhaps because of national political changes and their privatization programmes which will remove the affected industries from its coverage.

State aid control during privatization

Since the early 1980s, member states, starting with Britain, followed by France, Greece, Portugal, former East Germany and most recently Italy and again France, have been privatizing parts of their public sectors. Such privatizations are often preceded by injections of state aid in order to improve the marketability of the enterprise involved (for instance, state aid accompanied the privatization of Ilva Steel). Accordingly, the Commission has increasingly been called upon to determine whether aid is involved in the process of privatization.

To this end, it applies the 'investor in a market economy' principle whereby, if the enterprise receives a capital injection or write-off of debts from the state before privatization on conditions that would not be acceptable to a private investor, or if the state does not demand an adequate return on its capital invested in a public enterprise, aid may be involved. Aid is deemed not to be present if the privatization meets certain conditions: the sale is made through a public offer; to the highest bidder; and interested parties are given sufficient time to prepare their offer (Ehlermann 1993: 5, 14).

The Commission is concerned whenever a state grants aid to an unhealthy public or private enterprise. However, it is more difficult to detect such aid when it is granted to a public enterprise prior to sale to the private sector, owing to problems of transparency. The Commission requires such aid to be conditioned on the 'implementation of a sound restructuring or conversion programme capable of restoring the long-term viability of the beneficiary' and, when the sector has excess capacity, a capacity reduction. In industries with excess capacity, a *prima facie* case for authorizing aid is created if a capacity reduction is included in the plan (see *Spain* at paras 95, 98). This changes previous policy, which required only that state aid should not contribute to an increase in capacity in such industries.

This policy recently was applied to Italy's Ilva Steel. In conjunction with its privatization, a waiver of debts totalling 2,500 million ECU was conditioned on a cut in capacity of 2 million tonnes. The Commission has also applied the policy to Groupe Bull, for which it conditioned its 1993 interim order that aid should be suspended until receipt of a recovery plan from the French government (*Financial Times*, 18 February 1994: 1). Aid to Bull was also approved in July 1992, which was part of a restructuring plan under which Bull cut 18 per cent of its workforce and closed seven of its thirteen plants (*Financial Times*, 3 July 1992: 20).

The Commission also has adopted the 'one time, last time' doctrine, under which companies can receive one last grant of state aid to return them to viability. This has been applied in the airline industry by DG VII, responsible for competition matters in that sector. This programme was designed to help the airline industry in the deregulation process. However, DG IV officials assert that this situation is unique to the airline industry, and that DG IV has not applied it to any sector within its jurisdiction. Groupe Bull has argued that this doctrine should apply with respect to its latest proposed aid payments (*Financial Times*, 18 February 1994: 1). DG IV officials were sceptical, since Bull had applied for additional aid on various occasions. However, the aid payment of 1,000 million francs was ultimately permitted.

CONCLUSION

Prior to the formation of the Community in 1957, effective regulation of competition essentially did not exist in any of the countries which were to become the member states. The market mechanism was not accepted or relied upon as the means of controlling the economy. Instead, the member states all engaged in heavy interventionism, through either nationalization combined with uncontrolled state aid or the over-regulation of industry or some combination of the two.

An essential corollary to the creation of an economically integrated European Community was that the market mechanism would replace state intervention in controlling industrial economic relations. Thus, the Treaty of Rome incorporated this fundamental principle, and the substantive rules to regulate restrictive agreements, abuses of dominant positions and state aid incompatible with the common market. These rules were supplemented with the Merger Regulation in 1989.

Over the last four decades, Community competition rules have had an impact throughout the Community, not only because their enforcement has improved competitive conditions directly, but also because their beneficial effects served as a stimulus to legislators in the member states to enact national competition laws consistent with Community law. Moreover, the existence of the Community enforcement apparatus has provided a competitive incentive to member states effectively to enforce their competition rules. Member states have also come to understand that state aid, which distorts competition in the Community, must be controlled and used only sparingly to balance out regional differences, to promote social and economic cohesion or to correct market failures. These important developments would not have occurred without the influence of the Community.

To the extent that differences remain between Community law and national law, member states continue to re-examine the policy reasons which underlie their law. In Germany, for instance, major sectors of the economy had been at least partially exempted from coverage of national competition law, including insurance and utilities (see Chapter 10). However, these sectors are not exempt from Community law. This has caused German authorities to reconsider the wisdom of their policy, and Germany is currently considering harmonization of national law with Community law.

The influence has also begun to flow in the opposite direction, such that commentary from member-state authorities has caused European regulators to consider improvements to the Community system. Such critique is badly needed, in light of the isolation from public scrutiny in which DG IV has traditionally operated. For instance, the Bundeskartellamt's proposal for the creation of an independent European cartel office has been much debated. Thus, the dynamics of Community/member-state relations are inducing improvements at both levels.

Tensions have also developed in these relations, largely based on the Commission's desire to retain central control of competition policy and the member states' interest in increasing their powers to enforce the antitrust laws, pursuant to the principle of subsidiarity. For instance, these tensions are apparent in the debate as to whether the Commission's monopoly to grant exemptions under Article 85(3) should be dispersed, whether the Community's jurisdiction over mergers should be expanded through reduction of the thresholds and to what extent state aid should be permitted.

A number of obstacles continue to hinder pursuit of free and unfettered competition throughout the Community, both at the national level and at the Community level. The latest economic recession in Europe, and the resulting high rate of unemployment, were powerful forces driving political interference with enforcement of the antitrust laws. The flexibility of the Treaty's substantive provisions allows factors other than competition-oriented criteria to be considered in deciding cases. Flaws in the Community's institutional arrangement for antitrust law enforcement allow political pressures to influence the outcome of cases in a way that may not promote the goal of free competition. The absence of a firmly rooted antitrust tradition in most member states implies that political interference is not controlled by public demand for the unequivocal application of competition laws.

In the future, member states will probably play an increasingly important role in enforcement of both Community and national competition laws. Strong antitrust enforcement institutions are currently being developed in the member states, and the Community is making efforts to decentralize power to enforce Community law. This is likely to lead to a higher degree of antitrust enforcement throughout the Community.

NOTE

The author acknowledges the generous assistance of those DG IV officials who discussed at length many of the issues raised in this chapter. These individuals include: Dr Claus Dieter Ehlermann, Director-General; Philip Lowe, Director, Merger Task Force; Luc Gyselen, Assistant to the Director-General; Auke Haagsma, Head of Unit A1; Helmut Schroter, Head of Unit A2; Emil Paulis, Deputy Head of Unit A3; Anne Houtman, Deputy Head of Unit, Directorate E; Glyn Philip Owen, Rapporteur, Directorate E; Sergio Benini, Rapporteur, Directorate E; Fabiola Mascardi, Rapporteur, Merger Task Force; and Thalia Lingos, National Expert, Merger Task Force. The author also acknowledges the insightful comments of Professor Barry E. Hawk, Partner, Skadden, Arps, Slate, Meagher & Flom.

REFERENCES

Bechtold, R. (1993) 'Antitrust Law in the European Community and Germany – an uncoordinated co-existence?', in Hawk (ed.) *United States, Common Market and International Antitrust: A Comparative Guide*, New York: Fordham Corporate Law Institute 1992.

Forrester, I. and Norall, C. (1983) 'The laicization of Community Law –self-help and the rule of reason: how competition law is and could be applied', in Hawk (ed.), New York: Fordham Corporate Law Institute 305.

Ehlermann, C.D. (1993) 'Privatization and competition', speech delivered in Brescia, 29 March 1993.

Goyder, D. (1993) *EC Competition Law* (2nd edition), Oxford: Oxford University Press.

Hawk, B. (ed.) (1992) *United States, Common Market and International Antitrust: A Comparative Guide*, vol. II, New York: Fordham Corporate Law Institute 441.

House of Lords Select Committee Report on the European Community (1993) *Enforcement of Community Competition Rules: Report with Evidence*, Session 1993/4, First Report, London: HMSO.

Majone, G. (1991) 'Cross-national sources of regulatory policy-making in Europe and the United States', *Journal of Public Policy* XI, 1: 79–106.

Roundtable Two (1993) 'Investigatory powers, fact-finding, procedural guarantees, transparency and independence of antitrust authorities,' in Hawk (ed.) 1993 Fordham Corporate Law Institute 99.

Stockmann, K. (1992) 'Trends and developments in European antitrust laws', in Hawk (ed.), *United States, Common Market and International Antitrust: A Comparative Guide*, New York: Fordham Corporate Law Institute.

Van Miert, K. (1993) 'The granting of state aid and control of subsidies in the European Community', speech delivered in Bonn, 5 July 1993.

Zekoll, J. (1991) 'European Community competition law and national competition laws: compatibility problems from a German perspective', *Vanderbilt Journal of Transnational Law* 24, 75: 75–111.

STATUTES

Treaty on European Union, Together With the Complete Text of the Treaty Establishing the European Community, OJ C 224/1 (31 August 1992) ('EC Treaty').

Treaty Establishing the European Coal and Steel Community (18 April 1951) ('ECSC Treaty').

Council Regulation (EEC) no. 4064/89 of 21 December 1989 on the control of concentrations between undertakings, OJ L395 (30 December 1989) ('Merger Regulation').

First Regulation implementing Articles 85 and 86, 1959–62 OJ Special edition 87, as amended by Reg. no. 59, 1959–62 OJ Special edition 249; Reg. no. 118/63/EEC, 1963–64 OJ Special edition 55; and Reg. no. 2822/71, 1971 OJ Special edition (III) 1035 ('Regulation 17').

Commission Regulation (EEC) no. 2367/90 of 25 July 1990 on the notifications, time limits and hearings provided for in Council Regulation (EEC) no. 4064/89, OJ L.219 (14 August 1990) ('Merger Procedural Regulation').

Commission Directive 93/84/EEC of 30 September 1993 amending Directive 80/723/EEC on the transparency of financial relations between Member States and public undertakings, OJ L.254/16 (12 October 1993) ('Transparency Directive').

Commission Decision of 23 November 1990, on the implementation of hearings in connection with procedures for the application of Articles 85 and 86 of the EEC Treaty and Articles 65 and 66 of the ECSC Treaty, Twentieth Competition Report, Article 2: 312–13.

Commission Communication to the Member States regarding Application of Articles 92 and 93 of the EEC Treaty and of Article 5 of Commission Directive 80/723/EEC to Public Undertakings in the Manufacturing Sector, 91/C273/02 (18 October 1991) ('State Aid Communication').

Notice on Co-operation Between National Courts and the Commission in Applying Articles 85 and 86 of the EEC Treaty, OJ C.39/05 (13 February 1993) ('Notice on Co-operation').

Commission of the European Communities, Report from the Commission to the Council on the Implementation of the Merger Regulation, COM(93) 385 final: 4 (Brussels, 28 July 1993) ('Commission Merger Report').

Commission of the European Community, XXIst Report on Competition Policy 1991: 57 (Luxembourg, 1992) ('XXI Competition Report').

Commission of the European Community, XXIInd Report on Competition Policy 1992: 75 (Luxembourg, 1993) ('XXII Competition Report').

CASES

French Republic *v.* Commission, C33/93 (12 October 1994) ('Groupe Bull').

Federal Republic of Germany *v.* Commission, C324/90 and C342/90 (13 April 1994), at I-7 ('Pleuger Worthington').

Spain *v.* Commission, Joined cases C278/92 to C280/92, Opinion of Advocate General Jacobs (23 March 1994) ('Spain').

Commission *v.* Mannesmann/Vallourec/Ilva, Case no. IV/M.315 (31 January 1994) ('DMV').

French Republic *v.* Commission, OJ C325/91 (16 January 1993) ('French Republic').

Società Italiana Vetro, SpA *v.* Commission, Joined Cases T68/89, T77/89, and T78/89 (10 March 1992) ('Flat Glass').

Ahlstrohm Osakeyhtio *v.* Commission, Joined Cases C89/85, C104/85, C114/85, C116/85, C117/85 and C125/85 to C129/85 (31 March 1993) ('Wood Pulp').

Automec *v.* Commission II, Judgement of the Court of First Instance, 18 September 1992 ('Automec II').

French Republic *v.* Commission, OJ C301/87 (14 February 1990), at I-356 ('Boussac').

Gebr. Lorenz GmbH *v.* The Federal Republic of Germany, C120/73, 1973 E.C.R. 1471 (11 December 1973) ('Gebr. Lorenz').

Van Gend en Loos *v.* Nederlandse Administratie der Belastingen, no. 26/62, 1963 E.C.R. 1 ('Van Gend').

Part III

Problems of the regulatory state

12 The future of regulation in Europe

Giandomenico Majone

INTRODUCTION

The case studies presented in the second part of this volume cover a limited number of countries and policy areas, but nevertheless raise, explicitly or implicitly, most of the important issues of regulatory policy-making in Europe today. Thus, they provide a most useful background for this chapter whose aim it is to assess the current situation and possible future developments of regulatory federalism in the EC.

Four central themes emerge clearly from the case studies. First, the extraordinary impact of European laws, policies and judicial decisions on the actions and behaviour of the member states. In the areas of Community competence, this impact is visible not only in specific legislative and administrative measures, but also in the choice of policy instruments and in subtle changes in national styles of policy-making. A less obvious, but in the long run perhaps more important, influence is the stimulus to policy learning. As several of our case studies show, Community actions force national governments to reconsider the rationale of traditional policies and institutional arrangements. Sometimes the induced adaptations are fairly marginal, at other times they are quite far-reaching.

A second important theme is the relations between national and European regulation. It is clear that these relations are far from having reached any sort of stable equilibrium. A trend toward greater centralization in some areas co-exists with signs of an evolution toward patterns of co-ordinated partnership in others. The picture of intergovernmental relations in the EC is complicated by several factors including a serious lack of mutual trust, the tendency of national governments to use European legislation to their advantage, striking differences in national regulatory capacities and, partly as a consequence, a very uneven level of implementation of EC regulations.

Third, the limits of the independence of national and European regulators have still to be clearly determined. All our case studies stress the importance of this issue, which is indeed central to the future of regulation in Europe. This is because agency independence is not only an effective means for achieving policy credibility, as has been argued in previous chapters, but also the necessary condition for a reform of the regulatory process in the direction of a co-ordinated partnership among national and European authorities.

The fourth theme – the legitimacy and democratic accountability of regulation – is particularly prominent in the chapter by Robert Baldwin, but is present, at least implicitly, also in the other case studies. The issue of political legitimacy is closely related to the question of political independence but will be taken up in the next chapter, partly because of its complexity, but also because of its normative character.

This chapter is mainly concerned with questions of efficiency and effectiveness. It analyses the political and institutional defects revealed by the case studies in the light of the theories developed in the first part of the volume, and suggests possible remedies. The main message is that a serious regulatory reform cannot be limited to measures of institutional engineering at the EC level, but must also involve the policies and institutions of the member states.

THE STIMULUS OF COMMUNITY ACTIONS

EC laws, policies and judicial decisions are not the only, but certainly the most important, stimulus to current regulatory developments in Europe. This conclusion emerges clearly from the preceding case studies. For example, Baldwin, in Chapter 5, quotes the Chairman of the British Health and Safety Commission saying that the Single European Act paved the way for a shift from national to Community primacy in policy-making in the area of health and safety at work. By now, the chairman notes, the Community must be regarded as the principal engine of health and safety regulations affecting Britain, not just in worker safety but in major hazards and most environmental matters. And Albert Weale notes, in Chapter 6, that an important stimulus for passage of the British Environmental Protection Act in 1990 came from the government's need to legislate in order to implement the EC's 1986 framework directive for the control of air pollution.

As is to be expected, the stimulus provided by Community law is particularly evident in the field of competition policy. Lluís Cases, in Chapter 9, shows how the new Spanish competition law enacted in 1986 was heavily influenced by European competition law, which Spain adopted almost in its entirety. Belgium, France, Italy, Ireland, Greece and Portugal also have competition laws which substantially resemble those of the Community (see Chapter 11). Thus, both in economic and in social regulation, policy initiatives in the member states are increasingly likely to derive from an agenda established at the European rather than the domestic level.

But the impact of Community actions is not restricted to agenda-setting and legislative innovations. The study by Michelle Everson (Chapter 10) of the regulatory regime of the German insurance industry demonstrates the capacity of the Community to change the rules of the domestic policy game and to upset historically rooted institutional equilibria. In refusing to acknowledge the traditional role of the Association of German Fire Insurers, and treating it as a private cartel rather than as a regulatory partner of the Insurance Authority, the European Court of Justice at one stroke upset an intricate arrangement. While such bodies as the Association of German Fire Insurers might be allowed to continue in their quasi-regulatory functions, they must now satisfy both EC and national law, and the German regulator must reckon with the active involvement of the European Commission in its own decisions. At the same time, consumers were finally given the chance to bring pressure to bear on the German industry to offer products as advantageous as those offered by, for example, British insurers. Thus, Everson concludes, the Community was the prime stimulus in the transformation of the regulatory regime of the German insurance industry.

National styles of policy-making and choice of policy instruments have also been affected by Community actions. These aspects of EC influence are particularly emphasized in the two chapters dealing with social regulation in Britain, a country known for its distinctive approach to regulatory enforcement. Both Baldwin and Weale note the tension between the precise and rigid approach to enforcement that emanates from the EC, and the flexibility that is central to the British approach. Regulatory philosophy in Britain traditionally pursued a compliance strategy in which negotiation and discussion played an important role in the relationship between inspectors and plant operators. The discretion granted to the inspectors under this approach meant that there was a lack of formality in terms both of the derivation of the standards and of the latitude of their implementation. On the other hand, the specific obligations imposed by EC directives (see also the discussion of regulatory complexity later in this chapter) do not leave much room for regulatory discretion.

The EC's influence on the choice of policy instruments can be seen in the preference of EC environmental directives for uniform emission limits over the environmental quality objectives in terms of the putative receiving capacity of the environment, favoured by the British. The British approach has the advantage of being more sensitive to the different environmental circumstances of the member states, but unfortunately it is also much harder for outsiders to monitor. Hence, other governments have tended to suspect that the British preference for environmental quality standards was due to an underlying unwillingness to implement EC directives (Gatsios and Seabright 1989).

Weale notes that by the mid-1980s this clash of approaches had become quite serious as the British government sought to withstand in a variety of proposed EC directives, in particular the Large Combustion Plant Directive, the imposition of inefficiently costly controls on sources of air pollution. A few years later, however, the official position began to change in the direction of the Community approach. Among other innovations, the Environmental Protection Act of 1990 introduced legally binding emission limits, in the EC (and German) style. These far-reaching changes in regulatory philosophy were a response to domestic factors, such as the electoral success of the Green

Party in the 1989 European elections, but also, as mentioned above, to the need to adapt British environmental legislation to European directives.

POLICY LEARNING

Quite aside from their immediate legislative and administrative impact, Community actions have often been a powerful stimulus for national governments to reconsider the rationale of their own domestic policies. We have just mentioned the British Environmental Protection Act which rationalized and modernized the British approach to pollution control, but practically all the case studies provide telling examples of policy learning induced by Community actions.

Thus, Laudati points out that in the field of competition a high level of harmonization of national policies has occurred spontaneously, that is, through mutual adjustments and 'bottom-up' convergence towards the EC model. To the extent that differences remain between EC law and national law, the member states continue to re-examine the policy reasons which underlie their roles. For instance, German authorities, stimulated by the Commission's criticisms and findings of the Court of Justice, had to reconsider the wisdom of exempting industries such as insurance and public utilities from the Cartel Law (see also Chapters 7 and 10). Again, Everson's study shows that Community action highlighted the tension between Germany's commitment to an open, competitive market economy and the restrictive nature of its traditional insurance supervision. With the consumers free, thanks to EC rulings, to seek the best price for an insurance policy outside the domestic market, the national regulator is now under pressure to bring its practices into line with the most flexible and cost-effective systems of prudential regulation prevailing anywhere in the Union.

It should not be thought, however, that critical inputs flow only in one direction. The dynamics of relations between the EC and member states are inducing policy learning at both levels: commentary from national authorities or evidence of policy failure have often caused European regulators to consider improvements to the Community approach. The adoption of the principle of mutual recognition – which stimulates competition among national regulators, but at the same time represents a major innovation in the regulatory philosophy of the Commission – is perhaps the best example of policy learning taking place at both the national and European levels.

The immediate reason for reforming the old approach was the mounting evidence that the attempt to harmonize a continuously growing body of national rules had failed. In the words of the 1985 White Paper on the completion of the internal market, 'experience has shown that the alternative of relying on a strategy based totally on harmonization would be over-regulatory, would take a long time to implement, would be inflexible and could stifle innovation' (COM(85), 310 final: 18). To overcome the limitation of the traditional approach, the White Paper introduced a new strategy with the following key elements: mutual recognition of national regulations and standards; legislative harmonization at the European level to be restricted to laying down essential health and safety requirements binding on all member states; and the gradual replacement of national product specifications by European norms.

In essence, the White Paper proposes a conceptual distinction between matters where harmonization is essential, and those where it is sufficient for there to be mutual recognition of the equivalence of the various requirements laid down under national law. This line of reasoning had been followed by the European Court of Justice in the famous *Cassis de Dijon* judgement of 1979. The Court had stated that a member state may not prohibit the sale in its territory of a product produced and marketed in another member state even if this product is produced according to technical or quality requirements which differ from those imposed on its domestic products – except when the prohibition is justified by the need to protect public health or the environment, or to ensure the fairness of financial transactions.

Unlike harmonization, mutual recognition does not involve the transfer of regulatory powers to the Community, except for the regulation of essential health and safety requirements. Instead, it stimulates competition among national regulators which, like competition among producers, should provide an efficient way of assessing the costs and benefits of different methods of regulation, as well as increasing the range of choice available to consumers. An instructive example of policy learning produced by regulatory competition is provided by the application of the new approach to the rights of establishment of professionals.

In the 1970s a number of sectoral directives had attempted to facilitate professional mobility by harmonizing the conditions for access to, and the exercise of, various professions. This approach was relatively successful for the medical and paramedical professions, but little progress was made in other areas, notably law, architecture, engineering and the pharmaceutical profession. The new approach is based on the following principles: mutual trust between member states; comparability of university studies between the member states; and mutual recognition of degrees and diplomas without prior harmonization of the conditions for access to and the exercise of the professions.

These principles find concrete application in Directive 89/48. Unlike the older, sectoral directives, the new directive does not attempt to harmonize the length and subject matters of professional education, or even the range of activities in which professionals can engage. Instead, it specifies methods by which the states can compensate for such differences. The way the methods are applied by national authorities may be appealed in the courts of the host country.

Directive 89/48 creates, for the first time in Europe, a single market for the regulated professions. A member state can no longer deny access to, or the exercise of, a regulated profession on its territory to EU citizens who already exercise or could legitimately exercise, the same profession in another member state. Equally important, the directive provides incentives for raising the level of professional education throughout the Union. This is because the citizens of a country that does not regulate a certain profession adequately are at a competitive disadvantage if they wish to use their professional skills beyond the national borders. Some countries have already taken actions to improve the quality of professional education in some areas (see, for example, Zilioli 1989 on the reform of dentistry in Italy).

THE LIMITS OF POLITICAL INDEPENDENCE

Together with the impact of the Community on domestic law and policy, the issue of the political independence of regulators is the other recurrent theme of the case studies. This is not surprising, since political independence is generally considered essential for the credibility of regulatory policies. As we saw in Chapter 2, credibility is problematic for politicians and the bureaucrats under their direct control, because in a democracy political executives tend to have a short time horizon and parliamentary majorities are not bound by the decisions of previous majorities. Hence the delegation of powers to a politically independent agency is an important means whereby governments can commit themselves to regulatory strategies that would not be credible in the absence of such delegation.

The case studies show that while European governments are aware of the importance of policy credibility in an increasingly interdependent world, and are thus prepared to accept the independence of national and European regulators in principle, in practice they are often driven by considerations of political expediency to interfere with the regulators' decisions or to limit regulatory discretion. This ambivalent attitude towards agency independence may be especially evident in the French and Spanish case studies, but is a general European phenomenon.

In Chapter 8, Demarigny argues that the way in which the French 'independent administrative authorities' are designed and their powers defined still leaves a considerable margin of influence to the central government. Thus, the old Competition Commission was carefully structured so that it could not impose penalties. Even the present, and considerably more powerful, Council for Competition does not have the power to initiate investigations; that power remains in the hands of the government. In fact, the 1986 competition law strengthens the power of the Minister of Economics in relation to mergers. In sum, the law fails to take its own logic to its ultimate conclusion, preserving a considerable margin of arbitration and discretion to the central government.

Similarly, under the Spanish competition law of 1989, the government, not the regulator – the Competition Tribunal – has been delegated the main power to control mergers. The Minister of Economics and Finance does not have to inform the Tribunal about mergers which the Minister approves. Also the important power to exempt particular industries or activities from the application of competition rules is reserved to the government. In this as in other cases such as the regulation of state aid to industry, the regulatory body can give only non-binding opinions. Like Demarigny, Cases concludes that the latest Spanish competition law, although a considerably improvement over the previous one, is still seriously incomplete and does not carry its own logic to its natural conclusion.

The German Cartel Office has considerably more extensive powers than the competition authorities of France or Spain, and indeed of any other European country – in part as a result of American pressures on occupied Germany at the end of the war (see Chapter 3). Yet, even here, as Baake and Perschau show in Chapter 7, the government retains considerable powers of intervention in competition policy and especially in merger cases. The case of the Daimler-Benz–MBB merger, in which the Minister of Economics overruled the negative decision of the Cartel Office and disregarded the opinion of the President of the Monopoly Commission, is instructive in this respect, despite its exceptional nature. Equally instructive is the observation of the authors of the German case study that in granting exemptions from the prohibition of mergers and cartels the Minister of Economics is driven more by political or social considerations than by efficiency criteria.

How the limits of the political independence of regulators are to be defined is still an open question in Europe (the American debate is more advanced in this respect, as we shall see in the next chapter), not only in competition policy but also, and even more, in the other areas of regulation. For example, Baldwin refers to the risk of 'devastating ministerial interference' in the field of occupational health and safety, while Weale argues that despite the formal separation of the National Rivers Authority from the British Department of the Environment, there can still be political pressures placed on the NRA not to pursue particular cases with vigour. In fact, the first Director-General of the NRA resigned allegedly because of pressures from a minister in the Department not to impose a stringent discharge consent on a textile firm near the minister's own constituency.

The reader will recall that the issue of ministerial interference has already been raised in Chapter 1, in discussing the design of the new bodies regulating the privatized public utilities in Britain. Many of the most important regulatory powers in this area are often given directly to government rather than to the new agencies. The danger, it was pointed out there, is that such powers of direction 'could be abused to exert behind-the-scenes pressure on the regulator in much the same way as pressure was put on the nationalized industries by government' (Prosser 1989: 147; see also Veljanovski 1991: 10–13).

The limits of the political independence of regulators remain uncertain not only at the national, but also at the EC level. This is even more worrying since the credibility and coherence of European regulatory law depends crucially on the perception that the Commission is able and willing to enforce the common rules in an objective and even-handed way. Precisely for this reason Article 157 of the Treaty of Rome states, in part, that 'the members of the Commission shall, in the general interest of the Community, be completely independent in the performance of their duties. . . . They shall neither seek nor take instructions from any government or from any other body.'

In practice, however, the Commissioners are not immune from political influences both from the member states and from within the Commission itself. Although they are not supposed to pursue national interests, European Commissioners are usually politicians who, after leaving Brussels, will return to their home country to continue their career there. This makes national pressures often difficult to withstand. On the other hand, the Commission is a collegial body, and the need to achieve a majority within the *collegium* has on several occasions produced flawed or inconsistent regulatory decisions.

Such concerns are reflected in the proposals to transform the Commission's Competition Directorate, DG IV, into a European Competition Authority, independent not only from the member states but from the Commission itself (see Chapter 11). A model often cited in this respect, and indeed one of the driving forces behind such proposals, is the German Cartel Office. It is true that, as noted above, the Cartel Office itself is not completely immune from political influences. However, the procedures which the German government must follow when it wishes to overrule a decision of the Office entail high political costs and make the interference plain for all to see. Relations between the Commission and the European Cartel Office, it is suggested, could be regulated in a similar way.

As Laudati notes, the idea of an independent European Cartel Office is still very controversial. Sceptics point out, *inter alia*, that the time for such an institutional innovation (which in any case would require revision of the treaties) is not yet ripe, and also that such an independent body 'would be a kind of political orphan. Its decisions could meet with stiff resistance in countries where the public is less committed to the competition principle than in Germany' (Ehlermann 1995: 479). It is admitted, however, that delegating powers to independent European agencies is one of the means of adapting the present institutional framework to the realities of an enlarged EU. Hence the next intergovernmental conference should create the legal basis for setting up, eventually, not only an independent European competition authority but also other bodies such as a European agency for Community-wide licensing of new medical drugs, or a European telecommunications agency (Ehlermann 1995: 484–5).

The current debate would be more productive if both advocates and critics would not focus their arguments exclusively on the Community level. Our case studies show that the problem of agency independence is at least as serious at the national level, and also that national and Community regulatory policies are highly interdependent. These considerations suggest that the problem should be tackled simultaneously at both levels. Indeed, the future of regulation in Europe depends crucially on the ability of finding co-ordinated, rather than disarticulated, solutions. One such solution seems to be emerging in the form of transnational regulatory networks.

REGULATORY NETWORKS

Although national regulators may be personally committed to the statutory objectives assigned to their agency, that commitment lacks credibility as long as the agency remains isolated and politically too weak to withstand ministerial interference on its own. However, we know from the theory of repeated games that commitments may be strengthened through teamwork (Dixit and Nalebuff 1991; see also Chapter 2 above). Although people may be weak on their own, they can build resolve by forming a group or network, and the same principle applies to organizations. Thus, a regulatory agency which sees itself as part of a transnational network of institutions pursuing similar objectives and facing analogous problems, rather than as a new and often marginal addition to a huge central bureaucracy, is more motivated to resist political pressures. This is because the regulators have an incentive to maintain their reputation in the eyes of fellow regulators in other countries; a politically motivated decision would compromise their credibility and render co-operation more difficult to achieve in the future.

The European System of Central Banks (see Chapter 2) may be seen as the prototype model of such transnational networks, and a network structure seems to be emerging also in the field of competition policy. As Laudati writes in Chapter 11, the Commission's Competition Directorate has recently initiated a decentralization project with the long-term goal of having one Community competition statute applied throughout the European Union by a network including DG IV itself, national competition authorities and national courts. Direct links already exist between Commission inspectors and national competition authorities as regards any investigation carried out by the Commission. Moreover, a high level of harmonization of national competition laws has already occurred spontaneously in the member states, while national competition authorities everywhere are becoming more professional and increasingly jealous of their independence.

A high level of professionalization is crucial to the viability of the network model. Professionals are oriented by goals, standards of conduct, cognitive beliefs and career opportunities that derive from their professional community, giving them strong reasons for resisting interference and directions from political outsiders (Moe 1987: 2). In turn, political independence is important because basic ideological differences concerning, for example, the role of competition principles in economic policy are likely to persist between the member states. However, such differences are much less pronounced between professional competition regulators from different countries, just as a commitment to price stability tends to be stronger among central bankers than among politicians. Without a common basis of shared beliefs, a co-operative partnership of national and European regulators could not function effectively.

There is no reason why the network model, given the right conditions, could not be extended to other areas of economic and social regulation, and indeed to all administrative activities where mutual trust and reputation are the key to greater effectiveness. An example is the emerging pattern of co-ordinated partnership between the Community statistical office, Eurostat, and the national statistical offices of the member states (McLennan 1995). As another indication of the same trend, at a meeting of the Council of Ministers of the Environment in 1991 it was agreed that member states should establish an informal network of national enforcement offices concerned with environmental law.

Moreover, the recent creation of a number of specialized European agencies (*Agence Europe* no. 6098, 31 October 1993) may be seen as a potentially important step in the same direction. The list of the new bodies includes, in addition to the European Monetary Institute, the forerunner of the European Central Bank, the European Environmental Agency, the Office of Veterinary and Phytosanitary Inspection and Control, the European Centre for the Control of Drugs and Drug Addiction, the European Agency for the Evaluation of Medicinal Products, and the European Agency for Health and Safety at Work.

These bodies are not (yet) fully fledged regulatory agencies. They neither make nor implement regulatory policies. For the time being, their functions are essentially limited to the collection, processing and dissemination of policy-relevant data and information. For example, the European Environmental Agency has been assigned the following tasks (Council Regulation no. 1210/90 of 7 May 1990):

- to provide the member states and the Community with information
- to collect, record and assess data on the state of the environment
- to encourage harmonization of methods of measurement
- to promote the incorporation of European environmental information into international environmental monitoring programmes
- to ensure data dissemination
- to co-operate with other Community bodies and international institutions

Similarly, the Agency for the Evaluation of Medicinal Products has been given such tasks as the co-ordination of scientific evaluation of the quality, safety and efficacy of medicinal products; the dissemination of assessment reports of product characteristics; the provision of technical assistance for the maintenance of a database on medical products, to be made available to the public; advising companies on the conduct of various tests necessary to demonstrate the quality, safety and efficacy of new medical drugs (Council Regulation no. 2309/93 of 22 July 1993).

The future activities of the European agencies need not be limited to such functions, however. First, the need to develop uniform assessment criteria for monitoring the implementation of Community regulations is at least as urgent as the development of common methodologies of data collection and analysis. Such matters can be only partially addressed in the formal texts of European legislation. Rather, the development of criteria for monitoring implementation is a task which only the new agencies can adequately perform. Second, the same agencies cannot be the passive and uncritical receivers of data supplied by the national administrations. Sooner or later, their officers will have to be given powers to visit member states to verify the accuracy and consistency of the methods followed by national and subnational governments.

Finally, as the House of Lords Select Committee on the European Communities argued in its 1992 report on *Implementation and Enforcement of Environmental Legislation* (House of Lords 1992: 40–1), there is a strong case for some form of Community oversight of the measures taken by the member states to monitor and enforce compliance. This is because common regulations lose credibility if they are not consistently implemented throughout the European Union. Hence the Committee suggests the creation of an 'audit' inspectorate to examine the policies and performance of national authorities – rather than seeking to supplant them – and publicly report its findings to the member states, the Commission and the European Parliament. Such an 'inspectorate of inspectorates' would also report on shortcomings in administrative arrangements, such as inadequacies of training or resourcing, leading to insufficient regulatory activity.

The House of Lords Select Committee rightly insists that these functions and powers should be formally distinguished from the Commission's own duty to enforce Community policies in the event of failure to do so by the member states. Thus, the environmental inspectorate should not be part of DG XI, the Commission's directorate responsible for environmental policy.

Rather, the 'logical home for an environmental inspectorate on the lines indicated is the European Environmental Agency, with whose functions the inspectorate would neatly dovetail' (House of Lords 1992: 41). Institutional separation from the Commission would enable the inspectorate to scrutinize the Commission's own role, for example in providing assistance to the member states through the Structural Funds or the Cohesion Fund: the use of such funds in the countries of southern Europe has been known to produce negative consequences for the environment. By the same token, we add, European inspectorates in other fields such as health and safety at work (see Chapter 5) should be organized within the corresponding agency rather than as offices of the Commission. In the case of the already existing competition inspectorate, this is one more argument in favour of an independent European Competition Office.

In a new report on the European Environmental Agency, the House of Lords Select Committee has reconsidered its previous recommendations with regard to an inspectorate 'in the light of the present activities of the Agency and the current political mood in the member states about the powers of EU institutions' (House of Lords 1995: 14). The Committee now thinks that 'an incremental and cautious approach to a European inspectorate would be politically more acceptable and less likely to put at risk the goodwill towards the Agency on which its future success depends'. It is still of the opinion that an inspectorate with the powers recommended in the previous Report should be established, but at this time does not wish 'to prejudge whether an inspectorate would sit better within the Agency or within the Commission' (House of Lords 1995: 14). The best solution of course depends on the way the Agency will develop, but, leaving contingent political considerations aside, the logic of the 1992 Report is still compelling.

In an earlier chapter we referred to Selznick's definition of regulation as sustained and focused control exercised by a public agency over activities that are valued by a community (Selznick 1985: 363–4). Regulation, Selznick suggests, is not achieved simply by passing a law, but requires detailed knowledge of, and intimate involvement with, the regulated activity; hence, specialized agencies entrusted with fact-finding, rule-making and enforcement are part and parcel of statutory regulation. Seen in this light, the transformation of the new European agencies into fully fledged regulatory bodies would appear to be a question of time. Incidentally, such a development would have the added advantage, from the viewpoint of the member states, of limiting the growth in size of the Commission despite an expanding membership of the EU. While the Commission would retain all the political responsibilities entrusted to it by the treaties, technical tasks would be delegated to the agencies. The latter would not operate in a political and institutional vacuum. First, national and Community representatives and experts would sit in the Management Board and in the Scientific Committee of each agency. In particular, the Management Board, whose task it is to provide strategic guidance to the agency (for example, in setting regulatory priorities) would comprise, as at present, one person from each country with membership in the agency, as well as representatives from the Commission and the European Parliament. Second, each European agency would operate in close partnership with the corresponding national regulatory bodies.

IMPROVING REGULATORY CAPACITIES

For a co-ordinated partnership involving national and Community regulators to operate effectively, two more conditions must be satisfied in addition to political independence: each participating organization must be able to perform the tasks assigned it, and there must be sufficient trust among the partners to keep the costs of transacting within acceptable limits. Both conditions are still problematic in the EC.

To begin with the first one, regulatory capacities – in terms both of delegated powers and of expertise – vary widely among the member states. In Chapter 11, Laudati observes that, where national enforcement of competition law was virtually non-existent in Europe until 1958, at present a number of member states have competition authorities with a satisfactory level of technical expertise and the power to impose significant remedies. However, as the case studies on France and Spain demonstrate, there are still significant exceptions, and these include not only these two countries, but also Italy and several smaller countries.

Overall regulatory capacities are even less adequate in other policy areas. Thus, few countries have a fully fledged environmental protection agency, specialized pollution inspectorates or agencies for the regulation of public utilities. Decentralized rule-making and enforcement remain problematic as long as wide differences in regulatory capacities persist. For example, in the next section we discuss early attempts to introduce mutual recognition of toxicological and clinical trials for the approval of new medical drugs. Now, these attempts failed, at least in part, because of the perception that some national regulators lacked the resources and expertise needed to deal competently with complex regulatory issues. Moreover, the very uneven level of implementation of European directives in the field of health and safety at work (see Chapter 5) is probably due less to deliberate resistance than to a lack of regulatory capacities and resources in a number of member states.

Close co-operation between European and national regulators in removing such obstacles would be an important step toward the development of a true partnership. The practice of regulatory federalism in America provides some suggestions about how such co-operation could be organized. For example, when the Occupational Safety and Health Act (OSH Act) was passed in 1970, few states had comprehensive laws dealing with safety and health at work and fewer still had adequate programmes to enforce them. In spite of this, the OSH Act did not provide for the complete federalization of this area. The objective of assuring safe and healthy conditions in the workplace was to be reached, in part, by 'encouraging the States to assume the fullest respons- ibility for the administration and enforcement of state occupational safety and health laws', by means of federal grants and approved state plans (OSH Act, section 2(b)(11)).

The Act incorporates special mechanisms for utilizing state resources. The most important of these are the provisions for 'state plans' contained in section 18(b–g). While the Act generally pre-empts state enforcement once the federal government regulates, section 18(b) provides that states wishing to regain responsibility for the development and enforcement of safety and health standards under state law may do so by submitting and obtaining federal approval of a state plan which meets the requirements set forth in Section 18(c). Approval of a state plan by the Occupational Safety and Health Agency (OSHA) permits the state to re-enter the field of occupational health and safety regulation. The agency is to approve a state plan only if the plan demonstrates the availability of adequate financial resources and the exist- ence of a sufficient number of trained personnel. States are entitled to receive federal funding for developing the plan and implementing it after approval.

Thus, the American approach has three attractive features: first, states retain the possibility to act if they see fit; second, in order for them to do so, they must meet precise standards; third, such a flexible solution takes due account of the fact that not all states enjoy a similar regulatory capacity: some of them need federal assistance in order to meet national standards. Could such a model be transposed at the EC level? The setting is of course radically different here. Far from being the exception, decentralized implementation tends to be the rule. Yet, to require the member states to draw up an implementation plan and to set up the means that are necessary to make it operational would force them to address the implementation issue more systematically than is currently the case. Resources from the structural funds could be used to assist those member states lacking sufficient resources to develop the plans and requisite structures.

It is clear, however, that such a system can work only if the Community is technically equipped to assess the adequacy of implementation plans, to monitor the activity of national regulators, to provide guidance – all activities that, by its own admission, the Commission is currently not in a position to carry out satisfactorily, but which could be entrusted to the new European agencies. Despite the practical difficulties, the proposed scheme is quite in line with the subsidiarity principle: member states would retain their primary responsibility, while the Community's main task would be to assist and supplement their action (Dehousse *et al.* 1992: 63–5).

On the other hand, while the network model favours decentralization in rule-making and enforcement, at the same time it increases the need for centralized oversight in order to ensure consistent and effective implementation. In areas such as competition policy and environmental protection, where many rules will continue to be set at the European level, the case for some form of centralized oversight of the measures taken by national regulators to monitor and enforce compliance is particularly strong. It will be recalled that the 1992 Report of the House of Lords Select Committee suggested that European 'audit' inspectorates should also report on shortcomings in administrative arrangements, such as inadequacy of training and resourcing, leading to insufficient regulatory activity. Something like the state implementation plans would provide the natural famework for such audits.

THE COSTS OF MISTRUST

Trust is a basic social mechanism for coping with system complexity and for sustaining long-term co-operation (Gambetta 1988). It is particularly important for a system like the European Community which depends on the loyal co-operation of the member states and of their administrations, for the formulation and implementation of common rules. The drafters of the founding treaties were well aware of this. Article 5 of the Treaty of Rome imposes an obligation of Community loyalty on the member states, who are required to facilitate the achievement of the Community's tasks and to abstain from any measure which could jeopardize the attainment of the objectives of the Treaty. Analogous prescriptions are contained in Article 86 of the Treaty of Paris establishing the European Coal and Steel Community, and in Article 192 of the Euratom Treaty.

The European Court of Justice has interpreted Article 5 of the Treaty of Rome in a way that goes well beyond the principle of international law that *pacta sunt servanda* and is in fact akin to the principle of *Bundestreue* or 'federal comity' of German constitutional law; see Article 35 of the German Basic Law. Thus, in the interpretation of the Court, Article 5 expresses a general principle of mutual trust not only between member states and Community institutions, but also among national governments (Due 1992).

As a specific application of this philosophy, the Commission's White Paper on the completion of the internal market, as we saw, mentions mutual trust as the first element of the new approach for the mutual recognition of university diplomas. Mutual trust and loyal co-operation among the member states are supposed to replace the impossible task of harmonizing vastly different national systems of professional training and licensing. Each state is to trust other states' courses of study as being generally equivalent to its own, and a competent national authority must accept the evidence provided by another member state.

As this example shows, the principle of mutual recognition is extremely demanding in terms of mutual trust. In fact, an American scholar has observed that the principle presupposes a higher degree of comity among member states than the Commerce Clause of the US Constitution requires among individual states. The Commerce Clause has been interpreted by the US Supreme Court to allow each state to insist on its own quality standards for goods and services, unless the subject matter has been pre-empted by federal legislation, or unless the state standards would unduly burden interstate commerce (Hufbauer 1990: 11).

The crucial importance of mutual trust between national administrations is demonstrated also by the failure of early attempts to introduce a decentralized system for the approval of new medical drugs (see above). In order to speed up the process of mutual recognition of toxological and clinical trials (which were to be conducted according to EC rules), a 'multi-state drug application procedure' (MSAP) was introduced in 1975. Under the MSAP, a company that had received a marketing authorization from the regulatory agency of a member state could ask for the recognition of that approval by at least five other countries. The agencies of the countries nominated by the company had to approve or raise objections within 120 days. In case of objections, the Committee for Proprietary Medicinal Products (CPMP) – a group which includes national experts and Commission representatives – had to be notified. The CPMP would express its opinion within sixty days, and could be overruled by the national agency that had raised objections.

The procedure did not work well. Actual decision times were much longer than those prescribed by the 1975 Directive, and national authorities did not appear to be bound either by the decisions of other regulatory bodies or by the opinion of the CPMP. Because of these disappointing results, the procedure was simplified in 1983, but even the new procedure did not succeed in streamlining the approval process since national regulators continued to raise objections against each other almost routinely (Kaufer 1990). As already mentioned, these difficulties induced the Commission to propose a centralized approval procedure and the establishment of the European Agency for the Evaluation of Medicinal Products. Both proposals were accepted by the Council in 1993.

As this example shows, mistrust and lack of co-operation among the member states contribute significantly to the centralizing trends at the EC level which national governments so often deplore. Also other defects of the European regulatory process, including excessive complexity, legalism and poor enforcement, may be explained in part as a consequence of insufficient trust among the member states and between them and the Community institutions. Many students of EC policy-making have pointed out that EC directives usually contain many more technical details than comparable national legislation. It is sometimes argued that such regulatory complexity reflects the technical perfectionism of the Commission, but this explanation lacks plausibility: the Commission is chronically understaffed, has no in-house research capabilities, and is largely composed of generalists, not of technical experts. Rather, regulatory complexity may be explained as another consequence of distrust among the member states. Doubting the commitment of other governments to implement European rules honestly, national representatives often insist on spelling out mutual obligations in the greatest possible detail, to the point of including chemical, mathematical or statistical formulas in the text.

Excessive legalism is another recurrent criticism of EC regulation. It is true that, at present, European regulators tend to pay more attention to rule-making than to the effective enforcement of the rules they produce. But this is because the Commission is not allowed to play a direct role in implementation, except for a few policy areas such as competiton. Thus, by excluding the Commission from the implementation process, the member states have encouraged a tendency to focus on the transposition of EC directives into national legislation, rather than on effective compliance and actual results.

To appreciate the role of mistrust in the problem of poor or non-compliance, one should keep in mind not only that member states are unenthusiastic about close monitoring of their own regulatory activities in the interest of Community objectives – indeed, as Baldwin points out in Chapter 5, national governments actually seek to use EC legislation to their domestic advantage – but also that their own determination to implement European rules vigorously is weakened by the suspicion that other national governments may not behave in the same correct way (Vervaele 1992).

To conclude, it is very unlikely that any reform in the direction of a more effective, flexible and decentralized regulatory system can succeed without a greater spirit of co-operation and mutual trust than national government have shown so far. The question is, how can the present unsatisfactory state of affairs be improved?

REFORM BEGINS AT HOME

The Maastricht Treaty on European Union contains two important political signals: first, the member states are not prepared to accept an unlimited expansion of Community competences; and, second, the Commission has been weakened. The 'three-pillar' structure of the Union signifies a refusal to 'communitarize' foreign policy and immigration matters. Even the new competences established by the treaty in fields such as education, culture, public health or consumer protection are replete with reservations: the Community can encourage co-operation among the member states, support and supplement their action, but harmonization of national laws is often excluded. As far as the Commission is concerned, not only were most of its proposals postponed or rejected, but its institutional status was weakened. One cornerstone of its power, the right of initiative, has been watered down in monetary policy where it enjoys only the right to put forward recommendations. It is bound to play a lesser role in the new co-decision procedure, where the Council of Ministers and the European Parliament are the main actors. Furthermore, some declarations attached to the treaty (declarations on transparency and access to information, and on the cost-benefit evaluation of Commission proposals) suggest that the Commission's legitimacy has been questioned (Dehousse *et al.* 1992: 8–10).

The Intergovernmental Conference on Institutional Reform due to start in 1996 is bound to reflect the current political mood in the member states about the powers of the European institutions. Political leaders will argue that the future of the Union lies not in more centralization, but in a stricter application of the principle of subsidiarity and more co-operation among the member states. Yet the same leaders are reluctant to admit that many, perhaps most, problems of the EC policy-making system have domestic roots. Lack of mutual trust, weak commitment to the common objectives, the temptation to gain short-term political advantages at the expense of policy credibility: these, as we argued in the preceding pages, are all factors contributing to more centralization than is required by efficiency considerations, to over-regulation, to regulatory complexity and to poor enforcement.

Again subsidiarity unaccompanied by a change in national attitudes and behaviour is not sufficient to resolve the dilemma of regulatory federalism. It will be recalled (see Chapter 3) that the dilemma arises from the fact that while lower levels of government are more attuned to individual tastes, they are unlikely to make a clear separation between providing public goods to their citizens and engaging in policies designed to advantage their jurisdiction at the expense of their neighbours. Centralization of regulatory authority at a higher level of government can correct such policy externalities, but its cost is the harmonization of policy across jurisdictions that may be dissimilar with respect to underlying tastes or needs.

Now, the pursuit of narrow and short-term advantages by national governments is often dictated by party political considerations or by pressures from domestic redistributive coalitions. We have argued that one important means of limiting the influence of such factors is to delegate policy-making powers to independent institutions. Under which conditions this delegation is compatible with democratic accountability is the issue to be discussed in the next chapter. Here it suffices to repeat by way of conclusion that the willingness to give up old habits of behind-the-scenes ministerial interference in regulatory decisions would have two positive consequences. It would increase the credibility of domestic policies but would also make possible the emergence of those networks of national and European regulators which alone hold the promise of resolving the dilemma of regulatory federalism.

Thus, in the post-Maastricht era institutional reform must begin at home. Failure to create the domestic conditions for greater trust and a closer partnership between national and Community institutions can only lead either to more centralization or to the progressive weakening of the economic and political foundations of the Union.

REFERENCES

Dehousse, R., Joerges, C., Majone, G., Snyder, F. and Everson, M. (1992) *Europe after 1992: New Regulatory Strategies*, Florence: European University Institute, EUI Working Paper Law 92/31.

Dixit, A.K. and Nalebuff, B.J. (1991) *Thinking Strategically: The Competitive Edge in Business, Politics and Everyday Life*, New York: Norton.

Due, O. (1992) 'Article 5 du Traité CEE: Une disposition de caractère fédérale?' in *Collected Courses of the Academy of European Law*, II, 1: 23–32, Dordrecht: Martinus Nijhoff Publications.

Ehlermann, C.D. (1995) 'Reflections on a European Cartel Office', *Common Market Law Review* 32: 471–86.

Gambetta, D. (1988) *Trust: Making and Breaking Cooperative Relations*, Oxford: Blackwell Press.

Gatsios, K. and Seabright, P. (1989) 'Regulation in the European Community', *Oxford Review of Economic Policy* 5, 2: 37–60.

House of Lords Select Committee on the European Communities (1992) *Implementation and Enforcement of Environmental Legislation*, London: HMSO.

House of Lords Select Committee on the European Communities (1995) *European Environmental Agency*, London: HMSO.

Hufbauer, G. (ed.) (1990) *Europe 1992 – An American Prospective*, Washington (DC): The Brookings Institution

Kaufer, E. (1990) 'The regulation of new product development in the drug industry' in Majone (ed.) *Deregulation or Re-regulation? Regulatory Reform in Europe and the United States*, London: Francis Pinter.

McLennan, W. (1995) 'Working together as partners in European statistics', in Crescenzi (ed.) *European Statistics in Perspective*, Rome: ISTAT, 24–48.

Moe, T. (1987) 'Interests, institutions and positive theory: the politics of the NLRB', *Studies in American Political Development* 2: 236–99.

Prosser, T. (1989) 'Regulation of privatized enterprises: institutions and procedures', in Hancher and Moran (eds), *Capitalism, Culture and Economic Regulation*, Oxford: Clarendon Press.

Selznick, P. (1985) 'Focusing organizational research on regulation', in Noll (ed.) *Regulatory Policy and the Social Sciences*, Berkeley and Los Angeles: University of California Press.

Veljanovski, C. (1991) 'The regulation game', in Veljanovski (ed.) *Regulators and the Market*, London: Institute of Economic Affairs.

Vervaele, J.A.E. (1992) *Fraud Against the Community – the Need for European Fraud Legislation*, Deventer: Kluwer.

Zilioli, C. (1989) 'The recognition of diplomas and its impact on educational polities', in DeWitte (ed.) *European Community Law of Education*, Baden-Baden: Nomos.

13 Regulatory legitimacy

Giandomenico Majone

INTRODUCTION

The deregulation debate of the 1980s has emphasized such defects of the regulatory process as the absence of a real budgetary discipline and the consequent tendency to over-regulate, legalism and unnecessary rule complexity, inflexibility in the face of technological and economic innovations, and poor co-ordination among regulators. However, the most persistent and fundamental criticisms of statutory regulation by independent agencies have been concerned less with such technical problems than with the normative issues of public accountability and democratic legitimacy. It seems therefore appropriate to conclude this book devoted to the rise of statutory regulation in Europe with a discussion of these issues.

Regulators wield enormous power, yet they are neither elected nor directly responsible to elected officials. How is their exercise of that power to be controlled? This, in a nutshell, is the question before us; the answer, we argue in this chapter, ultimately depends on the model of democracy one adopts. According to the majoritarian model, the main if not the only source of legitimacy is accountability to voters or to their elected representatives. Measured by this standard, independent agencies can be seen only as 'constitutional anomalies which do not fit well into the traditional framework of controls, checks and balances' (Veljanovski 1991: 16), even as challenges to the basic principles of constitutionalism and of democratic theory (Teitgen-Colly 1988).

Moreover, the debate about the democratic deficit of EC decision-making is informed by standards derived from the majoritarian model. Critics point out that the European executive (the Council of Ministers and the Commission), rather than the European Parliament, is responsible for legislation. Within the executive, the bureaucratic branch (the Commission) is said to be unusually strong with respect to the political branch (the Council), whose members are in the last instance subject to the control of the national parliaments. Finally, because of the supremacy of European law over national law, the governments of the member states, meeting in the Council, can control their own parliaments rather than being controlled by them (Vaubel

1995). Thus, the democratic deficit can be reduced only by expanding the role of the European and the national parliaments in the EC policy-making process.

Those who favour a non-majoritarian model of democracy agree that a problem of regulatory legitimacy exists at both the national and the European levels, but deny that a higher level of politicization of the regulatory process is the correct answer. The non-majoritarian model is particularly concerned with protecting minorities from the 'tyranny of the majority', and the judicial, the executive and the administrative functions from representative assemblies and from fickle mass opinion (for classic statements of this position, see *The Federalist*, nos 48, 49 and 71). Hence, instead of concentrating power in the hands of the majority, it aims to limit and to disperse power among different institutions. Delegation of policy-making responsibilities to independent bodies, whether at the national or supranational level, is viewed favourably as one important means of diffusing power. Such diffusion, according to the model, may be a more effective form of democratic control than direct accountability to voters or to elected officials.

Most democratic polities rely extensively on non-majoritarian principles and institutions. In fact, Lijphart (1984, 1991; Lijphart, Rogowski and Weaver 1993) has produced massive empirical evidence that majoritarian democracy is the exception rather than the rule, being mainly limited to the United Kingdom and to countries strongly influenced by the British tradition. In spite of this, the assumption that majority rule is the only source of democratic legitimacy is still generally accepted. This paradox may be explained in part by historical and cultural factors, such as the weight of British practices and traditions, but the following pages suggest a more general explanation. For reasons to be discussed below, but which are at any rate fairly obvious, in a democracy redistributive policies can only be legitimated by majority vote. Such policies have been central to the modern welfare state, and their overwhelming importance in the past explains the tendency to apply majoritarian standards of legitimacy to all policy types.

The crisis of the welfare state has reduced the political significance of redistribution relative to policies which aim to increase aggregate welfare, but the normative standards have not been reset accordingly. This chapter suggests that until this is done regulatory legitimacy will remain an elusive concept both at the national and the EC levels, impeding the search for suitable mechanisms of public accountability and political control.

Non-majoritarian institutions and democratic theory

Independent regulatory bodies, like independent central banks, courts of law, administrative tribunals or the European Commission, belong to the genus 'non-majoritarian institutions', that is, public institutions which, by design, are not directly accountable either to voters or to elected officials. The growing importance of such institutions in all democratic countries shows that for many purposes reliance upon qualities such as expertise, professional discretion, policy consistency, fairness or independence of judgement is considered to be more important than reliance upon direct political accountability.

At the same time, however, doubts as to the legitimacy of non-majoritarian institutions persist, and indeed increase, in direct proportion to the expanding role of these institutions. Probably the most important reason why the debate tends to be inconclusive is the failure to realize that a normative appraisal of non-majoritarian mechanisms – blatant violation of democratic principles or legitimate instruments of democratic governance – depends crucially on the model of democracy one adopts.

Democratic theorists distinguish two different conceptions of democracy, both compatible with Abraham Lincoln's notion of 'government of the people, by the people, for the people'. The first, represented by the majoritarian or populistic model of democracy, tends to concentrate all political power in the hands of the majority. According to this conception, majorities should be able 'to control all of government – legislative, executive and, if they have a mind to, judicial – and thus to control everything politics can touch. Nothing clarifies the total sway of majorities more than their ability to alter and adjust the standards of legitimacy' (Spitz 1984, quoted in Lijphart 1991: 485). Although majority rule is viewed here as the very essence of democracy, in practice it is usually admitted that the will of the majority must be restrained by minority rights. In a strict formulation of the majoritarian model, however, these restraints should be informal – a matter of historical tradition and political culture – rather than of a formal-constitutional nature which cannot be changed by bare majorities. The model also implies that the governmental system should be unitary and centralized in order to ensure that there are no geographical or policy areas which the Cabinet and its parliamentary majority fail to control (Lijphart 1991: 486).

By contrast, the non-majoritarian (or, as Dahl (1956) calls it, Madisonian) model of democracy aims to share, disperse, delegate and limit power in a variety of ways. The overriding objective is, to use Madisonian language, to protect minorities against the 'tyranny of the majority', and to create safeguards against 'factionalism' – the usurpation of government by powerful and self-interested groups – and the threat which factionalism poses to the republican belief in deliberative democracy. In particular, delegation – a non-majoritarian strategy which has played an important role in our analysis, see especially Chapter 4 – attempts to restrain majority rule by placing public authority in the hands of officials who have limited or no direct accountability to either political majorities or minorities.

Recent empirical research provides additional evidence in favour of the thesis that non-majoritarian decision-making mechanisms are more suitable for complex, plural societies than are mechanisms that concentrate power in the hands of the political majority. Lijphart defines plural societies as those which are 'sharply divided along religious, ideological, linguistic, cultural, ethnic, or racial lines into virtually separate sub-societies with their own political parties, interest groups, and media of communication' (Lijphart 1984: 22). The evidence collected by Lijphart and other scholars concerning the relationship between the needs of cleavage management in these societies and non-majoritarian mechanisms is quite strong (Lijphart, Rogowski and Weaver 1993).

This research is clearly relevant to the study of European integration (Taylor 1991). The European Union is split by a number of deep cleavages, the most obvious being the distinction between large and small member states. Linguistic, geographical (north–south), and ideological (protectionist versus free trade, and dirigiste versus more *laissez-faire* countries) cleavages also play significant roles in European politics. Indeed, many non-majoritarian features of the Community system are best explained as strategies of cleavage management. However imperfect, these strategies have been essential to the progress of European integration, while a strict application of majoritarian principles could produce only deadlock and possibly even disintegration.

It is therefore surprising to see that many current proposals to increase the democratic legitimacy of European institutions – associating the European Parliament with the appointment of Commission members, reducing the Commission (which would no longer include representatives of all the member states), generalizing and simplifying the use of majority voting in the Council, reforming the Presidency in a way which would *de facto* limit the role of small countries – all point in the direction of strengthening the majoritarian features of the European political system (Dehousse 1995).

Such proposals can be understood only in terms of a paradigm which equates democracy with majority rule. As the research referred to above shows, this paradigm is flawed both theoretically and empirically. It is particularly inadequate in the case of the European Union. The Union is not, and may never become, a state in the modern sense of the concept. It is, at most, a 'regulatory state' since it exhibits some of the features of statehood only in the important but limited area of economic and social regulation. In this area, however, non-majoritarian institutions are the preferred instruments of governance everywhere, as the preceding chapters have shown.

Regulatory legitimacy in America

Additional insights into the legitimacy problem of non-majoritarian institutions can be gained from the continuing American debate on the 'independent fourth branch of government', an expression used by political scientists and legal scholars to denote the regulatory branch of the federal government. Many of the arguments made today in Europe to criticize or defend the independence of regulatory bodies were first formulated in the course of the American debate, which thus provides a useful historical background to the current European discussion. That debate is also instructive for another reason. It is well known that the American Constitution incorporates a number of principles inspired by the Madisonian philosophy of government – separation and division of powers, checks and balances, the presidential veto and so on. These non-majoritarian features of the American political system explain why this country was the first to develop a tradition of judicial review and judge-made law, and also to create independent regulatory bodies. In spite of these precedents and of a generally favourable constitutional philosophy, doubts continue to be raised as to the democratic legitimacy of non-majoritarian institutions. The persistence of such doubts shows the complexity of the issue, but also the tenacity of the paradigm equating democracy and majoritarian rule.

Initially the expression 'fourth branch of government' was used polemically, to emphasize what already in the 1930s were considered major defects of the independent regulatory commissions (IRCs): violation of the principle of separation of powers, lack of political accountability and poor co-ordination. According to the Committee on Administrative Management (Brownlow Committee) established by President Franklin Roosevelt in 1936, the independent commissions

> [a]re in reality miniature independent governments set up to deal with the railroad problem, the banking problem, or the radio problem. They constitute a headless 'fourth branch' of the government, a haphazard deposit of irresponsible agencies and uncoordinated powers. They do violence to the basic theory of the American Constitution that there should be three branches of government and only three.
>
> (Brownlow Committee, cited in Litan and Nordhaus 1983: 50)

Writing almost a generation later, a political scientist expressed similar concerns in equally strong language:

> The theory upon which the independence of the commission is based represents a serious danger to the growth of political democracy in the United States. The dogma of independence encourages support of the naive notion of escape from politics and the substitution of the voice of the expert for the voice of the people ... The commission has significant anti-democratic implications.
>
> (Bernstein 1955: 293)

In fact, an independent regulatory branch appears problematic in view of the constitutional position of the American president as head of the executive branch and its agencies. Traditionally, liberal scholars have argued that strong presidential oversight was needed in order to keep the regulators democratically accountable. Moreover, Bernstein, for example, maintained that isolation from the presidency leads to a lack of political support, and this political vacuum leads to capture by the regulators by the supposedly regulated industries. Incidentally, the argument about the risk of a political vacuum has been used to oppose the creation of a European cartel office; see Chapter 12.

More recently, another scholar has argued that presidential control allows the government to respond to shifts in public opinion, reducing the likelihood that regulatory policy will become routinized and bureaucratized (Sunstein 1987). But what if shifts in public opinion lead to the election of a president with strong deregulatory views, like President Reagan? An important idea behind the creation of the IRCs was to ensure consistency in regulatory policy-making by insulating the regulators from the potentially destabilizing effects of the electoral cycle. However, because of the liberal critique of the IRCs, most of the regulatory bodies created in the 1970s – such as the Environmental Protection Agency, the Occupational Safety and Health Administration or the National Highway Traffic Administration – were organized as single-headed executive agencies, either reporting directly to the president (the case of the EPA) or in the line of command from the president down through the executive branch hierarchy.

Once elected, President Reagan tried to use his control of the budgetary process to reduce the activity of the EPA and the other social regulatory agencies, and to slow down enforcement of antitrust legislation. At the same time Congress, concerned about the mounting cost of social regulation and the consequent threats to employment and the international competitiveness of American industry, was not pushing the agencies very hard to implement the statutes of the 1970s.

Faced by a reluctant Congress and by a president who opposed any form of regulation, some liberal scholars and representatives of public-interest groups began arguing that not only the IRCs but also the social regulatory agencies should be viewed as an independent branch of government not answerable to either Congress or president but closely monitored by the courts. As Shapiro writes:

> If you don't trust Congress and know that the president is the enemy, who is left to love and nurture the health, safety and environmental legislation of the sixties and seventies? All that is left is the bureaucracy of the new federal agencies who were recruited only recently and retain their enthusiasm for doing what they were hired to do. They want to regulate on behalf of the great public values of health, safety and environmental purity. So it becomes attractive to those favoring regulation to turn the federal bureaucracy into an independent branch of government. Such a branch would be free of the president, even free of the Congress of the eighties, but loyal to the sweeping statutory language of the sixties and seventies.
>
> (Shapiro 1988: 108)

It is important to keep in mind, however, that the independence of the regulators is relative. Even the IRCs are independent only in the sense that they operate outside the presidential hierarchy and that commissioners cannot be removed from office for disagreement with presidential policy. All regulatory agencies are created by congressionally enacted statutes. The programmes they operate are defined and limited by such statutes; their legal authority, their objectives and sometimes even the means to achieve those objectives are to be found in the enabling laws.

Regulatory discretion is also severely constrained by procedural requirements. Since passage of the Federal Administrative Procedures Act (APA) in 1946, followed in 1976 by the Freedom of Information and by the Government in the Sunshine Acts, regulatory decision-making has undergone a far-reaching process of judicialization. Under APA, agency adjudication was made to look like court adjudication, including the adversarial process for obtaining evidence through presentations of the contending parties, and the requirement of a written record as the basis of agency decision. Clearly, these and similar procedural requirements greatly simplify judicial review of administrative adjudication.

On the other hand, APA requirements for rule-making are less demanding: before promulgating a rule, the agency must provide notice and opportunity for comments; when it promulgates the rule, it must supply a concise statement of the rule's 'basis and purpose'; the rule can be set aside by a court only if it is 'arbitrary, capricious, or abuse of discretion'. Such differences in requirements for adjudication and rule-making did not matter much as long as most regulation was of the rate-setting and permit-allocation types and hence relied largely on adjudication. However, with the growth of social regulation in the 1960s and 1970s, rule-making (for example, standard-setting) became much more important. Thus, the courts began to develop a large body of new procedural rules and strict standards of judicial review for rule-making proceedings: see the following section.

The progressive judicialization of regulatory proceedings makes the arguments in favour of an independent regulatory branch more plausible by making the agencies more and more court-like. After all, one of the most important characteristics of courts is their independence. If it is improper for a president or a member of Congress to interfere with a judicial decision, the same ought to be true with respect to the decisions of a court-like agency. This does not mean, of course, that regulatory decisions should be taken in a political and institutional vacuum. The authority of Congress to define broad policy objectives, and the responsibility of the president to co-ordinate the entire regulatory process to ensure internal coherence, are not questioned. Rather, the advocates of an independent fourth branch, but also some supporters of stronger presidential control like Sunstein, favour a bigger role for the courts in controlling agency discretion through procedural and substantive review of rule-making (Ackerman and Hassler 1981; Shapiro 1988; Edley 1990; Sunstein 1990; Rose-Ackerman 1992).

If a pro-deregulation president can mount a frontal assault on social regulation, and if members of Congress are too concerned with their own re-election to worry about the coherence of statutory programmes, only the courts can provide the necessary continuity of the regulatory process. They, more than any other branch of government, are committed to preserving continuity of meaning in statutory law. What is suggested here is a partnership between regulatory agencies and courts. By both procedural and substantive means, but especially by statutory interpretation, the courts should insist that regulators continue to pursue with vigour the objectives set by Congress in the 1960s and 1970s, even when other political forces try to use recently elected members of Congress and presidents to cut back on regulation in the name of economic development (Shapiro 1988: 127). In return, judges should protect the independence of the regulators.

But what about political accountability? Is government by judges and technocratic experts compatible with democratic principles? The writers considered here are well aware of the importance of these questions, but point out that government by elected politicians, too, suffers from a number of defects that have been extensively discussed by, among others, public-choice theorists (Mueller 1989). For example, in seeking re-election, legislators engage in advertising and position-taking rather than in serious policy-making, or they design laws with numerous opportunities to help particular constituencies. In either case, re-election pressures have serious consequences for the quality of legislation. On the other hand, pro-regulatory scholars ask rhetorically: if the courts require the regulatory process to be open to public input and scrutiny and to act on the basis of competent analyses, are the regulators necessarily less accountable than elected politicians? (Rose-Ackerman 1992: 34).

At any rate, the value of agency responsiveness to political principals begins to appear questionable once it is realized that new political forces can put pressure on Congress and the president to cut back on social regulation. Under such circumstances continuity with the policies of the past could be preserved only by reasserting the faith of the New Deal in the independence of the regulatory branch. However, while New Dealers viewed the courts with suspicion, the new advocates of an independent fourth branch see judicial review as the most effective means to ensure the public accountability of the regulators.

Procedural legitimacy

The American debate on the legitimacy of the regulatory branch reveals two distinct dimensions of the issue: a procedural dimension and a substantive one (for a similar distinction in the context of EC institutions, see Weiler 1992, and Chapter 5 above). Procedural legitimacy implies, among other things, that the agencies are created by democratically enacted statutes which define the agencies' legal authority and objectives; that the regulators are appointed by elected officials; that regulatory decision-making follows formal rules, which often require public participation; that agency decisions must be justified and are open to judicial review.

Substantive legitimacy, on the other hand, relates to such features of the regulatory process as policy consistency, the expertise and problem-solving capacity of the regulators, their ability to protect diffuse interests and, most important, the precision of the limits within which regulators are expected to operate. We shall discuss the substantive dimension of regulatory legitimacy in the following section. Here we examine the procedural dimension, focusing on the requirements of transparency and public accountability since this is the area where the democratic deficit of European regulators, at both the national and EC level, is most obvious.

The simplest and most effective way of improving transparency and accountability is to require regulators to give reasons for their decisions. This would in turn activate a number of other mechanisms for controlling regulatory discretion such as judicial review, public participation and debate, peer review, policy analysis to justify regulatory priorities and so on. As Shapiro (1992: 183) has written, 'giving reasons is a device for enhancing democratic influences on administration by making government more transparent. The reason-giving administrator is likely to make more reasonable decisions than he or she otherwise might and is more subject to general public surveillance'. The above-mentioned US Administrative Procedures Act is an excellent example of the potential of the giving-reasons requirement. It will be recalled that the APA provides two basic procedures for regulatory decision-making: trial-type or quasi-judicial hearings for formal adjudication; and 'notice-and-comment' requirements for informal rule-making. In the latter case there is no trial-type hearing and the decision is not 'on the record' since the agency is not required to base its decisions solely on the written comments submitted but may take into consideration any information which it finds relevant to the case.

However, as we saw, informal rules must be accompanied by a 'concise general statement of their basis and purpose', and may not be 'arbitrary, capricious, or an abuse of discretion'. Starting from such general and apparently innocuous requirements, federal judges have succeeded in formulating new principles to improve the transparency and rationality of informal rule-making. For example, they have demanded that both the essential factual data on which a rule is based and the methodology used in reasoning from the data to the proposed standard should be disclosed for comment at the time the rule is proposed. Moreover, the agency's discussion of the basis and purpose of its rule must detail the steps of the agency's reasoning and its factual basis, while significant comments received during the public comment period must be answered at the time of final promulgation (Pedersen 1975). Thus, today informal rule-making has to be accompanied by records and findings even more detailed and elaborate than had been initially envisioned for formal adjudication. To a large extent, these strict procedural requirements have been achieved by elaborating the giving-reasons requirement of the APA (Shapiro 1992: 185).

The importance of this requirement has not escaped the framers of the Treaty of Rome. According to Article 190 of the Treaty, 'Regulations, directives and decisions of the Council and of the Commission shall state the reasons on which they are based'. Furthermore, Article 15 of the Treaty of

Paris establishing the European Coal and Steel Community, provides that 'Decisions, recommendations and opinions of the High Authority shall state the reasons on which they are based', while Article 5 of the same treaty states that 'the Community shall . . . publish the reasons for its actions'. It is interesting to note that there is no *general* requirement to give reasons in the law of most member states, so that these Community provisions were, and to some extent still are, not only different from, but in advance of, national laws (Hartley 1988).

In the *Beus* case of 1968, the European Court of Justice introduced a distinction reminiscent of the APA's distinction between the strict reason-giving requirements for formal adjudication and the more limited require-ments for rule-making. According to the Court, in case of an act of general application (regulation) it is sufficient to indicate the general situation which led to the adoption of the act, and the general objectives which it is intended to achieve. This is because 'it is not possible to require that it should set out the various facts, which are often very numerous and complex, on the basis of which the regulation was adopted, or *a fortiori*, that it should provide a more or less complete evaluation of the facts' (Case 5/67, *Beus* v. *Hauptzollamt München* [1968] ECR 83: 95). On the other hand, much fuller reasons can and should be given in case of an individual act (decision) where all the relevant factors are known.

A question still debated by legal scholars is whether Article 190 of the Treaty of Rome, 'one of the world's central devices for judicial enforcement of bureaucratic transparency' (Shapiro 1992: 220), will be used by the European Court of Justice to move beyond formal requirements towards substantive judicial review of regulatory decision-making in the EC. Accord-ing to Shapiro the formula used by the Court in Case 24/62 (*Germany* v. *Commission* [1963] ECR 63) for expressing the transparency requirement 'constitutes a transition from procedural to substantive reasons that is strikingly comparable to the American transition from procedural to substant-ive due process in the famous *Minnesota Rate* case' (Shapiro 1992: 201).

Be that as it may, there is little doubt that the Community could usefully draw on the long experience of the American regulatory state in controlling bureaucratic discretion. The enactment of an Administrative Procedures Act for the EC would provide the Community with a unique opportunity to decide what kind of rules are more likely to rationalize decision-making, to what extent and in which form interest groups should be given access to the regulatory process and the possibility of dialogue with the Commission, or how judicial review could be facilitated. The proliferation of committees, working groups and agencies shows how urgent is the need for a single set of rules explaining the procedures to be followed in regulatory decision-making. The growth in the number of such bodies (close to a thousand, according to some estimates), the overlap of their activities and the diverg-encies between the rules governing their functioning create a real lack of transparency (Dehousse *et al.* 1992: 30). In such a situation, where it is difficult for the citizens of the European Union to identify the body which is responsible for decisions which apply to them, regulatory legitimacy is reduced to vanishing point.

As previous chapters have shown, the need for greater transparency and accountability in regulatory decision-making exists also in the member states. If the problem of regulatory legitimacy seems to be more acute at the European level this is also because, relative to other functions of government, the regulatory function is much important here than at the national level. Thus, a European APA would not only contribute to the legitimacy of the Community policy-making system, but also serve as a useful model for all the states of the Union.

Substantive legitimacy

As already noted, reliance upon qualities such as expertise, credibility, fairness or independence has always been considered more important than reliance upon direct political accountability – but only for some purposes. The substantive legitimacy of non-majoritarian institutions depends crucially on how precisely those purposes are defined. In essence, this is because accountability by results cannot be enforced when the objectives of an organization are either too vague or too broad. In this section, I argue that the familiar distinction between efficiency and redistribution (see Chapter 2) provides a sound conceptual basis for deciding whether the delegation of policy-making authority to an independent regulatory body has at least *prima facie* legitimacy.

The nineteenth-century Swedish economist Knut Wicksell (1967 [1896]), was probably the first scholar to emphasize the importance of this distinction and the need to deal with efficiency and redistributive policies through separate collective-decision processes. In a democracy, public decisions concerning the redistribution of income and wealth can be taken only by a majority vote since any issue over which there is unavoidable conflict is defeated under a unanimity rule. Redistribution is a zero-sum game since the gain of one group in society is the loss of another group. Efficiency issues, on the other hand, may be thought of as positive-sum games where everybody can gain, provided the right solution is discovered. Hence, such issues could be settled, in principle, by unanimity. The unanimity rule guarantees that the result of collective choice is efficient in the Pareto sense, since anybody adversely affected by the collective decision can veto it.

Naturally, unanimity is practically impossible in a large polity, but there are second-best alternatives. These include various non-majoritarian mechanisms such as consociational strategies, which encourage bargaining among elites of relatively well-organized cleavage segments, supermajorities and, of particular interest in the present context, delegation of problem-solving tasks to independent expert agencies (Lijphart 1984).

The main task delegated to regulatory agencies is to correct market failures so as to increase aggregate welfare. It is important to note that the adoption of efficiency as the standard by which the regulators are to be evaluated implies, *inter alia*, that regulatory instruments should not be used for redistributive purposes. Regulatory policies, like all public policies, have redistributive consequences; but for the regulator such consequences should represent potential policy constraints rather than policy objectives. Only a commitment to efficiency, that is, to the maximization of aggregate welfare, and to accountability by results, can substantively legitimize the political independence of regulators. By the same token, decisions involving significant redistribution of resources from one social group to another cannot be legitimately taken by independent experts, but only by elected officials or by administrators directly responsible to elected officials.

A criticism frequently raised against these normative arguments is that efficiency and redistribution – or 'value creation' and 'value claiming' in the suggestive terminology used by students of negotiations (Lax and Sebenius 1986) – cannot be separated in practice. Were this the case, Wicksell's analytic distinction would in fact have limited policy relevance. Indeed, the two issues *can* be separated under conditions which economists have succeeded in specifying with sufficient precision (Milgrom and Roberts 1992: 35–9). The main condition is that of 'no wealth effects', meaning that every decision-maker regards each possible outcome as being completely equivalent to receiving or paying some amount of money, and that he or she has sufficient resources to be able to absorb any wealth reduction necessary to pay for a switch from the less preferred to the more preferred alternative.

When there are no wealth effects, 'value creation' and 'value claiming' can be treated as distinct and separable processes, as advocated by Wicksell. In other words, decisions about resource allocations or about institutional arrangements are unaffected by the wealth, assets or bargaining power of the parties: efficiency alone determines the outcome. Only the decision of how benefits and costs are to be distributed is affected by the resources or power of the parties.

It is easy to think of situations where the condition of no wealth effects does not hold, that is, where the choice actually made depends on the decision-maker's wealth. For example, a poor person or a poor country may not have the resources to pursue some course of action that a richer one would. When the decision-makers are large organizations or governments of rich countries, however, the assumption of no wealth effect, and hence the possibility of separating efficiency from redistributive considerations, is often plausible. The history of European integration shows that such a separation is both possible and useful. A striking feature of the integration process is that all major efficiency-increasing strategies – from the creation of the Common Market to Economic and Monetary Union – were accompanied by *separate* redistributive measures in favour of the poorer member states: the Social Fund, the European Investment Bank, the European Regional Development Fund, the Structural Funds and finally the Cohesion Fund which the

Maastricht Treaty explicitly ties to the adjustments made necessary by monetary union. By this method it has been possible to achieve a remarkable level of economic integration, in which the richer member states are particularly interested, while distributing the benefits so as to induce all the members to participate in such projects.

I have insisted on the possibility of separating efficiency and redistributive concerns because such a separation is crucial to the substantive legitimacy of regulatory policies. To repeat, the delegation of important policy-making powers to independent institutions is democratically justified only in the sphere of efficiency issues, where reliance on expertise and on a problem-solving style of decision-making is more important than reliance on direct political accountability. Where redistributive concerns prevail, legitimacy can be ensured only by majoritarian means.

The same argument suggests that large-scale redistributive policies at the European level have been ruled out not only by the small size of the EU budget (see Chapter 4) but also by serious concerns about the democratic legitimacy of such policies. By comparison with the social policies of its member states, the Union remains a 'welfare laggard' while it continues to play a major role in the development of social regulation. This apparent paradox is discussed in the following section.

Efficiency, redistribution and the democratic deficit

The idea of a European welfare state somehow emerging as a transnational synthesis of national welfare systems has been discussed repeatedly in recent years. The advocates of this idea are generally motivated by an historical analogy, but particularly by concerns about the future of social entitlements in an integrated European market – the fear that competition among different national welfare regimes in an increasingly integrated market could lead to regime-shopping, social dumping and deregulation.

The analogy is with the integrative role of social policy in the development of the nation state in nineteenth-century Europe. Historically, social policy has made an essential contribution to the process of nation-building by bridging the gap between state and society. National insurance, social security, education, health and welfare services and housing policy were, and to a large extent remain, powerful symbols of national solidarity. It is argued that a supranational welfare state would provide an equally strong demonstration of Europe-wide solidarity.

How realistic are these expectations? Should there be a European welfare state or at least a coherent supranational social policy? Actual policy developments do not show any progress in these directions. The question is whether this lack of progress is due only to budgetary limitations or also, as suggested above, to deeper legitimacy problems.

To begin with, one should note that there is considerable ambiguity about the meaning of a European social policy in the Treaty of Rome itself. The section on social policy – Title III of Part Three of the Treaty – enumerates a number of 'social fields' (employment, labour law, working conditions; vocational training; social security; health and safety at work; collective bargaining and right of association) where member states should closely co-operate (Article 118, EEC). In the following article, member states are urged to 'ensure and subsequently maintain the application of the principle that men and women should receive equal pay for equal work'. The same Title III also established the European Social Fund with the goal of improving employment opportunities and facilitating the geographical and occupational mobility of workers.

What is arguably the most significant social policy provision of the Treaty of Rome – the social security regime for migrant workers – appears not in the section on social policy, but in the one on the free movement of persons, services and capital. Finally, one of the objectives of the common agricultural policy is, according to Article 39(b) of the Treaty, 'to ensure a fair standard of living for the agricultural community, in particular by increasing the individual earnings of persons engaged in agriculture'.

Thus, to the framers of the Treaty, 'social policy' included not only social security and interpersonal distribution of income, at least for certain groups of workers, but also inter-regional redistribution, elements of industrial and labour market policy (vocational training, measures to improve labour mobility) and social regulation (primarily health and safety at work, and equal treatment for men and women). However, the enumeration of matters relating to the social field in Article 118 and the limited role given to the Commission in Title III indicate that the social policy domain, with the exception noted above, was originally considered beyond the competence of the Community institutions.

In fact, Commission activity in the area of social policy and social regulation was quite modest between 1958 and the end of the 1970s, with one notable exception, environmental policy. As noted in Chapter 4, the terms 'environment' and 'environmental protection' do not even appear in the Treaty of Rome, but, in spite of the lack of an explicit legal basis, a Community environmental policy has been growing vigorously since 1967. The Single European Act (SEA) assigns a number of new competences to the Community in the social field. The main lines of development of Community activities in this field are beginning to emerge clearly: they are regional development (new Title V, Economic and Social Cohesion), and social regulation (Articles 100a and 118a, and the new Title VII, Environment). In particular, under Article 118a, directives in the field of occupational health and safety, which previously needed unanimity in the Council of Ministers, can now be adopted by the Council by qualified majority and with no proof needed that they are essential for the completion of the internal market. As an indication of the progress achieved in social regulation in a few years, one should also mention Article 100a(3) of the SEA, which states that the

Commission should start from a high level of protection in matters relating to health, safety, and environmental and consumer protection.

Finally, the Maastricht Treaty contains a new section on consumer protection; it introduces qualified majority voting for most environmental protection measures; it even adds transportation safety to the regulatory tasks of the Community. But the Treaty is silent about most areas of traditional social policy. These developments show that EC policies in the social field are evolving along quite different lines from those followed by the member states. National historical traditions have yielded a dense web of welfare institutions covering most citizens 'from the cradle to the grave', while the Community remains, and will very possibly remain, a 'welfare laggard'. In the field of social regulation, however, the progress has been so remarkable that, as we saw in Chapter 4, some recent directives surpass the most advanced national measures in the level of protection that they afford.

At this point it could be objected that the impressive growth of the funds allocated to regional redistribution in recent years shows that a European social policy is not entirely lacking. It is not clear, however, that regional redistribution should be considered an instrument of social policy rather than a side-payment to induce all member states to accept certain efficiency-enhancing measures. The problem with the former interpretation is that there is an important distinction between reducing inequality among individuals (the main objective of social policy) and reducing disparities across regions. Since most regions contain a mix of rich and poor people, a programme aimed at redistributing resources to a region whose average income is low may simply lead to a lowering of the tax rate. The main beneficiaries of the programme will thus be rich individuals within poor regions (Musgrave and Musgrave 1976). The problems of targeting regions to achieve a better individual state of income redistribution are particularly severe in federal or quasi-federal systems (Majone 1993). Even in the United States, where the federal government pays three-quarters of the cost of welfare assistance, states insist on defining the standards of need and setting the benefit levels. As a consequence, the level of welfare assistance among the American states varies widely, more so than interstate disparities in wage rates or cost of living (Peterson and Rom 1990). In Europe too the governments of the countries of the southern periphery, foremost among them Spain, are strongly opposed to individualized transfers of EU funds.

To conclude, the 'big trade-off' between economic efficiency and a more equal distribution of income and wealth has confronted every democracy since the dawn of industrialization. Today's social policies are the outcome of the struggles of the past over the division of the domestic product. However, the delicate value judgements about the appropriate balance of efficiency and equity which social policies express can be made legitimately only within fairly homogeneous communities. It is difficult to see how generally acceptable levels of income redistribution can be determined centrally in a community of nations where levels of economic development and political and legal traditions are still so different, and where majoritarian principles can play only a limited role. Thus, a more active role of the European Union in income redistribution would not reduce the Union's democratic deficit, as many people would, seem to think, but would on the contrary, aggravate it.

Conclusion: reconciling independence and accountability

Non-majoritarian institutions are bound to play an increasingly important role in Europe. The multiplication of regulatory bodies at the national and EC levels is a clear indication of this trend, but equally revealing are the growth of judicial review and the expanding role of courts in the policy-making process. The latter find their policy-making role enlarged by the public perception of them as guarantors of the substantive, as well as procedural, ideals of democracy when electoral accountability in the traditional spheres of government seems to be on the wane (Volcansek 1992). Similarly, the rise of independent agencies has been facilitated by the widespread perception that governmental powers are too concentrated, that public policies lack credibility, and that accountability by results is not sufficiently developed in the public sector.

In country after country, voters have expressed their opposition to an uncontrolled expansion of the welfare state, thus questioning the legitimacy of a model of democracy which has reduced politics to a zero-sum game among redistributive coalitions. What the majority of voters seem to demand, however, is less a general retreat of the state than a redefinition of its functions and modes of operation – greater transparency and accountability, more emphasis on efficiency and a clearer separation of policy and politics. Because of their insulation from partisan politics, their expertise, and their commitment to a problem-solving style of decision-making, independent regulatory bodies and other specialized agencies would seem to be in a better position than government departments to satisfy the new demands of the electorate.

Unlike judges, however, regulators cannot rely on a firm foundation of legitimacy. Regulatory agencies tend to be treated as constitutional anomalies in countries where the delegation of state power to independent institutions is viewed as a serious threat to democracy, parliamentary sovereignty and the hallowed principle that public policy ought to be subject to control only by persons directly accountable to the electorate. These traditional principles are used to justify ministerial interference in agency decision-making, and the retention of important regulatory powers by government departments.

Against these attempts to establish political control by means which contradict the very *raison d'être* of the agencies we must restate one of the central themes of this book: the root problem of regulatory legitimacy in Europe today is not an excess of independence but, on the contrary, the constant threat of politically motivated interference. With greater independence would go greater accountability.

In this connection, on should recall the experience of the nationalized industries. As was mentioned in Chapter 1, detailed ministerial interventions in the decisions of public managers, usually exercised through informal and even secret processes, reduced accountability to vanishing point. Indeed, who could be held accountable if it was unclear whether responsibility for decisions rested with the public managers or with the government, and if the multiplicity and haziness of the objectives of nationalization made it impossible to define clear criteria of evaluation? The danger today is that the powers of direction which governments exercise over the agencies may be abused to exert pressure on the regulators in the same way as pressure was put on the managers of nationalized companies (Prosser 1989).

The real question, therefore, is how agency independence and public accountability can be made complementary and mutually reinforcing rather than antithetical values. Our arguments, and the century-old experience of the American regulatory state, indicate that independence and accountability can be reconciled by a combination of control mechanisms rather than by oversight exercised from any fixed place in the political spectrum: clear and limited statutory objectives to provide unambiguous performance standards; reason-giving and transparency requirements to facilitate judicial review and public participation; due process provisions to ensure fairness among the inevitable winners and losers from regulatory decisions; and professionalism to withstand external interference and reduce the risk of an arbitrary use of agency discretion. As Terry Moe (1987) has remarked, when such a system of multiple control works properly, no one controls an agency, yet the agency is 'under control'. At that point the problem of regulatory legitimacy will have been largely solved.

REFERENCES

Ackerman, B.A. and Hassler, W.T. (1981) *Clean Coal, Dirty Air*, New Haven (CT): Yale University Press.

Bernstein, M. (1955) *Regulating Business by Independent Commissions*, Princeton (NJ): Princeton University Press.

Dahl, R.A. (1956) *A Preface to Democratic Theory*, Chicago: The University of Chicago Press.

Dehousse, R., Joerges, C., Majone, G., Snyder, F. and Everson, E. (1992) 'Europe after 1992: new regulatory strategies', EUI Working Paper, LAW 92/31.

Dehousse, R. (1995) 'Institutional reform in the European Community: are there alternatives to the majoritarian avenue?' Florence: European University Institute, EUI Working Paper, Robert Schuman Centre, RSC 95/4.

Edley, C.F. (1990) *Administrative Law: Rethinking Judicial Control of Bureaucracy*, New Haven (CT): Yale University Press.

Hartley, T.C. (1988) *The Foundations of European Community Law: An Introduction to the Constitutional and Administrative Law of the European Community* (2nd edition), Oxford: Clarendon Press.

Lax, P.A. and Sebenius, J.K. (1986) *The Manager as Negotiator: Bargaining for Cooperation and Competitive Gain*, New York: The Free Press.

Lijphart, A. (1984) *Democracies: Patterns of Majoritarian and Consensus Government in Twenty-one Countries*, New Haven (CT): Yale University Press.

Lijphart, A. (1991) 'Majority rule in theory and practice: the tenacity of a flawed paradigm', *International Social Science Journal*, 129/1991: 483–93.

Lijphart, A., Rogowski, R. and Weaver, R.K. (1993) 'Separation of powers and cleavage management', in Weaver and Rockman (eds) *Do Institutions Matter?*, Washington (DC), The Brookings Institution.

Litan, R.E. and Nordhaus, W.D. (1983) *Reforming Federal Regulation*, New Haven (CT): Yale University Press.

Majone, G. (1993) 'The European Community between social policy and social regulation', *Journal of Common Market Studies* 31, 2: 153–70.

Milgrom, P. and Roberts, J. (1992) *Economics, Organizations and Management*, Englewood Cliffs: Prentice-Hall International.

Moe, T. (1987) 'Interests, institutions and positive theory: the politics of the NLRB', *Studies in American Political Development* 2: 236–99.

Mueller, D. (1989) *Public Choice II*, Cambridge: Cambridge University Press.

Musgrave, R.A. and Musgrave, P.B. (1976) *Public Finance in Theory and Practice* (2nd edition), New York: McGraw-Hill.

Pedersen, W.F. Jr (1975) 'Formal records and informal rule-making', *Yale Law Journal* 85: 38–88.

Peterson, P.E. and Rom, M.C. (1990) *Welfare Magnets*, Washington (DC): The Brookings Institution.

Prosser, T. (1989) 'Regulation of privatized enterprises: institutions and procedures', in Hancher and Moran (eds) *Capitalism, Culture and Economic Regulation*, Oxford: Clarendon Press.

Rose-Ackerman, S. (1992) *Rethinking the Progressive Agenda: the Reform of the American Regulatory State*, New York: The Free Press.

Shapiro, M. (1988) *Who Guards the Guardians?*, Athens (GA): University of Georgia Press.

Shapiro, M. (1992) 'The giving-reasons requirement', Chicago: *The University of Chicago Legal Forum*, 180–220.

Spitz, E. (1984) *Majority Rule*, Chatham (NJ): Chatham Publishers.

Sunstein, C.R. (1987) 'Constitutionalism after the New Deal', *Harvard Law Review* 101: 421–510.

Sunstein, C.R. (1990) *After the Rights Revolution: Reconceiving the Regulatory State*, Cambridge (MA): Harvard University Press.

Taylor, P. (1991) 'The European Community and the state: Assumptions, theories and propositions', *Review of International Studies* 17, 2: 34–47.

Teitgen-Colly, C. (1988) 'Les autorités administratives indépendantes: histoire d'une institution', in Colliard and Timsit (eds) *Les autorités administratives indépendantes*, Paris: Presses Universitaires de France.

Vaubel, R. (1995) *The Centralization of Western Europe*, London: Institute of Economic Affairs, IEA Hobart Paper 127.

Veljanovski, C. (1991) 'The regulation game', in Veljanovski (ed.) *Regulators and the Market*, London: Institute of Economic Affairs.

Volcansek, M.L. (1992) 'Judicial policies and policy-making in Western Europe', special issue of *Western European Politics* 15, 3.

Weiler, J.H.H. (1992) 'After Maastricht: Community legitimacy in post-1992 Europe' in Adams (ed.) *Singular Europe*, Ann Arbour: The University of Michigan Press.

Wicksell, K. (1967) [1896] 'A new principle of just taxation', in Musgrave and Peacock (eds) *Classics in the Theory of Public Finance*, London: Macmillan.

Index

Yarrow, G. 21, 27

Zekoll, J. 251, 259

Zilioli, C. 270, 283
Ziller, J. 100, 101, 105
Zysman, J. 159, 179